Corporate Governance

Corporate Governance

How to Add Value

Ulrich Steger
Wolfgang Amann

John Wiley & Sons, Ltd

Other Wiley Editorial Offices

John Wiley & Sons Inc., 111 River Street, Hoboken, NJ 07030, USA

Jossey-Bass, 989 Market Street, San Francisco, CA 94103-1741, USA

Wiley-VCH Verlag GmbH, Boschstr. 12, D-69469 Weinheim, Germany

John Wiley & Sons Australia Ltd, 42 McDougall Street, Milton, Queensland 4064, Australia

John Wiley & Sons (Asia) Pte Ltd, 2 Clementi Loop #02-01, Jin Xing Distripark, Singapore 129809

John Wiley & Sons Canada Ltd, 6045 Freemont Blvd, Mississauga, Ontario, L5R 4J3, Canada

Wiley also publishes its books in a variety of electronic formats. Some content that appears in print may not be
available in electronic books.

Library of Congress Cataloging in Publication Data

Steger, Ulrich.
  Corporate governance : how to add value / by Ulrich Steger and Wolfgang Amann.
    p. cm.
  Includes bibliographical references and index.
  ISBN 978-0-470-75417-7 (pbk.)
  1. Corporate governance.   2. Value.   I. Amann, Wolfgang.   II. Title.
  HD2741.S763 2008
  658.4′2—dc22

                                                            2008004946

British Library Cataloguing in Publication Data

A catalogue record for this book is available from the British Library

ISBN 978-0-470-75417-7 (P/B)

Typeset in 10/12pt Times by Integra Software Services Pvt. Ltd, Pondicherry, India
Printed and bound in Great Britain by Antony Rowe Ltd, Chippenham, Wiltshire

Contents

About the Authors   ix

Preface   xi

Acknowledgments   xv

PART I   INTRODUCTION   1

1   **Corporate Governance – Beyond the Scandals and Buzzwords**   3
      1.1   Every company has a corporate governance   3
      1.2   The history of corporate governance – a tale of crime and crises   5
      1.3   What are the basic paradigms of corporate governance?   14
      1.4   Basic corporate governance institutions   15
      1.5   The shaping factors of corporate governance   16
      1.6   Types of corporate governance system   18
      1.7   The types of board   20
      1.8   Typical dilemmas for the board   23
      1.9   Corporate governance and financial performance   24
      1.10 Where does corporate governance specifically add value?   26
      1.11 The contingent role of boards   28
      1.12 Case study: Developing corporate governance at Highfly Logistics
            Software – but how?   32
      1.13 Case study: Did corporate governance fail at Swissair?   36
      1.14 Case study: ABB – corporate governance during a turnaround   49

2   **International Corporate Governance – Similarities across Systems**   63
      2.1   Do international differences matter?   63
      2.2   Case study: DaimlerChrysler – corporate governance dynamics in a
            global company   68

PART II   BOARDS' INTERNAL DYNAMICS   89

3   **Information Demand and Supply for Changing Board Roles**   91
      3.1   Do new board roles require different information?   91
      3.2   Case study: Conflicts of interest at the board of Khan AG   97

3.3   Case study: ICM – when hidden agendas enter the boardroom (A)   104
3.4   Case study: ICM – hidden agendas in the boardroom (B)   108

4   Navigating through Typical Conflict Patterns   111
4.1   Are tensions and clashes normal?   111
4.2   Case study: War at the helm of Elicor   115
4.3   Case study: Cobra vs. Commerzbank – can investors raid their own company?   120

5   Codes of Conduct – The Value-Added beyond Compliance   131
5.1   Codes of conduct as a panacea?   131
5.2   Case study: Boeing hits turbulence – is it worth losing a successful CEO for a code of conduct?   135
5.3   Case study: Codes of conduct at ConnectU2 – adding value, cost, or nothing at all?   142

6   Board Evaluation   153

PART III   CORPORATE GOVERNANCE IN SPECIFIC CONTEXTS   161

7   Corporate Governance Dynamics in M&A   163
7.1   Why governance as usual is not an option in M&A   163
7.2   Case study: The DaimlerChrysler merger – the involvement of the boards   166
7.3   Case study: DaimlerChrysler board – after the deal is done   180

8   Corporate Governance in and with Subsidiaries   191
8.1   Tension fields and central issues   191
8.2   Case study: Pharmagroup Int. and Fluvera – when subsidiary governance means losing competitive ground   195

9   Corporate Governance in Developed vs. Emerging Markets   203
9.1   The wild, wild East? The wild, wild South?   203
9.2   Case study: China Prime – corporate governance with Chinese traits   207
9.3   Case study: Compania Unidas de Argentina – fight for your right or vote with your teeth?   212
9.4   Case study: Starting from scratch – corporate governance at South East Bank Europe   215

10   Responsibilities in Alternative Forms of Governance   221
10.1   Differences in non-profit organizations   221
10.2   Case study: WWF International – a truly worldwide organization   223

PART IV   CORPORATE GOVERNANCE IN SPECIAL OWNERSHIP SITUATIONS   233

11   Corporate Governance in Family Businesses   235
11.1   Good news for family firms   235
11.2   Case study: Bata Shoe Organization   245

12   Corporate Governance Dilemmas in Private Equity Companies   **255**

12.1   Corporate governance in private equity firms: can it add value?   255

12.2   Case study: Automotive Machine Tool GmbH&CoKG – from ailing
       family business to accelerating private equity?   261

12.3   Case study: Biocast   276

12.4   Case study: Asian Car Part Holding – sold without the knowledge
       of the board?   280

PART V   CONCLUSION   **285**

Index   **287**

About the Authors

Professor Ulrich Steger holds the Alcan Chair of Environmental Management at IMD and is Director of IMD's research project on Corporate Sustainability Management (CSM). He is Director of Building High-Performance Boards and other major partnership programs (e.g., the DaimlerChrysler & Allianz Excellence Program). He is also a member of the supervisory and advisory boards of several major companies and organizations. He was a member of the managing board of Volkswagen, in charge of environment and traffic matters and, in particular, the implementation of an environmental strategy within the VW group worldwide.

Before becoming involved in management education, he was active in German politics. He was Minister of Economics and Technology in the State of Hesse, with particular responsibility for transport, traffic, and energy. Before that, he was a member of the German Bundestag, specializing in energy, technology, industry, and foreign trade issues. Previously, Professor Steger was a full professor at the European Business School, a guest professor at St. Gallen University, and a Fellow at Harvard University. He holds a PhD from Ruhr University, Bochum. He is the author or editor of numerous publications including, most recently: *Corporate Diplomacy* (2002), *Sustainable Development and Innovation in the Energy Sector* (2003), *Managing Complex Mergers* (2004), *Mastering Global Corporate Governance* (2004), *In the Mind of the Stakeholder* (2006), and *Managing Complexity in Global Organizations* (2007).

Dr Wolfgang Amann joined the University of St. Gallen in 2007 as the Executive Director of the MBA Program and member of the faculty. He worked for DaimlerChrysler and was a top management consultant before pursuing his PhD in international management at the University of St. Gallen. He subsequently joined IMD in Lausanne and thereafter became a professor and the director of the Henley Centre for Creative Destruction, which innovates strategies to drive markets, at the Henley Management College in the UK. He has held visiting academic appointments at the Wharton School of the University of Pennsylvania, the Indian Institute of Management (IIM) in Bangalore, and Hosei University in Tokyo.

Wolfgang Amann's primary expertise and interests lie in the areas of successful corporate governance in international companies, with specific attention to ownership differences. He has also directed, delivered, and contributed to open and in-company programs on complexity, strategy, internationalization, and governance in the USA, Europe, China, India, and Japan. He has (co-)authored more than 70 case studies for these programs and his case series on Unilever in India won the 2006 oikos case-writing competition. For two years in a row, his course 'Corporate Strategy and Governance: how to add value' received the top European teaching award when it was chosen as the CEMS course of the year among all CEMS business schools in 17 European countries.

Preface

What is this book all about? Why a textbook on corporate governance?

Within just a few years, the 'corporate governance revolution' has evolved from a theme for experts to the forefront of business news, and has entered the classroom of many executive education, graduate, and undergraduate courses.

Sweeping legislation, numerous codes of conduct, scrutinized in detail by rating agencies and financial analysts, have – especially in the USA – created a bonanza for lawyers and consultants. Nevertheless, the topic is not new. Since the birth of the modern corporation, great economics and business administration scholars – from Karl Marx to Joseph Schumpeter and Peter Drucker – have always examined the apex or structure of the company. Given the inherently hierarchical nature of any organization, top management 'matters' more than other levels of management, although the extensive diversification of business administration into ever more specialized fields has somehow disguised this basic fact.

The question is: how can corporate governance (CG) be taught? It is far from simple, even in senior management development programs. The topic is just too far removed from operationally involved executives' daily lives. And what can Master's students or even undergraduates learn? The legal conditions are not only boring, but far too general to provide empirical hints on what makes companies 'tick' at the top. Even the previously hyped difference between 'one-tier' and 'two-tier' boards (in the former, a single board consists of executive and non-executive directors, while there is a legal separation between the management board and the supervisory board in the latter) does not tell you much. The question whether, for example, the role of the chairman of the board differs from that of the CEO or not is more important for corporate governance in practice than the legal framework.

Today's CG style is pretty generic and focused on a couple of simple structural features, such as separating the role of the chairman from that of the CEO (with the USA as the only holdout), ensuring a majority of independent directors, and installing a powerful and competent audit committee. This is all well and good as far as financial analysts ticking boxes in their analysis and communicating the results to investors are concerned. The bad news is, however, that none of these fashionable structural features has any relation to financial performance – which is supposed to interest investors most. What could students learn from this?

Our learning approach to corporate governance

We therefore decided on a different approach and focused this book on typical boardroom dilemmas. Dilemmas are the reality of managerial life. A managerial dilemma occurs when two or more (legitimate) goals conflict and, with the given resources, it is impossible to achieve both simultaneously. A priority decision needs to be taken, but this will result in constant tension. Dilemmas cannot always be solved; they need to be managed – especially in the boardroom. The more complex – and, thus, the more uncertain and ambiguous – the issues are, the further they move up in the hierarchy, ending with the board, where the corporate buck stops. These dilemmas reveal much about boardroom practice, and their impact is felt throughout the organization. In this book, we frame boardroom dilemmas as cases to provide students with a learning platform that allows a structured, interactive dialog, role-playing, and debriefing by means of our ambassador principle, as depicted below. The learning goal is to provide a fundamental understanding of dilemmas faced by the company top management and to demonstrate that, within legal limits and fundamental ethical standards, there are few clear-cut right or wrong decisions.

The course participants' attention is directed to the circumstances in our contingency approach, the identification of decision-making criteria, the pros and cons of the different options, and the way that certain structures, processes, and personalities influence decisions. Given the subject, the cases differ unavoidably from the 'usual' teaching cases, which often focus more on one functional and operational issue (and with good reason, as this facilitates students' learning). The instructor might therefore feel the need to give the students more guidance than usual. Consequently, teaching notes are available from the European Case Clearing House (www.ecch.com/).

This book has no specific information on the legal preconditions in specific countries, as even a rudimentary attempt would have made the book both cumbersome and almost immediately out-of-date. As we will see later on, legal situations do not actually explain how companies 'tick' or how boards work. We therefore only refer to a few general sources and websites that could be perused if a specific company has to be analyzed.

Course participants might ask why so many of the cases have been disguised. The answer is: to keep them real. Few companies, if any, are ready to release a case describing, for example, an escalating conflict between the CEO and chairman of the board. The only option to maintain real storylines that have not been censored by numerous legal and political considerations was to disguise them. Some of the cases are very sensitive indeed. In one instance, a US corporate lawyer had his company provide a press release on a current lawsuit, arguing that in the context of the case, the court might give it a different interpretation. For learning, the names of the real persons or companies are unimportant. What is far more important is whether a case captures a typical pattern, one that can be regarded as representative of the dilemma under discussion. Sometimes we 'distill' a case from several interviews, observations during board retreats, reviews of the media, etc. In all the disguised cases, various thorough checks have ensured that the case can serve as a learning platform and is more than just a 'war story'. We always describe the conceptual framework behind the cases and build on empirical evidence provided by interviews with CEOs, board members, and stakeholders regarding the dilemmas described and supported by surveys.

We therefore hope to 'reduce to the max' (as a popular car slogan demanded) a far-reaching and complex theme, whose cases sometimes lead to more questions than answers – on paper and in real life . . .

GUIDING PRINCIPLES

1. Allowing maximum interaction and learning.
2. Limiting repetition to a minimum.

PROCESS

1. The assigned groups must have discussed the assigned tasks.
2. Each individual group's 'hosts' remain in their specific room, while the others become 'ambassadors' and go to other rooms, ideally within 'their' scenario.
3. The hosts stay in their specific rooms and, in turn, give a 10-minute (maximum) presentation of their business model and solution to the ambassadors of each of the other groups.
4. The ambassadors discuss this solution with the host (10 minutes).
5. All ambassadors then return to their specific room.
6. The original groups then discuss what they have learned:

   (a) Hosts: what feedback did they get from the visiting ambassadors?
   (b) Ambassadors: what did they learn from the other hosts' presentations?

7. The groups then review their business model design and prepare a one-sentence summary (15 minutes for steps 6 and 7).

The Ambassador System

Our research approach. It is important to note that the cases are the result of comprehensive and (in the IMD tradition) global research efforts undertaken since 2001. We conducted truly international, large-scale surveys on codes of conduct, subsidiary corporate governance, board information, and corporate secretaries to name just a few recent ones. We furthermore conducted more than 250 interviews with chairmen of the board (no women to date), board members, company secretaries/corporate governance officers, and other experts. Much learning occurred during biannual board programs ('Building High-Performance Boards') and numerous board retreats that we facilitated from Shanghai to Bucharest and New York. They always served as the immediate reality check for our research.

Methodologically, we have chosen a contingency approach, as we are more interested in finding governance systems' shaping factors – their real underlying pattern, and their 'fit' with other corporate characteristics – than preaching *the* best practice. Our focus is clearly on the board as the central corporate governance organ, the way it works, and how it adds value to the company. This book presents our latest insights, thus following its predecessor *Mastering Global Corporate Governance* (John Wiley & Sons, 2004).

Acknowledgments

As always, this book is a convergence of many readings, thinking, debating, listening, and building on impressive foundations laid by others. We are grateful for every contribution that we received. A special note of gratitude goes to Peter Lorange and Jim Elbert, who make IMD a great place for innovative research on global, complex issues (which includes having the required resources and infrastructure). In addition, Peter contributed to this book as an academic colleague, especially on the chairman–CEO relationship. Fred Neubauer, who conducted the IMD Board Programs for more than a decade, has been an exceptional academic researcher and teacher, friend, and colleague. Although much has changed, his pioneering book *The Corporate Board* (together with A. Demb, 1992) is still regarded as a masterpiece of research on complex and confidential issues. His wisdom enriched us tremendously.

Furthermore, it is great to be surrounded by colleagues who share our interest in corporate governance: Paul Strebel, John Ward, Stewart Hamilton, and Preston Bottger challenged us as much as they provided feedback, support, shared their knowledge, and contributed to the success of the program 'Building High-Performance Boards'. Gertrud Erismann-Peyer, the newly retired UBS Company Secretary and now Executive-in-Residence at IMD, helped us to understand the board work's underlying processes and infrastructure much better, as well as the different roles that company secretaries or corporate governance officers can play. We also extend our thank-you note to the other members in the Global Corporate Governance Research Initiative: Helga Krapf and George Raedler were the 'first generation', later followed by Jochen Brellochs, Oliver Salzmann, and Christoph Nedopil. It was a real pleasure to work with them. John Evans and his information center team, our colleagues from Case Administration, the editors, as well as Emma Cranfield and Kathy Schwartz deserve a special thank you.

Acknowledgments

Part I
Introduction

1
Corporate Governance – Beyond the Scandals and Buzzwords

1.1 EVERY COMPANY HAS A CORPORATE GOVERNANCE

The corporate governance (CG) of large, stock market-listed corporations dominates the academic and public debate. This has actually created the (wrong) impression that CG is predominantly an issue for these types of companies. Every organization – not only corporations – has a governance system: governance concerns the distribution of power and responsibilities and, consequently, accountability for the organization's performance.

We distinguish, however, between the governance of different types of organizations such as membership vs. capital-based organizations, and public vs. private companies. CG concerns companies that, in modern economies, are characterized by specific features:

- The license-to-operate is fundamentally an economic one: to competitively provide goods and services to customers who are willing to pay. This does not mean that companies should ignore the social and environmental impact that is the side-effect – 'externalities' – of their task.
- The central benchmark of success and survival is a profit – the monetary value added comprised of the difference between the costs incurred and attained revenues.
- Corporations are hierarchical organizations that may differ in their degree of hierarchy (e.g., number of layers, power distance, etc.), but always have an identifiable 'apex'.
- The ultimate 'say' in a company is based on property rights, not on (democratic) principles such as 'one vote per person'.

The license-to-operate depends on compliance with the many restrictions that society has placed on companies: competition rules, national security, protection of creditors, of employees, of natural resources and/or of the environment, etc., but within this 'corporate life space' the company is free to act.

However, what may appear as restrictions on the enterprise level, are often essential preconditions to make a market-based capitalism work on the macro level. To name just a few: defined property rights, enforcement of contracts, a predictable 'level playing field', social and political stability. As the situation in emerging markets clearly indicates, these market preconditions are not easy to develop and synthesize. The economic system in Europe and the USA is by no means 'natural', but relies on a sophisticated legal infrastructure and fundamental values, developed over centuries, to guide behavior.

One of the fundamental principles of this economic system is that all people are responsible and held accountable for the decisions that they (or the institutions that they represent) take. The principles are intended to guarantee the responsible use of power and respect for others' interests.

These principles have been partly codified in laws and regulations and are partly unwritten but understood as expected behavior. On the whole, they ensure 'freedom with accountability', although societies vary in how they implement these principles in detail. The extent to which someone is accountable to a variety of stakeholders for corporate actions' results or for violating restrictions differs. In a small business, it might just be the owner who has to account for a loan that has not been serviced or labor laws that have been ignored. In large, specifically global companies, this accountability might be more complex and not easy to relate to a specific person. Whatever the case, it is CG's key task to establish this accountability and create transparency in this regard for stakeholders.

Our 'managerial' definition of CG is therefore:

Corporate governance establishes clear structures regarding accountability, responsibility, and transparency at the head of the company, and defines the role of boards and management

This definition differentiates CG from other management themes in several ways:

- First, it deals only with the company's top management (but sometimes also with *specific* CG implications further down the corporate ladder, such as subsidiary governance or compliance insurance).
- It does not deal with the content of a specific strategy and the organization as such, but specifically with how accountability and responsibility are allocated – especially between the top management and the board – and how this is made transparent to the stakeholders. In short: who is responsible for what.
- Transparency is not only concerned with the accountability dimension, because it would be difficult to hold someone accountable without being able to benchmark performance. CG does not, however, justify this benchmark, it simply describes the process; how a specific corporation has identified this benchmark.

The definition of cultural governance is also culturally neutral and, consequently, globally applicable, as it does not favor one form of governance over another, such as a two-tier or a one-tier board, or specific types of ownership.

Definitions cannot be either right or wrong; they can only be useful for a specific purpose or not. Our definition is shaped by our focus on examining real-life corporate governance processes and shedding some light on the working of boards. If one were to examine the definition from a primarily compliance perspective, the definition might have a different focus. One example of a compliance perspective is the OECD CG Guidelines, which were the foundation, as well as the umbrella, for many national CG codes. The OECD definition reads as follows: 'Corporate governance is the system by which business corporations are directed and controlled. The corporate governance structure specifies the distribution of rights and responsibilities among different participants in the corporation, such as the board, managers, shareholders, and other stakeholders, and spells out the rules and procedures for making decisions on corporate affairs. By doing this, it also provides the structure through which the company objectives are set, and the means of attaining those objectives and monitoring performance.'

1.2 THE HISTORY OF CORPORATE GOVERNANCE – A TALE OF CRIME AND CRISES

Although the term 'corporate governance' only appeared in the mid-1980s, the underlying problem started with the modern corporation's evolution after 1840. The huge investments required by the railroads and the growth of banks separated investors from those who were running the company, creating what is today called the 'principal–agent theory' or the Means–Berle dilemma after the two Harvard professors who first suggested separating management from ownership in 1932.

Until then, practically all major US companies were either family businesses or state owned. It was early industrialization with its tremendous and intransparent risks and uncertainties, as well as its potentially high stock growth rates and attractive dividends, that lay at the heart of the first UK/USA stock market crash in 1856. At that time, the continental European markets were not sufficiently developed to have a crash of any significant proportion and remained relatively unscathed. Eventually, however, they usually followed the USA and the UK in the big crashes.

It should be noted that the pattern of, and the behavior during, asset price inflation have not changed since then, as revealed by the dot.com bubble: the huge speculative gain in the stock market attracted many hit-and-run investors interested in getting rich fast. Once the bubble burst, the scam was discovered with many (especially small) investors losing substantial sums. Although German historian Heinrich von Treitschke already noted the 'unlimited stupidity' of these get-rich-quick investors in 1873, the incentive to participate has not changed in 150 years: one should know that the assets are overpriced, but everybody hopes to soon find a 'bigger idiot' to sell the assets to at an even higher price. Only when this stops, does the bubble burst and punish those who arrive too late at the party, normally small investors.

Government reaction too has remained unchanged in 150 years: punish the 'bad apples in the basket' to restore investors' confidence and draft new regulations. The stock market crash of 1873 eventually resulted in the external auditing of company books, and the crash of 1929 in regulatory stock market supervision.

The response to the dot.com crash did not differ from this pattern. One could, however, argue that the crime was more sophisticated and required a bending of the rules.[1] For economists and everyone else with common sense, the main point is rather to prevent bubbles instead of adding even more regulations, which merely generate creativity in circumventing them. This leads to the discussion whether central banks should not only prevent customer price inflation, but also asset price inflation. It also casts a critical eye on the role of (investment) banks, which have always fueled bubbles. And last but not least, if regulations are needed, is there an intelligent design that can enforce the rules and provide incentives to comply? There are good reasons to assume that the US rule-based system is not the optimal framework.[2] It is also a never-ending story: in 1970, when regulation was still relatively light, 117 of 1043 US companies (or 11%) had contravened the regulations. This ranged from straightforward fraud, price fixing, to bribery, etc., and was not just limited to restatement of the books.

The following description of corporate governance rules should therefore be regarded in the light of the criteria: did they really work and achieve their set goal? The latter is

---

[1] For details see Hamilton, S. and Mickethwait, A. (2006). *Greed and Corporate Failure.* Palgrave Macmillan, Houndmills.
[2] Also see Hamilton's book for a more detailed discussion.

sometimes difficult to answer when a new regulation is driven by public outrage – usually as a vent for frustration after another bubble fiasco. A related question is therefore: did the law of unintended consequences lead to counterproductive side-effects, which might have outweighed the regulation's benefits? This last point is especially relevant when national regulators do not take into consideration that we are living in a global economy . . .

Diffusion of corporate governance regulation

The beginning of the 21st century has experienced great 'excitement' with regard to corporate governance. Many corporate governance issues are currently regulated and regulators don't seem to tire of introducing new legislation to govern the relationship between companies' stakeholders and their management. Furthermore, there are sufficient codes and best practice catalogs with regard to corporate governance in the business community to satisfy a variety of stakeholders.

Even though the topic of corporate governance is as old as managed entities themselves, it splits ownership and management, giving rise to a principal–agent problem. The term 'corporate governance' was not used until the 1980s, despite prior recognition of the need for shareholder and owner protection against management fraud, as the establishment of the Securities and Exchange Control in 1934 illustrates.

At the beginning of this century, investors' trust was severely shaken, not only by the collapse of Enron in 2001 – a trite if useful example – but also by other corporate disasters such as Vivendi in France in 2002. Table 1.1 gives an impression of how extensive the major business scandals were.

Table 1.1 Corporate governance scandals

Company	Year	Country	Detail
Daewoo	1998	South Korea	Accounting fraud and embezzlement by former CEO
Flowtex	1999	Germany	Insolvency after exaggerating sales figures
Enron	2001	USA	Bankruptcy of the seventh largest US company due to accounting fraud
Marconi	2001	UK	Bankruptcy due to overpriced acquisitions and to neglecting of controls
Swissair	2001	Switzerland	Insolvency due to wrong strategy, inefficiencies of the board
HIH	2001	Australia	Stock market manipulation
OneTel	2001	Australia	Overstretching of budget for overambitious acquisitions
Allied Irish Bank (AIB)	2002	Ireland	Loss of $691m in unauthorized trading
Worldcom	2002	USA	Company collapses with $41bn debt due to fraudulent accounting
Tyco	2002	USA	Overstretching of budget for overambitious acquisitions leading to bankruptcy
Vivendi	2002	France	Overstretching of budget for overambitious acquisitions leading to losses of $23.3bn
Royal Ahold	2003	Netherlands	$500m accounting fraud
Parmalat	2003	Italy	Undisclosed debts of €14.3bn
Volkswagen	2005	Germany	Abuse of corporate funds to provide inappropriate benefits

The incidents did not stop there though. After recognizing the gravity of these scandals, authorities felt the need to react and to create and amend corporate governance regulations. The most prominent corporate governance regulation is the United States' Sarbanes–Oxley Act, which became effective on 30 July 2002 and is still being amended.

One cannot help thinking that in order for change to happen, crises have to happen, but was it only due to the scandals that corporate governance became this regulated? The following sections analyze the pattern of corporate governance regulation's diffusion in France, Germany, the UK, and the USA – four of the world's major economies – over the last 40 years and explore the drivers of, as well as the barriers to, corporate governance regulation convergence.

Developments in corporate governance regulation in the 1970s

At the beginning of the 1970s, Mace (1971) challenged the abilities of the board – probably the most important instrument of corporate governance – to fulfill its following functions:[3]

- Establishing basic objectives, corporate strategy, and board policies.
- Asking discerning questions.
- Selecting the president.

In order to re-establish the board's control and supervising functions, there was a strong call for independent outside directors and for more checks and balances at board level in the USA. This appeal originated from investors, as well as the Securities and Exchange Commission (SEC), with the SEC even calling for standing audit committees to be composed of independent outside directors. This regulatory movement was followed in the UK where, based on Sir Brandon Rhys-Williams' call for the employment of non-executive directors and the use of audit committees, a Green Paper was produced to this effect.[4] This Green Paper, however, failed to find supporters in Parliament.

On a European level, the European Economic Commission's Fifth draft Directive suggested replacing the unitary boards system with the two-board system, as practiced, for example, in Germany. In the UK, this proposal was criticized for requiring employee representatives on the board. Furthermore, English directors regarded the one-tier board as viable and therefore could not see the need for change. Following this European directive, the Bullock report was published in the UK, suggesting that the unitary board be continued but with worker representation. Again, this report was not received well by British directors.

These demands and suggestions for changes in corporate governance behavior and corporate governance regulation, although the term 'corporate governance' was not yet used at that time, were driven by a number of issues: in the USA, shareholders had become more litigious and started to sue companies and their auditors when investors thought this was lucrative. To be better protected against such lawsuits, it was suggested that the control should be improved, with checks and balances being provided between the supervisory and executive part of the company. In Europe, the main driver of corporate governance regulation was the aim to create a harmonized European market.

---

[3] See Mace, M. (1971). *Directors: Myth and Reality*. Harvard Business School Press, Boston, MA.
[4] See Rhys-Williams, B. (1976). The Case for Audit Committees. *Accountancy Age*, London.

Developments in corporate governance regulation in the 1980s

In the 1980s, the term 'corporate governance' first appeared, spreading through the literature, indicating a growing awareness of corporate governance issues. This attention was partially due to a number of high-profile initial public offerings (IPOs) in conjunction with the privatization of state-owned companies. In order to increase state-owned companies' profit orientation and, obviously, to fill the treasury, the telecommunication, mining, and electricity industries were privatized in the UK, creating revenues of US$96.7bn for the UK treasury between 1985 and 1995. In the following years, other developed nations followed this approach in order to increase shareholder-value. Germany, for example, privatized its telecom industry in 1995, almost 10 years later than the UK.[5]

The increased attention on corporate governance issues was also due to a number of corporate failures and scandals. In the USA there was Ivan Boesky, Michael Levine, and Michael Milken's insider trading and in the UK, the Guinness share-trading fraud, which attempted to influence the stock market to increase the value of Guinness stocks. Furthermore, a growing number of people depended on the stock market, either directly as a result of personal investment or through pension fund investments, etc. This is best illustrated by the equity market value in the UK, which increased from £36bn in 1971 to £514bn in 1989 or the growing number of shareholders in the USA, which grew from around 31 million in 1970 to around 51 million in 1990.

Developments in corporate governance regulation in the 1990s

As can be seen in Figure 1.1, the late 1990s saw a further rise in the awareness of corporate governance in all the focal countries. A host of reports, guidelines, and best practice codes calling for more transparency, checks and balances, conformance, and compliance at board level were issued in various countries.

In 1992, the Cadbury Report was published in the UK, which dealt with directors' service contracts, interim reporting, the effectiveness and perceived objectivity of auditing, and the role of institutional investors. This was a landmark event for corporate governance, as this report's recommendations became obligatory for companies listed in the UK in 1993. This was what is called a 'comply or explain' regulation, meaning that any divergence from it had to be explained from 30 June 1993 onwards.

In France, a number of embarrassing business scandals led to the creation of the Rapport Viénot, which was further spurred by the Cadbury Report. The Viénot Report suggested that cross-shareholdings and cross-directorships should be prohibited and that nomination and remuneration committees should be established. In 1995, the Greenbury Report on directors' remuneration was published in the UK, recommending full disclosure of management payment.

In 1998, more reports were published on corporate governance: the Hampel Report ('Combined Code: Principles of Good Governance and Code for Best Practice') in the UK and in France the second Viénot Report. The Hampel Report combined the Cadbury and Greenbury codes and concluded that in general, corporate governance regulations shouldn't be

---

[5] This time lag was partly due to a different perception of the market for corporate control, as, especially in the UK, the constant threat of hostile takeovers was regarded as an incentive for strong board-level performance [see Tricker, B. (2005). Corporate governance – a subject whose time has come. *Corporate Ownership & Control* **2**(2): 11–19]. In Germany and France, however, this market didn't exist to this extent, due to a less diffused stock-ownership structure and the banks' stronger role, nor was the market for corporate control regarded as a threat for German companies' strategy.

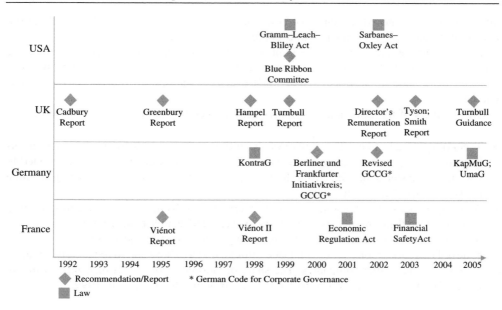

Figure 1.1   Major laws and reports on corporate governance 1992–2005

mandatory, but followed voluntarily. It furthermore suggested that the board should only be accountable to the company's shareholders – a clear statement in favor of corporate governance's shareholder orientation instead of a broader stakeholder approach. The report also suggested that the role of the CEO and chairman of the board should be separated.

The second Viénot Report of 1998 aimed to change the secondary goal of achieving shareholder value in French companies by stressing greater transparency in response to investors' demands. This report also called for a pay-for-performance type of remuneration for top managers, as well as the disclosure of the directors' remuneration policy (not the disclosure of individual directors' compensation). The second Viénot Report thus again embraced the Anglo-Saxon practices of good corporate governance.

In Germany, two laws that were passed concerning corporations' transparency and control (KonTraG) and their access to capital (KapAEG) demonstrated that there was movement with regard to corporate governance. The KonTraG was the first major company law reform since 1965 and had to satisfy the prevailing demands for shareholder protection, as well as effective employee representation on supervisory boards required by codetermination laws. The law dealt with, for example, cross-shareholding, the use of 'golden shares', which allowed for disproportionate voting rights, transparency, and shareholder democracy. It was passed after a number of corporate scandals like that of Daimler-Benz AG, which disclosed losses of more than a billion dollars when its annual report was published with GAAP calculations after reporting profits under German accounting rules.

In 1999, the USA too saw changes to corporate governance regulations through the Gramm–Leach–Bliley Act and through the recommendations of the 'Blue Ribbon Committee'. The latter provided 10 suggestions about issues such as transparency, external auditors' accountability, and external directors' independence with regard to audit committees and aimed to improve the effectiveness of corporate audit committees. The NYSE, NASDAQ, and AMEX made the recommendations compulsory in 1999.

These reports on and laws for the improvement of corporate governance, as well as the growing awareness of corporate governance issues, were driven by the economy that had changed worldwide, as well as by individual events or the described crises in the various countries.

Other drivers of the diffusion of corporate governance regulation in the 1990s were:

- Technological advances. The spread of the Internet rendered communication and information sourcing easier, faster, and cheaper. The boundaries of information continued to vanish ever faster and, with it, the barriers to international investment, leading to more internationalized capital markets.
- A stronger focus on shareholder-value. In Germany the banks, which had formerly been more interested in companies' long-term success and which held a high proportion of seats on supervisory boards, became increasingly interested in short-term benefits. They believed that more money could be made through underwriting and in the lucrative market for buying and selling companies. The share of German banks' chairmanships of the 40 largest German companies therefore fell from 44% in 1992 to 23% in 1999.[6]

Development of corporate governance since 2000

In January 2000, after much criticism from international investors because of its opaque corporate governance regulations, the Frankfurt Commission for Principles on Corporate Governance and the Berlin Initiative Group started to document the German corporate governance system. The 'German Code of Corporate Governance' was introduced in June of that year. It deals with the responsibilities of the Vorstand – the executive part of the German two-tier board – and makes recommendations on issues like performance-linked remuneration, the use of the Internet for reporting and annual meetings, the use of international accounting standards, the creation of audit committees, and the use of a sufficient number of independent directors. A 'comply-or-explain' regulation was passed for the compliance with the code in its revised form in 2002.

The creation of this code was driven by international shareholder pressure but also – again – by corporate failures such as Flowtex AG, Cargolifter, and Philipp Holzmann AG. Losses of DM 2.4 billion surfaced in November 1999 at Philipp Holzmann AG; Flowtex had to file for insolvency after a debt of DM 3 billion and years of dramatically exaggerated sales figures were revealed. In 2001, the French legislative passed the Economic Regulation Act, giving shareholders the right to sue members of the board in cases of company bankruptcy due to management mistakes and conflicts of interest.

In 2002, the US legislation passed the Sarbanes–Oxley Act (SOX), the most far-reaching reforms of American business practices since Franklin Roosevelt's presidency from 1933 to 1945. This Act had a serious impact on the corporate governance of US companies, as well as foreign companies listed on American stock exchanges. Major regulatory changes that SOX brought about by amending prior regulations included:

---

[6] See Hoepner, M. (2001). Corporate Governance in Transition: Ten Empirical Findings on Shareholder Value and Industrial Relations. Discussion Paper 01/5, Max-Planck-Institut für Gesellschaftsordnung, Cologne.

- CEO and CFO have to certify the accuracy of corporate financial reports.
- Companies are required to publish information related to material changes in their financial situation in a timely manner.
- Companies must prepare reports that assess and describe the effectiveness of their internal control structures and financial reporting procedures.

The Act's drivers were a number of major corporate failures in 2001 and 2002, of which Enron, Tyco International and Worldcom, all involving accounting frauds, were the most (in)famous.[7] The US legislation felt the need to pass this comprehensive act in order to enhance corporate responsibility, financial disclosures, and to combat corporate and accounting fraud and certainly to re-establish investors' trust.

On the other side of the ocean, the EU pushed the harmonization process of the European market by issuing a number of directives and recommendations in 2005. These directives dealt with the disclosure of management remuneration, management's personal internal liability with regard to the company (external liability is subject to state regulation), the publication of half-year and full-year reports as well as interim reports when necessary, the use of international accounting standards as well as the use of nomination, remuneration, and audit committees. The directives furthermore affirm the freedom to choose between a one-tier or a two-tier board. Some of these directives (e.g., the publication directive) resemble the Sarbanes–Oxley Act. According to the Winter Report, the European Union is merely interested in harmonizing national regulations through directives and recommendations and not in the establishment of a European Codex for Corporate Governance.

A number of the EU recommendations and directives, such as the management's personal liability in respect of shareholders, became law in Germany in 2005. Filing lawsuits on behalf of small investors has become easier, thus increasing minor shareholders' power. Furthermore, the German government required managers' remuneration to be published, a highly controversial decision in Germany. The French legislature also introduced a law requiring publicly traded companies to disclose directors' and general managers' remuneration, as well as retirement bonuses in 2005. Furthermore, sociétés anonymes (limited liability companies) were required to publish information on their board organization as well as the company's internal control procedures, similar to what the Sarbanes–Oxley Act required. Unlike the other focal nations, France does not yet have a corporate governance code.

Analysis of corporate governance regulation diffusion, its drivers and barriers

Corporate governance regulation convergence and its drivers

Table 1.2 shows the evolving nature of corporate governance and the diffusion of corporate governance regulation over the last 10 years. The latter does not converge in just one direction, i.e. from the Anglo-Saxon model to the continental-European model. A more differentiated view has to be taken, as corporate governance approaches and rules do sometimes diffuse from the Anglo-Saxon model – as, for example, with remuneration disclosure, regulation regarding transparency, and the use of audit committees. Other issues diffuse from continental Europe, like the distinction between the executive and the supervising members

---

[7] Accounting problems and fraud visible, for example, in financial restatement announcements became increasingly significant in the USA, increasing from only 92 financial restatements in 1997 to an estimated 250 in 2002 [see Coffee, J. (2005). A theory of corporate scandals: why the USA and Europe differ. *Oxford Review of Economic Policy* **21**(2): 198–211].

Table 1.2 Diffusion of selected corporate governance issues 1994–2005

CG issue	Country	1994	1995	1996	1997	1998	1999	2000	2001	2002	2003	2004	2005
Remuneration according to performance	Germany												
	France												
	UK												
	USA												
Remuneration disclosure	Germany												
	France												
	UK												
	USA												
Audit committee creation	Germany												
	France												
	UK												
	USA												
Audit committee independence	Germany												
	France												
	UK												
	USA												
Board independence	Germany							*)					
	France	**)			***)							
	UK												
	USA												
Removal of cross-shareholding	Germany												
	France												
	UK												
	USA												
Liability of board	Germany												
	France												
	UK												
	USA												
Comply or explain	Germany												
	France												
	UK												
	USA									****)			
Separation chairman/CEO	Germany												
	France												
	UK												
	USA												

Recommended

Statutory/common practice

*) 'Sufficiently independent'
**) 2 independent directors
***) 1/3 independent directors
****) Law driven

of the board, as well as the division between the chairman of the board and the CEO. While the USA had only 8% split roles between the CEO and chairman in 1998, this number rose to 29% in 2005 for S&P 500 companies. A variety of drivers, as described above, led to this diffusion of corporate governance regulation. The main drivers identified were:

- Scandals and corporate crises.
- Internationalized capital markets.
- The harmonization of capital markets through political powers.
- The growing importance of investment for a broader part of the population.
- Privatization.

Persistent corporate governance differences and the barriers to diffusion

Differences do, however, still prevail in corporate governance. Barriers to the further assimilation of corporate governance laws and manifold differences in the regulations have been specifically mentioned in this chapter. The main barriers can be summarized as:

- Differences in the capital/financial structures.
- Differences in remuneration policies.
- Differences in the law system.
- Differences in the economic systems and economic environment.

In the Anglo-Saxon system, the financial community culture is characterized by a highly dispersed ownership structure and arm's length investment. The continental system, on the other hand, is still characterized by a long-term commitment to block-shareholding and cross-shareholding, the state's strong involvement (France), and that of banks (Germany). In Germany, for example, cross-shareholding has just experienced a new increase, with Porsche AG having bought a sufficiently large enough stake in Volkswagen to avoid the necessity of a full takeover offer. The various approaches to controlling an economic entity through either the market or major shareholders' influence do differ and, hence, the need for regulation.

Remuneration policies differ significantly between the various countries. US and, to a lesser extent, British managers still receive a much higher proportion of their compensation in equity (in 2001 it was 66% for US CEOs) than their German or French counterparts do. Furthermore, senior management income expressed as a multiple of the average employee compensation is essentially higher in the USA and the UK (531:1 in the USA in 2004, 25:1 in the UK in 2004) than in France (16:1) or Germany (11:1). Managers whose remuneration is partly in equity feel the need to push the stock price, even by means of artificial and illegal financial statement inflation, so that they can sell the options/stock profitably. A different approach to corporate governance might therefore be necessary, as governance protection that works in one system may easily fail in another.

Another barrier to corporate governance regulation's unitary diffusion that has not as yet been mentioned, is the difference between the UK/US and German/French law systems. The UK and the USA have a body of common law, in which precedent decisions and their analogies mostly determine the law. As long as there are no incidents or scandals, laws will not be enacted within this common law system. This is exemplified by the corporate governance system in the UK to date generally relying on guidelines, whereas corporate scandals have triggered the SOX in the USA. This does not imply that the other focal countries, for example Germany, do not have statutory regulations with regard to corporate governance systems, but rather that the US corporate governance system 'prefers the hammer of Sarbanes–Oxley, while the Europeans lean towards a voluntary approach' (Melnitzer, 2003, p. 36). Germany and France, on the other hand, have a body of civil law with codified laws. In Germany, for example, many of the issues addressed in the German Code of Corporate Governance are a summary of already existing laws amended with recommendations with regard to best practices (currently a comply-or-explain regulation). From this point of view, a unitary diffusion of corporate governance regulation is unlikely, since the regulating approaches already differ in the various systems.

The last barrier to be discussed here concerns the cultural differences in the economic system. The most important of these differences lie in the differing perceptions of the market and the individual. The Anglo-Saxon corporate culture emphasizes self-responsibility; the individual is therefore able to act without immediate state constraint. Consequently, the USA and the UK are classified 'liberal market economies'. Germany and France, on the other hand, are considered 'coordinated market economies', as the state regulates many issues – in an effort to integrate a variety of stakeholders – and self-determination and self-responsibility are more limited. This again makes the need for differing corporate governance regulations apparent.

Summary

Overall, the diffusion of corporate governance regulation is found in many issues, but a global convergence towards one corporate governance model – whatever it may be – is unlikely, due to the number of cultural, regulatory, and structural barriers. Convergence is therefore unlikely to occur within the near future.

1.3   WHAT ARE THE BASIC PARADIGMS OF CORPORATE GOVERNANCE?

There are two dominant CG paradigms. They are, however, not alternatives – but in fact, often combined. The first is the (neo-classical) 'principal–agent' theory. In its most basic form, it states that the principal (for example, the owners of a company) cannot trust the agent (for example, the management) to act in the principal's best interest, but to follow her/his own. The principal's problem is that the agent knows the situation much better than she/he does, due to the information asymmetry, and that, furthermore, supervising the agent means that the principal incurs costs, which are called agency costs. The principal is therefore focused on how to specify the right incentives for the agent in a contract so that she/he acts in the principal's best interests, who can then minimize her/his agency costs. This was also the theoretical foundation of stock options. Corporate governance is therefore concerned with a typical agency problem: how can the owners ensure that management, which is mostly separated from ownership in larger companies, acts in their interest, maximizing shareholder-value and not building 'empires' at the owners' expense?

The theory has been refined, detailed, and varied in many aspects. Today's versions often use game theory's mathematical models to simulate the outcome of specific principle–agent dynamics. The theory has, however, also been heavily criticized. The main arguments are:

- The assumptions about human behavior are too simplistic; for example, the agents are regarded as only being ruled by opportunistic self-interest. Furthermore, the theory does not explain how the players' perceptions of their interests are formed in situations of uncertainty.
- By assuming that the firm is a 'bundle of contracts', power relations are overlooked (which explains, for example, the practice of 'repricing' stock options once they are 'under water').
- It applies only to specific types of ownership. For example, the thousands of shareholders in a widely held stock-listed company can hardly be regarded as 'principals', given individual shareholders' limited rights; they have more incentive to exit and sell their shares than to take the trouble to voice their concerns.

But the principal–agent proposition is a useful framework when CG is viewed as a broad range of different principal–agent situations that can occur in different circumstances and guides an analysis of the situation. Questions in this regard are, among others: what are the players' different interests? Based on the incentives provided, what are the agency costs? Such agency situations are relevant in respect of institutional investors and their clients, which the aftershock of the corporate scandals in the USA revealed, in respect of boards and top management, and corporate management at the headquarters and subsidiary management, etc.

This specific, more applied, approach to the principal–agent theory is often combined with contingency theory. Basically, this conceptual principal–agent framework requires an analysis of a specific situation, the influencing factors, and the interests. All of these often shape a company's articles of foundation and the different players' incentives, restrictions, and interdependencies. The contingency framework looks for a fit between the outside factors, which cannot be influenced, and the decisions taken to adapt to these – changing – factors, thus, for example, developing a specific organization to fit volatile market conditions.

In this book, we thus apply the principal–agent proposition as the dominant framework, combining it with contingency theory. Together, they form the conceptual underpinning of the cases and concepts.

1.4   BASIC CORPORATE GOVERNANCE INSTITUTIONS

As the principal–agent theory implies, you need at least two players or institutions: the principal (in the case of companies, the owners) and the agent (the management). This description might suffice for smaller, closely held companies in which the ownership and management are obviously separated. For most global, larger companies this description is not adequate, as you need four basic entities for a comprehensive analysis:

- **The general assembly/annual meeting**, where all owners meet (or to which they are invited) and take decisions as described in the corporate articles of foundation, or receive reports for which they have asked. The content and duration of these meetings vary considerably. In a widely held stock market company, there is very little that the shareholders can decide or approve. In a limited partnership with few owners, this gathering will make major decisions regarding investments or strategy, and if it meets regularly, it can even function as a board. The differentiating criterion is, however, the meeting (or, at least, the invitation) of *all* owners.

- **The board**. In our terminology, the board is the apex that carries the company, 'it's where the buck stops', whether this is legally described or not. A board has several characteristics: (1) regular meetings (more than once a year); (2) defined tasks and rights, but no operational or functional tasks, it therefore does not 'run' the company; (3) it is elected or appointed by the owners and there is no higher authority other than the owners. According to the criteria, the meeting of the limited partners can act like a board. However, common practice and legal foundations specify that it is the meeting of the owners, if they meet regularly, that has the final power to make decisions that go beyond mere operational decisions. The issue of power goes beyond a one-tier vs. a two-tier board, or whether boards only represent owners. The decisive criterion is who is ultimately responsible, both towards society (regarding compliance with the laws) and with regard to the company's performance, even if owners or boards have delegated the daily business to the management. This delegation of power does not release the principals from their responsibility. They need to prove that they have lived up to the professional standards required of those in authority. In an individual case, this can be controversial – but the principle is clear. No wonder, therefore, that boards are regarded as the central CG body and that their work – such as selecting a successful CEO – has the greatest influence on corporate development.
- **Management** (either a CEO or a board of management) is defined as having to report to the board (even if the chairman of the board and the CEO are one person) and is held accountable by the board for its actions and results.
- **Outside stakeholders** include a wide variety of interest groups: regulators, employees, financial analysts, local communities, and society at large. There is no generally accepted answer to the question regarding the extent to which stakeholders should or could influence the decisions taken in the CG system. Even in the US states, corporate law allows the board to consider or represent other interests than that of shareholders. In the spirit of the contingency theory, this question can be left open and specific situations can be analyzed.

1.5   THE SHAPING FACTORS OF CORPORATE GOVERNANCE

Much of the corporate governance discussion is focused on legal and 'soft' regulations such as codes of conduct. Compliance with these rules and regulations is, of course, important, but does not really indicate how a board or a company 'ticks'. Take the example of the much-discussed one-tier vs. two-tier board systems. BP, for example, has an independent chairman with a majority of independent, non-executive directors serving on the board and the CEO and CFO acting as executives. The chairman and the independent directors regard their roles as basically (1) defining 'space' for the CEO by, for example, approving strategy, large acquisitions and (2) monitoring performance and ensuring that boundaries are not crossed. This is very much what a two-tier board does. The supervisory board, which by definition has an independent chairman and directors, rarely meets without the management board if the executives know that trouble is brewing. But if the chairman of the supervisory board, who goes to his corporate office every day, is a significant shareholder and perhaps even a former CEO, which happens in larger, family-controlled businesses, then the current CEO is at best a 'managing director' and the shots are called by the chairman. In such a case, one could argue, even if this does not comply with corporate law, it is at least a gray area – but who is going to complain when the company is performing?

Consequently, it makes sense to go beyond the formalities and look at the important drivers, the shaping factors of a specific corporate governance system. Through our research, we found four determinants. They are:

- **Personalities**. To take an extreme example: US management hero and guru Jack Welsh was definitely an outstanding industrial leader, but not a CG standard bearer. He left it to his successors to comply with the new 'best practice' standards. Nobody ever complained as long as GE was delivering double-digit profit growth. Who would have dared – either inside or outside the boardroom – to challenge a CEO with such a stellar 20-year track record? Whether formalists, purists, or legalists like it or not, personalities do matter. A CEO with an outstanding performance or a towering, resilient chairman with long experience, wisdom, and diplomatic skills will shape boardroom discussions – and the resultant decisions – whatever the formalities may be. As our colleague Stewart Hamilton has shown, the formalities and the directors' qualifications were close to perfect in most of the widely held companies that went down the drain as a result of fraud, e.g. Enron and Worldcom, or without fraud, e.g. Swissair. But where were character and stamina when the very visible warning lights were ignored?
- **Business model and industry context**. Companies are successful in the market because they are different and try to differentiate themselves (otherwise we would have a static commodity market). This is also reflected in their business models, which we define as a combination of strategic value drivers and a selection of markets with a good fit providing a company with sustainable economic survival. Companies operate in different stages of a lifecycle – start-up vs. mature – and are confronted with very different strategic challenges. A mature company might struggle to regain momentum and avoid decline, a start-up struggles with the impact of growth: how to move from 'friends of innovation' to a well-organized company? A good business model also reflects the specific needs of an industry: risk management is paramount in the financial service industry, where rapid innovation is required for survival, just as is the case in the mobile phone industry. Heavy assets industries – steel, automotive, and chemical – need different capital structures than entertainment services do. All of this is also reflected in a specific company's CG – and in the persons who act as directors or corporate officers. Any 'one-size-fits-all' standard would neglect these differences and would therefore lead to many non-value-added activities: a bank might have good reasons to install a risk management committee on the board, while this would be pretty useless for a food retailer.

  On a personal level: can a retired manufacturing manager from a commodity industry bring value to a rapidly growing service start-up's board discussions? The question is more than rhetorical, because, on the one hand, diversity in the boardroom is a way of avoiding 'groupthink'. But how much diversity is required? How large can the business and cultural distance be for you to still understand and 'feel the beat of business'? This question has been raised recently, as there seems to be a trade-off between a director's 'independence' and the industry expertise in widely held public companies. CG might therefore be perceived to run counter to the many efforts to establish CG codes of conduct. This perception is only true to a certain degree, as the codes are for large, widely held public companies and focus on transparency and reporting requirements, the board's composition, and certain minimum standards. These issues are only relevant for these groups of companies.

- **Ownership**. As discussed before, most of the corporate governance themes are derived from the 'principal–agent' situation that regards ownership and management as very often being separate. However, company ownership can take a wide variety of forms: from one owner to hundreds of thousands; in all possible variations, from founder-owned, family-owned; with varying degrees of institutional investors, such as, for example, pension funds; can be fully owned by a private equity fund, be majority privately held, be a minority on the stock market and vice versa; be listed on all stock markets, or on one or several markets, etc. Since CG should align owners' and managers' interests and provide adequate monitoring while minimizing agency costs, the owner composition has to be reflected in the design of CG systems. A rule of thumb is that the more disperse the ownership is, and the less aligned the owners' interests are, the more crucial the board's role is. Furthermore, there is a difference in the board's role if a company is fully family-owned, or if it is fully stock market quoted.
- **Legal and political environment**. Last, but not least, companies – even global ones that are often described as 'footloose' – do not operate in a vacuum. There are many ties to the non-business environment in a specific country: local communities, regulators and authorities, industry associations, and professional organizations. In the process of globalization, some of the links have loosened, but on the whole they still matter. Complying with complicated legal frameworks is often not a simple question of 'yes' or 'no', but a matter of interpretation and discretionary decision by the enforcement agency, its readiness for dialog, and consensus solutions. Beyond written rules, there are certain dos and don'ts in any culture. Decisions can be perfectly legal, but nevertheless regarded as completely unacceptable by society at large and the relevant stakeholders. In the USA, for example, it is quite normal for companies to sue government agencies. In Japan, this would be unthinkable. History and cultural tradition influence laws and their enforcement in subtle but lasting ways. In Europe, you still have different legal approaches between 'Latin Europe', 'Germanic Europe', and 'Anglo-Saxon Europe' that date back to Roman times. These differences influence companies' framework conditions, but do not explain individual CG systems. There is always the 'Gaussian law of equal distribution' and the variety of CG systems within one legal system is considerable, given the other shaping factors.

If one dares to look at the (fictitious) 'median' company, one finds CG systems as described below.

1.6   TYPES OF CORPORATE GOVERNANCE SYSTEM

These four shaping factors, with their many variations, lead to an infinite number of company-specific CG systems and even if you cluster the variations on a Likert-scale of 1–7, more than 65,000 versions of CG result. As far as it is possible to use the four shaping factors as a framework to analyze the specific governance system of a company, it would not make much sense to describe here many unlikely, unrealistic, hardly seen variations. From our research, we found four relevant clusters around one dominant feature – that means, these clusters do not exist in a pure form – which influences most of the work of the board and other governance institutions. So these clusters can help to kick off the CG analysis of a company, not replace it.

The involvement of the board is highly dependent on the basic CG model. Figure 1.2 and Table 1.3 capture the differences between a CEO-centered model and a check-and-balance model in detail. Consistent with the basic features of the CG models, in the latter case, the board is far more involved, but with specific value-adding contributions and in an interactive

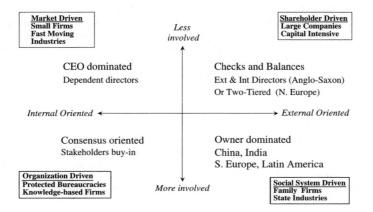

Figure 1.2   Characterization of corporate governance systems

Table 1.3   Typical board involvement in the strategizing process

	CEO-centered model		Checks-and-balances model	
	Top management/ staff	Board	Top management/ staff	Board
Scanning/early awareness	Done by management and specific functions (e.g. marketing), hired outside experts	More informal input, often at social occasions	Brings own and board input together	Systematic input expected
Deciding on strategic options	Management debates alternatives, tests robustness, etc. and then 'sells' results to the board	Only after management has come to a conclusion and presented to the board limited possibilities to compare options and test robustness	Preparation of options, but final decision after strategy retreat of the board	Thorough evaluation of assumptions, consequences, consistency with business model, mostly during a strategy retreat
Detailed planning	Done by management in negotiation with subsidiaries, functions	Submitted by management for approval	Driven by management in negotiation with subsidiaries	Review of consistency with options chosen, resources, and financial restrictions

Table 1.3   (Continued)

	CEO-centered model		Checks-and-balances model	
	Top management/ staff	Board	Top management/ staff	Board
Implementation	Driven by management, as part of regular meetings reporting to the board	Supervision based on key performance indicators, no 'hands-on' knowledge	Driven by management, reporting to the board, review part of regular meetings	Supervision based on key performance indicators, but also first-hand experience through personal discussion with line management, visit of subsidiaries
Design of strategy process	Design by management only	More informal input	Proposed by management	Assessed and agreed

dialog with management. The space for management is unavoidably smaller than in the CEO-centered model, where the board is more approving of what management proposes as strategy and actions. Our point is not to argue in favor of one model or the other, but to indicate what a board's strategy work could look like when it is consistent with the basic CG model.

These classes are not stable over time. A long-time successful CEO might today dominate the board, but this may change rapidly. A crisis might shift power back to the board as in Disney's case, after a shareholder revolt. A change in the business model or the core strategy might alter the governance model too, as, for example rapid decision-making may become more urgent now compared to the hitherto prioritized checks-and-balances model.

Also, political and economic trends affect the preference for certain clusters: before the dot.com bubble burst, the clearly preferred model of Wall Street was the CEO-dominated model. The crash, and a recession that revealed what auditors did not, made institutional investors push for a checks-and-balances model with more transparency. That is the basis of the new mantra of the more vigilant board.

1.7   THE TYPES OF BOARD

It is pretty obvious that the role of the board varies widely in the different variations of CG systems. We can take the classification one step further and outline a typology of boards in the following. In any case, to add value to the company, the board's contribution has to be unique. This means that only the board can perform such tasks. Three typical board tasks stand out in this perspective:

(1) Monitoring and supervising

In this role, the board is concerned with compliance ensuring and performance monitoring. Even if it delegates the operational implementation to the CEO/management, it has to decide on the compliance mechanism and controls and has to be sufficiently involved to see if the system is working or not. Compliance covers a wide range of issues: legal compliance, meeting financial reporting requirements, codes of conduct, compliance with own policies, ranging from travel costs to safety standards, etc. The previous practice that the external auditors report first to management has been scrapped, now the board (or specifically the Audit Committee, which is responsible for the daily grind of financial compliance) is in charge of hiring and firing the external auditors, the setting of their mandate, and the amount of additional consulting work, and receiving their reports. In some cases, in the USA through Sarbanes–Oxley or in banks, even the internal audit reports to the Audit Committee. Performance monitoring is the definition of Key Performance Indicators (KPIs) for the company and observing them over time – and of course acting, if there are serious deviations. It is not an easy task to differentiate early between noise, random fluctuation, and an emerging trend.

This task of compliance insurance and performance monitoring is the baseline of any board work. To fail here can have disastrous consequences for the company. The recent legislation (especially in the USA), the stock market listing requirements, and the code of conduct for CG have detailed this task by an order of a magnitude – up to the point where more bureaucracy and box-ticking might be generated than effective supervision.

(2) Selecting, evaluating, and coaching top management

The days when an outgoing CEO picked his successor are over, at least in many more cases than some years ago. Most of the boards today would claim that they are in charge of the CEO succession planning, but also of other senior corporate officers as well. This includes regular evaluations of the CEO. This is not only focused on financial performance, but also on leadership behavior, communication style, and interaction with the board – a 'Balanced Scorecard' approach – however, prominently focused on financial performance and most bonuses are solely dependent on financial performance. As a rule, one could state: as long as the financial performance of the company is good, a CEO gets away with a lot of bad behavior, but as soon as the performance declines, the lack of soft skills undermines the CEO.

Coaching should be part of the normal work process of the board, when directors give the CEO feedback and advice. However, to separate the coaching part is not easy. Given the importance of the top management performance for a hierarchical organization like a company, any mistake in the selection of the top team can be costly – not only in financial terms. Therefore the right selection and good coaching can be an important value added by the board.

(3) Substantive input in the corporate evolution

The work of the board should also lead to better decisions. The formal process of approving budget, strategy plans, investments, etc. does not ensure this. Take strategy: after all the executives, expert staff, plus consultants have worked on this document for months, what can the board add that is specific and unique? But there are other areas of opportunity for adding value, too: one is the development of a specific code of conduct that spells out clearly the core values of a company, its vision, and mission – hopefully both beyond the usual 'motherhood and apple pie' statements – and mechanism of conflict resolution. The basic organizational design, e.g., the dominant axis of management, the headquarters–subsidiaries relation, is another area, where the board could give substantial input.

Value-adding board work is therefore a good balance between the 'supervising/monitoring' task and the 'substantive input/coaching' dimension. However, depending on the governance system and the role of the board, this balance can be very different, depending on which axis the emphasis is laid on (see Figure 1.3).

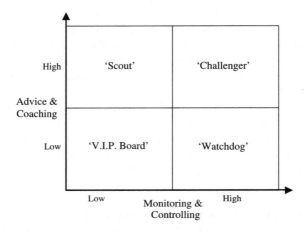

Figure 1.3   The four main types of board

The 'watchdog' board is the type now required by Sarbanes–Oxley and institutional investors. It loads its Audit Committee with heavy control tasks and predominantly examines the financial figures of past performance.

The 'scout' board is often found, for example, in privately held companies, where the owners themselves look after their money and use boards to alert them to new trends, bring new ideas, and challenge the management to avoid complacency.

For the 'VIP' board, the performance on both axes is low. We call it the VIP board as such a board is often stuffed with VIPs, who have little intention of looking at the nitty-gritty of the business. One recent example was the board of Hollinger International, where Henry Kissinger – former US Secretary of State and an eminent historian – served next to other, mostly retired, but still to all intents senior government officials.

The 'challenger' board combines high performance with the 'scout' and the 'watchdog' dimension of board work. But honestly, we haven't seen many practical examples of such boards performing very highly on every axis, as the integration of the two tasks represents a dilemma.

But whatever type of board is a good fit for a company, in the end it matters how the directors and corporate officers all work together and are able to contribute. This personal dimension is especially important when, in tough situations, the players have to stand and act together.

1.8   TYPICAL DILEMMAS FOR THE BOARD

As far as board work differs, depending on the shaping factors of CG, there are some typical dilemmas, which any board of a global company has to address in one way or another:

1. *Drive for shareholder value in global markets vs. expectations of society regarding the corporate license to operate.*
   Especially in Europe, but increasingly in the USA too, companies are confronted by dilemmas resulting from the different expectations in the home market and the pressure of capital markets. Closing a factory in Europe despite its profitability can easily end in a PR nightmare. To shift manufacturing to China can invite political pressure groups in the USA to call for a boycott. The reason is always that the perceptions of the opinion leaders and the public at large differ widely from the management elite and their perceptions about needed actions for survival in a cut-throat competition. The board also has no solution to this dilemma. Remember, dilemmas cannot be solved, but they need to be managed. But the board has to give guidance and define the space in which management has to make its decisions. Clear values and strategic priorities from the board at least allow a company to appear thoughtful and honest, even if not everybody can agree with the decision.

2. *Eroding boundaries in global companies vs. national and cultural framework.*
   The boundary-less organization with a seamless flow of information in global processes has become the ideal of many organizational theorists. But national boundaries as a cultural divide between customers still call for a segmented organization. This makes most global companies unbelievably complex, as we will illustrate, for example, in Chapter 8 on subsidiary governance. How can these conflicting demands be reconciled? How can needed differentiation be allowed, but 'fiefdoms' not? How can such a complex organization be supervised? This is definitely the area where the board has to guide the organizational development, set criteria, and step in from time to time to reduce the naturally growing complexity.

3. *Risk taking vs. tight financial control.*
   Companies want their local leaders to take risks, otherwise profitable growth opportunities are missed and the subsidiary declines into a bureaucracy. But what is the difference between an expected, entrepreneurial risk taking and betting the company? At the fringes of the wide spectrum it is easy to tell, in a larger gray area it is not. What are the (financial) control mechanisms to ensure accountability and create organizational transparency but not burden the organization with huge reporting and other transaction costs and restrict opportunity taking? Again, here the board has to be clear on the balance to be struck.

4. *Micromanagement vs. detachment.*
   In any checks-and-balances model, but also in the ownership-centered or consensus model, it is vital to define the space in which management can act and that for which they are held accountable. Boards can err on both sides: to micromanage and get involved (not to say immersed) in operational decisions. On the other hand, boards can be too detached, and not really know what's going on – to the point where it is too late for a smooth correction. Again, here the board has to find a transparent and shared understanding. The board then has to ensure management knows about it. It must be crystal clear what space the board will give to the management and where the board is in full control.

As we have seen in previous sections, the corporate governance revolution with more active boards has clearly narrowed the space for management in recent years. A case in point is that CEO succession is now much more under board control than it used to be. In respect of the USA it would be fair to say that tight financial control has increased and the impact on risk taking will be felt in the years to come. Few companies will be able to combine an 'HP culture', which was said to be the role model for an entrepreneurial spirit, with tight financial controls.

The ongoing process of globalization and complexity drives the dilemmas. If one observes declining or failed companies, one often sees that the board failed to develop a workable answer to the four dilemmas. Often boards flip-flop, switching from one extreme to another, accompanied by dramatic changes in top management. The focus on the – indeed horrible – fraud cases both in the USA and Europe tends to see only the tip of the iceberg, and not the lurking widespread problem of non-performing boards that do not violate any laws.

One case which stands out is the bankruptcy of Swissair, once one of the most admired airlines in the world (see Section 1.13 for a full report). The board never addressed the question whether Swissair could be a profitable international carrier in a deregulating market without a relevant home market. The first-tier position was a national mandate, but this idea was never tested against its economic feasibility. This was the first dilemma. The board allowed an acquisition spree into third-tier airlines, which carried huge liabilities as the second dilemma, which the board did not understand. Ultimately, it was too Swiss in its mentality. Remember, the case takes place in a country where the last serious strike was in 1936. It was obviously unthinkable that the unions would fight the company and go on strike, even if it sank the company, which was the third dilemma.

And most of the board was too detached and ignored red warning flags, except the one board member who had developed the strategy in his previous job, as a McKinsey consultant, and pushed it through with the CEO to the bitter end, which represented the fourth dilemma.

Nevertheless, from the outside, the Swissair board met all the criteria of 'best practice'. It had – by law – almost exclusively independent members, which represented the Swiss business elite, including the top banks. It had committees such as an audit committee, met regularly, and followed the accounting rules. At least the external auditors, one of the top four, did not balk, and the board met reporting requirements. Illegal operation could not be detected in a criminal investigation. But the bankruptcy was spectacular . . .

1.9   CORPORATE GOVERNANCE AND FINANCIAL PERFORMANCE

Ultimately, the additional cost of corporate governance should be overcompensated by the added value, which ultimately should be seen in the financial bottom line. But it is notoriously hard to detect there.[8] In empirical studies, a wide range of board aspects have been explored, such as board composition, the impact of committees and their structures, role and effects of independent directors, ownership issues, the role of individuals, and diversity among top managers, to name but a few. In the quest for 'low-hanging fruit' on insights into

---

[8] For an overview, see Dalton, D., Daily, C., Elbstrand, A. and Johnson, J. (1998). Meta-analytic review of board composition, leadership structure and financial performance. *Strategic Management Journal* **19**: 269–290.

corporate governance, a plethora of studies have been conducted to identify a few corporate governance aspects with larger performance. However, these studies too often relied on:

- Convenience sampling in individual studies in terms of a smaller set of easy-to-collect indicators, instead of a more comprehensive set.
- A large variety of indicators overall, making integration and comparability of results across studies difficult.
- Only data for public listed companies being available, overlaid by many other influencing factors such as business cycle, industry trends, M&A activities, etc.
- The lack of expected analysis of measurement properties for selected corporate governance indicators.
- Shortcomings in the understanding of the number of dimensions (or constructs) necessary to comprehensively depict or assess corporate governance.
- Weaknesses in the conceptualization of proxies, e.g., percentage of external board members for independence.
- The incomparability of samples used.
- The preoccupation with the statistical significance of results instead of explanatory power, especially the 'scientific' ones.
- And last, but certainly not least, a too linear thinking (do A to achieve B, always, in all settings, at all times), during which interactions between governance aspects are hardly considered.

But as Wharton Professor Larcker and his colleagues show, the empirical foundation is indeed weak. He screened the 39 most important factors commonly linked to performance, reduced them to 14 governance factors through principal component analysis, and could only explain 6% of the cross-sectional performance variation.[9] In other words, even the most established variables cannot explain a noteworthy part of performance.

As a result, one can easily question the importance of corporate governance based on the simplistic success hypotheses currently proposed and measured. What is needed is a revised understanding of such studies that board performance is heavily contingent upon specific factor constellations in each company. The role of boards and individuals, such as the CEO, varies over time. Simplistic calls for undifferentiated to-dos beyond compliance will lag behind their inherent potential if they remain unadapted to each case. There are further key points to bear in mind.

The notion of what good CG means in detail is shifting. Depending on the research question and methodology, or the time frame and selected indicators, a lot of contradictory and difficult-to-interpret results are available. Sometimes CG is defined in a way that is hard to distinguish from good management in general. Only one thing is certain: none of the individual characteristics of today's 'good CG practice', such as independent directors, audit committee, etc., lead to superior financial performance, but obviously do not harm it either. Exceptions abound. In the global auto industry, General Motors ranks top in CG, but is unfortunately a lousy financial performer. Toyota and Porsche are the notorious and deliberate violators of the best CG practice on various dimensions, but their financial performance is top in the industry. The influence of CG is more indirect and mediated.

---

[9] Larcker, D. *et al.* (2005). How important is corporate governance? Working Paper, The Wharton School, University of Pennsylvania.

It should lead to better decisions in terms of strategy, organization, and selection of top management, but it is hard to detect a linear, mono-causal relationship.

Suggested further reading

Colley, J. *et al.* (2003). *Corporate Governance*. McGraw Hill, New York.
Demb, A. and Neubauer, F. (1992). *The Corporate Board – Confronting the Paradoxes*. Oxford University Press, New York.
Hilb, M. (2004). *New Corporate Governance*, Springer, New York.
Melnitzer, J. (2003). US presses Europeans to implement governance reforms. *Corporate Legal Times* **13**(137): 36–37.

Suggested key websites

The Conference Board: http://www.conference-board.org
The Institute of Directors: http://www.iod.com

1.10   WHERE DOES CORPORATE GOVERNANCE SPECIFICALLY ADD VALUE?

The last section concluded with the cautious finding that the relation between CG, board performance, and corporate (financial) performance is probably looser than we would like to see, given the importance of CG for companies. Although we are not able to detect statistically meaningful correlations, or even cause–effect relations from the structured feature of CG, does not mean that the value of CG cannot be discovered and specified or not quantified on the level of an individual company. Here is where contingency theory comes in, not least because it is also important to know not only how but also for whom this value added is created. It is in the foundation of a pluralistic society that interests can and will differ. Markets are platforms where the different economic interests are reconciled between creditors and investors, customers and suppliers, employees and owners, etc. But the rules of the game must be transparent and sufficiently stable. How CG contributes to answering the question 'who is creating what value added and for whom' is the core of this chapter, which goes beyond the analysis of structural features.

What are the potential areas of value-added?

(1) *Corporate evolution.*
Corporations are often described as living organisms, they evolve – they not only grow, but also regress. They constantly adapt to a changing business and political or social environment. As in nature, this process is dangerous. Many companies fail to reach the next level, miss the needed adaptation, or change too slowly. If this happens, the root cause is never operational ineffectiveness – such failures start at the top. Normally the board had not seen the indicators for adaptation and changed too early, or failed to act accordingly, or did not understand the dilemma with which they were confronted correctly, and had to balance and manage the conflicting goals. Companies in such situations often flip-flop, moving from one extreme to the next, or send confusing, even contradictory, signals about their strategic intent. The board has to be a guardian of permanent vigilance to ensure the evolution of the company. What options are available to achieve this goal?

(2) Values and code of conduct.
Companies have to make a profit to survive in a market economy – but the how, the conduct, the way by which these goals are achieved is by no means determined. Companies can be ruthless, aggressive, and selfish or be honest, caring, and compassionate – and both behaviors can be successful as long as everybody in the organization knows what the values are which guide behavior and customers accept certain behavior. The 'tone at the top' communicates the values for which a company stands, and the expected business conduct in one way or another. Actions, decisions, the way people work together at the top speak most loudly. In a hierarchical organization only the apex, the board, can set the values and define the code of conduct. If this is not clear, confusion and political infighting are a very likely result.

(3) Transparency and accountability.
A key precondition for corporate evolution and value-based decisions is – internal as well as external – transparency and accountability. Especially in global – and that means always – complex organizations this is not a trivial task, and in a hierarchical organization it either starts at the top or not at all. The questions are simple. What should be known by whom, and when? Who is accountable for what? But the answers are not straightforward and can only be found in a design that serves the business (remember: structure follows strategy) and is as simple as possible. The reason why boards need to get involved in the basic design of an organization lies exactly in this responsibility to establish accountability and transparency – not allowing the proliferation of headquarters bureaucracy to blur the lines and generate too much politics.

But the transparency and accountability includes the board itself. In today's mobile, networked society, conflicts of interest are nearly unavoidable for board members. As an example, one favorite question that recently arose: does it already constitute a conflict of interest if you are a board member and also a major investor? If you try to bring only people to the boardroom who cannot, according to their CV, have any potential conflict of interest, then you end up with the US problem of selecting a jury in a high-profile murder: you have to choose the most ignorant people. Therefore the question is, when (as early as possible) and how (as openly as expected by the most critical stakeholder) to reveal cases of conflict of interest when they emerge and how to solve them – thereby setting a standard for the whole organization. The more clearly the board has defined its own role and that of its individual members, the better the issues around the conflict of interest can be managed.

(4) Core processes.
Standardized, and this does not mean centralized, processes are one of the effective simplifiers in complex, global organizations and the only means to ensure transparency and accountability throughout the whole organization. The board needs to evaluate those processes and the principal designs on which they are built. This makes life for a board easier, since it is easier for board members with diverse business backgrounds to evaluate the effectiveness of processors than to go into the detailed content. It also helps board members to understand the basic underlying assumptions and the risks of a strategy better, as they examine the process of strategizing. But given the complexity of today's CG, the board is well advised to design its own processes as a role model for the organization. It starts with the sensitive issue of CEO and top management succession to the evaluation of its own performance, the way conflicts of interest are handled, the chapter of committees, etc.

(5) Select top management and set incentives.
One of the areas most difficult to quantify, but with an extremely high value-adding potential, is found in just making the right personnel choices. This is a question which, unfortunately,

can only be answered in hindsight. But to select a wrong CEO can cost the organization dearly, as many examples indicate, especially when companies suddenly find themselves in a turnaround situation – or worse. As we will discuss in Chapter 6, it is not a one-time decision, but a constant process of monitoring, evaluating, giving feedback, providing coaching – and setting the right incentives to keep the CEO and his top team on the right track. Especially the setting of incentives is more difficult than usually appreciated. The example of stock options indicates, however, how easily things can go wrong. Remember the law of unintended consequences, especially if you naïvely apply a theory. Perhaps even the principle–agent theory is a bit naïve here, assuming that the principal can set incentives through his own enthusiasm and not be manipulated by the agent.

How do stakeholders benefit from good CG?

'To restore the trust of investors' were the magic words motivating the US Congress to embark on the massive regulation named after the congressional co-sponsors Sarbanes–Oxley. However, trust is not a category of the principal–agent theory, which is built on the assumption that agents behave opportunistically according to their own interests. Trust might be a result of longer experience, but is never per se the core of a regulation. In economic terms, it would be more precise to talk about lowering the risk premium for investors and with that lift share prices up – again – through higher price–earnings multiples. When investors see their investments are at additional risk, because they can be 'ripped off' through manipulation by managers, majority owners, or regulators, they demand a higher return from that investment to compensate for the risk. This is the simple reason why the price–earnings ratios in most emerging economies are much lower than in more developed countries. Hence, good CG simply lowers the risk premium for investors as they can look inside the company through the reporting requirements and assume that their interests are institutionally protected. This is the fiduciary duty of the board.

But to comply with a defined and known set of rules of the game is not only beneficial for investors, but the fundamental precondition for a market economy – otherwise transaction costs would be simply too high (e.g., if one cannot assume that the company will pay its invoice for a delivered product or service) – and a lot of commercial transactions would be more costly. Similar considerations are valid for M&A, any supply chain, and other cooperation agreements. And it helps that the government not only enforces laws, but that compliance is also institutionalized in the company itself.

As far as good CG leads to better corporate decisions – as argued before this is hope, not a certainty – everybody would be better off: the employees, the customer, the local communities within which a company is operating, and society at large, e.g., through higher taxes.

1.11   THE CONTINGENT ROLE OF BOARDS

The previous sections examined possible contributions, value-added, and financial performance. In the following, we outline how this matters when designing roles for boards. Many discourses on boards and directors often emphasize such roles and responsibilities, as the relationship among the various participants in determining corporations' direction and performance is central to corporate governance. Previous research indicated the large variety of roles boards can play.[10] In particular, the role of the board in firm strategy has long been the subject of debate. There is a frequent call for more active and contributing boards, and criticism of mere 'rubber stamp boards' limited to signing off CEOs' decisions.

In addition, each corporate governance model, in which boards operate, shows distinctive strength and weakness profiles and can adapt to new requirements over time, thus alluding to dynamics within boards' roles over time. In general, there is no lack of normative studies calling for improvements in boards' performance, but there is a lack of studies and of a comprehensive framework describing the actual dynamics in boardrooms based on rich description, triggered by a strong mono-method bias in the corporate governance field.

Such a framework for boards' contingent role that considers dynamics over time was proposed by our colleague at IMD, Paul Strebel.[11] Depending on various conditions, boards' driving role can vary between an auditing, supervising, coaching, and steering role, as described in Figure 1.4. 'Driving role' therefore refers to the subset of activities that dominate, but never completely replace, others.

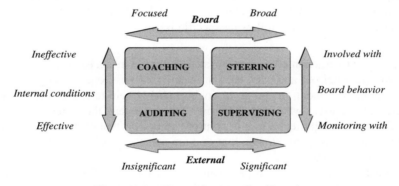

Figure 1.4   The contingent role of boards
Source: Strebel (2004), p. 62.

The framework allows for less board involvement in the execution of decisions whenever the management in place appears to be effective, and externalities' scope and nature appear rather insignificant. Sound auditing would suffice in this phase. But more board involvement is called for when the management functions ineffectively, necessitating true coaching. When externalities such as, for example, safety or pollution risks become more significant, the board can either adopt a more supervising role whenever management seems to function rather ineffectively, or needs to become involved with the execution of decisions, adopting a steering role as long as needed. The board perspective must therefore be larger and more long-term than just focused on auditing. This holds especially true when the board's perspective is too narrow and the board is encouraged to act more as a coach whenever the management appears ineffective, while externalities tend to be insignificant. The ABB case presented in Section 1.14 will demonstrate how this model works in a specific case.

[10] See, for example, Demb, A. and Neubauer, F. (1992). The corporate board: confronting the paradoxes. *Long Range Planning* **25**(3): 12–17.
[11] See Strebel, P. (2004). The case for contingent governance. *MIT Sloan Management Review* **Winter**: 59–67. Also: Amann, W., Brellochs, J. and Steger, U. (2005). The contingent role of boards – the case of ABB's turnaround. European Academy of Management, May, Munich.

Learning nuggets from the cases

As a learning platform for this consideration, we present two cases here. The first, 'Developing corporate governance at Highfly Logistics Software – but how?', presented in Section 1.12, deliberately did not choose a public quoted company, but a venture capital setting, to underline the notion that CG is not just an issue for public, stock market-listed companies, but an issue for every company (and not a potential distraction for students by focusing on legal requirements that should be avoided). It should really concentrate on the question: what, in the specific situation, is the value-added of a more developed CG system? What can better CG contribute to the further corporate development? And for whom is this a value-added, and for whom not?

Contingency theory can help to identify the misfit between the shaping factors of CG and the current situation. Usually the growth of a company requires different CG frameworks and models for leadership accountability, while an enlargement of the investor base requires more transparency. But this general notion does not determine what exactly should be done. The core of the controversy is the evolution from a CEO-centered model to a checks-and-balances model. This raises the following specific issues:

- Are the higher transaction costs compensated by the better decision-making process? As this is uncertain upfront and even hard to quantify ex-post, one can argue – sometimes very emotionally – about this point. It would probably help to clarify the different roles and personal interests ('what is in it for me?') to understand the different positions: that of the CEO, who might feel a loss of control and power; that of an investor, who might regard it as a less risky investment; that of a top management team, who asked for more a rational decision, etc.
- CG unavoidably has to do with personalities, and therefore the issue is always if key people can make the move to the 'next level' of CG or if they are so fixed in their current role that the change in CG means also a change in key people (here the CEO).
- But also the board has to ask what its new role means in terms of workload, processes, responsibilities, and – last but not least – what this means for the behavior and contribution of an individual board member and his personal responsibility (if not liability) that goes hand-in-hand with a more active and involved board.
- Last, but not least, it depends on the design of the processes and the level of elaboration, e.g., of risk management, which are chosen. The 'what' cannot be meaningfully decided without looking at the 'how', which is not only true for CG. It might be helpful for such a decision to rapidly develop a prototype of the process, which is envisioned, for example, regarding risk management, focusing on key design characteristics, and the benefit such a process would generate.

We have already outlined the dilemmas in the Swissair case. The subsequent ABB case, 'Corporate governance during a turnaround', presented in Section 1.14, focuses on one specific issue of the value-added by CG: the role of the board in strategy formation. A turnaround is a moment when the previous conventional wisdom and the 'way we do things around here' needs to be fundamentally challenged as it probably contributed significantly to the downfall. But a more active board role in strategy formation raises some fundamental issues too:

- First and foremost here is: how? After all, boards are less informed than management. At least, this is a basic assumption of the principal–agent theory and if this assumption does not hold true – well, then the company has an additional problem. Can boards, or in this case the strategy committee, obtain and process the necessary information unbiasedly, in time, and can the board members make sense of it? How much information do they need to understand the specific market segments of a business unit, the specific value drivers, the technology trends, etc. to make a meaningful contribution? On the other hand, can their different knowledge and expertise add value by giving the strategy a fresh perspective (after the old one obviously didn't work) and push through the needed strategic shift, which the previous 'insiders' had been unable to do as they were too locked into an unworkable paradigm and unable to change in time. But to make such a different perspective work needs more than just a challenging idea. It needs time-consuming detailed work to think through the application within the specific unit and the competences and resources for implementation. The board members' unavoidable time expenditure can easily become the real bottleneck in this process, as this work is more time-consuming when boards challenge the robustness of the strategic planning assumptions or look at the way the strategy process is organized.
- The second issue is the division of labor between management and the board – and the responsibility and accountability that goes with it. If management proposes a strategy, the board approves it after some debate but it basically remains unchanged – the 'usual' situation. The board can still hold the management accountable if their strategy does not work for whatever reason. But what if the board has designed the strategy to a large degree, and it did not work? The question can only be raised here as in the ABB case, the redesigned strategy seems to work. Also, from the management perspective, it should be considered what it feels like if the board were to move too much into the management's 'territory', degrading them, in the worst case, to mere implementers of what others have decided.
- Third, in a turnaround situation much can be accepted, as every manager has a very personal struggle to improve nearly every aspect of management and keep morale high despite layoffs. Every helping hand is welcome. But as soon as things get back on track, how sustainable is a solution that was acceptable in the stress of a turnaround? Probably it needs – as contingency theory will recommend – another adjustment to the new business situation, but without repeating the old mistakes.
- Fourth, the strategy work of the board has to fit into the dominant CG model and the way other decisions are made. Section 1.11 outlines our main contingency framework on how boards work.

Conclusion

The 'learning nuggets' from the two cases could therefore be summarized. CG is – beyond the legal requirements – a value-adding institutional set-up, which needs to be negotiated between the key players in a company (including investors) and answers the question: value-added for whom? The CG system also depends on contingency factors such as size, business situation, personalities, and ownership, and therefore evolves over time. There is a need for synchronization with corporate evolution. The board has to be specific in the value-added of its work, establishing transparency and accountability as two outcomes of its work, which need to be ensured under all circumstances. Selecting the right people for top management, setting the values and incentives according to the fundamental strategic direction, and ensuring the integrity of the core process designs are other areas where a board can add significant, but hard-to-quantify, value-added.

1.12   CASE STUDY: DEVELOPING CORPORATE GOVERNANCE AT HIGHFLY LOGISTICS SOFTWARE – BUT HOW?

6 JUNE 2005, IN HIGHFLY'S BOARDROOM AT 11:47AM. Tom was angrily looking at Arno, not even trying to hide his emotions:

> More corporate governance...?! You want to bring bureaucracy to us, killing the entrepreneurial spirit and speed that has made this company so successful?

Loosening his tie, Tom looked around at the other members of the board of directors. Reminding himself that he wanted to become a team player, he stopped and asked:

> What do you think?

There was no immediate response, as the members of the board of directors were obviously unsure and needed time to reflect. Tom was the co-founder, chairman, CEO, and master brain of Highfly Logistics Software, a London-based software company specializing in logistics solutions since its inception seven years ago (see Figure 1.5 for Highfly's organizational structure). Surviving the burst of the dot.com bubble, Highfly had grown rapidly in its market niche, doubling headcount and revenue year by year. The fast growth seemed to be slowing down the organization as some of the board members had pointed out during the discussion around the previous agenda item. To better serve its customers, the original 'one-size-fits-all software program' had been split into three distinct product lines for: truck companies, retailers, and warehouse companies. Highfly employed a highly qualified and technically trained sales force, which not only installed and upgraded the software, but also helped customers with a broad variety of issues: training for their workforce, 'fire fighter

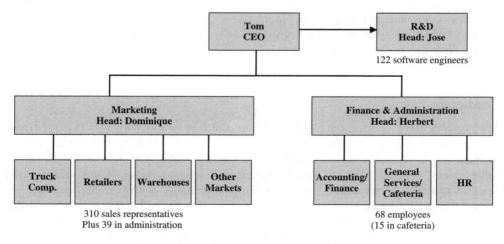

Figure 1.5   Highfly's organizational structure

teams' for emergency situations, adaptation to company-specific needs, etc., all very much to the satisfaction of its customers.

Recently the company had ventured into other geographic markets, establishing sales and support offices in four bigger European countries. Competition was gearing up slowly, but continuously, from both a French and a German competitor. Now, a team was working on entering China, but Tom's real dream was to conquer the USA – if Highfly could afford it.

Highfly's need for organizational adaptation

Herbert, the CFO and the longest-serving executive next to Tom, with three years of Highfly experience, warned a month ago that if revenues and profit margins continued to fall, as they had over the last six months, the company would slide deep into the red by the first quarter of 2006.

For Tom, Highfly's success – which had largely been his own success story – had to continue. He had seen too many start-ups disappearing almost at the same speed as they had mushroomed in the first place, and he did not want Highfly – and himself – to become the next victim. After analyzing recent developments, Tom determined that Highfly's costs were outpacing revenue growth for several reasons. He then developed what he called a corporate fitness program that included the following points, which he communicated in a 'letter from the CEO' to his key people:

- Too much duplication in adapting efforts for customer needs.
- The customer did not cover the full cost of additional services and developments.
- The marketing and sales organization wanted to keep the customer in 'their domain' instead of involving R&D for specific applications. As they were lacking sufficient technical competence, this resulted in quality problems, which were expensive to fix.
- The newly established country organizations still lacked sufficient access to the R&D base and occasionally bought expensive software modules and consultants on the market instead of using the available in-house resources.
- The general overheads (HR, cafeteria, accounting, etc.) had been exploding after moving into a new office building nine months ago. The much appreciated and frequented cafeteria costs alone were a considerable £144[12] per employee per month.

To conclude his most recent 'letter from the CEO' to his key people, Tom proposed the following:

- To impose a hiring freeze.
- To close the cafeteria.
- To outsource the HR, accounting, and general services function to external providers.
- To demand that subsidiaries rely on internal solutions exclusively and participate in more knowledge sharing.
- To establish a goal of reducing administration costs by 5% and R&D costs by 10%.

But closing the cafeteria and cuts in R&D were strongly opposed by José, an old buddy of Tom's with a similar 'techno-freak' background. José was responsible for R&D and strongly

---

[12] £1 roughly equaled €1.45 or US$1.82.

defended any move which could possibly have a negative impact on his domain. After all, R&D was 'his baby', which he had to protect.

Dominique, the youngest member of the executive team, joined Highfly as chief marketing officer in late 2002. As an exception, Dominique had been allowed to join the ongoing board meeting in order to provide an update on the international expansion. He was also opposed to Tom's ideas as he was unsure if they had been well thought through or if Tom was merely 'shooting from the hip'. Dominique definitely did not want to narrow the managerial discretion of the subsidiaries, which needed the freedom to get established to ensure a lasting return on investments.

Arno was one of the most active members of the board of directors. He understood Tom's desire to continuously develop the organization but also saw room for improvement elsewhere. As Tom was about to close the meeting by asking if there was any further business to discuss, Arno came up with the proposal to re-examine the actual contribution of the board of Highfly. Half an hour earlier, Arno had commented to Herbert during a coffee break for the board in the cafeteria:

> Tom is a real incarnation of the classic imperial CEO. Ok, I have heard he does delegate if someone comes up with a promising idea, but what do we as the board actually do? We have no checks and balances in place – no real outside experts on the board level, no annual evaluation, simply nothing. We are no longer a start-up – one brain cannot do it all alone. Our challenges are just too complex – and it will get worse. We need to change something; we need to become better and better. While we tend to demand greater efforts from others, nothing is moving in this part of the organization. It is not right. Our real value potential is not in internal restructuring, but with our clients out there. We need to provide fresh stimuli – on an ongoing basis. Don't you agree?

Herbert nodded with a sigh, sipping from his hot latte macchiato, for him the best there was among all cafeteria offers. He did not know what to add.

Corporate governance at Highfly

The initial business success overshadowed an area of Highfly that saw few changes in the last seven years – corporate governance. Tom felt he had a clear vision of where Highfly needed to be 10 years down the road, so he tried to avoid having long and tedious board meetings. Highfly's board usually met four to five times a year for no more than two or three hours. While attendance was quite good, it was not unusual for a member to be absent. The board consisted of five people:

- Tom Svensson, Chairman & CEO.
- Herbert Jones, Chief Financial Officer.
- Van Chu, First Stages Capital.
- Arno Levin, Venture Partners.
- Kevin Garzias, Independent Director with several board assignments.

Van and Arno represented two private equity investors. First Stages Capital originally invested £5 million in exchange for a 30% stake. Venture Partners came on board later and financed the second round of expansion, with £25 million, and now owned 40% of Highfly.

In contrast to Arno, who had just recently replaced a retiring colleague, Van had been on the board for almost seven years. Herbert remembered Van's comment during one of the previous board meetings:

> We are more like passive investors. We really try to understand the business model and market opportunities, but then we have to let the CEO and his team run the show. Strategies need years to fully deploy. We stay in the background and can hopefully watch how the value of our investment increases. Tom has done a good job so far.

Tom and his co-founders (most of whom had left the organization) owned the rest of Highfly. Tom thought back to the moment when he decided to open the company to outside investors to spur growth:

> If only I had kept it within my family and group of friends . . . then I would not have to deal with all of this.

Things went pretty well for Tom in general. He had great relationships with the independent directors, especially the two representatives from the investor side. Also Arno, who was extrovert and still rather young, fitted in perfectly shortly after joining the board. Both Arno and Van knew that every business required special knowledge that was gained from being 'at the pulse' of the business to sense the intricacies of new developments. They were happy with the performance of Highfly so far, and Tom never had a problem keeping them impressed with his convincing style and charisma.

Kevin was the remaining person on the board. After retiring from his professorship at London Business School, he continued to have several board assignments. The other co-founders and co-owners brought him in when they significantly reduced their shareholding in Highfly and left the board in 2004. They trusted Kevin's neutral stance and long-term view. After all, he was a renowned business professor and author of a range of business books for managers. Kevin liked the intelligence hidden in Highfly's software and was keen on promoting start-ups and entrepreneurship in general. As Kevin had board experience to offer, he was deemed to be a highly suitable candidate for the board. In spite of being retired, he seemed to continue to be extremely busy with speeches and social engagements.

A moment of truth in Highfly's boardroom

Tom usually navigated smartly through the board meetings. He set the right tone at the top, which had always been frank and positive – until today. While his style was sometimes perceived as too fast, he nonetheless succeeded in checking off items on the agenda quite efficiently. For a surprisingly long time, there was little trouble on the horizon as Highfly emerged as a key player from the vanishing heydays of the Internet boom, and corporate governance at Highfly saw few changes.

Arno's proposal was rather clear and simple. He suggested the following:

- Double the number of board meetings.
- Increase the involvement of the board in the strategy process.
- Build a risk management system.
- Introduce an audit committee, which would also be responsible for the risk management system.

Everybody in the ongoing board meeting knew that Tom truly hated conflicts and 'administration' (as he called everything outside of product development and delivery). After personal coordination, he 'let everybody run their own show'. His usual recommendation to any suggestion was:

Grab the ball and run!

And now this . . .

Tom looked into the faces of the board members, waiting for a response. Nervously ticking his Mont Blanc on the table, he was still breathing hard after the unusual outburst towards Arno. There was no ambiguity in the room – he wanted to know from them what Highfly should do now about corporate governance, if anything needed to be done at all.

1.13   CASE STUDY: DID CORPORATE GOVERNANCE FAIL AT SWISSAIR?

[By Ulrich Steger and Helga Krapf]

4 OCTOBER 2001. The protestors were walking down Zurich's Bahnhofstrasse. Many held placards with one word: 'CHaos'. Tabloids that day exclaimed:

What a shame. Switzerland is a banana republic. Everything we are proud of went down the drain. Honesty. A sure eye. Dependability.[13]

The reliability of Swiss trains, airlines, and watches is legendary and seen as a synonym for the functioning of the country. The Swiss could not understand why one of their national icons – and their whole country – was suddenly hit by crisis.

What had happened? On 2 October 2001 Swissair, Switzerland's national airline, had suspended all flights because of liquidity problems. Some 40,000 angry passengers worldwide were stranded.

On October 3 bank officials and Swissair executives blamed each other for the grounding. Christoph Blocher, Swiss politician and entrepreneur, commented:

The disastrous linkage of politics, country, cantons, trade associations, big companies and the ruling parties turned Swissair into an untouchable symbol. Swissair was a temple, a god and a juggernaut.[14]

But who was responsible for the grounding? Was the corporate governance system overstretched as a result of managing a company whose corporate boundaries had begun to erode because of strategic alliances? Or was national politics too involved in a global business? Would tighter financial controls have been necessary to control risks taken in implementing a global strategy? Could the board have balanced the aims of a charismatic CEO? Had the board been too detached from management and could they have prevented such a disaster?

---

[13] Scotsman (Edinburgh), 4 October 2001.
[14] Aargauer Zeitung (Aargau), 5 November 2001.

Consolidation in the global airline industry

The still heavily regulated aviation industry was the subject of liberalization worldwide. The American aviation industry had been going through a deregulation process since 1978, which encouraged more than 50 new companies to enter the business. The resulting overcapacity triggered strong price competition. Most of the start-ups, as well as some of the older airlines, eventually went out of business.

The European market for air transport had grown dramatically over the years – in 2000 it was 32 times bigger than it had been in 1960. The European Community gradually established a single market for air transport. Between 1980 and 1993 issues such as market access, capacity control, and fares were deregulated, with similar effects as in the United States. New 'no-frills' airlines added further pressure on prices. In 2000 these airlines accounted for 5.2% of the intra-European air travel market. A rapid growth in their market share had been forecast. Despite the liberalization, mergers and acquisitions were difficult due to complex legal situations. Airlines tended to join European or global alliances instead (refer to Figure 1.6 for membership and global ranking).

Too big to be small: Swissair in search of a new strategy

In 1992 Swissair flew to 109 destinations in 66 countries when the Swiss voted against integrating the country into the European Economic Area. Swissair had to remain globally competitive or run the risk of becoming an insignificant regional airline, since it was no longer operating under the same conditions as airlines in the European aviation market. At that time Swissair was part of Swissair Group, with:

- Crossair, a regional European airline.
- Balair and CTA, two Basel- and Geneva-based charter airlines.
- Swissair associated companies, which included hotels, catering, etc.

The board and management were challenged in a new way as a result of the Swiss vote. In 1993 an initial merger plan with Scandinavian Airlines (SAS), Austrian Airlines (AUA), and KLM Royal Dutch Airlines met with resistance from the public, the governments involved, and trade unions. Heated debates began, especially in Switzerland, where one Bundesrat (Swiss government) member claimed:

Replacing the William Tell[15] statue in Altdorf with a statue of the Dalai Lama would give rise to the same political feelings as if Swissair merged with a foreign airline. But politicians cannot ensure the survival of a company with today's competition; it's the market that decides in the end.[16]

---

[15] William Tell: Swiss legendary hero who symbolized the struggle for political and individual freedom against Austrian authority in the 13th and early 14th centuries. However, the historical existence of Tell is disputed.
[16] *Neue Zuericher Zeitung* (Zurich), 17 June 1993.

	MEMBER From...	1999 PAX (mill)	WORLD TRAFFIC Rank	% Share	HUBS
STAR ALLIANCE					
United Airlines	May-97	87.0	2		Chicago, Denver, Los Angeles, Washington
LUFTHANSA	May-97	41.9	8		Frankfurt, Munich
Air Canada	May-97	16.2	20		Montreal, Vancouver
Thai Airways International	May-97	16.0	21		Bangkok
SAS	May-97	22.0	14		Copenhagen, Oslo, Stockholm
Varig	Oct-97	10.3	31		Rio de Janeiro, Sao Paulo
Air New Zealand	Mar-99	7.2	38	18.5	Auckland
Ansett Australia	Mar-99	11.8	29		Melbourne
All Nippon Airways	Oct-99	42.7	7		Tokyo, Osaka
AUSTRIAN AIRLINES GROUP	Mar-00	6.2	44		Vienna
Singapore Airlines	Apr-00	13.5	26		Singapore
Mexicana	Jul-00	7.8	36		Mexico City
BMI BRITISH MIDLAND	Jul-00	6.5	40		London Heathrow
ALLIANCE		**289.3**			
oneworld					
American Airlines	Feb-99	81.5	3		Dallas, Miami, Chicago
BRITISH AIRWAYS	Feb-99	36.6	10		London Heathrow
Qantas	Feb-99	16.8	19		Sydney
Cathay Pacific Airways	Feb-99	10.5	30	11.8	Hong Kong
IBERIA	Sep-99	21.9	15		Madrid
FINNAIR	Sep-99	6.1	45		Helsinki
LanChile	Jun-00	4.3	62		Santiago
AER LINGUS	Jun-00	6.3	42		Dublin
ALLIANCE		**183.9**			
SKYTEAM					
Aeromexico	Jun-00	8.7	34		Mexico City
AIR FRANCE	Jun-00	37.0	9		Paris CDG, Paris Orly
Delta Air Lines	Jun-00	105.5	1	11.1	Atlanta, Dallas, Cincinnati
Korean Air Lines	Jun-00	20.4	17		Seoul
CSA Czech Airlines	Apr-01	1.9	95		Prague
ALLIANCE		**173.5**			
The Qualiflyer Group					
SWISSAIR	Mar-98	13.3	27		Zurich
SABENA	Mar-98	10.0	33		Brussels
TAP	Mar-98	4.8	56		Lisbon
TURKISH AIRLINES	Mar-98	10.1	32		Istanbul
AOM	Mar-98	2.9	80		Paris Orly
Crossair	Jul-98	2.7	82		Basel-Mulhouse
Air Europe	May-99	1.2	110	3.5	Milan Malpensa
LOT	Jan-00	2.1	89		Warsaw
PGA	Jan-00	0.8	132		Lisbon
Volare	Jan-00	0.7			Milan Malpensa
Air Littoral	May-00	1.6	100		Nice
Air Liberté	Sep-00	4.0	66		Paris Orly
ALLIANCE		**54.2**			
WORLD WIDE RELIABILITY					
KLM	Nov-92	15.5	22	4.7	Amsterdam
Northwest	Nov-92	57.5	4		Minneapolis, Detroit, Memphis
ALLIANCE		**72.9**			
World Total Scheduled Traffic		**1,560.0**	≅ 100%		

Source: AEA/ICAO/IATA

Figure 1.6   Airline alliances: membership and ranking

In spring 1994 McKinsey Switzerland, headed by future Swissair Group board member Lukas Mühlemann, presented three basic directions:

- Stay an independent airline.
- Buy stakes in smaller airlines to become number three or four in Europe.
- Become a partner of a bigger European airline but give up its independence.

Swissair Group decided on a dual strategy:

1. Grow Swissair (then commonly referred to as the 'flying bank') and become an attractive partner for Delta Airlines.
2. Become a global player in airline-related businesses such as catering, ground handling services, and maintenance.

Management decided to pursue an aggressive acquisition strategy rather than entering into lengthy talks about cooperations. The first acquisition target was Belgian state airline Sabena, which had chronic financial problems and a reputation for bad service. Fleet and workforce reductions, as well as customer service training for the remaining employees, had failed to improve the financial situation. In May 1995 both airlines finally agreed that Swissair would take a 49.5% stake in Sabena, a foothold for the Swiss airline in the European market. The Belgian government withdrew from the operational level. Swissair appointed 5 of the 12 directors and sent a new CEO. He soothed some of the problems, but at the cost of increasing staff from 6900 employees to more than 12,000.

In 1997 McKinsey developed plans to form another airline alliance in competition with StarAlliance and OneWorld. The consultants advised Swissair Group to behave like a 'hunter', aiming for 10%–25% stakes in the European partners of Delta (Austrian AUA, Portuguese TAP, Finnish Finnair, Hungarian Malev, Irish Aer Lingus). They estimated the investment volume to be SFr 400 million. Swissair's board decided to implement the Hunter strategy.

Corporate governance in a globalizing company

Responsibility in Swissair Group was split in accordance with Swiss law. The day-to-day business was left to executive management but the board had ultimate responsibility for leading the company (Gesamtleitungsfunktion). Board members (Mitglieder des Verwaltungsrates) were entitled to request information from management and had the right to apply to the chairman to be shown books and files. The chairman played a critical role in ensuring communication and the exchange of information between executive management and board members. However, industry insiders questioned the backgrounds of the chairmen:

- Hannes Goetz, chairman 1992–2000, had no previous experience in the aviation industry.
- Eric Honegger, chairman 2000–2001, had a civil service background but no previous international experience.
- Mario Corti, chairman 2001–2002, had previously worked in banking and as chief financial officer at Nestlé but had no turnaround or operational experience.

In 1997 Swissair Group adopted a holding structure and changed its name to SAirGroup. SAirLines then consisted of Swissair, Crossair, and Balair/CTA Leisure. Figure 1.7 shows the development of group structure and executive management between 1997 and 2001.

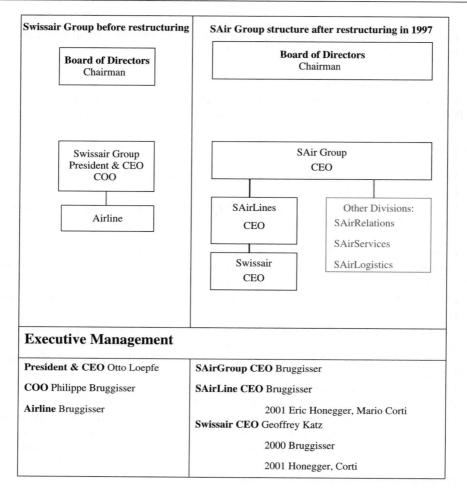

Figure 1.7   Development of group structure (simplified)

The board

Swissair Group's board members were elected for a period of three years, with the possibility of re-election. Bénédict G.F. Hentsch, managing partner of a private bank, who joined the board in 1989, remembered:

> The Swissair board was like a legion of honor. When I joined it had 32 members and I was told point-blank that it would be clever not to ask too many questions during my first two periods of tenure since I was still young. The real decision makers were the members of the executive committee of the board of directors.[17]

---

[17] *Cash*, 16 November 2001.

The complete board met about five times a year for half to one day. The executive committee, which consisted of the chairman, the two deputy chairmen, and four or five other board members, met monthly. The financial, organizational, and remuneration committees each had three members and usually met twice a year for half a day (refer to Figure 1.8 for duties of board and committees).

In 1999 Swiss aviation law changed and public representation on the board was no longer necessary. The board was reduced to 10 members, who met every month. The three committees remained but the executive committee was abolished. Instead, an advisory board

---

The duties of Swissair's board were stated in the company's Articles of Association:

1. To ultimately direct the corporation and issue the necessary directives.
2. To determine the corporate organization.
3. To organize the accounting, financial control, and financial planning to the extent that such organization is required for the overall management of the corporation.
4. To appoint and dismiss the person entrusted with the management and representation of the corporation.
5. To ultimately supervise the persons entrusted with the management of the corporation, including their compliance with the law and the corporation's Articles of Association.
6. To prepare the annual report and the shareholders meeting, and to implement the latter's resolutions.
7. To inform the legal authorities in the event of overindebtedness.

Financial Committee

The duties of the Financial Committee shall comprise in particular:

1. Considering issues relating to accounting, financial, investment, and fiscal policy, and the Group's operating accounts and associated strategies.
2. Monitoring the efficiency of management and information systems and other internal controls.
3. Defining the duties of the external and internal auditors, and assessing the scope and results of their audits.
4. Monitoring the efficiency of the audits conducted.
5. Assessing the Report of the (external) Auditors and the internal auditors' reports.

Organization Committee

The Organization Committee shall familiarize itself with the business and operations of the Group subsidiaries and form an opinion of whether the Group divisions are suitably equipped to meet future business needs. The Organization Committee shall also monitor Group personnel policy.

Remuneration Committee

The Remuneration Committee shall determine:

1. The remuneration of the Chairman of the Board and the salary and other terms and conditions of employment of the Group President & CEO.
2. The salaries and other terms and conditions of employment of the other members of Group Executive Management and the heads of business units within the Holding Company (based on recommendations by the Group President & CEO).
3. Any salaries in excess of an upper limit set by the Remuneration Committee. The Remuneration Committee shall generally meet twice a year, or additionally at the request of at least two of its members.

Figure 1.8   Board of directors and committee duties

Source: Organization Regulations of the SAirGroup; issued by the Board of Directors on 22 November 2000 (supersedes the version of 6 May 1999).

Size		**1997** **Hunter strategy**	**2000**
	Industry	14	11
	Public Inst.	4	0
Executive Committee	**Chairman**	Goetz	Honegger
	Deputy Chairmen	Hoefliger Schmidheiny	Hentsch Schmidheiny
	Other Members	• Hentsch • Honegger • L. Mühlemann • Staehelin	*Committees*: **Members not in committees**: Corti, Fischer **Financial**: Hentsch, Staehelin, Spoerry-Toneatti **Organization**: Hoeflinger, Leuenberger, L. Mühlemann **Remuneration**: Honegger, Staehelin, Schmidheiny

Corti, Mario: Swiss, born 1946; joined SAirGroup board in 2000. **Current**: Chairman of the board Swissair. **Career**: *Kaiser Aluminium and Chemical Corporation*, California: 1972–76 corporate planner. *Swiss National Bank Zürich*: 1977–86 director and deputy head of the banking department. *Federal Office for Foreign Economic Affairs*, Berne: 1986–90 ambassador and delegate of the Swiss government for trade agreements. *Nestlé*: 1991–93 senior VP and chief administrative officer, USA; 1994–95 executive VP and CFO, USA; 1996–2001 executive VP and CFO, Switzerland.

Goetz, Hannes: Swiss, born 1934; joined Swissair board in 1991, chairman from 1992–2000. **Career**: *Sika AG*: 1961–70 different positions in Switzerland and USA; 1971–79 CEO; 1979 board member and president. *Georg Fischer AG*: 1981 board member; 1983–92 board member and CEO.

Gut, Rainer E.: **Current**: Chairman of the board Nestlé. **Career**: *Lazard Frères & Co*: 1968–71 general partner, New York. *Swiss American Corporation* (Credit Suisse investment banking): 1971–73 chairman and CEO, New York. *Credit Suisse*: 1973–82 executive board member; 1982–83 president of the executive board; 1983–2000 chairman of the board of directors of Credit Suisse; 1986–2000 chairman of the board of directors of Credit Suisse Group (formerly CS Holding – renamed 1 January 1997).

Hentsch, Bénédict: Swiss, born 1948; joined Swissair board in 1989. **Career**: *Morgan Guaranty Trust of New York and Sao Paulo*: 1976–82. *Hentsch & Cie private bankers*, Geneva: 1982, 1985–2001 managing partner.

Hoefliger, Paul-Antoine: Swiss, born 1939; joined Swissair board in 1978. **Current**: Chairman of the board and president of Comptoir Suisse, Lausanne. **Career**: *Comptoir Suisse*: joined 1969; 1978 general manager; since 1990 board member, CEO and general manager.

Honegger, Eric: Swiss, born 1946; joined Swissair board in 1993, chairman 2000–2001. **Career**: *Municipal council of Rueschlikon*: 1974–78 member. *Parliament of the Swiss Federal State of Zürich*: 1979–87 member, 1983–87 president of the finance committee. *Government of the Swiss Federal State of Zürich*: 1987–91 head of construction, 1991–99 head of finance.

Figure 1.9 Members Swissair/SAirGroup committees 1995–2000
Source: Public information.

Leuenberger, Andres: Swiss, born 1938; joined Swissair board in 1995. **Current**: Vice chairman of the board and deputy CEO of Roche Holding Ltd, Basel, chairman of the board Swiss Life Insurance and Pension Company. **Career**: *Roche*: joined 1968; 1970 manager (Pharma Marketing), Tokyo; 1973–80 president and CEO. *F. Hoffmann-La Roche Ltd*, Basel: 1980 member of executive committee; 1982 vice chairman of the executive committee; 1983 board member and managing director; 1986 COO; since 1989 present position.

Mühlemann, Lukas: Swiss, born 1950; Swissair board 1995–2001. **Current**: Executive chairman and CEO of Credit Suisse Group, Zurich. **Career**: *IBM*, Switzerland: 1973–75; *McKinsey & Company*: 1977 management consultant; 1982 principal; 1986 director; 1989 managing director for Switzerland. *Swiss Reinsurance Company*: 1994 CEO and MD; 1996 also deputy chairman. *Credit Suisse*: 1997 CEO; 2000 also chairman.

Schmidheiny, Thomas: Swiss, born 1945; Swissair board 1980–2001. **Current**: Chairman of executive committee and chairman of board of directors of Holcim Ltd (formerly Holderbank), Switzerland. **Career**: *Cementos Apasco*, Mexico: 1970–71 technical management; *Holderbank Group*: 1975 managing director of Swiss cement companies; 1976 responsible for Middle East cement companies, member Holderbank executive committee; since 1978 chairman of executive committee of Holderbank; 1980 deputy chairman of board of directors of Holderbank Financière Glaris Ltd.; 1984–2001 executive chairman of Holcim AG; since 2002, majority shareholder of Holcim AG and president of the board of directors of Holcim AG.

Spoerry-Toneatti, Vreni: Swiss, born 1938; Swissair board 1989–2001. **Career**: *Municipal council of the city of Horgen*: 1978–86 member. *Prefectoral council of the canton of Zürich*: 1979–83 member. *National councillor*: 1983–95. *Councillor of state*: since 1996.

Staehelin, Gaudenz: Swiss, born 1923; Swissair board 1984–2001. **Current**: President Swiss National Committee, International Chamber of Commerce. **Career**: *Advocate*: in Basel: 1953–59. *Swissair*: 1960 assistant to chief legal advisor; 1961 deputy secretary general; 1981–86 secretary general. (Also, *Advocate*: 1984; *Lecturer in civil and comparative law*: 1985.)

Figure 1.9   (Continued)

with 15 members from multinational companies, the Swiss government, and cantons advised on strategic and aeropolitical issues. This group met two or three times a year.

Swissair's board read like the *Who's Who* of Switzerland (refer to Figure 1.9 for an overview of board and committee members). The interconnectedness of Swiss companies had been the subject of criticism. A 1980s study came to the conclusion that Switzerland was effectively run by an elite of 300 people from industry, banks, and trade associations.[18] Board members were often invited by their friends or because of their connections to politics or banks. Swiss law required the majority of board members to be Swiss nationals or residents. As a result, some Swiss held up to a dozen board seats. Ultimately, this led to situations where the CEO of one company was the chairman of the board in another and vice versa.

In the case of Swissair, chairman Eric Honegger was a director of UBS. UBS's chairman of the board, Robert Studer, was a Swissair board member. Financial committee member Vreni Spoerry-Toneatti and deputy chairman Thomas Schmidheiny were directors at Credit Suisse (CS). In turn, Rainer E. Gut, CS chairman and mentor of Lukas Mühlemann (who later also became CEO of CS), sat on the Swissair board.

---

[18] *Bilanz*, October 2000.

ruggisser: developing into a dominant leader

*.mann and two other board members stimulated discussions about the need for changes .xecutive management to implement the new strategy. In October 1995 the board appointed Philippe Bruggisser as chief operating officer (COO) of Swissair Group. At the end of 1996 he became CEO of the Group.

Bruggisser faced a dilemma right from the start. He had advised against taking a stake in Sabena, but he also knew who had made him COO. In 1997 an internal study came to the conclusion that it would be better to write off the Sabena stake. However, Mühlemann, who had only joined the board in May 1995, used his dominant influence and defended the strategy.

Bruggisser had to accept the decision but succeeded with his second goal, an international management team at Swissair. He planned not only to break up old structures in the management but also to be revolutionary and appoint a non-European CEO of the airline.

Table 1.4 Consolidated financial results SAirGroup (SFr million)

	2000	1999	1998	1997
Operating revenue				
SAirLines	7,166	6,414	5,925	5,619
SAirServices	3,183	2,412	1,941	1,805
SAirLogistics	1,712	1,346	1,280	1,221
SAirRelations	6,218	4,839	3,863	3,663
Holding company	154	83	81	42
Intragroup revenue	(2,204)	(2,092)	(1,793)	(1,794)
Total operating revenue	16,229	13,002	11,297	10,556
Total operating expenditure	(15,626)	(12,328)	(10,694)	(9,997)
Net profit/loss	(2,885)	273	361	324
Net cash inflow from operating activities	1,809	2,196	1,427	969
Net cash inflow from investment activities	(2,237)	(3,172)	(1,021)	(677)
Net cash inflow from financing activities	933	1,291	153	(431)
Net (decrease)/increase in disposable funds	505	315	559	(139)
Assets				
Current assets	7,201	5,986	5,080	4,628
Fixed assets	13,014	11,868	8,620	8,002
thereof intangible assets/goodwill*	2,274	1,767	503	446
Total assets	20,215	17,854	13,700	12,630
Liabilities				
Current liabilities	4,624	2,955	2,157	2,091
Non-current liabilities	8,161	6,853	5,418	5,030
Accrued liabilities & provisions	6,078	3,653	3,126	2,857
Liabilities	18,863	13,461	10,701	9,978

* This item consists largely of the goodwill acquired via various acquisitions since January 1995.
Source: SAirGroup Financial Statements 2000, pp. 8, 9, 11, 12, 22; SAirGroup Financial Statements 1998, pp. 10, 11, 13, 14, 22.

Geoffrey Katz, who had worked all his professional life for American Airlines, was signed as CEO for Swissair.

After net losses in 1995 and 1996, Bruggisser had managed to turn Swissair around by the end of 1997. The press celebrated him as a national hero – the company achieved a profit of SFr 324 million (refer to Table 1.4 for 1997 results).

The new CEO was not universally popular, despite his successes. His decision to stop inter-continental flights from Geneva was met with massive public criticism. But at least Zurich would be saved as international hub, which many thought was essential for Switzerland's status as an international financial center. Internally, Bruggisser controlled the flow of information to the board. But the board liked and trusted him as the sole source of power and major source of information in SAirGroup.

Implementation of the Hunter strategy

In 1998 Bruggisser started his hunt for partners with the aim of achieving 20% market share in Europe. Talks with Aer Lingus and Finnair failed, but by the end of the year shares in national, regional, and charter airlines amounted to SFr 3.2 billion – the equivalent of a 20% stake in BA. Most of these airlines joined the new Qualiflyer alliance, while continuing to operate under their own brand. The group planned to achieve economies of scale by combining all necessary back-office activities such as a common booking system, maintenance, and catering. Swissair played a key role by providing all these services to the remaining group.

SAirGroup continued to acquire stakes in different airlines (refer to Table 1.5 for an overview of SAirLines holdings acquired from 1995 to 2000). Outsiders openly questioned the value of some of these investments. Not only were some of the targets experiencing financial difficulties, but they were also operating in lower market segments. Some analysts thought SAirGroup should concentrate on diversifying into its successful airline services like catering, retailing, and cargo handling rather than increasing global alliances. The Qualiflyer members also started to voice criticisms, but Bruggisser continued to pursue new acquisitions. Deputy chairman Hentsch remembered:

> Some of the board of directors thought Bruggisser was playing a lonely powergame when he suggested acquiring airlines in France. He was the leader but his strengths were also his weakness: he didn't leave much room for others.[19]

In 1999 Bruggisser secretly discussed taking over a 9% stake in Austria's AUA from another airline. The negotiations were not successful but Bruggisser lost AUA's confidence. When AUA's board started discussions about joining another alliance, Bruggisser did not intervene, although he was a member of AUA's board. In September AUA finally decided to leave the Qualiflyer alliance. Soon afterwards Delta announced it was forming another alliance, with Air France–Sky Team.

The year was not only a difficult one in terms of managing alliances. Fuel costs for European airlines increased by more than 40% but SAirGroup still showed a net group

---

[19] *Aargauer Zeitung* (Aargau), 16 November 2001.

Table 1.5   SAirLine holdings acquired 1995–2000

Amount (SFr million)				Profit/(loss) from associated undertakings		Book value	
Airline	Stake since	Home base	Holding(%)	2000	1999	2000	1999
National airlines							
LOT Polish Airlines	2000	Poland	37.6	7		154	
Sabena	1995	Belgium	49.5	(51)	35	0	50
South African	1999	South Africa	20	16		169	355
Regional airlines							
Air Littoral	1998	France	49	(3)	(31)	0	0
AOM + Air Liberté	1999	France	49.5	(237)	(104)	0	0
Charter airlines							
LTU	1998	Germany	49.9	(498)	(167)	0	0
Volare Group + Air Europe	1999	Italy	49.79	(30)	(134)	0	19
Agreed, but not executed							
TAP	2000	Portugal	20				

Source: SAirGroup Financial Statements 2000, pp. 18, 24.

profit of SFr 273 million (compared with SFr 361 million in 1998). Other divisions compensated for the increased costs at SAirLines (refer to Table 1.4 for SAirGroup results in 1999).

Into the new millennium with baggage

Increasing fuel prices and a strong dollar exchange rate added to problems in 2000. Chairman Goetz resigned in April. Potential candidates for his succession were L. Mühlemann, Hentsch, and Honegger. However, the first two could not assume the responsibility on top of their other duties. Honegger became chairman due to his political skills and national connections. In July, Katz resigned as CEO of Swissair, and Bruggisser took over again. Although some thought he had the ideal background and knowledge to implement the Hunter strategy, others feared it would stretch management resources too much.

In October 2000, Honegger was still vaguely optimistic for the coming year:

We have fuel costs, which are still a major item. We have some restructuring costs in France and with Sabena and Delta. But we've made provisions for all those problems, it should be a normal 2001.[20]

---

[20] *Scotsman* (Edinburgh), 27 October 2001: 4.

Nevertheless, the board started debating future prospects and the direction of the Hunter strategy. Hentsch commented in November:

> You would have to be blind not to notice that the current strategy is proving more difficult to implement than expected.[21]

The troubled airlines LTU, Sabena, Air Liberté, Air Littoral, and AOM required further financial aid. Analysts estimated a demand of around SFr 3 billion within the next two years. However, it was not clear whether that would lead to profit. The necessary restructuring measures also faced heavy political and social opposition, especially in France, where militant trade unions organized strikes frequently (in Switzerland, by contrast, the last public strike had taken place in 1936). The board decided in November 2000 to continue with Hunter. A public opinion poll concluded that 92% of Swiss thought Switzerland needed a national airline. This result led one Swissair manager to the optimistic conclusion that the survey was the best thing that could have happened. He reckoned that after that there would be only little scope for the board. He was mistaken. Hentsch remembered:

> We asked Bruggisser the crucial question in December: had the Group enough liquidity to solve the problems with Sabena? Bruggisser didn't seem to be able to admit the whole situation. He had never been so lonely before, he didn't really listen to anybody anymore.[22]

Fighting crisis

SAirGroup reported a net loss of SFr 2.9 billion for the previous business year in January 2001 (refer to Table 1.4 for SAirGroup results in 2000). The board finally decided to abandon the Hunter strategy due to financial, time, and management capacity restraints. This decision and its results had far-reaching management consequences. Chairman Honegger, who lacked Bruggisser's entrepreneurial drive, became temporary CEO of SAirGroup. On 15 March 2001 'Super Mario'[23] Corti took over as chairman and CEO of SAirGroup. Later it was made public that he had been paid five years' salary in advance as compensation for professional and personal risks associated with his new assignment.

The annual general meeting (AGM) in April was eagerly awaited. Corti had to present the worst results ever in the company's history. The shareholders at the meeting voted against legally discharging the directors, with the exception of Corti. Pascal Couchepin, the Swiss economy minister, summarized their feelings:

> Voting against the normal legal discharge was a way to say that I have a number of questions and I am awaiting a special audit to decide whether I will start a civil suit.[24]

[21] *The Times* (London), 20 November 2000: 26.
[22] Touristik R.E.P.O.R.T., 30 November 2000 (Reuters).
[23] The media dubbed Mario Corti 'Super Mario'. The first video games featuring this action hero were released in the 1980s and built the foundation for Nintendo's global gaming empire.
[24] *Aargauer Zeitung* (Aargau), 16 November 2001.

Seven of the ten board members resigned at the AGM – among them the four longest-serving board members (who had been on the board between 13 and 23 years) and ex-chairman Honegger. When asked whether he thought that the board had acted with due diligence, L. Mühlemann justified:

> The board of directors has to rely on management, which is responsible for the operational business. The board has to have a careful look at management's ideas and proposals, it has to ask critical questions and if necessary demand alternative scenarios. Our trust in the management was justifiable with the record results of 1997 and 1998. Directors cannot know as much about the market, competition, customer requirements and organization of the company as the management.[25]

The working style of the board changed in the months following the AGM. The members received the financial figures every month and met every other month for half a day to discuss all the details about Swissair Group. A number of desperate rescue measures were initiated. In April, Swissotel Hotel & Resorts was sold to Raffles Hotels for SFr 520 million. The sale of non-core activities and minor airline stakes, including holdings in French AOM and Air Liberté, was announced. In June and July, Swissair discussed with Sabena being released from increasing its 49.5% stake to 85%. The parties finally agreed on a payment of SFr 430 million.

In June 2001, PricewaterhouseCoopers resigned as auditors of Swissair Group after many years of service. For four years their statements had been identical – not even minor deficiencies had been reported, especially with regard to risk associated with the different holdings or activated goodwill (refer to Table 1.4 for consolidated SAirGroup results 1997–2000). Observers wondered why the board did not question this – did they simply not know or were they ignoring the writing on the wall?

On 31 August 2001 the new auditor, KPMG, published re-audited 2000 accounts. Among other items, aircraft leases, which had previously been off balance sheet as operating leases, were then classified on balance sheet as finance leases. The previous accounting for pension funds and own shares was adjusted and reduced equity. The presentation of the figures for the first half of 2001 revealed that Swissair's financial position was much weaker than previously reported:

	End of year 2000	Revised end of year 2000	End of June 2001
Net debt position	SFr 6.4 bn	SFr 9.4 bn	SFr 10.4 bn
Equity	SFr 1.2 bn	SFr 716 m	SFr 555 m

Passing the buck

The terrorist attacks in the USA on September 11 aggravated Swissair's situation. On October 1 the company filed for bankruptcy protection. The same day, UBS agreed to take over 51% of Swissair's stake in Crossair, and Credit Suisse (under CEO Mühlemann) the remaining 49%. With the change to the winter flight schedule Crossair was supposed to

---

[25] *Financial Times* (London), 19 April 2001.

take over two-thirds of Swissair's flight operations. However, on October 2 Swissair's cash requirements skyrocketed when all suppliers demanded cash payment. Swissair did not have enough liquidity to maintain its services. The complete fleet had to be grounded. Thousands of passengers were stranded and left to organize alternative transportation.

Two days later Swissair resumed its flight operations with the aid of a government lifeline of SFr 450 million. But the image of Swissair and Switzerland had been damaged.

On October 5, L. Mühlemann, who had been a member of the Swissair board for six years, resigned. The board of directors had only three members left: Corti (on the board for 1 year), Hentsch (12 years), and Leuenberger (6 years). Controversial, often acrimonious, debate accompanied every step in the massive restructuring, such as who should form the new leadership and board.

A Swiss private banker commented:

> This incident will be remembered as a watershed. From now on corporate governance in Switzerland will be divided into pre- and post-Swissair.[26]

1.14   CASE STUDY: ABB – CORPORATE GOVERNANCE DURING A TURNAROUND

[By Paul Strebel, Ulrich Steger, and Wolfgang Amann]

ABB HEADQUARTERS, ZURICH, 3 MARCH 2004. Jürgen Dormann leaned back in his chair as he reviewed the media response to his announcement the day before that he would be stepping down as CEO. Fred Kindle (44), the previous CEO of the Swiss technology concern Sulzer, would succeed him at the beginning of 2005. Dormann would stay on as chairman of the board. What a contrast with the coverage when he became CEO after Jörgen Centerman's sudden resignation on 5 September 2002. Then there had been talk of a 'spiralling crisis',[27] 'dangerously close to collapse',[28] combined with the lingering question 'can the new boss of ABB stop the burnout in the rotten technology company at the last second?'[29] Now, it was 'return to stability'[30] – no mean feat after four CEOs in seven years, and three major reorganizations in five years. The financials looked reasonable, but Dormann knew that ABB was like a patient that had just left hospital – not yet fit enough to compete in any industry Olympics.

He felt confident that due to the massive improvements in corporate governance, the fundamental changes triggered would last, and their positive effects would continue to be felt as the new values and behaviors trickled down through the organization. But how would the new division of labor – and power – between him and the CEO work out? What new dynamics would emerge? Could, and indeed should, board involvement remain as high as it had been during the turnaround? What kind of contributions could be expected as the new strategy was formulated in the near future? A high-performing business model was still under construction – now was not the time to rest on his laurels . . .

---

[26] *Cash*, 4 May 2001.
[27] *Financial Times*, 6 September 2002.
[28] *The Economist*, 26 October 2002.
[29] *Wirtschaftswoche*, 12 September 2002.
[30] *Financial Times*, 3 March 2004.

'From admired to mired: a powerhouse adrift'[31]

As an industry leader in power and automation technologies resulting from the merger of ASEA (Sweden) and Brown Boveri (Switzerland), ABB generated US$18.78 billion of revenues in 2003 with its 105,000 employees worldwide. Dormann remembered only too well that until the late 1990s, ABB had always ranked near the top of the list of most-admired companies. Percy Barnevik, ABB's chairman (up to 2001) and CEO (up to 1996), was widely praised as the European equivalent to the US management hero Jack Welch, the former head of General Electric. However, with hindsight,[32] it became clear that ABB's fortunes had started to wane with the crisis in Asia in 1997, an area where ABB had seen massive expansion. Overpaid acquisitions and a botched and costly attempt to position ABB as an e-business had added to the company's woes.

Then came 'the perfect storm', reducing ABB's market capitalization by 95%. The hangover from the e-bubble affected the technology industry in particular, as investments slowed across the world. The asbestos liabilities in the USA exploded, as did the pension scandal – the discovery that two former CEOs, Percy Barnevik and Göran Lindahl, had amassed US$160 million of pension benefits without proper board approval.

The intention of the Financial Services Division to finance long-term obligation with short-term debt turned sour. ABB's largest shareholder, Martin Ebner, pushed for a share buyback in early 2001 to raise ABB's share price – not least to get him out of a squeeze as falling stock prices turned his double leverage financial business model against him. Not only did his conflict of interest trigger a liquidity crunch, but his persistence as a shareholder advocate finally made the board aware of the pension issue. Jürgen Dormann summed up his experience as a new board[33] member:

> The ABB board was not really performing effectively. There were too many boys' games between Barnevik and Ebner, a continuous influence of Swiss and Swedish investors, which did not reflect the global activity of the Group and too little challenge and serious debate. It was all about the chairman and the CEO, and their interactions. Barnevik had patriarchal tendencies and clearly monopolized the flow of information. It is today clear that too much power was concentrated in the hands of one person for too long.

Immediately after assuming the role of chairman of the board on 21 November 2001 and then suddenly being appointed CEO on 5 September 2002, Dormann deemed that an overhaul of the corporate governance system was vital for ABB's turnaround.

Things got worse before they got better

Dormann remembered:

> The problems were bigger than I imagined. I had to realize that from a financial point of view things were becoming pretty narrow and dangerous. However, I underestimated the complexity and mind-set of the company. People in the factories, even middle

---

[31] *Financial Times*, 11 March 2003.

[32] For a full account of ABB's development, see the IMD case series by Paul Strebel and Nanci Govinder (IMD-3-1241, IMD-3-1242, IMD-3-1243, IMD-3-1244).

[33] Board refers to the Board of Directors or Supervisory Board or Verwaltungsrat in the Swiss corporate governance context (which consists primarily of non-executives), in contrast to the Group Executive Committee at ABB, which consists exclusively of inside executives.

management, did not realize that we were close to bankruptcy and that nobody would come to our rescue. We are not in France. But nevertheless, under such circumstances, one can act very quickly and decisively.

Or, as one newspaper put it, 'Jürgen Dormann's job: to save ABB from itself'.[34] It was not an easy ride: barely six weeks into his tenure, on 28 October 2002, Dormann was forced to deliver a profit warning. The figures his top team had presented and he had come to believe were too optimistic. An outcry from financial analysts and the downgrading of ABB by the Standard & Poor's (S&P) rating agency accompanied the unfolding drama. As one observer noted:

The business community loves nothing more than a hero becoming a loser.

Three top priorities

First, ABB had to retain customers and ensure liquidity. Dormann, along with members of top management and the board, visited customers extensively, while the new CFO, Peter Voser, worked on stabilizing the financial side. Tom Sjökvist, Head of the Automation Products business area, remembered:

We had to convince our customers that we were going to be around. After one year we were out of the doldrums.

Second, the overly complex 'hybrid front/back-end organization', the darling of organizational consultancies for the attractive fees it earned them, needed to be abolished. Björn Edlund, Head of Corporate Communication, pointed out:

It simply did not work. Instead of dynamics, we had confusion. Everybody was doing what they wanted. And a lot of turf wars.

Within weeks, Dormann had restructured the previous four sales divisions and the two manufacturing divisions into two, abolished the Group Processes Division, which produced more overhead cost than results, and put parts of Financial Services, the Building Systems business in various countries, and the Oil, Gas & Petrochemicals Division up for sale. Within the remaining core divisions, the relevant unit of strategic consideration was the business area. Under the new structure, these were reduced from 33 to 9, which achieved integrated responsibility for both the important production lines and the markets. Dormann described the emerging structure as 'back-to-basics and reality', which was urgently needed to revive ABB's former entrepreneurial spirit, which had drowned in bureaucracy and convoluted reporting lines.

   Third, a new leadership team had to be formed: within weeks, half of the executive team left. The simplification of the organization did away with more than one-third of senior executive positions, the Executive Committee was down to five, with only two of the old committee remaining. The three newcomers (including Dormann) were able to bring a new perspective (see Dormann's letter on his ideas for communication among them in Figure 1.10).

---

[34] *Fortune*, 18 November 2002.

Letter from the CEO No. 7:
Clear, concise and direct communications

Oct. 11, 2002 – In his latest letter to employees, CEO Jürgen Dormann emphasizes the need for clear, concise and direct communications. We should stop presenting to each other, rather discuss, analyze and find solutions, he says.

Dear Colleagues,

Today I'd like to share with you some reflections of a newcomer into the operational management culture of ABB. The newcomer is me, of course.

. . .

Last week, I wrote about trust and leadership – about saying what we mean and meaning what we say, about showing as leaders that decisions are taken on merit, with the Group interests put first, and our own unit's second. Now, nearly every time I have asked for information in the past month, I have received a sizeable PowerPoint file. Is this the corporate language? I thought it was English.

I know we need presentation materials, and we need presentation skills. But consider this: somewhere among the dazzling presentation techniques, which ABB people steeped in a good engineering culture, have mastered, I sense a creeping loss of substance. I don't want to be sold to when we are discussing real-life business issues within the company – I want facts, views, arguments, context. I don't want self-promotion, I want someone to lay out the issues at hand so we can examine them and find solutions.

You may feel it is frivolous to talk about such matters. I don't think so – the constructive search for solutions starts with setting the right expectation levels. And if what I see is typical, which I'm fairly sure it is, how much time is spent – and lost – in our company as we spin stories to each other across the world?

I know one thing for sure. The world around us, our customers, the families of our employees, the media and the financial markets, have limited interest in us spinning a story. They don't want to be sold a story. They want to understand what our situation is, what we are doing about it, and when we will deliver what results and implement what actions. A plan of action, explained in clear and simple terms.

This starts with removing all the fanciful trappings. These can be virtual/physical trappings – the PowerPoint effects. Or it can be those too-familiar lists of excuses, exceptional items that we are invited to ignore when we review ABB problems.

I know this may sound harsh. So, let me summarize what I mean in a positive way:

- Let's start exchanging information instead of just presenting to each other.
- Let's concentrate on facts – both hard and soft – and analyze their context.
- Let's share, understand, discuss, weigh options and decide.
- Let's stop boiling down complex managerial reality to charts, which few understand.
- Let's cultivate the art of concise memos, with complete sentences.
- Let's listen to each other and practice assuming each other's points of view.

I'm not saying we should ban PowerPoint slides and stop presenting to each other. I'm saying, let's minimize it. Let's build a culture of analysis, dialogue, decision-making and disciplined action. Not my plans against your plans. Our plans.

Cultures don't change easily. I'll do my best to set an example. I never use PowerPoint unless it is absolutely necessary. In my experience it very rarely is. Instead I write down what I want to say, and, in doing so, discover small inconsistencies or get new ideas and insights, as the thoughts become words and sentences.

I'm sure I'll be seeing some of my words on PowerPoint slides soon. OK, as long as they help us increase the operating margins and the cash flow. Otherwise, where's the Power? And what's the Point?

. . .

Kind regards
Jürgen Dormann

Figure 1.10   Selected extracts from a letter from the CEO
Source: Company information.

A rigorous evaluation was needed to answer the following questions: what are ABB's competitive advantages? What is a truly sustainable strategy? And, above all, how to drive the changes necessary to move from crisis management to excellent performance – and make the changes last? This affected the interactions in the upper echelons of ABB and corporate governance patterns in general. Dormann explained:

We needed to focus on corporate governance in this situation for three reasons. Firstly, only the board can provide the orientation on the future, the required values, and the core strategy. Secondly, we needed to give leadership examples at the top for more honest communication, transparency, and focus on performance. Thirdly, the way we wanted to work together and to design an organization that supports this kind of accountable leadership needed to penetrate the organization – with no exceptions – and definitely starting at the top. The development of the new strategy is an example.

Dormann reflected on what kind of process would be appropriate for deciding on the strategy and what role, if any, the board should play.

ABB (B): The formation of the strategy committee

[By Paul Strebel, Ulrich Steger, and Wolfgang Amann]

ABB had to form a new strategy. As part of his 'back-to-basics' approach, Dormann had a weekly letter to all employees posted on the company's intranet in the 15 key local languages to keep the people of ABB informed of the key issues and the progress already made (refer to Figure 1.11 for a key sample). In his letter from 15 November 2002, he wrote:

Letter from the CEO No. 28:

We are charting a new strategic roadmap

Mar. 21, 2003 – In his weekly letter, Jürgen Dormann, says that while ABB concentrates on strengthening its core businesses, a longer-term strategic review is also being undertaken to ensure profitable growth. He spells out the next steps, and outlines some of the key questions that need to be answered. 'Everyone in ABB will feel the positive effects once our new strategy is acted upon', he says.

Dear Colleagues,

Today, I'm going to write about ABB strategy.

. . .

Let me now turn to ABB, and to our future. It lies in our core businesses – getting more value out of what we know best. It lies in doing what we do best even better.

We are waging an intense 18-month campaign to repair ABB's finances, focus our portfolio through divestments and restore our competitiveness. But we must also use this period to shape ABB for 2005 and beyond – so that once again we can actively lead industry developments. For that, we need a clear strategy.

The strategy starts with a broad idea – focus on the core and blossom from the core. It offers guidance and direction. It must be externally focused: what do our customers rely on ABB for? Strategy also means taking certain risks to counter the biggest risk of all – standing still.

Figure 1.11   Selected extracts from a letter from the CEO
Source: Company information.

What is our strategy for profitable growth over the next 10 years? We will use this year to find the answer. Here is how: Strategy formulation is the duty of the Board of Directors, under Swiss corporate law. So, as chairman of the board, I recently initiated a strategy review, which will unfold at three different levels. It will remain a central issue for the board. At the Annual General Meeting of shareholders on May 16, we will propose the election of two new members – two experienced industrialists – in addition to our current directors. And after the shareholder meeting, the board will create a new strategy committee.

I'm also driving this strategy project at the group management level, together with my colleagues on the Executive Committee. At the market level, top managers from Zurich and around the world are involved – from growth markets such as China and India, as well as mature markets like the U.S. and Germany, where we need to improve. Naturally, the project will build on our existing strategies, challenging them where necessary. At each level, we are supported by consultants from Bain & Company.

Implementation will begin after the board members have formulated our future strategic roadmap, based on the strategic options put before them. Not one single strategic route, but alternative roadmaps. More roads than one lead into the future. In our unpredictable world, alternative strategic scenarios are a must.

This week, we held a kick-off meeting with key managers, so I wanted to share our aspirations with you. I will continue to keep you informed as we proceed. Let me now revisit some basic issues, so you can see why we embark on this project.

ABB is a technology-based provider of power and automation products, systems, solutions and services to utilities and industry.

Our core strengths rest on three pillars – technology leadership, a pioneering spirit, and a sustainable approach to business, possible because we are at home where we do business. In other words: strong technologies, strong market presence, strong people. But despite our leadership in power technologies and automation technologies, our core businesses do not achieve the operating margins of our best competitors. Why? Are we in the right sections of the right markets? What are the right markets? Should we concentrate on solutions and service or on products and systems, or on all? Do we have too many factories, or too few, or in the wrong places? Where are the future key value-adding technologies? Do we have access to them? Do we shape them? Are our businesses linked logically, or strung together based on our historical development? Where will our customers invest? How are their value chains developing? Beyond market share, where does profitable growth come from?

As you can see, the strategy review will look at our business beyond organizational or geographical boundaries – at customer needs, market dynamics, industry life cycles, competitor dynamics, capabilities, technology and value chain. It would be arrogant – even foolish – to think that anyone holds the answers already, or that the choices we will make will be easy to implement. That's where the proof of any good strategy lies; making change happen and making it stick.

Asking questions is always the best start. We approach this with open minds, from the outside in. Relatively few people will be involved in seeking the answers and plotting our future course. But everyone in ABB will feel the positive effects once our new strategy is acted on. This is an investment in our future.

Figure 1.11   (Continued)

There are many ways to define a strategy. I, for one, save this word for the most important things, that I, as the CEO can do with the executive team. Strategy to me is a pattern of action that takes an organization to its goals. It's not planning, it's not vision. It's concrete action, making the most of our strength. Building on our leadership in power and automation technologies for utilities and industrial customers – that's our strategy put in clear, simple terms. The pattern of action – that's the execution of this strategy.[35]

---

[35] Letter No. 12, 15 November 2002.

As a first action step, the Strategy Department, which was 'buried' somewhere in the Finance Department, started to report directly to him. But this clearly did not suffice to cope with the challenges.

Tobias Becker, Head of Corporate Strategy, was convinced:

> When Dormann assumed responsibility, he certainly had a vision for ABB, but also needed to keep options open – at least for some time.

Dormann already encouraged direct interaction between board members and the executive committee when he became chairman in November 2001 (refer to Figure 1.12 for changes in the relationship between the board and the executive committee). He was pondering about setting up a strategy committee on the board, headed by Louis Hughes, 'someone with extensive industrial experience' (refer to Figure 1.13 for the intended new structure of the board). Peter Smits, Head of the Power Technology Division, would make a good secretary of this committee.

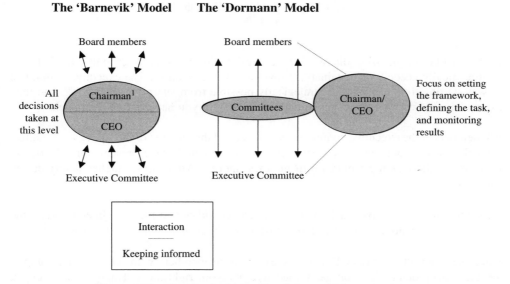

Figure 1.12   Changes in the board and the executive committee

[1] In case of separation of CEO and chairman, the two interact closely with each other and relay then to the organization and the board.
[2] These board committees represented both board members and managers from the executive committee.
Source: IMD.

ABB (C): The strategy committee in action

[By Paul Strebel, Ulrich Steger, and Wolfgang Amann]

Overall, the first meeting of the strategy committee went extremely well. Hughes analyzed the strategizing process:

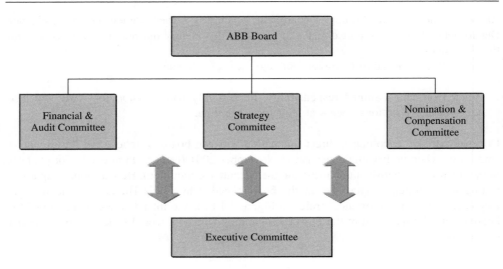

Figure 1.13   Intended structure of the board
Source: IMD.

> It was like an intensive dialog. The strategy committee's starting point was: What is strategically needed for sustainable growth and value creation? The executive committee was starting to think: What is strategically possible from an operational view? And then you have to work on the issues in depth – in the end you have to find the match.

All members of the executive committee were to attend the meeting of the strategy committee, but only the full members of the strategy committee could make presentations. Dormann wondered if the meeting would fulfill his expectations. Afterwards, Hughes described the balancing act:

> In this dialog, you need flair or *Fingerspitzengefühl* not to blur the lines between the board and executive committee's responsibilities in such an intensive process.

Since the committee consisted of highly experienced members with relevant and complementary backgrounds, it could get started with its work right away. Hughes, for example, especially contributed international experience (e.g., for North America). Michael Treschow ensured the fit between strategy and organizational design, and Hans Ulrich Märki added the structure for multiple profit and loss accounts, while the entire team agreed on a systematic approach from the very beginning. Following a clear scheme, the committee started by gathering facts as a basis for deriving prospects and priorities for the portfolio as well as the implementation phase. Progress was closely monitored. Smits remembered:

> It was true teamwork. As the crisis was primarily on the financial side, it turned out to be helpful in determining where we wanted to head. Based on an in-depth analysis of facts, it crystallized very soon what was the core of the business and what wasn't. We wanted to grow further and needed to find an answer to where and how to do it. We jointly identified key enablers for future success to be tested in selected markets.

Smits also remembered how the necessary input for the strategy development process was gathered:

> We proceeded with a high degree of bottom-up involvement. People from various crucial countries and functions contributed. This turned the results into more solid ones and decreased the risk of unwanted surprises. We also scrutinized the details with the Board of Directors much more than had previously been the case. Regarding the board's interaction with the executive committee, it was true coaching. Nobody stepped over his lines of responsibility.

As a consequence, the extensive interaction between the board and the executive committee at the top level entailed more involvement from the entire organization in general. Input came from throughout the organization.

The board welcomed this approach, but wanted to have Bain consultants accompanying the process from the beginning to ensure that the proceedings always remained systematic. As the entire board was more involved than before, an even better understanding of key pressure points was created. It was primarily due to this widely shared basis and understanding that good dialogs and consensus were reached more easily. Some follow-up meetings were held, together with all board members. The latter received detailed information upfront, while the actual meetings were highly focused (refer to Figure 1.14 for a formalized structure of the new strategy development process).

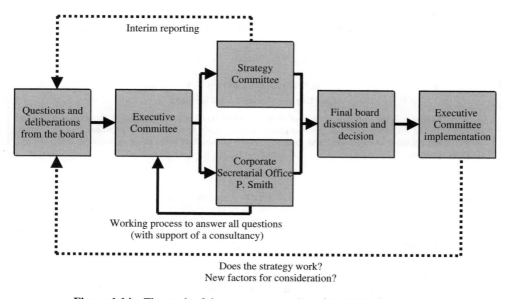

Figure 1.14   The work of the strategy committee (simplified flow chart)
Source: IMD.

During the time of the turnaround, all members of ABB's executive committee knew that the coming months would test their competence in strategic thinking, mastery of the issues and, above all, ability to implement the strategy. The committee chairman, Hughes, wrote the extensive protocol for each meeting, which he admitted sometimes took longer than the meeting itself. Dormann was kept informed, but not leading the process. As Hughes described:

> He knew what was presented and we discussed the results so far in between the meetings. We also talked about the way forward.

One issue was rigor in evaluating the facts and being ready to draw radical conclusions. One example was the Oil, Gas & Petrochemicals Division: despite previous assumptions, the potential synergies with ABB's core business were estimated at only US$36 million. The consequence was clear: divestment. To ensure the openness of the process and thinking in terms of scenarios rather than 'right' or 'wrong', Dormann stressed, time and again:

> We do not have the answers, sometimes not even the questions.

Tobias Becker, Head of Strategy, described the new process:

> Strategy is more like strip mining than blast mining, meaning it is a continuous process where you work on the issues systematically one by one, depending on the life cycle of key products, which vary between 2 and 25 years, not a one-time-every-five-year event, where you turn everything on its head.

(For more details on how Dormann kept the staff up to date with the new strategic roadmap, core businesses, and strengths such as technology leadership, a pioneering spirit, and a sustainable approach to business, see the letter in Figure 1.15.) The organization understood the message. Tom Sjökvist, Head of Automation Products, shared his experience:

Letter from the CEO No. 49:

Charting the strategic road forward

Sept. 5, 2003 – A wide-ranging review of ABB strategy has been continuing, with consultations in recent weeks at different levels of the company. In his weekly letter, Jürgen Dormann looks at some of the issues raised and discussed, and says the review shows that units need to improve their ability to work together.

Dear Colleagues,

During the summer months, we have pressed ahead with our global strategic review, looking at ways of increasing profitable growth in our core power and automation technology businesses. We are seeking to define the best customer segments for our core businesses, and our ability to win within each segment. The process is driven by fundamental questions. How can we improve the way we work? How can we reach our leadership potential in markets where we are already strong?

How can we improve in those markets where we are not strong enough? How can we position ourselves better with some of our products and markets, and capitalize on key competitive advantages, such as speed? In addition, we are examining what needs to get done to increase transparency between our units that collaborate on bigger projects, and how we can speed up our internal processes.

The review is still ongoing, but there are a number of very positive indications I would like to share with you.

Figure 1.15   Selected extracts from a letter from the CEO
Source: Company information.

The way the review is being carried out has been very heartening. Working with an independent company, we conducted a deep analysis of our businesses, markets and our ability to capitalize on our strengths, at all levels – country, business area, regional, executive committee, and board of directors. The teamwork is truly global. We started at country level. Previously such research had always started at business area level. The new approach proved beneficial, drawing in another set of information and opinion.

The findings are highly informative and thought provoking. For example, our discussions with the board, both with individual members and the board's strategy committee, resulted in great input from 'outsiders' with strong business and industry backgrounds.

As part of the review, an extensive customer survey was carried out. The results confirmed our image as a market leader. ABB's quality, service and products are highly regarded by our utility and industry customers. The survey also confirmed that the ABB brand is very strong, particularly in Europe and Asia. Now, we need to translate our customers' appreciation into increased market share and profitable growth, and improve in areas where we are not so strong.

Two pieces of news this week showed how powerful the ABB brand can be. The Power Technologies division won a contract with a mid-western utility in the United States that turned to us to act as an asset management consultant on ways of strengthening grid performance in the Ohio region, and to manage the utility's transmission and distribution equipment, in the wake of the power outages in mid-August.

My colleague Dinesh Paliwal this week visited a customer based in San Diego to confirm a frame agreement. It was won against strong competition because of our brand quality. Also as part of the strategy review, a benchmark of competitors was also carried out, raising question marks about our performance in such areas as strategic cost management. This will be addressed.

It is also clear there is potential for greater synergies across our businesses, in areas such as R&D, manufacturing, raw materials, sales and technical skills, and the customer base. We could identify significant top and bottom line potential in our current businesses, allowing us to define ambitious goals. All data has now been collected and we are examining the different scenarios in detail. We will conclude this before the end of the year.

The current strategy is the correct one going forward, but it needs to be refined. Strategy never stops. There will be changes as a result of the strategy review, but they will be done in a well-planned manner so as not to upset our business progress. We are talking about evolution not revolution. The past year has shown that everyone, at all levels of ABB, is open and prepared for change – when it is clear to our people what we are changing and why.

. . .

Figure 1.15   (Continued)

The new management drives strategy along the lines of clear thinking. No 'strategy of the year', it's a no-nonsense approach. Better have the facts ready and know your market.

The strategy development process was only one example of how the board and executive committee worked together. A similar process was set up to develop a new HR policy. Gary Steel, member of the executive committee, described it as follows:

It aimed to link people to strategy. We spent much more time physically together, very interactive, but also with social events. We know our roles, especially that we are responsible for making the strategy work. But this mutual involvement creates commitment and the ability to tie everything together at the top.

ABB (D): Leadership in a decentralized governance structure

[By Paul Strebel, Ulrich Steger, and Wolfgang Amann]

The decentralized governance structure at ABB very much fit the leadership style Dormann developed at the helm of Hoechst. There, he had been the CFO for a long time, and subsequently CEO. At that time, he redirected Hoechst to focus on Life Sciences activities while decreasing its industrial chemical exposure. He divested specialty chemicals, and merged the pharmaceutical division with Rhône-Poulenc to create Aventis, where he first became Chairman of the Management Board and later Chairman of the Supervisory Board. Dormann had extensive experience with such restructuring. In an earlier interview he described it as follows:

> My job is – besides setting the tone – to impart the principle of competition, bring in values, and exert an influence on important personal and strategy decisions. Beyond this, I tried to keep out of the business. For most issues, there is someone in the company who can do what has to be done better than I can.[36]

When referring to competition at ABB, Dormann meant to trigger a 'competition for more responsibility, not more turf; for more opportunity, not bigger teams; for more real results, not a bigger share of an internal cake'.[37] He clearly emphasized:

> This is definitely not 'soft'. First the transparency we create by not neglecting the formal process side is the basis for clear accountability and responsibility of individual managers. And secondly, it focuses on performance, results delivered and confronts everybody with the questions: Is my behavior promoting our performance? Are the values I live promoting our strategy?

This focus on the values and behavioral side explains why, in the new 'people strategy' for the first time after the crisis, one essential part concerned the values and business principles (refer to Figure 1.16).

Referring to a string of irregular, questionable, or even illegal activities, which caused negative headlines for ABB in 2002, Steel observed:

> It was urgently needed, as the standards for the conduct of business were eroding dramatically.

As the person responsible for the Step Change Program, ABB's productivity improvement program initiated in October 2002 (and to be finished by 2004), Steel's message was clear:

> A major and increasing part of the actions in Step Change will aim to achieve organizational and cultural change. If all we do with Step Change is to take out $900 million, and nothing changed in ABB, we have totally failed.

---

[36] Scharmer, O. (2002). Leadership is about setting the tone: an interview with Jürgen Dormann. *The Society for Organizational Learning Journal* **4**(2): 19.
[37] Letter No. 6, 4 October 2002.

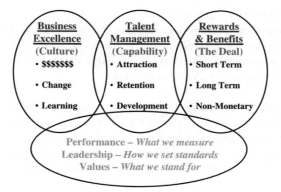

Figure 1.16 ABB people strategy
Source: Company information.

At the top of the list of changes were:

Fewer rules, but more compliance, less bureaucracy and more responsibility. This is what the board expects us to deliver – rightly so.

Another subtle change needed to get these leadership values trickling down through the organization was the style of communication. One tool was Dormann's weekly letter to all employees, addressing critical issues (e.g., the downgrading of ABB's rating, but also future growth; refer to Figure 1.17 for an example), but also setting the tone for debates

---

Letter from the CEO No. 51:

A plan for profitable growth

Sept. 19, 2003 – Profitable growth is key to ABB's lasting success, Jürgen Dormann writes in his weekly letter. To get there, we must recognize our strengths, simplify the way we operate, and make the most of opportunities in growth markets.

Dear Colleagues,

As we press ahead with our efforts to put ABB on a better course for the future, let us not forget the key to sustained success – growth. We must, and we will, settle the asbestos issue once and for all. We will also make our planned divestments, and ensure a sound economic base for the company. But now, as the first signs of a broader recovery are showing up in the world economy, I would also like you to think about the next chapter. And that is profitable growth.

Why is it important for a company to grow? I'll share my view with you. In the next few years, I think we will see a change in how companies are perceived by the markets. I think that given sound fundamentals, which are a must, the ability to grow organically and profitably will again be recognized as a real measure of a company's leadership, and the basis for its valuation in the markets. And here is the underlying reason for the strategic review of ABB's portfolio. We want to create a high-growth strategy. How can we do this?

. . .

That's how we begin to position ABB for real growth.

Figure 1.17 Selected extracts from a letter from the CEO
Source: Company information.

and good standards for interacting with one another. His criticism of the excessive use of PowerPoint presentations became legendary in the organization. In addition, Dormann believed that the focus on strategy formation at the board level perfectly fitted the Swiss model of corporate governance, where the board explicitly had overall responsibility, the so-called *Gesamtleitungsfunktion*. As he explained:

> In the German model, the Management Board develops the strategy and gives notice to the Supervisory Board. In the US system, the CEO prepares, but gets real input from the Board. But in the end he does what he thinks is right. In France, in a two-tier system, the Board often changes what Management proposes and they comply. In Switzerland, the strategy is defined by the Board – and that is what I will focus on in the future.

As he sat at his desk at ABB's headquarters in Zurich, Dormann reflected on his 18 months as CEO and the challenges that lay ahead in the next 9 months as he prepared to hand over the reins of CEO to Kindle. ABB had two extremely strong fields, power technologies and automation technologies. He knew that the key question for him would be how to turn these two ships into a fast catamaran, able to outpace others. And to ensure the best navigation possible for this catamaran, he also wondered about what role the board should play after this crucial turnaround phase.

International Corporate Governance – Similarities across Systems

2.1 DO INTERNATIONAL DIFFERENCES MATTER?

Governance systems vary across nations, although certain basic rules about transparency and accountability have gained momentum around the world. For companies to deal with such differences, it is often not the big picture but the legal 'fine print' and the varying cultures across nations, industries, and companies that matter, which leads to different expectations, working procedures, and performance criteria. The case of DaimlerChrysler (DC) is a good example, as few companies have become so global, so rapidly. Starting with the latest merger with Chrysler, Daimler-Benz evolved from a German-based export-oriented company to a German–American player, extending its reach through the alliance with Mitsubishi into Japan within three years. Although DC was the controlling shareholder of Mitsubishi, it was called an alliance in order to avoid consolidating Mitsubishi's huge debt on DC's stretched balance sheet. The case does not primarily look at the merger or the economic performance specifically. Instead, it focuses solely on the discussion of the following issues:

- How can different legal and board systems be effectively integrated?
- What are the issues and intricacies of CG in a global company?
- What are the different expectations and work modes?

Surprisingly, the Sarbanes–Oxley focus on compliance has pushed the managerial issues of CG in a global company a bit on the back burner for many global companies incorporated outside the USA, i.e. for the majority. However, Sarbanes–Oxley and – to follow up – the NYSE listing requirements was part of the headache: how could partly conflicting legislation and expectations be reconciled? Just one example to illustrate our point: whereas by US rules all members of the audit committee should be independent, German law requires an employee – by definition not independent – to sit on the audit committee. The extraterritoriality of US laws – an 'evergreen' for its European and Asian allies – caused additional problems. The national governments were reluctant to accept the US claims (e.g., that European audit companies also fell under the supervision of a newly created board overseeing accounting practices, basically pushing European companies to comply with US laws more than with their domestic laws). In response, Europe specifically started its own more detailed regulation.

But beyond the legal complications, the managerial practicalities were not to be underestimated. For a global company, a central question for the board was whether to adapt the control focus of the US legislation or state with its current balance of activities. Could there be different levels of ensuring compliance – one meeting US standards, one the domestic or corporate internal standards? And should special consideration be given to emerging economies, especially Asia, as this might contain specific risks? However, such a complex design raised the question: how would domestic, European stakeholders respond to those proposed changes? Would they (e.g., the workers' representatives or the regulators) feel their issues were neglected?

There is as yet scant evidence of how boards of global companies have changed their working procedures and priorities recently. One issue has become clear: there is no simple 'best practice' to follow, but every company has to evolve a specific fit with the four shaping factors of CG previously outlined, not only with the legal requirement. Some trial and error is probably unavoidable in this process, though.

Core insights

The integration of very different board philosophies is key; as argued before, this is not shaped by the legal framework alone. As one observer described the clichés:

> US boards are often more informal and freewheeling in the discussion, like jazz bands, and the CEO takes home what he thinks was useful advice. In Germany, the joint supervisory and management board meetings – with more than 30 persons present – is symbolized by an opera: everything is well prepared. Everybody knows his or her 'score/role' and at the end there is a clear result. Japanese boards are an evolving ceremony with even more people and if you are unable to understand what the ritual means, you don't understand anything. But you can be sure that the outcome is ambiguous and evolving.

In the DaimlerChrysler case presented in the following, this led to experimenting with several types of committees. After the merger, a shareholder committee was established, consisting of DC supervisory board members from the owner side and the former Chrysler board. It also contained a labour committee that would partly compensate for the majority of German labor representatives on the supervisory board as only German citizens are entitled to vote for their representatives. The basic goal was to keep the former Chrysler board members, who did not get a seat on the DC supervisory board, involved in the information and decision-making process. But after more than three years – and with Chrysler in a severe crisis – this committee had obviously run its course. The need was no longer clear and the redundancies with the supervisory board high. It would not develop a meaningful purpose of its own as it could have only an advisory and information-sharing role. An additional factor might have been that the shareholder base moved back to Germany. Whereas after the merger the US and European shareholder base was roughly equal (around 45%), today DC is owned about 55% by German shareholders, including institutional investors, and less than 10% of shareholders are from the USA.

This committee was a succeeded by a chairman's council, a pretty unique structure. It was chaired by the CEO; however, the chairman of the supervisory board and five other members served on this committee as did four eminent industrialists (e.g., the CEO of BP or the owner of CEMEX). As the company explained:

> The council will provide advice to management and global business strategy issues. Elements of American and European corporate governance structures are combined to meet the specific requirements of a truly global company and the interest of the different stakeholders. The legal rights and responsibilities of the supervisory board will

remain untouched. The chairman's council is complementary to the current governance structure.

Over the years, the chairman's council met roughly with the same frequency as the supervisory board. As far as could be observed from the outside, the legal rights of the supervisory board were untouched and in the crises in early 2005 regarding further capital injections to Mitsubishi, it was the supervisory board that 'pulled the plug'. But this was in line with the way many supervisory boards work: more controlling and not as such initiating strategic moves and formulating strategy. The chairman's council accentuated that tendency for DC.

Some critics of CEO Schrempp argued that the chairman's council was an attempt to tame Schrempp's appetite for bold, but risky, decisions. However, this is not plausible as, if this had been the goal, the CEO would not have chaired the meetings and the chairman of the supervisory board and his powerful colleagues would have served as ordinary members on the committee. More of an issue was the two classes of supervisory board members, which were created with the inauguration of the chairman's council: one was more involved in strategy formation than the other. The two other relevant committees of the supervisory board (the mediation committee is only used for issues of severe disagreements between labor and owner-representatives) were the audit committee and the presidential committee.

The latter is formed by the chairman and his deputy from the labor side plus one more representative from each side. It is important for two reasons: first, it coordinates the agenda topics and normally detects disagreements between the two sides early on. Secondly, it sets the remuneration for members of the board of management (and with that implicitly or explicitly evaluating their performance).

The audit committee had to make some difficult decisions due to the shifting legislation in accounting and auditing, which are hugely complex in such a far-flung empire. Although often technical, they could have far-reaching results. But the highly respected CFO enjoyed the confidence and trust of the committee members and they normally backed his proposal.

It should be noted that in co-determined supervisory boards, the owner and the labor side often meet separately before the plenary meetings to discuss their positions. Mostly, a member of the management board attends the labour meeting to answer questions, provide additional information, and alert the chairman of both the management and the supervisory board to trouble ahead.

On the management side there was also an attempt to reduce the overwhelming workload and complexity through committees. After the post-merger integration phase was concluded in late 1999, an automotive and a sales & marketing council was established, the first for the technical, manufacturing, and purchasing decisions, and that latter for the product portfolio, timing, and distribution decisions. The non-automotive activity had shrunk significantly, so no separate committee was formed. The goal was to organize the cooperation between Mercedes and Chrysler on the passenger car side and to do the heavy and detailed work of raising synergies (the Freightliner Division of the Commercial Vehicle Division managed to keep its independence at that time). However, as one insider put it, the 'meetings rather resembled a UN General Assembly' and therefore the two councils were dissolved and succeeded by an 'executive automotive council', co-chaired by the CEO and the head of Mercedes, one of Europe's most respected automotive engineers. This personal setting and the term 'executive' had to stress the focus on corporate-wide decision-making regarding all products and the implementation of decisions, leaving the board of management basically with 'all other corporate issues'. The executive automotive committee had a 'sister committee', called the alliance committee, in which the strategy and product decisions with Mitsubishi were coordinated. The main reason for that distinction was – apart from playing to Japanese pride – legal, as DC did not want to consolidate Mitsubishi's huge debt and therefore could not treat Mitsubishi as a subsidiary.

The executive automotive and alliance committees had subcommittees, dealing with product portfolio, technology, and the core functions of production planning, global purchasing, and sales and marketing organization. The overriding theme was always to reap economies of scale, avoid double activities, and remove complexity from product design and manufacturing.

However, in CG, the committee is a double-edged sword. On the one hand, they have to organize an effective division of labor, allowing the full meeting to focus on the top priorities. But committees can develop a life of their own and lead to fragmented, uncoordinated decisions. In addition, the individual and collective responsibility of the board of management and the supervisory board (or, in general, the board and management) remains unaltered. Therefore, it is of utmost importance to link the committee work and create transparency of the work through a 'charter' and the outcome, such as minutes to be distributed to the full board.

In the DaimlerChrysler case, the pragmatic solution was to have all meetings for both boards prepared and documented by the Strategy Department, the head of which sat on the board of management, so someone had an overview and could detect contradictions or issues that fell between the cracks.

Besides the complex governance process and its impact on strategy decisions in a global company, an additional aspect of global CG is the risk management dimension, as it can give an idea about information asymmetry between management and board in general, regardless of the specific institutional design. Just consider the areas of risk in a global company: there are – always – currency risks despite attempts to have a natural hedge via globalization of activities in a car company with many leasing and credit contracts to promote sales. There are financing risks, technology risks (e.g., should one follow the hybrid wave or push for a leap forward to fuel cells – and, which one?), product liabilities (especially in the USA) from recalls and the associated brand risk. As the assets are very specific, it is difficult to calculate an exit risk – but factory closings had already cost billions. Then there are organizational risks (e.g., non-compliance with regulations) and what can only be called 'surprise risks' or white space risks (e.g., when Kirk Kerkorian sued DC for US$8 billion over the 'Merger of Equals' notion). The brief and incomplete list indicates one result: no (supervisory or very independent) board could understand these issues in depth, or check if management is in control of a specific risk. Similar information asymmetry occurs in the 100-plus markets in which a global company operates. Of course, not all asymmetries are of equal importance, but to know the five or seven most important ones is already a stretch. Competitor dynamics represent another vast field.

Learning nuggets from the case

The DC case 'Corporate Governance Dynamics in a Global Company' is not a traditional case study on decision-making. It just describes how a company, which is on an accelerating globalization path, tries to adjust its CG system to the new realities of different cultures and traditions, diverse expectations, and the resulting dramatically grown complexity. It also indicates how the legal specifics and political conditions of the home country influence the work of CG, but do not determine the decision-making process.

There are three main 'learning nuggets' in the subsequently presented DaimlerChrysler case:

- **Learn as you go**: as there is no standard 'best practice' that globalizing companies can follow, they have to develop their own specific fit between the shaping forces of CG (now with many more players and influencing factors). A certain 'trial and error' approach is unavoidable and the issue is not if errors occur (only sheer luck can avoid them for a time), but how quickly they are corrected once it becomes clear that certain arrangements do not work as expected or the 'law of unintended consequences' ensures that the (negative) side-effects overcompensate the good things achieved.
- **Becoming global, the hour of the executives**: the case also indicates that the information asymmetry between management (and its staff) and non-executive board members increases with globalization (this is regardless of the legal framework of the one-tier or two-tier system). Issues are becoming too complex, too fast-moving for a 'part timer' to follow. Even for the board of management it is difficult to stay informed and manage the dilemmas (as we will see in Chapter 8, they have to cope with their own information asymmetries). Lack of information depth also impedes the (timely) involvement in strategy formation and therefore shifts the board more into a 'watchdog' role, looking at past performance and financial figures that are easier to process – and to attribute to the persons responsible. Even in shaping the CG processes and institutions, the management takes more initiative.

  There is an interesting symbol for this development. In much of Northern Europe the board of management is by law a collegial body, the chairman (in previous times often called the spokesman) was the first among equals. Huge companies – such as Deutsche Bank or Unilever – even had two spokesmen, usually male, in certain periods. The emergence of an 'imperial CEO' – as in the case of DC – is a recent development, which came along with the globalization of companies. This CEO often accumulates more de facto power than the corporate law originally envisaged – but his personal accountability has also grown to a degree not foreseen by the law. Personalization should therefore not be regarded as a copy of US habits, but as a means to reduce complexity and information asymmetry by outsiders, whether these are stakeholders or non-executive board members.
- **You cannot be everybody's darling**: as the perceptions of different stakeholders (including employees) are often volatile, contradictory, and can lead to massive bureaucratization, it is impossible to meet all expectations. Financial analysts would love a degree of transparency, which would go beyond any reasonable limit, as would national regulators who would like only their design to be implemented and couldn't care less about their peers across the Atlantic (this works both ways . . .). It is important, though, for global companies – within legal limits or standards (e.g., the OECD code) – to experiment and learn how to optimize their CG system and adjust it to new circumstances and experiences. What can be expected, however, is for the companies to explain why they have chosen a specific governance design and what it should deliver in terms of value-added for the company and its stakeholders.

2.2   CASE STUDY: DAIMLERCHRYSLER – CORPORATE GOVERNANCE DYNAMICS IN A GLOBAL COMPANY

[By Ulrich Steger and George Raedler]

We need a new, dynamic global partnership of business and politics. The dust of the trust crisis has settled somewhat. And many national governments have demonstrated their ability to act swiftly within their own territories. Now we should join forces in leading the way towards a wider, increasingly multilateral approach to Corporate Governance rules.

Jürgen Schrempp, CEO, DaimlerChrysler AG, 2003

Ever since the announcement of the merger between Daimler-Benz AG and Chrysler Corporation in May 1998, the company had been in the spotlight. The merged company, DaimlerChrysler (DC), was a full-range provider controlling six car brands and eight truck brands. In addition, DC acquired strategic holdings in Mitsubishi Motors of Japan (37% stake) and Hyundai Motors of Korea (10% stake). Besides this global push, DC divested many of its non-core businesses as recommended by the financial community. Nevertheless, the dividend dropped from €2.35 in the first three years to €1.00 in 2001. By 2002 the turnarounds at Chrysler and Mitsubishi had led to profitability, and the dividend was raised by 50%. However, by 2003, an ongoing price war in North America, with average rebates of $4500 per vehicle, was proving costly and the outcome uncertain.

Over the years, DC became an international benchmark for global operations and management. As for all corporations, corporate governance was of special importance. New regulations, a lack of shareholder and public confidence in big business, and general uncertainty increased the pressure on companies to consider their governance structures. How could a company such as DC reconcile regulatory differences and the diverse expectations of various stakeholders around the globe? There was agreement that corporate governance 'had to be lived', but how?

Background: understanding the DaimlerChrysler merger

When the merger of Daimler-Benz AG and Chrysler Corporation was announced on 6 May 1998, this 'merger in heaven' came as a total surprise to everyone in the industry. Both companies seemed to complement each other well on geographic and product dimensions,[1] and both had outstanding reputations. Forbes had even selected Chrysler as 'company of the year 1996':

> You may think of Chrysler as an old-fashioned metal bender in a mature industry, cyclical as hell. You may think it's just lucky with all those Jeeps and minivans when everyone happens to want a Jeep or minivan. Jeeps and vans go out of fad, Chrysler flops. That's the perception – which is why Chrysler stock sells at less than seven times earnings. But perceptions notoriously lag reality, and we think the reality here is that Chrysler's good luck is being leveraged by a superb management team that has made smart, disciplined decisions.[2]

---

[1] See Rädler, G., Neubauer, F. and Steger, U. (2000). The DaimlerChrysler Merger: The Involvement of the Boards. Case No. IMD-3-0771, for detailed corporate governance issues during the merger negotiations in 1998. The present case only covers the developments after the deal had taken place.
[2] Flint, J. (1997). Company of the year: Chrysler. *Forbes*, 13 January, p. 82 ff.

Chrysler was perceived as a very efficient producer, thereby earning more cash than any other major car maker. Daimler-Benz's luxury car division (Mercedes-Benz) was the envy of the industry. This was a 'merger of equals', with anticipated synergies of $1.4 billion for a combined revenue of $132 billion in its first year of operation. The merger of these two icons also caught the attention of the public right from the beginning. This $36 billion merger became a symbol for what is generally described as a complex business environment for global players: total transparency, Wall Street formulating earnings growth, and immense scrutiny of all stakeholders involved.

With hindsight, the merger developments between 1998 and 2003 can be split into five phases. Figure 2.1 gives an overview of the five phases.

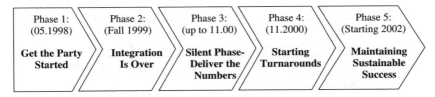

Figure 2.1   Overview of phases

Note: While reading this case, please refer to Figure 2.2 for the representation of the phases and the creation/elimination of various committees.

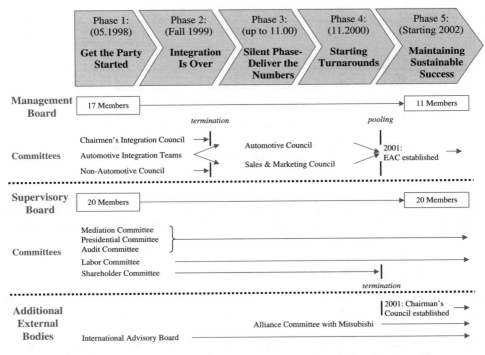

Figure 2.2   Overview of phases and the creation/elimination of various committees

Source: IMD analysis.

	1998	1999	2000	2001	2002
Revenues	131.782	149.985	162.384	152.873	149.583
Operating profit	8.593	11.012	9.752	(1.318)	6.854
Operating margin	6.5%	7.3%	6.0%	(0.9%)	4.6%
Net operating income	6.359	7.032	4.383	1.647	4.335
Net operating income as % of net assets (RONA)	12.7%	13.2%	7.4%	2.5%	6.7%
Net income (loss)	4.820	5.746	7.894	(662)	4.718
Cash dividend per share in €	2.35	2.35	2.35	1.00	1.50
Employees (in 000's)	442	467	416	372	366

Sales and operating profit by division 2002 (in € billion)

	Sales	Operating profit
Mercedes Car Group	50.170	3.020
Chrysler Group	60.181	0.609
Commercial vehicles	28.401	(0.343)
Services	15.699	3.060
Other activities	2.723	0.903

Regional sales distribution 2001

	Daimler Chrysler	Global GDP distribution
NAFTA	53%	36%
Western Europe	31%	27%
Asia	11%	27%
ROW	5%	10%

Figure 2.3   DaimlerChrysler fact sheet 1998–2002 (in € billion)
Source: DaimlerChrysler.

Revenues increased from €132 billion in 1998 to €162 billion in 2000, before falling to €150 for 2002 (refer to Figure 2.3 for a fact sheet on DaimlerChrysler for the five years up to 2002).

Phase 1: Merger announcement 1998 – 'get the party started'

Initially, the rationale for the deal was clear. In an interview on 5 October 1998, Dieter Zetsche, board member of Daimler-Benz AG, explained:

Our problem has been that costs are high for these new technologies because of our low volume. We always lost the technology to competitors. (. . .) Like with ESP (electronic stability program), we wanted one year of exclusivity [from our suppliers]; but they gave us three months, and we had to fight for it. Chrysler will give us the volume. We can stay No. 1 in developing technology – and take it as soon as possible to Chrysler.[3]

The synergy target of $1.4 billion (around 1% of gross revenue) was generally seen as low, but there was only a limited overlap of products. Helmut Petri, executive VP Production for Mercedes cars, explained at the time: 'There will be no platform sharing. We can share parts and components, but we won't share platforms.' However, competitors in the industry considered platforms as the 'holy grail' for reaping synergies.

17 November 1998 marked the first day of stock trading for the DC share, which rose by around 30% to the high €90s in the spring of 1999. Executives and board members were trying to turn DC into one company, not just a company name. The integration was organized around 17 clusters (Issue Resolution Teams or IRTs) and dealt with both automotive and non-automotive issues (refer to Figure 2.4 for an overview of the integration structure and IRT clusters). A corporate airline was set up to shuttle executives between Stuttgart (home of Daimler-Benz) and Auburn Hills (Chrysler), with video or telephone conferences complementing the integration efforts.

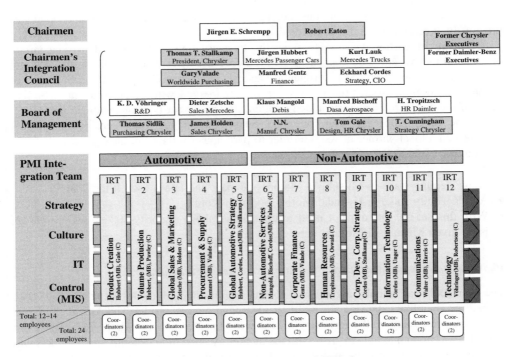

Figure 2.4   Integration structure and IRT clusters
Source: Company information, Case IMD-3-0771.

---

[3] Merger details, from 'autonomy' to 'Zetsche'. *Automotive News*, 5 October 1998, Vol. 73, Issue 5787, p. 41.

As part of the strategy to become a truly global company, managers at DC continued to develop strategies for Asia. Asia was going to be *the* growth market for automobiles, but it was a missing link for DC. DC identified two possible partners and even performed due diligence for acquiring a stake in Nissan Motors. However, after a lively discussion among the management board, this idea was dropped.

As integration got off the ground, second-quarter earnings (1999) failed to meet Wall Street expectations and the stock started to fall. In addition, the share was refused from the American S&P 500 index, a move which took the stock off the shopping list of many funds. By July, the company had to reduce its earnings growth expectations and suddenly synergies became very important. *Automotive News*, an industry journal, stated: 'Meanwhile, Wall Street, underwhelmed by the company's performance to date, is expecting much more from DaimlerChrysler'.[4]

Phase 2: September 1999 – 'integration is over!'

On 27 September 1999, Jürgen Schrempp announced the completion of the integration of both companies. The formal integration with its 17 IRTs was concluded and the chairmen's integration council was abandoned (after two of its eight members left the company). One of them, Tom Stallkamp, the president of North American Chrysler operations and the executive in charge of integrating the company, was replaced by James Holden. Holden was previously executive VP Sales & Marketing.

Following its earlier decision to focus its business lines, DC decided to concentrate on the automotive and trucking business. Non-core activities (ADTRANZ trains, Debitel telecommunications, European Aeronautic Defense and Space Company [EADS, maker of Airbus]) were either sold, prepared for sell-off, or merged with other companies. Selling some of the non-core businesses added financial flexibility for possible acquisitions.

But the geographic expansion continued. Schrempp and his team were convinced that they needed a local partner in Asia in order to participate in the forecasted growth there. In the summer of 2000 DC ultimately bought:

- A 34% equity stake in Mitsubishi Motors of Japan, and later raised it to 37%.
- A 10% equity stake in Hyundai Motors of South Korea.
- With this set-up, DC did not need to consolidate these minority stakes, which was an issue given Mitsubishi Motors' debt.

Phase 3: Up to November 2000 – 'silent phase – deliver the numbers'

The year 2000 was actually a good year for the car industry. Mercedes-Benz cars benefited from its product line extension and maintained strong financial results. The American market was performing very well and a new record was expected for the whole year. However, Chrysler was no longer able to grow with the market. A flood of new competitive models was expected in the minivan segment for which Chrysler had up to 55% share (in the USA). As a result, Chrysler loaded its new minivan with expensive options and prices rose accordingly. However, sales of the new minivan were below expectations and the vehicles needed sales

---

[4] Kisiel, R. (1999). Gale: D/C won't share platforms. *Automotive News*, 4 October, Vol. 74, Issue 5841, p. 1.

incentives/price reductions early on. For Chrysler's other pillar of profitability, SUVs, a wide range of competitive products was suddenly eating into Chrysler's market, too.

The results soon became visible: Chrysler's US market share fell from over 16.2% in 1998 to 13.5% in 2000 and no miracle cure was to be expected from international demand. In order to move the vehicles, cash rebates/incentives of up to $3000 had to be paid. At the same time, production costs spiraled out of control, as production capacity could not be reduced fast enough (refer to Figure 2.5 for a comparison of manufacturing hours by make). In late 2000, *Fortune* reported:

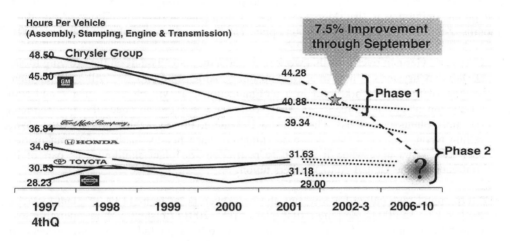

Figure 2.5   Perception vs. reality at Chrysler
Source: *Harbour Report 2002*; Wolfgang Bernhard, presentation at JP Morgan/Harbour Auto Conference, 7 August 2002.

(...) after its merger with Daimler-Benz, Chrysler was in the midst of one of its once-a-decade swoons. Having ridden the crest of the 1990s boom with popular minivans and sport-utility vehicles, the company's American managers had allowed costs to careen out of control and big gaps to open in Chrysler's new-product program. Despite record U.S. auto sales, the company reported an operating loss.[5]

Within DC, divisions had to meet prearranged profit and sales targets ('deliver the numbers'). This approach made it relatively easy to compare different divisions and several executives hoped it 'would bring back the Chrysler spirit'. Holden argued that Chrysler could not make money because of the huge incentives that were bringing down transaction prices. When the Chrysler Group missed a set of prearranged goals (and profit levels), a supervisory board meeting was held on 17 November 2000 and the decision taken to dismiss Holden – after only one year. DC brought in Dieter Zetsche, who had been running the commercial vehicles division, and he started three days later. However, in the fall of 2000, the share price fell below €50.

---

[5] Taylor, A. (2003). Just another sexy sports car. *Fortune*, 17 March, p. 32.

Phase 4: November 2000 – 'starting turnarounds at Chrysler, Mitsubishi, and Freightliner'

The situation facing Zetsche when he arrived was complicated. According to Ward's *Autoworld*, 'to say that Zetsche inherited a mess is an understatement'. He arrived in Detroit with only his chief operating officer (COO), Wolfgang Bernhard, to a welcome that was any-thing but friendly. During a press conference, Zetsche was asked how many more Germans they should expect in Detroit. He replied: 'Four. My wife and three kids.'

Excluding one-time write-offs, Chrysler Group lost $1.8 billion in the last two quarters of 2000. Within DC, the Mercedes Car Group was producing strong cash flows and in Stuttgart, the public opinion was that Mercedes was financing the rest of the Group. After three months, Zetsche presented his turnaround plan. *The Economist* reported on 3 February 2001:

> Chrysler's German overlords this week mounted a dramatic assault on the growing losses at DaimlerChrysler's ailing American subsidiary. At least 26,000 jobs will go [equivalent to 20% of the total workforce] in a reorganization that will close six plants and trim production at seven more. (...) Analysts (...) noted the absence of any American assembly plants on the list. The plant in Belvidere, Illinois, which produces the slow-selling Neon, seemed a sure bet to be shuttered, but Chrysler inadvertently outsmarted itself two years ago, when it agreed to restrictions on plant shutdowns as part of its contract with the United Auto Workers union.

The turnaround plan called for lowering the breakeven point from 113% of plant capacity in 2001 to 83% in 2003.[6] Zetsche's first quarter (Q1, 2001) finished with an operating loss of €1.4 billion, and the full year saw a loss of $5 billion (including one-time effects) at Chrysler.

The equity stakes in Asia (Hyundai and Mitsubishi) developed differently. While Hyundai was becoming highly profitable due to very successful cars and trucks, Mitsubishi required more management attention. Rolf Eckrodt, formerly CEO of ADTRANZ trains (a DC subsidiary that was sold off in 2001), became COO of Mitsubishi Motors in January 2001 and in summer 2002, he left DC and took over as CEO of Mitsubishi Motors.

Mitsubishi Motors had too many models and no real success. The company was plagued by a set of issues. *Manager Magazin*, a German publication, commented:

> No controlling, inefficient structures and processes, which killed the company due to excessive harmony. After two failed turnaround attempts, the company was unable to reform itself.[7]

The turnaround plan at Mitsubishi was drastic. Within three years, the production capacity was going to be cut by 28% and material costs by 15%. The turnaround was also a test for the DC merger, as it dispatched a group of 35 executives from both companies to Japan. The financial year 2000 ended with a loss of $750 million at Mitsubishi.

Neither of the equity stakes in Asia were limited to cars. In 2002 both Mitsubishi and Hyundai spun off their truck and bus divisions. Soon afterwards, DC announced the acqui-

---

[6] Taylor, A. (2003). Can the Germans rescue Chrysler? *Fortune*, 30 April, p. 47.
[7] Hirn, W. (2002). Die Revolution von Tokio. *Manager Magazin*, November, p. 88.

sition of a 43% share in Mitsubishi Fuso Truck and Bus Corporation for €760 million. In Korea, the 'Daimler Hyundai Truck Corporation' was expected to be founded in 2003 with both companies holding equal shares.

DC's truck division, with revenues of €28 billion in 2002, also saw considerable changes. In 2000, DC acquired Detroit Diesel, a highly regarded supplier of heavy-duty engines, and Western Star Trucks of Canada for $877 million. But around the same time, Freightliner, DC's trucking division in North America, was facing problems. The American market for new trucks decreased by 50%. This slump hit Freightliner, as market leader for heavy trucks, especially hard. The demand for new trucks collapsed, and at the same time, leasing models were returned. 'Easy credit' and market values dropping below the book values led to a huge loss on each leasing truck returned. In the case of Freightliner, Jim Hebe, the CEO overseeing the leasing deals, was replaced by Rainer Schmückle. Schmückle knew the company quite well from a previous assignment as CFO of Freightliner.

Phase 5: 'Maintaining sustainable success'

By 2002, both Mitsubishi and Chrysler were profitable again. Chrysler recorded an operating profit, and Mitsubishi Motors recorded an after-tax profit of $290 million for 2002 – the highest ever in the history of Mitsubishi Motors! Although budgets were cut in many cases, the number of products increased. In the case of Chrysler, capital spending was reduced by about 30% – while eight additional new models were added. Chrysler even developed a new model with the help of the Mercedes Car Group, the Chrysler Crossfire. Executives had high hopes for the new vehicles, as sales of Chrysler had fallen from 3.2 million units in 1999 to 2.8 million in 2002. Nevertheless, Chrysler set a growth target of one million additional units by 2011.[8] Table 2.1 summarizes the results between 1998 and 2002.

Table 2.1 Financial summary in € billion (at year-end)

	1998		2002	
	Sales	Operating profit	Sales	Operating profit
Mercedes Car Group	32.6	1.9	50.2	3.0
Chrysler Group	56.4	4.2	60.2	0.6

Source: *Der Spiegel*, 8 September 2003, p. 117.

However, 2003 remained a challenging year. The *Financial Times* reported on 5 June 2003:

> Chrysler's incentives for buyers have reached $4500 per vehicle, almost doubling in a year. (. . .) The company said Chrysler's second-quarter operating loss would be about €1 billion – against analyst forecasts of a €500 million profit. Most of the difference was accounted for by an estimated $400m–$500m writedown in the value of 500,000 cars in dealers' lots and by a cut in the second-hand value of cars held by rental companies.

---

[8] Smith, D. (2002). Is this the next chairman? *Ward's AutoWorld*, November, p. 48.

By Q3, 2003, Chrysler was able to rebound into profit, but the focus on controlling cost continued. The share price remained at around €30.

In order to reap the synergies, Chrysler and Mitsubishi also evaluated the development of a joint platform with an annual volume of one million cars. This was expected to enter the market by 2005. For the same year an annual capacity of 1.5 million units was expected from a 'global four-cylinder engine'. Of this, 600,000 units would be made in a new factory that would be jointly owned by Chrysler, Mitsubishi, and Hyundai. The engine would also be built in a Hyundai factory in Korea and at Mitsubishi in Japan.

In summary, DC had considerably streamlined its portfolio. Table 2.2 outlines major acquisitions and divestitures since 2000.

Table 2.2   Major acquisitions and divestitures (year, company, value)

Acquisitions			Divestitures		
2000	Mitsubishi Motors (34%, later 37%)	€2 billion	2000 and 2002	Debis Systemhaus (IT Services)	€5.5 billion
2000	Hyundai (10%)	$428 million	2001	Debitel (mobile phone operator)	€300 million
2000	Detroit Diesel and Western Star	$877 million	2001	ADTRANZ trains	$725 million
2003	Mitsubishi Trucks	€760 million			

Note: DC owns 33% of EADS. This stake was estimated at around €5 billion at the time of the IPO in 2000.

Corporate governance at global corporations post-Enron

Manfred Gentz, DC's chief financial officer, commented as early as 1999 on the corporate governance challenges:

> The merger of the former Chrysler Corporation and the Daimler-Benz Aktiengesellschaft presented us with a number of integration challenges, including how to combine two different legal systems in such a way as to meet the differing expectations of each company's shareholders and management. With DaimlerChrysler AG's corporate governance, which was already finalized in the Business Combination Agreement of 6 May 1998, we tried to find a solution that combines German and US forms of corporate management.

While the merger was taking place and requiring considerable management attention, the external environment for corporate governance changed dramatically. Although DC was legally based in Germany, it was traded on the New York Stock Exchange (NYSE) and hence had to adhere to many rules and regulations: the Sarbanes–Oxley Act, SEC regulations, and the German Corporate Governance Code. On top of that, DC had to comply with German co-determination rules and other peculiarities in the different countries where DC operated. The effort and bureaucracy involved were considerable:

- **The Sarbanes–Oxley Act (SOA)** aimed to improve investor confidence and the accuracy of financial statements. It stated that CEOs and CFOs should certify the 'appropriateness of the financial statements . . . ' and that the audit committee should be totally independent.

- **American Securities and Exchange Commission (SEC)** stipulated more detailed requirements for audit committees (e.g., committee members had to prove their familiarity with US-GAAP accounting rules). The chief regulators also wanted a better power balance between managers, board members, and shareholders.
- **The German Corporate Governance Code (Cromme Code)** provided an overview of various existing laws and regulations in order to create transparency for foreign investors (as opposed to creating new laws). This resulted in about 50 recommendations (e.g., deductible liability insurance for directors and officers, or the need to disclose financial reports within 90 days). By law, publicly traded companies had to state whether they complied with each recommendation (refer to Figure 2.6 for the main headings of the code). If not, management was requested to publish reasons for not doing so. In addition, there were several suggestions covering items such as individual salaries of management board members.

Chapter 1: Foreword
Chapter 2: Shareholders and the General Meeting
    2.1 Shareholders
    2.2 General Meeting
    2.3 Invitation to the General Meeting, Proxies
Chapter 3: Cooperation between Management Board and Supervisory Board
Chapter 4: Management Board
    4.1 Tasks and Responsibilities
    4.2 Composition and Compensation
    4.3 Conflicts of Interest
Chapter 5: Supervisory Board
    5.1 Tasks and Responsibilities
    5.2 Tasks and Authorities of the Chairman of the Supervisory Board
    5.3 Formation of Committees
    5.4 Composition and Compensation
    5.5 Conflicts of Interest
    5.6 Examination of Efficiency
Chapter 6: Transparency
Chapter 7: Reporting and Audit of the Annual Financial Statements
    7.1 Reporting
    7.2 Audit of Annual Financial Statements

Figure 2.6   German Code for Corporate Governance

Source: Government Commission, German Corporate Governance Code, version 21 May 2003;
www.corporate-governance-code.de.

Generally, the code was seen as an opportunity to evaluate control and management structures. Moreover, according to the code, members of the management board could be on a maximum of five different supervisory boards of listed companies if they held executive functions in (other) listed companies. The code also suggested more personal liability (including personal assets) and a maximum of two members could immediately transfer from the management board to the supervisory board. The code also strongly encouraged the creation of different committees. The chairman of the commission, Gerhard Cromme, explained: '[After all], an efficient and confidential discussion is not possible at regular supervisory board meetings.'[9]

---

[9] Wiskow, J.-H. (2003). Beschränkter Durchblick. *Capital*, 6 March 2003.

Intricacies of the German corporate governance system

The German system had some special features:

- The size of board meetings in this two-tier system was considerable. With 20 members of the supervisory board, plus the board of management, plus staff, there could easily be up to 40 people at the table. As an American board member put it, 'A German supervisory board meeting is like an opera'.
- Increasingly, the salaries of German supervisory board members were heavily debated among the general public. The lowest paid head of a supervisory board (Lufthansa Airlines) earned €21,000[10] – the highest paid (Schering Pharmaceuticals) received €343,000. Karl-Hermann Baumann, former CFO of Siemens and now on the supervisory boards of six big German companies (Siemens, Deutsche Bank, Eon, Linde, Schering, Thyssen-Krupp), earned a total salary of €589,000. In comparison, a board member at Nestlé earned on average €371,000 in 2002 (for one seat). At DC, the 2003 annual assembly voted for an increase from €51,000 to €75,000 for regular members of the supervisory board and from €102,000 to €225,000 for the chairman.
- German corporate law was written with the aim of protecting creditors and thereby allowed companies to accumulate hidden reserves, using book values rather than market values in accounting, etc. This was in sharp contrast to the American system, where corporate laws were aimed at creating transparency for the shareholders, allowing them to control management, and thereby limiting principal–agent conflicts.

Corporate governance at DaimlerChrysler

At DC, trying to adhere to the different codes caused regulatory conflicts. While Sarbanes–Oxley increased the personal responsibilities of CEOs and CFOs, in Germany the members of the management board had collective responsibility (refer to Table 2.3 for more conflicts).

Table 2.3   Managing conflicts

	Germany	USA
CEO/CFO certification (Sarbanes–Oxley Act)	Collective responsibility of the board of management	Personal responsibility of CEO and CFO
Disclosure of deviation from regulation (German Code, NYSE)	Disclosure of deviation from German Code	Disclosure of significant differences from CG practices*
Audit committee appointment of auditors (Sarbanes–Oxley Act, NYSE)	Annual general meeting of shareholders	Audit committee
Public company accounting oversight board inspections	Secrecy agreement between company and auditor	Right to request confidential records from auditor
D&O insurance policy	Introduce suitable deductible/excess	Deductible/excess not common

* Not yet in effect.
Source: DaimlerChrysler.

---

[10] Salary levels are for 2001 or 2002.

As part of this collective responsibility, the board met as a 'legal entity' rather than as a set of individuals. At the same time, Sarbanes–Oxley also led to considerable organizational adjustments, in order to comply with the comprehensive requirements. Schrempp explained:

> In this context, several international initiatives designed to improve corporate governance and restore public confidence in the corporate sector have been undertaken. (...) I can tell you:
>
> 1. There can be no barriers to information.
> 2. The whole company has to be as committed to DaimlerChrysler's balance sheet as Manfred Gentz [CFO] and I are. It is obvious that with their signature on those documents, the chairman and the CFO are accepting certain obligations for the company. Therefore, it is also clear that every senior executive must feel this obligation as well.
> 3. This means that we will install a cascade signing system. Starting with every General Manager and CFO of every business entity within DC and going to the top via every principal.

Due to the changes in the corporate governance landscape, considerable challenges lay ahead. As Dr Manfred Schneider, member of the supervisory board at DC, explained:

> We have to anticipate that in the future less people will be willing to become members of the supervisory board or even head of the supervisory board.[11]

For a global company like DaimlerChrysler, corporate governance was center stage. But corporate governance went far beyond the newly introduced six-page special in the 2002 annual report. This special feature covered the functioning of the annual meeting, a short explanation of the two-tier system, and some of the legally non-binding arrangements: executive automotive council (EAC), chairman's council and the international advisory board (IAB). The implications of the new corporate governance system were far-reaching, as can be seen by the developments on both boards and within various committees.

The management board: running DaimlerChrysler

Developments

Strong leaders, such as Lee Iacocca, often dominated the board of former Chrysler Corp. Their ability was to get designers to 'think outside the box' while getting their managers to meet budgets and cost targets. In 1999, key executives of former Chrysler Corp. left the DC management board, including Stallkamp (President), Gale (Design), Cunningham (Strategy), and co-chairman Bob Eaton followed in March 2000. On the former Daimler-Benz side, two members had left the board: Lauk (Trucks) and Tropitzsch (HR). After Holden's dismissal in November 2000, two former Chrysler executives remained on the board (both in purchasing functions).

Between 1998 and 2003 the board shrank from 17 members to 11, and by 2003 only two members retained their original positions (Hubbert, Mercedes Car Group and Gentz, CFO). In the process, the structure of the board was also changed. The organizational chart

---

[11] Neue Aufsichtsräte sind nur noch schwer zu finden. *Handelsblatt*, 1 April 2003.

showed clear separations between operating and functional divisions (refer to Figure 2.7 for the evolution of the organizational chart). Several former board members remained as advisors to the company (Mangold, Bischoff, Valade). Interestingly, new board members appointed were only 'deputy board members', with a three-year contract rather than the usual five-year contract for regular board members (the norm in Germany). Company policy generally required board members over the age of 60 to have their contracts renewed on an annual basis.

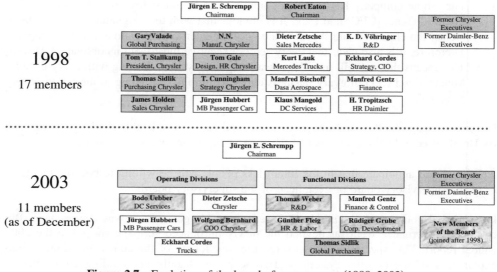

Figure 2.7   Evolution of the board of management (1998–2003)
Source: Company information.

Working style

Initially, the meetings were held in Stuttgart and Auburn Hills, but most American meetings were soon moved to New York (for travel reasons). English was the management language. Annually, there were between 22 – in 2003 – and 35 – in 2000 – meetings (refer to Table 2.4 for the frequency and location of meetings).

Table 2.4   Frequency and location of management board meetings

	1999	2000	2001	2002	2003*
Germany	11	13	17	16	16
USA	17	18	9	7	6
Other	1	4	1	1	–
Total	**29**	**35**	**27**	**24**	**22**

* Planned.
Note: Some of these board meetings lasted for two days. In this case, they were counted twice. This list also includes meetings of the strategic and planning process.
Source: Company information.

Creation of new committees

In the first year of the merger, the chairmen's integration council (CIC) was a central point of the integration. However, the overlap between the CIC and the board of management could not be avoided (refer to Figure 2.4) and all members of the management board were also allowed to join the meetings of the CIC. On the CIC, votes had to be unanimous, while on the management board they could be majority-based. The CIC ceased to exist in September 1999, as the integration was officially completed. Instead, two councils (automotive, and sales and marketing) were set up to coordinate possible component sharing, etc. However, both councils were abandoned.

The potential for sharing components and parts increased fundamentally with the addition of partners in Asia. In order to reap 'potentially huge synergies' (*Wall Street Journal Europe*) from economies of scale and to improve the decision-making procedure, the executive automotive committee (EAC) was set up. This committee, co-chaired by Schrempp and Hubbert, normally met before each board meeting and prepared recommendations regarding the product portfolio, technology, production capacity, and sales and marketing. The EAC's recommendations were then taken to the board (refer to Figure 2.8 for an overview of the EAC). Besides Hubbert and Schrempp, EAC members included Zetsche (Chrysler), Cordes (Trucks), Bischoff (head of the alliance committee with Mitsubishi), and Grube (corporate development). All of them were board members, too.

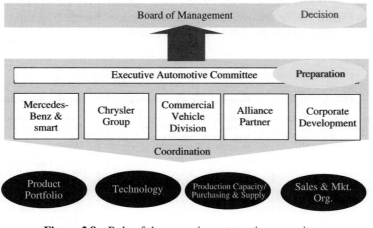

Figure 2.8   Role of the executive automotive committee
Source: Company information.

Grube's staff members prepared the materials for the EAC. Early on in the process, the team considered corporate governance implications. Grube explained:

Strategic initiatives, e.g., our new efforts in China, are discussed on every aspect of our corporate governance system. Strategy depends on feedback and consensus in our governance structure.

For cultural and legal reasons, a similar EAC structure was set up for the minority stakes in Asia. The 'alliance committee' functioned in a similar way to the EAC. In 2002, a similar structure to the EAC was also created for trucks (truck product and decision committee).

Supervisory board: keeping up in a changing industry

In the German two-tier system, the main function of the supervisory board was to supervise, advise on, and monitor business developments. At the same time, this board was also responsible for hiring board members (for which a two-thirds majority was required). The spoken language was German, but all documents were prepared in both German and English, with simultaneous translation at the meetings. The meetings remained driven by the issues. Lynton Wilson, former board member of Chrysler and current board member of DC, explained the style of these meetings:

> Schrempp is a very American-style leader. He is open and [knows] he has to make sure to have relationships and support in the company. So the discussions are matter of fact, issue-related and [end with a decision] on what to do.

The DC supervisory board was led by Hilmar Kopper, former CEO and chairman of Deutsche Bank, who also sat on the boards of Akzo Nobel, Xerox, Solvay, and Unilever. The media reported on the close working relationship between Kopper and Schrempp.

The supervisory board had seen few membership changes on the capital side over the years (refer to Figure 2.9 for the evolution of the supervisory board). The supervisory board met six times in 2003, both in the USA and in Germany.

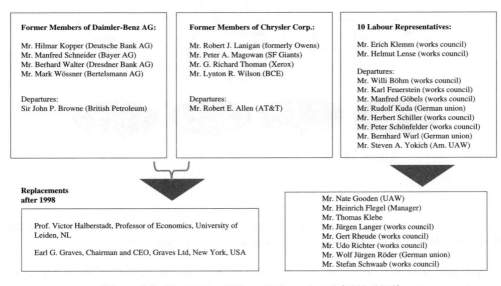

Figure 2.9   Evolution of the supervisory board (1998–2002)
Source: Company information.

Corporate governance in action

DC, like any other global company, had to deal with increasing complexity. However, its corporate governance system had to combine both the American and German governance systems. Wilson explained:

> We are talking here about two very different systems. In North America, non-executive directors are much more involved and have certain responsibilities. In the German system, you have co-determination. Nevertheless, both systems work.

Three committees were established, each consisting of two shareholder and two employee representatives:

1. Presidential committee: employment terms and remuneration for board members. It also conducted 'preliminary discussions on key decisions to be taken by the supervisory board'.
2. Audit committee: examination of annual and semi-annual statements of accounts. This committee also ensured the independence of the auditors. The committee's work became a lot more important due to Sarbanes–Oxley.
3. Mediation committee: in case of disagreement between supervisory board members with regard to the nomination of the new board (this was required by law).

Over the years, however, DC developed several legally non-binding committees.

Shareholder committee and labor committee

The shareholder committee was a big change for the German establishment. CFO Gentz explained:

> A shareholder committee modeled on the US-style board of directors was set up alongside the supervisory board. The committee included the two chairmen, all ten shareholder representatives as well as four prominent outsiders. [This committee] has no decision-making powers, which rest solely with the supervisory board, but instead restricts itself to debate and counseling and provides fact-based recommendations to support opinion-forming among the shareholder representatives.

The committee met six times a year and had two subcommittees. The audit subcommittee dealt with the examination of financial accounts and dividend policy, while the nomination and compensation subcommittee dealt with remuneration of board members and senior executives. The aim was to ensure competitive packages on a global scale, for which outside advisors were hired. However, the issues discussed in the shareholder committee were too similar to those discussed in the supervisory board – it was seen as a duplication, and the committee ceased to exist in January 2001.

Members of the workforce formed the labor committee to accommodate the needs of American and Canadian labor unions, which had only one seat on DC's supervisory board. In addition, employees formed various international committees that were independent of the supervisory board; they met around five times in 2003.

Additional committees

Chairman's council

A new council was started in the fall of 2001. The *Financial Times* reported in September 2001:

> DaimlerChrysler, the international automotive group, is to become the first German-based company to embrace Anglo-Saxon corporate governance rules by forming an independent chairman's council of non-executive directors. (. . .) Officials describe the project as a 'unique hybrid' between Anglo-Saxon corporate governance and the co-determination preferred by most German companies.[12]

The chairman's council consisted of six selected members of the capital side of the supervisory board and selected external members, including CEOs from blue chip companies. In a press statement, DC formalized the council:

> The council will provide advice to management on global business strategy issues. Elements of American and European corporate governance structures are combined to meet the specific requirements of a truly global company and the interests of the different stakeholders. The legal rights and responsibilities of the supervisory board will remain untouched. The chairman's council is complementary to the current governance structure.

International advisory board

The IAB replaced the Daimler-Benz international advisory board, which was started in 1995. It usually met once a year. The IAB's activities were outlined in the annual report:

> The IAB of DaimlerChrysler advises the DaimlerChrysler Group on questions relating to global economic, technological, and political developments and their effect on the business activities of the group. It supports the DaimlerChrysler board of management but is not responsible for making business decisions. The meetings are private to encourage frank and open discussion.

(Refer to Figure 2.10 for members of the chairman's council and IAB.) Figure 2.11 summarizes the various levels of supervision and management in DC.

Outside view: financial markets

Right from the beginning, there was a strong focus on pleasing the financial markets. DC tried to create awareness about the stock price and installed TV screens showing stock prices around HQ. DC had done a lot to cater to the needs of institutional investors. Even before the merger, both companies had used US-GAAP accounting rules; afterwards, DC added detailed reporting according to business segments, value-based stock option plans, and employee

---

[12] Burt, T. (2001). First German-based firm to adopt Anglo-Saxon corporate governance rules. *Financial Times*, 28 September.

Chairman's Council		International Advisory Board (IAB)	
Jürgen E. Schrempp	Chairman		
Internal Members		**Internal Members**	
Victor Halberstadt	Prof. of Economics, Leiden University	DC Board of Management	
Hilmar Kopper	Chairman of the Supervisory Board DCX	**External Members**	
Robert J. Lanigan	Chairman Emeritus of Owens-Illinois	12 members with various backgrounds in academia, politics and business.	
Dr. Manfred Schneider	Chairman of the Supervisory Board of Bayer AG	The members are based in Asia, Europe and the Americas.	
Lynton R. Wilson	Chairman of the Board of Nortel Networks		
Dr. Mark Wössner	Former CEO and Chairman of Bertelsmann		
External Members			
The Lord Browne	Group CEO of BP Amoco		
Louis V. Gerstner, Jr.	Former Chairman and CEO of IBM		
Minoru Makihara	Chairman of Mitsubishi Corp.		
Dr. Daniel Vasella	Chairman & CEO of Novartis AG		
Lorenzo H. Zambrano	Chairman and CEO of Cemex		

Figure 2.10   Members of the chairman's council and international advisory board
Source: Company information.

Controlling the Management...	Managing the Company...	Advising the Management...
Supervisory Board 6 meetings p.a.	Board of Management 22 meetings p.a.	Chairman's Council 5 meetings p.a.
International Employee Committees 5 meetings p.a.	Executive Automotive Committee 10 meetings p.a.	International Advisory Board 1 meeting p.a.
...according to German Law & Co-Determination Principles	...combining German legal requirements and global business needs	...combining elements of US and European Corporate Governance

Figure 2.11   Levels of supervision and management (scheduled number of meetings in 2003)

profit-sharing based on operating profits. Nevertheless, the base of American shareholders was rapidly decreasing. By 31 December 2002, American shareholders accounted for only 14% of total DC shareholders (down from 44% in 1998). Most shareholders were based in Germany (57%), with 21% in the rest of Europe and 8% in the rest of the world, other than the USA. The reduction in the number of American shareholders could have been the result of DC's removal from the S&P 500 index or, as an industry expert explained, 'Americans don't trust the two-tier boards'. The stock price development was unsatisfactory, but it was in line with that of major competitors (refer to Figure 2.12 for the share price development of DC and some competitors).

DaimlerChrysler AG (in $)   General Motors, GM (in $)

Figure 2.12   Share price developments of DaimlerChrysler vs. major competitors
Source: www.comdirect.de.

Deutsche Bank remained the largest shareholder, owning 12%, followed by the Emirate of Kuwait, with 7%. Institutional investors held 54%, private investors 27%.

Understanding risks

The globalization of DC created many opportunities. However, for corporate governance purposes, it was also essential to understand the business risk. Besides risks originating from *off-balance sheet activities* or *bad debt*, DC and other car companies faced considerable industry-specific risks. Being a global player and consolidating in euros, any drastic *exchange rate fluctuations* could severely impact the financial results. At the same time, large parts of the operating income resulted from *financial services* (e.g., car leasing), a business dependent on many 'outside' forces. DC also faced considerable *technology risks* (e.g., fuel cells, fuel efficiency, lightweight materials). Missing one trend could mean suffering for half a decade. The increasing number of brands brought with it the risk of wrong *brand positioning*. Also, because the factory assets were so specific to the industry, the *exit risk* was considerable. And since the merger, the company was also increasingly subject to North American risks such as *product liability* issues or court cases from *disgruntled shareholders*.

In 2003, Schrempp commented on the merger and corporate governance:

> When Daimler-Benz and Chrysler merged, there was no textbook written on how to do it. I admit, we were not as efficient from day one as we could have. But now the international cooperation and the implementation of the strategy work very well.[13]

And they broke new ground in corporate governance, too.

---

[13] Ein hartes Stück Arbeit, interview with Jürgen Schrempp. *Der Spiegel*, 8 September 2003, p. 120.

Part II
Boards' Internal Dynamics

3

Information Demand and Supply
for Changing Board Roles

3.1 DO NEW BOARD ROLES REQUIRE DIFFERENT INFORMATION?

'Knowledge is power' is an old Roman saying that still rings true today – particularly in the corporate world. Around the world, the effects of past corporate scandals have left their mark in the form of new legislation – with a greater onus on the company's board of directors to provide sound governance systems. The 'right' information at the 'right' time is crucial for a board to be effective. But are company boards equipped to succeed in their new, more powerful role?

The effects of past corporate scandals (e.g., WorldCom in the USA and Parmalat in Europe) were significant and appear lasting: investor, consumer, and employee confidence in corporate behavior were shaken to the core. Most countries reacted with fundamental new legislation targeting corporate organizational structures, disclosure requirements, or directors' and officers' liabilities. The board's role has changed and become even more crucial for companies' government systems. Clearly, boards today play a predominant role in modern corporate governance. As a result, board members' responsibilities and tasks are broader and the complexities and dynamics surrounding the board's work have increased tenfold. But with global corporate governance activism fading, the bad taste of past scandals remains: Will the 'new corporate governance' work out and will the board succeed in its crucial, more powerful role?

Cause for concern?

Businesses spend millions on organizational development, but how much do companies invest in educating and updating their boards? Knowledge is power according to the old Roman saying, and it seems more important than ever. The availability of information, sources, and knowledge determines how the board can influence and monitor management and its decisions, and how involved the board is in the company in general. Information supplied to the board indicates what is expected from its members, and whether it meets the standards that the board needs to fulfill its expected tasks. Information flows and sources are significantly representative of how powerful the board is. Furthermore, the timeliness of information is essential. Overall, information gives the board a strong and influential role, but when lacking, missing it can equally put the board out of action.

General aspects

Our research indicates that 50% of boards meet between four and six times a year. However, another 44% meet more than six times a year. For the large majority of board members

(>60%), only a very small part of the information they receive during the course of their full-time jobs is relevant to their board work. The board book of documents provided for every board meeting is usually kept small, and for 80% of boards, it does not exceed 50 pages. Surprisingly, 44% of board members also receive less than 10% of the information for every board meeting electronically.

When board members were asked whether or not they felt well informed about several fields relevant to their business, considerable differences showed up (see Figure 3.1). About 90% claimed they were well informed about corporate and business strategy and financials. In respect of organizational and human resources, more than 70% still agreed. In topics 'external' to the company, boards have different roles and influence. More than two-thirds are well informed about the company's markets and the political, legal, and societal issues related to the business.

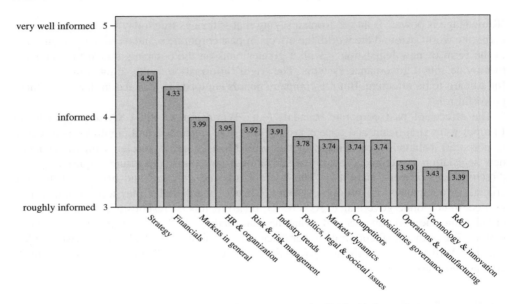

Figure 3.1   Satisfaction of board members by field of information

However, about one-third of board members felt uninformed about direct competitors, market dynamics and developments, and industry trends. It remains questionable whether this is sufficient to describe the 'bigger picture' about the company's business. In several strategic, forward-looking fields, the results should ring warning bells. In the case of technology and innovation and the company's operations and manufacturing, more than 50% have only rough knowledge or no knowledge at all. Moreover, regarding strategic research and development, more than 50% of board members said they were poorly informed.

The information provided to the board is still mainly focused on the past. Less knowledge of the fields important to the company's future and strategic success portends severe difficulties for board members in anticipating the future development of the company. New fields of information seem to be integrated rather slowly into the board's information systems: though past crises had a huge impact on the board's role, more than 30% of board members only have vague knowledge or less about the company's risks, risk management efforts, or the main activities of the company's subsidiaries.

Different board positions, different information?

Roles and information inside boards also vary: different board members have different functions and are supplied with different information. Corporate strategy and financials are core information fields for every position. However, for both fields, board chairmen showed slight informational advantages compared to ordinary board members. This trend grew stronger for the company's markets, market dynamics, and industry trends: in all of the fields mentioned, board chairmen had significant informational advantages compared to ordinary board members.

Concerning risks and risk management, both CEOs and chairmen were on a comparable knowledge level, whereas ordinary board members stood apart. On the subject of technology and innovation, operations and manufacturing, an apparent chain of information could be perceived: CEOs know the most, then other officers, chairmen of the board, and then ordinary board members. Again, research and development turned out to be the field with the greatest information asymmetry, with both chairmen and ordinary board members indicating much less expertise than CEOs and other officers.

Quality of board information

As assumed, about 40% of board members feel overloaded with information. This does not seem to be a problem of badly structured information. Regarding fields of information, the result is different: 63% stated the information supplied was too general and did not highlight specific key issues. Thus, most board members (>60%) would prefer to receive more information external to the company (e.g., about markets and competitors). 67% would prefer less detailed financial figures for their board work. Also, for nearly 80%, the information provided is not forward-looking enough and deals too much with the past. Consequently, a large majority of 80% agreed that given current informational practices, board members could not envisage the 'bigger picture' of the company.

Board members generally do not suspect the information supplied to be guided by hidden agendas. Yet, 31% still felt that it was at least a little biased and shaped by management's opinion; 37% even said the information supplied was fairly or more biased and shaped. Figure 3.2 presents the respective overview.

Additional influences on informational levels

Despite an increase in demands and responsibilities, the overall board information systems continue to remain unchanged. 80% of board information systems have been developed by management and then simply adapted over time. Only in one-third of the cases did the board define any criteria for how it should be informed. One in every three respondents clearly indicated that their board information system definitely does not apply best practice standards. See Figure 3.3.

There is a significant relationship between the time someone spends on the board and the overall level of information, specifically knowledge of markets. Long-term board members see through hidden agendas more easily and benefit from easier information sharing with colleagues. Thus, tenure has its advantages. Also, information exchange among colleagues improves over time. On the other hand, this means that new board members need initial advice and help and a considerable amount of time on the board to reach full efficiency. In creating high-performance boards, it is, therefore, a primary task to bridge these information gaps as soon as possible. Regular and more frequent board meetings provide board members with significantly better

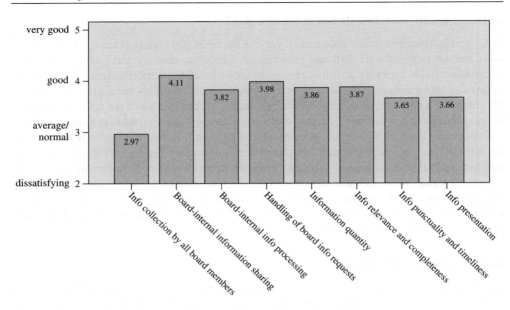

Figure 3.2   Satisfaction with board information characteristics

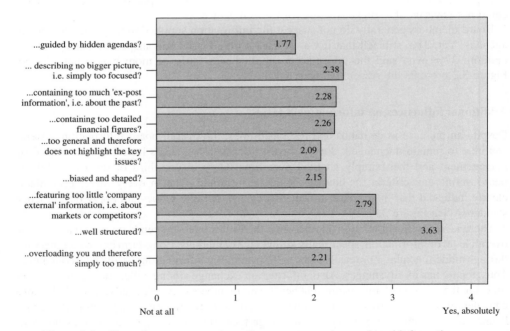

Figure 3.3   Given the current practices of your company, is your board information . . .

levels of information, especially regarding the core corporate governance fields of risks and risk management and subsidiaries' governance, but also general market and industry knowledge. A clear relationship links the strategic influence of the board and the number of meetings. The bottom line is that the more frequently the board meets, the more value-adding potential it has.

Overall understanding of board roles and tasks

By and large, board members have embraced their dominant role of adding value at the upper echelon of organizations. Boards emphasize strategic influence beyond monitoring and supervising. Controlling financial performance and providing checks and balances for the CEO and management continue to be highly essential tasks. Mere representational tasks or VIP status – without actually tackling real issues – do not take center stage. However, they need a certain basic level of information, and this can only be achieved through a minimum number of board meetings.

Information sources and potential implications

The results showed that there is considerable room for improvement regarding the information sources board members use for their daily work. For 54% of board members, more than 90% of the information for their board work came from the company; it was not sourced by themselves or externally.

Over 90% receive two-thirds of the information relevant for board meetings only from the company. Overall, board members mostly rely on the information that is sent to them, rather than looking for their own. Figure 3.4 depicts the results of the investigation of board members' most important information sources.

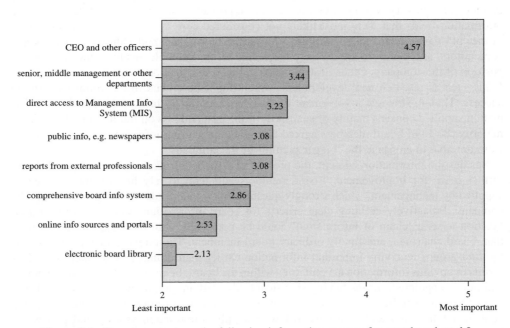

Figure 3.4   How important are the following information sources for your board work?

For an overwhelming majority, the CEO and other officers represent the most important information suppliers – far more important than any other source. Going directly to the company's middle, department, or line managers came in second, but did not have a significant lead compared to electronic information systems or other information sources. The board, therefore, should be aware that neutrality in content and information field selection is not guaranteed if the supervisors receive their information mainly from the body they are supervising, i.e. the top management.

Impact of recent corporate governance scandals and new regulation

It is no surprise that the recent scandals and failures in corporate governance, along with the plethora of codes and regulatory adjustments, have had an impact on how boards work, perceive their role and tasks, and ensure they have the proper information to deliver. 43% indicated these scandals and regulatory adjustments fostered independence of boards from management. More than 50% of boards now monitor management more intensively. As a result, almost half (46%) of the boards have succeeded in increasing the efficiency of board work and meetings. Board information improved significantly in almost 50% of cases. 60% of boards now exert more strategic and operative influence. Simultaneously, 56% of board members indicated that their tasks have become fundamentally more complex. For only 18%, scandals and regulations had no impact at all.

Conclusion

The role of board members has changed since the wave of corporate scandals triggered new regulation. More far-reaching board involvement, beyond monitoring and supervision, altered the information demand fundamentally. However, board members clearly indicate that they are not very well informed on several important issues. The key problems here are information fields that were most likely not considered core to the board's responsibilities in the 'old days': board members lack information on markets and industry dynamics and competitors, and therefore are unlikely to be able to, for example, evaluate the competitive position of the company. Other strategic gaps in board information concern forward-looking fields such as research and development, which might be crucial to the company's future success. Though strategic involvement is considered a primary task of the board, the information supplied consists mainly of snapshots of the past and less on future outlooks. A large majority (80%) of board members agreed that given the current informational practices they were not able to envisage the 'bigger picture' of the company.

Besides the information content, the process of how board members are informed shows further room for improvement. Board members still tend to rely heavily on information supplied by management, which strongly questions their independence and power within the company. Proactively defining clear criteria for board information systems is still a rarity. Position-wise, a 'chain of information' could be perceived, with the CEOs informed best, then board chairmen, and finally ordinary board members. These results also point towards the first groups receiving important information earlier than ordinary board members. This results in obvious information asymmetries within the board: being an ordinary board member and newly appointed, means having significant difficulty in getting necessary information.

Since board members regard their role as enhanced, new information demands regarding content, quality, and tools must be met with supply. Information sharing and processing between management and the board, and among the board members themselves, remain unused sources for adding value. Here the chairman's relationship to other board members is often neglected. To create and maintain a high-performance board, these informational gaps must be closed successfully.

Learning nuggets from the cases

The following two cases – Khan AG and ICM – illustrate the importance of board information in real life. 'Conflicts of interest at the board of Khan AG' captures a typical information and conflict pattern between the controlling owner and representatives of the minority shareholders, and what is acceptable and what not. The crucial role of information is outlined as the CEO has a clear-cut agenda, but a board member is left in the dark. Even if our heroine of the case were motivated and up to the challenge regarding the competencies, it takes more to solve the business dilemmas – the ambiguities she has to cope with are overwhelming. For her, obtaining clarity is a challenge and risky endeavor. But how to play the game and where to draw the line in games of manipulation, hidden agenda, and a CEO who benefits if some board members have no information clarity, is up to the decision of each current and future board member . We added the ICM case as we saw value in shedding light on factors that can complexify board work further. 'ICM: when hidden agendas enter the boardroom' centers around an intrigue triggered by the CEO and management against the chairman of the board to pursue their own interests against the formally agreed-upon objective. There is a reason for the intrigue, but we leave it to the reader to detect it.

3.2   CASE STUDY: CONFLICTS OF INTEREST AT THE BOARD OF KHAN AG

[By Ulrich Steger, Wolfgang Amann, and Jochen Brellochs]

I'm the elected hostage. Whatever happens, it will be a no-win situation.

These were the thoughts of Annie Knauf, the 53-year-old vice chair of Kahn AG's board. Otto Wilder, the tall, heavyset chair of the board, had just left the board meeting, citing a conflict of interest, leaving Annie to chair the meeting. Wilder's personal lawyer, whom he had installed as a corporate adviser to Khan, remained in the room. With no advance warning to the board, Wilder, who owned 49.9% of Kahn's shares, had proposed a complicated 'sub-merger' of the technology divisions of his own empire, the privately held Güldner AG, and Kahn's. After a bitter debate, during which the lawyer read some important paragraphs aloud (e.g., that Kahn had to pay for the Güldner division with its shares, bringing Wilder's share ownership above 75%), Wilder said that it was now time to decide. Annie, who had been brought in to represent the interests of small shareholders, was pondering her options. Refusing the deal could lead Wilder to 'pull the plug' on Kahn, as he had threatened to do. Accepting the deal might lead to a merger with a company that had liquidity problems and could probably harm Kahn's interests.

Annie was convinced that Kahn needed a period of consolidation rather than a merger, which would entail new problems. The deal currently under scrutiny ran the risk of squeezing out Kahn's small shareholders, and it would not be the first time that Wilder, who claimed to have built his empire as a self-made man with 'two empty hands', had ridden roughshod over smaller shareholders with his bold moves. And now that rumors were circulating that Güldner AG was facing liquidity problems, it would demonstrate that the board had made a decision to benefit the biggest shareholder at the expense of all the other shareholders. This would never benefit Kahn, and would make the shares less liquid on the stock exchange. Were there other options? Could Annie minimize the damage with some changes? Annie pondered her options as she considered her obligations as a board member along with her own values and integrity.

The vice chair's challenge

Things started happily two years ago when Wilder bought 49.9% of Kahn AG. At the time, he was perceived as a 'savior' especially among the employees, because Kahn had been close to bankruptcy. This was the result of an acquisition in the USA that had turned sour, been a drain on the company's resources for years and, ultimately, had to be sold for a huge loss. Although some analysts claimed that Wilder – as always – got Kahn for a 'fire sale' price, the original shareholders were hoping for a better future, after years of a declining stock price, by agreeing to a capital reduction (refer to Figure 3.5 for key data and the shareholder structure).

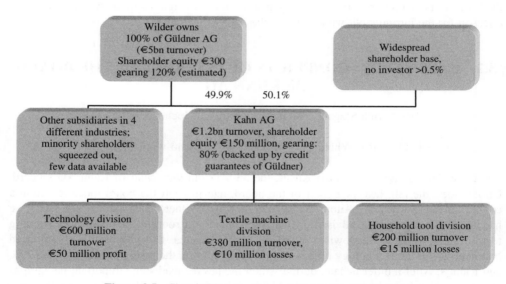

Figure 3.5   Shareholder structure and divisions of Kahn AG

Upon his arrival, Wilder promised fair treatment of small shareholders and presented Annie Knauf as vice chair with the explicit task to look out for their interests. After a 15-year career in a variety of multinational companies, with her last assignment as a member of the European executive committee and corporate legal counsel of a large multinational company, she could contribute substantial industry experience. Three years ago, she became a leading partner in a well-reputed law firm, specializing in corporate legal affairs. She therefore seemed uniquely positioned to represent the fragmented base of Kahn's majority and, guided by Wilder, the nomination committee voted for her. However, as one employee representative pointed out:

> The mother of two teenagers will not have access to Wilder's hunting parties, as he never takes women with him on such endeavors.

The employee representative also had some doubts that the lawyer would have sufficient understanding of Kahn's culture – engineering driven and traditionally seeking consensus with the Workers' Council (refer to Figure 3.6 for the composition of the board of Kahn AG).

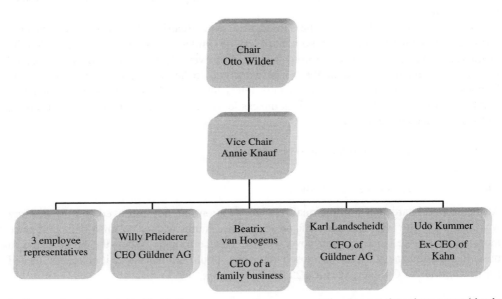

Audit committee: Landscheidt (chair), Kummer, one employee representative, has met three times a year (shortly before the board meeting).
Personnel committee: van Hoogens (chair), Pfleiderer, one employee representative, committee has not met yet.
Members of the management board routinely attend board meetings.

Figure 3.6   Composition of the board of Kahn AG

Nevertheless, the honeymoon lasted six months. Then, just before the first quarterly board meeting, Wilder called Annie Knauf and asked her 'to run the show' as he had another important meeting to attend. As nothing important was on the agenda, the board session was running smoothly. At the end of the session, Annie wanted to trigger a debate on how to structure the board meetings more efficiently, so that they could focus more on strategy, better transparency of numbers, and fewer presentations by members of the management board. She met with passive resistance.

The first board meeting goes awry

Walter Brinkmann, who had been put in place by Wilder two years previously, explained at length the accounting system and detailed budget process for the three divisions. While he did not reject Annie's suggestion, he did indicate that there was little room for board involvement. Udo Kummer, the former CEO and now a board member, went into a lengthy explanation about why Kahn was different from Anglo-Saxon companies, closing with what he thought was a joke:

Lawyers and women don't understand numbers anyway.

At the time, Annie decided to ignore Kummer's comment, but privately she thought that he had messed up Kahn and did not belong on the board. Only the employee representatives and Beatrix van Hoogens expressed interest in Annie's suggestion, the first more cautiously than the latter.

Annie decided, therefore, that she should meet with Beatrix. They had dinner during a business trip, which turned out to be a discovery of similar approaches and business/family challenges, typical for high-performing women. However, Beatrix indicated that she could not get very much involved in the board work due to her obligation to run her family business. At the end of the evening, Annie felt a bit irritated when Beatrix told her that Wilder had invited her for dinner at his home castle – an invitation Annie had never received. But Beatrix laughed and said:

Don't worry, I won't fall victim to his charm.

The second board meeting goes awry

At the second board meeting, the quality of preparation had not improved and the meeting was again overrun with management presentations. Annie wanted to raise her point once more under 'miscellaneous'. She never got the chance though. When the board came to miscellaneous business, Wilder proposed that Kahn should sell real estate it no longer needed for its factories to Güldner AG for €25 million, noting:

This is a very good price for Kahn.

Annie was shocked, as she expected there would have been an announcement for this type of matter beforehand. She demanded that an independent expert prepare a report. The CEO, Brinkmann, tried to appease Annie by assuring her that everything had been checked and the price was good. When she asked if the external auditor would agree to the terms of this transaction, she noted some unease in the room. But Wilder's personal lawyer, who was attending the meeting in his capacity as a corporate adviser to Kahn AG, raised his hand and confirmed that he had checked with the auditor and that everything was fine. In the end, Annie abstained from voting and she demanded to see a note from the auditor. She also insisted that details of the discussion be recorded in the minutes of the board meeting, which raised the tension in the room. It was clear that management was playing games with the information it provided, and under these circumstances Annie wanted some proof that she had abstained from the vote.

Beatrix had been silent during this exchange, but after the vote, she proposed that such deals should be on the agenda and more information sent to the board in advance. Wilder agreed to this. When leaving the room, he turned to Annie without shaking hands and said with his predator smile:

I don't understand what you're doing – but it will definitely not help our cooperation.

However, Annie had discovered a powerful weapon:

By raising questions and documenting the answers, I am taking away the 'good faith' of the board. I am making the board more accountable.

The only glimpse of hope for Annie was her ongoing good relationship with Beatrix. However, during a coffee break, Beatrix told Annie that Wilder was not as tough as he may appear in board meetings. She went on in his defense to explain that he did substantial charity work together with his wife. Annie, however, was not impressed by Wilder's charity work, because she believed that he was probably motivated by the tax reductions rather than helping people. She also didn't buy Beatrix's explanation that he had a different perspective on how to contribute to Khan – or that well-prepared board information delivered in a timely fashion was bureaucracy!

Board meetings never return to normal

Future board meetings at Kahn were a nightmare for Annie. Wilder brushed her off at every turn. Before the third meeting, the external auditor sent a note confirming that the property transactions were 'within the range of market prices, but probably at the lower end'. When Annie called the auditor before the meeting, he refused to elaborate on the note and, especially, the timing of his involvement. At the third meeting, Annie wanted to discuss the discrepancy with the original estimates presented by Wilder and Brinkman, but Wilder cut her off, saying that it was a done deal and the board should not waste its time on it. Beatrix did not attend this meeting, but when one of the employee representatives supported Annie's inquiry with a follow-up question, Brinkmann brushed him aside, saying:

We've already been through this. It's history, so let's move on.

Although Annie had been elected for a two-year term, she was pondering whether she should leave the Kahn board. She knew that her withdrawal would cause a disturbance in the press, as a reason would have to be disclosed. To avoid harming the company, she decided to stay until the next general assembly. In the meantime, she was determined to honor her integrity and obligations as a board member.

The final board session

In the meeting before the general assembly, however, Wilder surprised Annie with the proposal to merge the two technology divisions (refer to Figure 3.7 for an abridged version of the resolution).

Wilder's strategic intention was clear. The deal would bring Wilder's shareholding to 75%, enough to squeeze out smaller shareholders, when Kahn's stock price was falling. The share price was stagnating after a brief peak nearly a year ago, when Wilder's investment in Kahn was announced. In addition, this deal could be the next step in bringing the valuable technology divisions under the umbrella of Güldner AG, leaving Kahn with two

Board Resolution 2005/02 (abridged)

Re: Merger between the Technology Division of Kahn AG and the IKW GmbH

1. As the technology sector is rapidly consolidating and globalizing, the need for economies of scale is rising. In addition, there is an urgent need to respond to new business opportunities.
2. Both the technology division and the IKW GmbH, fully owned by Güldner AG, are too small to compete in this new business environment and can be – if forces are joined – a strong partner in the further consolidation process.
3. Therefore, the board of Kahn AG agrees to a merger of its technology division under the following criteria:

   - Both business units are of equal value, especially with regard to the high intellectual property of IKW, according to the preliminary results of a value estimation by Güldner's AG auditors.
   - Kahn AG buys the IKW GmbH for €100 million, paying it with the emission of new shares, valued at €4.20 per share.
   - The new division will be a separate legal entity, incorporated as Kahn IKW Technology AG.
   - The Management Board of Kahn AG is asked to continue the negotiation on the contract with Güldner AG and sign it before the General Assembly.
   - The General Assembly will be asked to ratify the deal as far as its legal responsibilities are concerned.

Figure 3.7   Board resolutions

low-performing divisions, a huge pension liability, and debt. As Annie pondered this, she thought:

The banks would not mind because Güldner AG was clearly a bigger concern for them.

Given the rumors of a liquidity crunch at Güldner AG, they could have an interest in an IPO of the technology division. This would allow Wilder to finally pay back some of the money he had spent on his acquisition spree. For Annie, the impact for Kahn's improving results, consolidation, and its small shareholders was the same – especially as Annie could not imagine that the Güldner technology division was as valuable as the Kahn division. In fact, she had no information at all about Güldner's technology division. She tried to remember:

Was there even one? And what worthwhile innovations and competencies did they actually have?

Instinctively, she tried to go the legal route, politely arguing that such a deal should have been on the agenda before the board meeting. Wilder, leaning back, asked her – with his predator smile:

But due to the urgency – if we *all* agree to waive this requirement, what then?

For the first time, Annie felt fearful of Wilder's ability to steamroll her. If she wanted to stay the legal route, she had to admit that this was possible but that it would probably leave the board vulnerable to shareholder lawsuits of negligence or even willful misconduct.

Instead of debating the unspecified urgency, she decided to demand more information for the board – and make sure it was documented in the minutes. To her satisfaction, the demand for information was met by support from the other board members, with the exception of Wilder's proxies.

At this point, Wilder's lawyer and Kahn's corporate adviser took over the discussion. His tactic was clear: he challenged Annie's and the board's right to know and then under pressure revealed some news. The discussion dragged on for more than three hours; even ex-CEO Kummer asked some critical questions and the employee representatives were obviously feeling uncomfortable as well. Beatrix participated a little in the information gathering, but stayed demonstratively neutral.

As the facts emerged, they painted an unpleasant picture. In order to be of equal value with Kahn's technology division, IKW GmbH was propped up by some smaller acquisitions, completed earlier by Wilder, and by the activation of intellectual property. When pushed to disclose and explain specific paragraphs of the draft contract, the lawyer admitted that it would give Wilder direct control over the newly merged entity.

Pondering her options, Annie thought that the majority of the board might vote against the proposed deal – the three employee representatives, ex-CEO Kummer, Beatrix, and herself. However, if Wilder then decided to withdraw with immediate effect some credit guarantees – which he had given to back up Kahn's still fragile finances – or sold his shares, Kahn might collapse.

The more Annie thought about this, the more she was convinced that Wilder would not go so far because he needed Kahn in order to save his own privately owned conglomerate from its liquidity problems. She regarded the situation as critical for Kahn. She decided to ask a question that nobody in the board had ever dared ask before, even though they might have thought about it frequently during the last two years. She stood up and asked Wilder directly:

> Do you need the deal to stabilize your own company? There are a lot of rumors in the market.

Wilder had long stopped smiling. He leaned forward with all his weight, his face turning redder than usual, and answered coldly:

> If you have no argument left except to spread offensive rumors, for me the debate is over. It's time to make a decision. To satisfy our legally sophisticated colleagues, I will leave the room now, as I might be accused of having conflicts of interest, despite all the support I have given to Kahn.

As he was leaving the boardroom, Annie thought about some advice an old friend had given her:

> When you join a board, never think of nor hope for re-election.

She knew she was on her way out, but that was currently the least of her problems.

3.3   CASE STUDY: ICM – WHEN HIDDEN AGENDAS ENTER THE BOARDROOM (A)

[By Ulrich Steger and Wolfgang Amann]

ICM'S BOARDROOM, DOWNTOWN TEL AVIV, 14:00, 23 NOVEMBER 2004: Nathan Adar's eyes opened wide in astonishment. Normally, very little surprised the highly decorated 57-year-old former colonel in the Israeli army. But this bowled him over: how could the board of Integrated Circuit Manufacturing (ICM) have voted against the joint venture in the USA, which was – in his mind – to all intents and purposes a *fait accompli*? After all, ICM's owners had brought him in as chairman of the board because of his international business experience to push growth and expansion in the USA. And now all the other board members had voted against a proposal that would have ensured swift access to the US market via a joint production venture with a strategic partner.

With shaking hands and breathing heavily, he moved on to the next point on the agenda, even though his mind was elsewhere. What had happened for the board to change its views so abruptly and how had he – with all his experience in army intelligence – not noticed this? Despite the air conditioning, he began sweating. How could he have understood what was in fact silent opposition to be agreement? And why had none of his fellow board members warned him in advance? What should he do: fight for the JV or resign? Or was someone about to oust him, as had happened to his predecessor – but now for exactly the opposite reason?

Company background

ICM was founded in the early 1980s by an Orthodox Jewish kibbutz – a typical Israeli cooperative – which wanted to diversify its business to ride the booming electronic industry's wave of growth. Focusing on microprocessors and related software applications within high-precision steering typically used in CNC[1]-controlled machine tools, it rapidly developed a market niche, broadening the company's existing know-how and gaining manufacturing and software expertise. But in the early 1990s, when management initiated an export drive by creating six subsidiaries in Europe and the USA, the company paid a high price to learn the ropes of global business. Between 1993 and 1997 its losses almost equaled all of its previous profits. It became especially clear that the US market could only be served via a manufacturing site in the USA itself.

After conducting a thorough strategy review, the kibbutz's coordinating committee – which basically acted as the owner-representative and was headed by an Orthodox rabbi-turned-manager – decided to go ahead as planned. Most noteworthy was the fact that they hired Jacob Eden, the former CEO of a privately held, smaller rival that could not be bought, as vice president of marketing in 1998.

ICM's expansion plan in the USA

Jacob soon developed a special plan for profitable business expansion in the USA. Despite the generally strong competition there, the niche that ICM would occupy could be made

---

[1] CNC = computer numerical control.

profitable. But time was running out. There was no alternative to manufacturing in the USA, as the logistics (shipping by air to save time) and market penetration would otherwise be too costly. Jacob therefore recommended that a strategic US partner be identified in order to (1) reduce the risk of the considerable investment required for a new factory; (2) accelerate the market penetration in this huge market; and (3) provide a better service in respect of the customized products.

Although the entire estimated investment of US$24 million would be financed through loans, the expectation of being profitable within three years greatly appealed to management.

The importance of the undertaking was underlined when the CEO, Yoav Granzach, promised:

If necessary, I'll go to the US myself in order to ensure the success of our endeavor.

By the end of 2000, the board had in general approved the investment and asked management to come up with a detailed plan, including proposals for a suitable JV partner.

At the annual general meeting in the spring of 2001, 53-year-old Gad Ariav had been elected as the new chairman of the board. With a domestic consumer goods background, he was not only a highly respected businessman but also a fellow Orthodox Jew. Soon, however, he started expressing his concerns over a strategic US partner. The crux of his argument was that any kind of JV would most probably be with a larger US partner and would sooner or later end in ICM being acquired by this partner, which would mean that the owners would lose control. This was significant because members of the kibbutz – representing a number of shareholders – worked in professional and management functions at ICM.

ICM's management, especially the CEO and the VP of marketing, Jacob Eden, were rather unhappy with this view of the strategy, but tried to avoid open conflict with the chairman. In discussions with him, Jacob time and again underlined that the JV would only be focused on manufacturing and logistics.

All customer relations and marketing factions remain here,

he assured Gad,

otherwise my job will also disappear.

It soon became clear, however, that even at the peak of the boom, ICM's current circumstances meant that at best it could only achieve breakeven in the US market (refer to Table 3.1). But, to maintain pressure on the board, sales to the USA were continued. On the pretext of needing to collect more data, the CEO had the board appoint a senior project manager, Shmuel Ellis – an old friend of his – whose secret agenda was clearly to search for partners and locations for the new investment. In 2003, the CEO and Shmuel made two long trips to the USA to visit potential locations and hold preliminary talks with possible cooperation partners.

The new chairman of the board

After the second trip, Yoav decided to stage a boardroom coup. He rallied the management behind him and pressured the owners to ask Gad to relinquish his position as chairman of

Table 3.1   ICM sales and profit: overall and in the USA ($ million)

Year	Sales (overall)	Profit (overall)	Sales (USA)	Profits (USA)
1993	100	13	17	−2
1994	109	11	22	−2
1995	121	10	25	−4
1996	132	11	25	−5
1997	137	10	28	−4
1998	145	12	31	−2
1999	157	14	39	−1
2000	169	15	45	+/−0
2001	175	13	47	−3
2002	179	14	52	−3
2003	186	15	59	−6
2004	192	17	61	−4

the board. Gad offered surprisingly little resistance and resigned during the annual general meeting in the spring of 2004.

However, the owners did not appoint the candidate chairman that Yoav had suggested, but brought in someone from outside – Nathan. Although he was a secular Israeli, the owners selected him on the grounds of his broad experience in the USA: he had just completed a large Israeli–US JV in the manufacturing industry. Even during his 20-year stint in the military, he had spent several years in the USA and still maintained a broad network there. Introducing the new chairman to the board and management, the owners made clear that they had 'chosen Nathan to fulfill the vision outlined in the strategic plan of establishing a plant in the US with a competent partner'.

In June 2004, soon after taking over, Nathan called a one-day board retreat, with the CEO and all four vice presidents in attendance as well. To prepare for the meeting, a consultant was hired to review the data collected and the strategic plan that management had developed. The result was very clear: there was an extremely urgent need to establish a factory in the USA. It was also obvious that a partner would be needed to share the high cost, which had risen to US$28 million. Nobody objected, and the various management members specifically reconfirmed their commitment and necessary action at the end of the retreat. The CEO was ready to go to the USA if needed; Jacob explained how the US sales force would be organized and coordinated from Israel, and the project manager presented the first draft of the potential layout of the factory.

Approaching a US partner

On another business trip to the USA soon afterward, Nathan met Charles Heyssen (the CEO of Semiconduct, a large manufacturer of electronics) at a private dinner. Charles coincidentally mentioned that after the Internet bubble had burst they had been forced to close a factory after demand declined drastically. It struck Nathan that some of the capacity could be transformed for ICM's production at a far lower cost than a 'greenfield' investment would require. He discussed this with Charles over a beer at the hotel bar, and they agreed to set up a joint task force to look at the details and conduct a feasibility study.

Fourteen days later, the ICM team – consisting of Shmuel as the project manager, the consultant who had handled the board retreat, and an internal expert on manufacturing – met their counterparts from Semiconduct. The results were even more promising than Nathan had expected. One-third of the factory was in a separate building and consisted of two production lines, which could be transformed at a cost of approximately US$3–4 million to suit ICM needs.

After the results from the task force had come in, Nathan and Yoav returned to the USA to negotiate a letter of intent with Charles. A 50:50 joint venture, called ICM Semiconduct USA, would produce ICM's product range, which Semiconduct's sales force would then distribute as a separate brand, since fortunately the two companies' product lines did not really compete. Semiconduct would contribute the manufacturing facilities, and ICM the patented technology, the customer relations, and own parts of the distribution network.

An audit company chosen by both companies would evaluate the non-cash investments. Any differences in the investment value would be compensated in cash to maintain the 50:50 balance. A team would be set up to develop a business plan with ambitious growth targets, since the factory's capacity could easily double ICM's sales in the USA, and the company would thus reap important economies of scale.

Reaching closure – or not?

While the experts were negotiating the details in a series of meetings and document exchanges between August and October 2004, Nathan and the CEO met individually with each of the four other board members (three were external business people, one a representative of the owners) as soon as possible to tell them about the evolving JV, relying on their discretion. A routine board meeting in late September 2004 did not lead to any discussion of the reported negotiation results.

By the end of October, however, Nathan had a feeling that the impetus was slowing down. The negotiations became mired in detail and he had the impression that no real progress was being made. He met the CEO for lunch at an industry fair in Europe, urging him to put all the remaining issues on the table at the next board meeting that would take place in two weeks' time, and to close the negotiations within a month. Gad agreed reluctantly, saying he was 'not euphoric' about this project and the idea of pushing it that fast, but also had no other solution to offer.

At the board meeting in mid-November 2004, support for the US JV seemed unchanged, although some board members raised concerns regarding – in Nathan's view – minor issues. Another member wanted to know if ICM's independence was ensured and if the Americans would also sell the JV products in markets outside the USA. Nathan confirmed that the US-produced products would only be sold in the USA. He then received a mandate from the board to push for the closure of the negotiations with Semiconduct as soon as possible. In the next two weeks, Nathan took part in the negotiations, making several telephone calls to the negotiation team in the USA. He found himself in a surprising discussion with the CEO, as Yoav raised the question of whether it would not be better 'to freeze' the project, given the many unsettled issues. In the ensuing conversation, Yoav admitted that the economic logic in favor of the JV was compelling and that at that time he had no alternative to suggest. But he was nevertheless uneasy and noted:

The US partners are impatient and aggressive.

Nathan replied:

> No wonder, we are really putting pressure on them with our even more detailed requests.

> They eventually agreed to move forward and conclude the negotiations within a week.

> All the open issues are of minor importance and can be settled when the JV is in operation.

Nathan concluded the discussion and informed the CEO of the content of the detailed board book. He also requested that the board consultant be allowed to review and assess the results of the negotiation and that this opinion be presented to the board.

To be on the safe side, Nathan met with the board consultant, who – although he had some reservations over the 50:50 model – confirmed that the economic logic was compelling. He also presented a written recommendation, stating that it was vital to finalize all coordination with Semiconduct, leading to a signature as soon as possible. At the board meeting, based on the consultant's detailed analysis, Nathan wrapped up the results by analyzing the pros and cons, but ended:

> If ICM wants to serve the US market, the JV with Semiconduct is the only economically viable option. We can sign the contract within a week. Let's move!

Nathan did not expect any negative responses – but when he called for votes in favor of the JV, the board members looked at each other reluctantly. The situation became, after all, awkward. He was stunned when not a single board member raised his hand...

3.4   CASE STUDY: ICM – HIDDEN AGENDAS IN THE BOARDROOM (B)

[By Ulrich Steger and Wolfgang Amann]

The day after the board voted against ICM's joint venture in the USA with Semiconduct, Nathan handed in his resignation. ICM continued to look for a US partner throughout the winter of 2004/05. There was even worse news than the company's inability to find a partner: no financial institution was ready to finance a solo investment by providing approximately US$30 million up front. But Nathan was still curious to know why his project had failed so spectacularly. Through the company's network he discovered that:

- The CEO had lobbied all other board members – except Nathan – intensively and had threatened to resign if the board approved the JV. The motivation for his behavior was that Nathan's project would have meant the end of his plan to relocate to the USA with his family, as he felt that he could only do so if there were an 'independent' US plant.
- Project manager Shmuel opposed the agreement with Semiconduct because without a new 'greenfield' plant, his consulting project with ICM would have been terminated immediately.

- The vice president of marketing, Jacob Eden, opposed the JV, because he would not have been in control of the US sales force, and he would have had to attend many coordinating meetings with Semiconduct in the USA.

And, finally, nobody had told Nathan any of this, as he was not part of the religious community.

4
Navigating through Typical Conflict Patterns

4.1 ARE TENSIONS AND CLASHES NORMAL?

Corporate governance should add value to the company through better decision making, but what are better decisions, and why is this such a specific issue at the apex of an organization? Again, in principle, the answer is simple but complex to implement. In hierarchical organizations such as companies, a decision's importance correlates with the hierarchical level at which it is made. The most important decisions – those that shape the company's destiny – are taken by those at the top of the hierarchy. However, these decisions are not only more important, they are less well structured than operational decisions and mostly very uncertain. They often have to take dilemmas, such as conflicting goals that cannot be reconciled in a given timeframe or with the available resources, into consideration. This results in disagreements.

To add to the complexity, the interests of the different actors in a corporation – the management, owners, board – are not naturally aligned; this is the core of the principal–agent theory. The different interests, which the question 'for whom is this decision made?' reflects, can lead to conflicts, obstructions, and even significant damage to the corporation. As decisions are made under conditions of uncertainty, it is difficult to convince opponents of the appropriateness of certain of these decisions. Uncertainty, differing interests, and dilemmas result in a highly charged situation in which smooth decision making can easily be derailed. Although every dilemma and conflict situation has its own specific characteristics, there are also certain typical patterns or constellations. The following are of interest:

- The board vs. the management (or the chairman vs. the CEO).
- Conflicts within a board (or management).
- The board and management vs. the owners (or some of them).
- Conflicts between the owners.

In the following subsections we examine the nature of typical conflict constellations, which is also reflected in the case studies.

Board vs. management

Given the allocation of power, responsibility, and accountability – and despite the legal framework – the division of labor between the board and management is neither obvious nor fixed. A change in one of corporate governance's shaping factors influences the board's power structure. This is one of the most likely occasions for conflict: regulators force boards to be more vigilant and the CEO defends his prerogatives; a new CEO fights a dominant board to enlarge his scope; or a CEO pushes for a strategic shift, although the board is reluctant or opposed.

There are no simple guidelines on how to handle these types of emergent conflicts, on how to negotiate compromises, or resolve conflicts. But three preconditions seem to be indispensable for such situations to be managed effectively:

- Everybody has to be aware that tension between the top structures can ripple through the organization, triggering politics and distracting people.
- These conflicts do not disappear if one ignores them. In fact, they tend to worsen by the day. Addressing them head on, and as early as possible, are key success factors in any conflict resolution.
- Conflicts are a test of a board's core culture with regard to cooperating. Is voicing dissent and disagreement accepted – or even expected – or is any deviation from a dominant CEO or towering chairman's opinion regarded as disloyalty?

Again, this sounds like basic common sense (and it is), but we have seen this being ignored too often. The pressure to conform is strong, as time is precious, there are too many items on the agenda already, and it is always difficult to be the wet blanket. There is, moreover, anecdotal evidence that headhunters are worsening this tendency. 'Looking for a team player' means: will this person cause trouble on the board or will he/she conform? It is sometimes amazing how much remains undetermined at an organization's top, despite the maxim: transparency, openness, and fix the problem first time around.

Two situations should be discussed in more detail: the strategic shift and the emergence of the 'toxic' CEO. When a strategic shift is contemplated, the CEO is well advised to inform the board at an early stage so that it can get behind the reasons for such a shift. The CEO should be able to answer the following questions: what are the assumptions? What are the indicators that the current business model has run its course? Why is organic growth not sufficient for the strategy and/or the business environment? After all, setting the strategic direction and determining the business model are two of the board's core responsibilities. It would be wrong of the board to simply rubber stamp major strategic changes. The CEO needs a commitment, not only a formal agreement, from the board. Questions and feedback from the board could test the new direction's robustness, as they could help to improve it.

The board should also determine schedules and timetables to deal with these issues according to their priority. Our main recommendation is to never allow an adviser (consultant or investment banker) to make presentations; instead, insist that management itself makes the presentations on these topics.

The second issue deals with the dark side of success: the emergence of the 'toxic' CEO. Normally, these are CEOs who have been extremely successful over a long time. They often become celebrity CEOs, enjoying the same popularity as movie stars do, but unfortunately displaying similar behavior. Since they have been so successful, they think that they are invincible and always right. They have heard everything, so they stop listening; they adopt a pompous lifestyle and use corporate resources. They harass and intimidate their subordinates, only allowing yes-men around them, and driving away every potential competitor or successor. They 'poison' an organization.

It is not easy for a board to deal with such a situation. First, the changes that take place in the CEO's behavior emerge slowly but surely and might not be easy to detect. Second, the company's figures are still good (at least for now). Third, these CEOs are very powerful, having ensured that their proxies have been appointed to the board. Staying calm is an easy option until the 'toxic' CEO's reign collapses and everybody asks: where was the board?

It is therefore essential for the board to see – and stop – such a dynamic person at an early stage (when it might still be possible to stop him/her). Observing is the easiest bit, however. Expressing concerns and challenging behavioral changes in the regular feedback and evaluations are the more difficult bits, but also the most effective ones.

Conflicts within the board

Here, again, three typical' constellations can be observed:

- Lack of a dedication to a culture to cope with disagreements.
- A CEO (less frequently the chairman) who tries to split the board.
- Board members who represent irreconcilable interests.

The first constellation is based on the empirical evidence that teams work best on the shop floor, but this becomes increasingly difficult the further one moves up in the hierarchy: team members become competitive, the tasks become more complex, with individual contributions being more difficult to recognize and compare. In order to form a team in which the members trust and respect one another (although they only meet occasionally), a (time-consuming) debate is encouraged, dissent is accepted, and consensus is nevertheless reached. This is the true art of leadership. The responsibility to achieve this lies mostly with the chairman of the board. It can, however, also go wrong very easily: low tolerance of dissent, personal animosity, stress, and arrogance are not unknown features in boardrooms.

The second constellation represents the application of the old Roman saying: 'divide et impera'. A CEO who dislikes a strong board because it restricts his/her reign can easily be tempted to create a fractious board, playing one faction off against the other as it suits him/her. The spreading of rumors, selective information, encouraging doubts as to the opposing side's honest intentions are typical tactics used (not only in boardrooms) to prevent a board from uniting against a powerful CEO. However, not only a CEO can resort to such petty plotting, but also a chairman who wants to manipulate the board and its decisions. This is especially likely to occur when a former CEO is appointed chairman of a board, and he/she can continue the power game that he/she had perfected in his/her previous role.

The third constellation is a fractious board that becomes an immediate threat to the company. The power game is then not engendered by a powerful prince (in the Machiavellian sense), but is the result of different factions' irreconcilable interests, which hinder decision making. Many political maneuvers are undertaken, which infect the entire organization, as the factions jockey for an opportunity to influence management in their favor and for information providers. Such a constellation would emerge from a conflict between the representatives of the owner groups (see below) and the representatives of the former companies after a merger. Everybody is dissatisfied and feels shortchanged by the other side, which is aggravated if these groups are different nationalities as in the case of the Hoogovens–British Steel merger or the Pharmacia–Upjohn one.

Board/management vs. owners

These are typical insider vs. outsider conflicts. They occur if an institutional investor or block holder outside the majority tries to change the corporate governance rules or the shareholders' policy direction while the board and management defend the original policy.

The policy direction could be changed with regard to, for example, dividend payouts, share buyback, or splitting the company (or threatening to organize a split up) via a proxy vote during the annual general meeting. Such conflicts are typical of Anglo-Saxon countries that have more institutional investors and a more fragmented shareholder base (which means fewer dominating or controlling shareholders). All shareholder lawsuits also fall under this category.

Another constellation might occur during the (sometimes prolonged) transition to a new ownership. One of the defensive measures against takeovers is staggered boards, which means that the new owners cannot remove the board to replace the existing board members with their own loyalists. This results in a majority owner having to live with a hostile board for a while. Normally, such conflicts are settled with the payment of fees. However, the Mannesmann–Vodafone trial in Germany indicated that this sometimes has unforeseen repercussions when former board members and executives have to stand trial for fraud.

In some cases, such conflicts can occur when, by law or contractual agreement, the majority of board members have to be natives of the hosting country (e.g., in Australia or Switzerland). In such cases, the board may defy the owners'/headquarters' decisions, as in the case of Axa Australia when the Australian subsidiary board rejected and impeded the ousting of the minority shareholders, or in the case of British Steel, when the Dutch board of the Aluminium subsidiary rejected the spin off.

Conflict between owners

Company owners can differ greatly, even in the case of companies listed on the stock market. One of the myths in the shareholder value debate is that all shareholders are treated alike. This myth is mostly perpetuated by financial analysts, investment bankers, and others who want to sell shares and who have to cope with their own principal–agent problem. Whether one is a majority owner, an individual minority block holder, a pension or hedge fund institutional investor, a day trader or a widow and orphan retail investor makes a significant difference to what one perceives as shareholder value.

Whereas retail investors often don't voice their interest, but simply withdraw if they are dissatisfied, owners with significant stakes tend to fight if they see their perception of shareholder value violated. This can happen in a family business, when one group wants to cash in and sell, and the others don't. This also often occurs between majority owners who control a company via multiple voting rights and minority owners when they clash over strategy, but also over evaluations, the suspicion that value will be transferred to associated companies at conditions that are favorable for the majority owners, board representation, and so on. In respect of emerging or closed markets in shareholder-unfriendly economies (countries like France, Italy, or Germany from an Anglo-Saxon investor perspective), this can lead to considerable, even political, conflicts.

Learning nuggets from the cases

We present two cases in the following. 'War at the helm of Elicor' has at its center a conflict between a new chairman and a successful CEO, who might be on a trajectory to become a 'toxic leader'. 'Cobra vs. Commerzbank' A and B looks at the conflict between the board and a group of raiders, who want to push the company into a merger or an acquisition, which is rejected by management and the board. It is a platform to discuss the responsibilities and obligations of owners, boards, and management regarding the company. In all these cases, the principal–agent theory (looking at the interests and behavior of the players) and contingency theory (what is the context? What are conflict drivers?) offer a highly suitable framework for analysis. Neither case is intended to be discussed with moral outrage, although one might judge some behaviors and strategies as more or less responsible and value-adding. But never forget to ask the question: for whom? Most cases pose a dilemma (e.g., even if you are right, how do you win?). Our cases invite course participants to role-play and negotiate an outcome.

As diverse as these cases are, three – again, common sense – learning nuggets can be derived in general. First, matters do not get better when postponed; in the majority of cases, they get worse. This goes back to what we have discussed before. The difference between a high-performance and a non-value-adding board lies to a high degree in the ability to detect emerging issues, new patterns, or changes early on – as well as the ability to act on those findings immediately.

Second, the distinction between legitimate representation and 'crossing the line' is blurred, often interpreted differently by different players. This explains why it is so difficult to define ethical behavior. It is much easier to elaborate on what is unethical and counterproductive to adding value. The question: does the corporation as a legal entity have its own interests and rights? will be answered differently in different cultures and legal environments. In the USA, this question is rather negated, but not so in Europe. That is why a context matters so much.

The third nugget is becoming important: why is so much emphasis put on the transparency of values – and are they lived? Values and their anchoring in an organization are a good predictor or leading indicator of how behavior will develop when things get rough. When everything is running smoothly this might not be as important. Is fairness then still regarded as important? And commitment honored? Or are corners then cut and information disregarded?

4.2   CASE STUDY: WAR AT THE HELM OF ELICOR

[By Ulrich Steger and Helga Krapf]

6 JULY 2002, EDINBURGH, ELICORE HEADQUARTERS. Chairman Lord Winston Heath had just read the long-awaited proposal from a corporate governance consultant. It described a detailed formulation of Elicore's corporate bylaws, the establishment of several committees, and the performance evaluation process for the board of management.

Heath immediately sent a copy to Paul Simon, the chief executive officer (CEO), noting that he wanted to send the paper to the whole board before the next meeting. Three hours later Simon called. His voice was as cold as ice:

I have read your proposal. I still think we are creating too much bureaucracy, but OK, we can discuss the details. But if you push the proposal for my evaluation, I will resign.

He hung up without waiting for Heath's reply. Heath felt trapped. Tensions between Simon and him had been growing ever since he became chairman at the beginning of 2001. His proposal for a new corporate governance structure and Simon's arbitrary decision to change the accounting rules so that Elicore would still show double-digit growth rates had been the latest incidents.

Heath's business instincts told him something was brewing. But the numbers would probably only deliver a clear picture at the end of the year. As he mulled things over, the telephone rang. It was Walter Dale, a member of the board of directors:

Hello, I am eagerly awaiting the new corporate governance proposals, to be discussed at the upcoming board meeting . . .

What could Heath do? What should he do?

Corporate governance at Elicore

Elicore was a global manufacturer of ventilation and cooling equipment. The company had been in a turnaround situation when Simon joined as CEO in 1993. Then, only 25% of the company's sales were generated abroad. He had a reputation for being a pushy executive, who got things done. He had grown up in a working-class family, and quickly learned that he had to be tough if he wanted to succeed. Previously he had worked for domestic companies, but his lack of international experience was not an issue when he joined Elicore. Simon staged a bloody, but successful, turnaround and drove the company on an accelerated growth path. For more than five years, every quarter had shown double-digit growth in revenue and profits, with major acquisitions along the way. Now 60% of revenue was generated outside the home country and close to 40% of the assets were located abroad. Elicore was one of the nation's top 25 companies.

Simon shared responsibility for Elicore's day-to-day business with chief financial officer (CFO) Hank Silver and chief operating officer (COO) Roger Hasting. The board of directors, chaired by Heath, had five non-executive members who were up for re-election annually at the AGM.

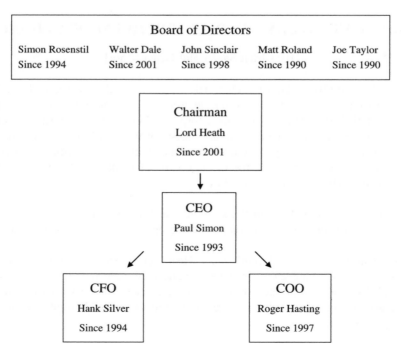

Heath had been chairman of the company since January 2001. This 'semi-retirement' role was a fitting conclusion to a long and successful career. Brought up in a well-off family, he had been educated at the best colleges, gained significant international experience in a well-known multinational, and even spent three years in the Foreign Office.

I didn't build my career on being aggressive or proffering my advice,

Heath reflected, trying to understand why Simon was opposed to his ideas. As he reviewed their interactions over the year, he could see that tensions between them would continue to grow.

From bad to worse

20 January 2002

Heath's lunch with his predecessor took a disappointing turn. He could not discuss his concerns about Simon's behavior. The retired chairman's advice was simple:

Let Simon run the show, his track record is unmatched – headhunters for the 'bulge bracket' companies of our nation are watching him closely. We have to be careful that we don't lose him. Just support Simon and enjoy your job.

Then the conversation turned to cars and politics. At least Heath now knew that he could not expect much support from the two longest-serving members on the board. They were old buddies of his predecessor and had been on the board for more than 10 years. The three kept close contact in the 'old boy network'.

3 February 2002

At the board meeting, Heath and Simon clashed openly. Simon bluntly brushed aside a proposal from Dale, a banking executive who had joined the board at the same time as Heath, calling it 'too analytical and not applicable to our business'. Heath and Dale were more embarrassed by Simon's tone and body language than his words. However, the proposal could not have been completely irrelevant. At least CFO Silver had cautiously expressed interest before Simon trashed the idea. Heath forced Simon into a half-hearted apology, but the mood remained tense for the rest of the meeting, despite another year of double-digit growth, profits, and earnings – the board should have been in a cheerful mood instead.

28 February 2002

Heath had another heated debate with Simon while preparing the meeting prior to the AGM in April. Heath felt obliged to propose some improvements in corporate governance and to increase reporting transparency. He suggested:

- Forming audit, nomination, and remuneration committees with only external board members.
- A formal evaluation of the performance of the entire board, including the CEO, COO, and CFO.
- More detailed reporting by business unit and geography.

Simon opposed the ideas, arguing that this would create bureaucracy, impede quick decision making, and make the share price more volatile, since dents in individual unit performance could push the stock market in the wrong direction. At the end of the argument, Heath ran out of patience: 'You run the company, I run the board', he told Simon and stormed out of the corporate dining room.

However, Simon's resistance motivated Heath to consult Elicore's six biggest shareholders. Most of them were institutional investors, who held more than 40% of the stocks and who had proposed him as chairman of the board. The group agreed that Heath should discuss the idea of improving corporate governance to meet 'best practice' in his opening speech at the AGM. Later on, the board could work out the details. Simon took a conciliatory approach when Heath told him about the shareholder resolution:

Let's sit down together and work this out,

he said,

I don't think that we fundamentally disagree.

How charming he can be, if he wants to, Heath thought.

17 April 2002

The days leading up to the AGM were filled with rumors that Elicore was facing a hostile takeover bid by its larger rival, which had recently been troubled by leadership problems. According to one rumor, the main shareholder of the rival company intended to make Simon the new CEO of the merged company. At the evening meeting before the AGM, originally scheduled to do some routine and last-minute tasks, the board informally discussed the idea of a potential merger. No one seemed to be enthusiastic about the idea, but Heath was surprised that Simon did not explain his position with his usual 'bang-bang' clarity. Heath volunteered to communicate to the AGM that the board saw the future of the company in the current framework. Nothing remarkable happened at the AGM, given the great business results. The board was unanimously re-elected.

26 May 2002

Over lunch outside Elicore, Heath met informally with Dale and John Sinclair, who had been on the board for four years, to discuss the new design of corporate governance. When Heath very carefully put out feelers to ascertain opinions on Simon, Sinclair's response was surprising:

I have observed this guy over time and am shocked by his increasing arrogance. He hasn't listened to the board for nearly two years. If he doesn't listen to us, who will he listen to?

Dale supported him:

I have seen this time and again: when executives are very successful they begin to be detached. Normally that is the beginning of their downfall – and the longer they have been successful, the more they take the whole company down with them.

Heath tried to balance his response by sharing their concerns, but also stressing Simon's leadership qualities. However, they agreed on the need to challenge Simon more – and that the appropriate tool was the board performance evaluation.

4 July 2002

While reading the incoming results of the second quarter in his home office, Heath discovered by chance that the earnings had been calculated differently. Although this was probably legal, it was not in line with Elicore's long-standing accounting tradition. A back-of-the-envelope calculation convinced Heath that without the accounting revision, Elicore would not have had double-digit growth. He called the CFO, but Silver was very guarded:

> It was Simon's decision. Please discuss this matter with him,

he said drily. Heath's telephone conversation with Simon escalated into a shouting match. Simon threatened to hold Heath accountable for any negative developments in the stock price; Heath finally accused Simon of 'cooking the books' and threatened to bring the matter to the attention of the whole board and to propose that they did 'not sign off the second-quarter results'. Then he hung up. An hour later Silver called and proposed solving the issue by asking the auditors to give their professional opinion on the accounting change. Silver told Heath that this was what he had proposed to Simon after Simon had told him about the clash. 'He was pretty upset, but agreed', Silver told Heath, who then also agreed. Personally he was happy that they had avoided a shootout.

The auditor came up with another proposal, which was more in line with Elicore's tradition and just made 'double digits'. Heath called Samuel Rosenstil, who had the most accounting experience on the board. Rosenstil had been brought in during the turnaround, to use this knowledge in the clean up. However, he had always been more cautious than Simon, and had become increasingly silent. Rosenstil was not happy:

> We have piled up huge risks with the accelerated growth strategy – and now we are trying to avoid the consequences by a change in accounting. But nobody listens to me anyhow. If these accounting tricks continue, I will resign pretty soon.

Heath could not help telling him that at the next board meeting he would propose the changes in corporate governance in detail.

> You have my word this will increase our proactive involvement, and in particular any changes in accounting rules will have to be approved by the audit committee.

With this assurance, Rosenstil gave his blessing to the accounting changes proposed by the auditors.

Pressing questions

Heath was convinced that Elicore needed to improve its corporate governance processes. He was confident about the consultant's proposal and also about his own instincts. The board meeting would be the ideal opportunity to discuss everything. But could he have avoided the deterioration of his relations with Simon? Would the CEO really resign or would he fight?

Heath knew Simon could command the vote of the COO and of the two longest-serving board members, which – including himself – amounted to four out of the nine votes. Heath could probably count on the other three non-executives as well as the CFO, but he could not be 100% sure. Simon probably knew that Heath had a small majority. But should Heath really take the risk of splitting the board? Was his proposal too far-reaching? Should he make a last attempt to seek a compromise, if not reconciliation?

And last, but not least, if the board agreed on the changes, how would the stock market receive the news of the corporate governance changes? How could he explain them? Heath had to find answers, quick.

4.3   CASE STUDY: COBRA VS. COMMERZBANK – CAN INVESTORS RAID THEIR OWN COMPANY?

[By Ulrich Steger, Wolfgang Amann, and Helga Krapf]

PART A

MONDAY MORNING, 21 MAY 2001. Martin Kohlhaussen, long-serving CEO of Commerzbank, was on his way to the office. The bank's AGM was due to take place on May 25. Uneasily he remembered the AGM in 2000 – a public clash between Cobra, a group of shareholders, and himself.

In 2000 Cobra, an investment group, had acquired a stake in Commerzbank and gained the support of other shareholders; together they held 17% of the voting rights. Their aim: to sell Commerzbank. The group admittedly wanted to make a premium of about 30% per share, but no buyer had been found so far.

How long could this continue? As he made his way to work, Kohlhaussen considered what further damage this group could do to the bank. In any case, they could spoil his last AGM before he retired to a non-executive position as chairman of the supervisory board. Cobra had warned that it would reveal 'management corruption, incompetence, balance sheet fiddling and delaying of negotiations'. There were a number of counter-motions on the AGM agenda. The share price had already suffered as a result. Customers, employees, and investors were nervous about the unclear but continuing activities of Cobra to take over the company or to split off parts and sell them.

But how could he put a stop to this sort of uncertainty? Kohlhaussen knew that the upcoming AGM would be vital for the future of the bank.

Consolidation in the European financial sector

The stage was set for a European single market in banking as early as 1958. However, specific directives followed only in the late 1980s and mid-1990s. The nations of Europe had fragmented banking systems characterized by relatively small size, high concentration, excess capacity, and lack of competition. A PriceWaterhouse report[1] came to the conclusion that gains could be made if the average size of banks was larger (economies of scale) and

---

[1] PriceWaterhouse (1988). The cost of non-Europe in financial services. *Research on the Cost of Non-Europe: Basic Findings*, Vol. 9, European Union, Brussels.

if products and services offered by banks in many countries were expanded (economies of scope). Greater efficiency could be achieved by adopting 'best practice'. To ensure that all of these gains were passed on to bank customers, barriers to competition would have to be removed. The consultants deemed that if their suggestions were implemented, the benefits to customers would be substantial – an estimated 0.7% of gross domestic product (GDP) for the nations studied.

The banks realized that with the emergence of a single market in banking, formerly big banks in the member states would be reduced to medium-sized institutions in the European market, and would be even less significant compared with global giants such as Citigroup, Goldman Sachs, and Morgan Stanley Dean Witter. The introduction of the euro, new technology, and globalization were the main drivers of consolidation from 1999 onwards. There was much discussion of the options: defensive alliances to prevent being taken over, or mergers between banks in the same country – or on a European or even worldwide scale.

However, such plans proved to be difficult to implement because of different IT, legal, and tax systems. Therefore most of the consolidation in Europe took place within nations or across borders between homogeneous regions such as the Benelux countries or Scandinavia (refer to Table 4.1 for the biggest European banks). One of the rare exceptions was HSBC Group, which had developed into a global banking and financial services organization during the 1990s. However, even domestic mergers usually turned out to be difficult. At the beginning of April 2000, the much talked about merger between the two biggest private German banks, Deutsche Bank and Dresdner Bank, crashed amid much acrimony between the top players. After these failed talks, Kohlhaussen commented on speculation about a potential merger between Dresdner and Commerzbank:

> We're doing just fine on our own. At the moment I don't see a national solution to merger speculations. Commerzbank will continue its current strategy to build a common investment bank with our network of European partners – France's Credit Lyonnais, Spain's BSCH Santander, and Italy's Intesa.

Table 4.1   Top 15 European banks 1999

Rank	Company	Country	Assets 1999 (€ billion)
1	Deutsche Bank	Germany	839.9
2	BNP Paribas	France	698.6
3	UBS	Switzerland	610.8
4	HSBC Group	UK	566.5
5	HypoVereinsbank	Germany	503.2
6	ABN AMRO Bank	Netherlands	457.9
7	Credit Suisse Group	Switzerland	449.8
8	Société Générale	France	406.5
9	Crédit Agricole Group	France	401.7
10	Barclays Bank	UK	397.0
11	Dresdner Bank	Germany	396.9
12	Westdeutsche Landesbank Girozentrale	Germany	393.4
13	ING Bank	Netherlands	349.6
14	Fortis Bank	Belgium	326.1
15	National Westminster Bank	UK	285.5

Source: *The Banker*.

Commerzbank

Commerzbank was the fourth largest bank in Germany (refer to Table 4.2 and Figure 4.1 for key business figures and structure). It took pride in being the premier financier of the German 'Mittelstand', the mostly family-owned or family-operated small and medium-sized companies that formed the backbone of the German economy. More than 40% of these companies conducted business with Commerzbank.

Table 4.2   Commerzbank: key figures

	FY 1999 (€ million)	FY 2000 (€ million)
Pre-tax profit total	**1.371**	**2.234**
Geographical breakdown		
Germany	697	1.839
Europe (excl. Germany)	485	215
America	146	175
Asia	33	2
Africa	10	3
Net profit	911	1.342
Employees (Germany)	27,068	27,124
Branches (Germany)	1,064	1,080

Source: Company information.

Since 1991 Kohlhaussen, dubbed a 'representative of the old money aristocracy' by *Der Spiegel* newspaper, had been at the helm (refer to Figure 4.2 for background information on the main players). Commerzbank shared one basic problem with all its German competitors: a low financial return on investment. The problem, which was institutionalized and therefore difficult to tackle, was shared by the Sparkassen – publicly owned by local municipalities – by the cooperatively owned Volks- und Raiffeisen Banken, and by private banking. Mergers within Germany were therefore almost impossible.

A new main shareholder

In April 2000, the always active grapevine in Europe's financial centers was fueled by media reports that 'Cobra Beteiligungsgesellschaft GmbH' had built up a 9.9% stake in Commerzbank by buying some shares and acting as a proxy for other shareholders. The name 'Cobra' inspired the same sort of fear as the real 'King of Snakes', with its venomous and paralyzing bite. A spokesperson for Cobra even confirmed their intention to raise the stakes:

> We are a group of strategic investors who, as a rule, don't comment on the investments we make. However, 20% is a stake we have often built up in the past.[2]

Cobra's front man was Hansgeorg Hofmann, a former board of management member of the rival Dresdner Bank, who had to resign because of tax fraud (he had to admit that he had not declared his foreign assets to the German tax authorities, which is illegal). He

---

[2] Germany: Cobra could raise Commerzbank stake to 20%. Dow Jones Newswire, 19 April 2000.

Head Office

Board of Managing Directors				
Corporate Divisions				
Group Management	Retail Banking and Real Estate	Corporate Banking and Institutions	Investment Banking	Services
Staff departments	Banking departments			Service departments
Accounting and Taxes Compliance and Security Corporate Communications and Economic Research Credit Risk Management Human Resources Internal Auditing Legal Services Risk Control Strategy and Controlling	Retail Banking Real Estate	Corporate Banking Corporate Finance International Bank Relations Relationships Management	Asset Management Securities Treasury/Financial Products	Global Operations Investment Banking IT Development IT Production IT Investment Banking Organization Transaction Banking

Domestic Branches

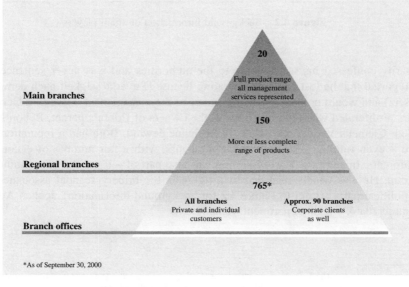

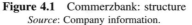

Figure 4.1   Commerzbank: structure
Source: Company information.

Martin Kohlhaussen – CEO/chairman of the board Commerzbank

Born in 1935, Kohlhaussen earned a degree in law and completed an apprenticeship at Deutsche Bank afterwards. He was at Deutsche Bank and then Westdeutsche Landesbank before joining Commerzbank in the early 1980s. He had been chairman of the board of management since 1991.

Hansgeorg Hofmann – managing director Cobra

Hofmann was considered a self-made man. He held no academic degree but completed an apprenticeship at Deutsche Bank. Afterwards he worked for Credit Commerciale de France, and US investment banks Merrill Lynch and Sherason Lehman. He had been working abroad for 24 years (London, Paris, New York, Boston) when he joined Dresdner Bank in 1989. He was promoted to the board in 1994. Hofmann masterminded the purchase of UK Kleinwort Benson in 1995. In December 1997 he stepped down from Dresdner's management board over personal tax irregularities.

Clemens Vedder and Klaus-Peter Schneidewind – controlling investors in Cobra's parent, Rebon

The German investors Vedder and Schneidewind each held 50% of Cobra's Dutch parent, Rebon. Vedder had been active in investment and real estate business. He met Schneidewind in 1987 when he began taking stakes in companies. Schneidewind's career in the retail sector had been meteoric. The pair quickly earned a reputation for secretly building up stakes in companies and selling them at a profit within one or two years. There were rumors that Vedder did not even consider investing in a company if he did not have someone in mind to take over his stake later.

Karl Ehlerding – occasional Rebon ally

A German billionaire, Ehlerding was the majority shareholder of WCM, an investment and real estate company. The company had a reputation for ruthlessly asset stripping companies. WCM and Rebon had already bought and profitably sold stakes in the retailer Spar. Commerzbank seemed to be another joint engagement – Ehlerding privately held 4.9% and WCM held 1% in the bank.

Figure 4.2   Background information on main players

voluntarily confessed his wrongdoing to the authorities and was never sentenced, but the press reported that he lost his bank-operating license (Zuverlaessigkeit nach dem Kreditwesengesetz) and would not stay on as a member of the management board of a German bank. Rumors proliferated when the identities of the owners of Cobra's parent, Rebon N.V., were revealed: Clemens Vedder and Klaus-Peter Schneidewind. Both had a reputation for being shrewd – even ruthless – dealers and arbitrageurs, with a fair number of encounters with law enforcers. In addition, Karl Ehlerding was also part of – if not the mastermind behind – the group. He was widely regarded as a figure in the bribery scandal associated with the CDU political party[3] (refer to Figure 4.2 for background information). Jochen Appell, head of Commerzbank's legal department, remembered:

---

[3] The Christian Democratic Union of Germany (CDU) and Germany's ex-chancellor Helmut Kohl were embroiled in a scandal about anonymous donations to the party in 2000. In the investigations that followed, it became apparent that Ehlerding had given the biggest ever donation to the CDU, presumably in exchange for being treated favorably when he bought property that the German Railways was selling off.

We were never quite sure how many of the things we read in the press were true. Had Hofmann really lost his bank operating license? Was Ehlerding really involved with Cobra? We never received confirmation of these rumors. We were never told precisely the shareholder's position they pretended to control.

The king of snakes shows its fangs

Cobra had increased its voting rights in Commerzbank to 17% in May 2000. Before the AGM on 26 May 2000, Cobra had repeatedly told Kohlhaussen in person and over the phone that it would sell its position very soon, and that the bank had to get ready for this move.

Shareholders expected a public clash between the bank and the Cobra group. Attendance at the meeting was therefore much higher than in previous years, at around 56% (compared with between 45% and 50% in the past). The investor group put together by Cobra reared up and bared its poisonous fangs for the first time at the AGM by abstaining from a trivial vote on reappointing the bank's auditor. The move emphasized Cobra's control of 87 million shares, almost 17% of the total voting capital, but 30% of the capital present at the meeting – enough to block major proposals by management. Moreover, Hofmann declared Cobra had enough offers from existing and potential investors to increase its voting rights to 30%! Hofmann explained Cobra's position:

> We are aiming to bring silent reserves into the market valuation through a better return on investment. Not through exercising influence on the policies of the bank – directly or through a seat on the supervisory board – but through an alliance of the bank with a strong partner. Our stake is key to that. We are receiving interesting signals for an alliance with Commerzbank from international capital markets which are promising advantages for all involved parties – customers, employees, shareholders – which will result in an increased shareholder value.

Hofmann valued Commerzbank at €50 per share – as opposed to the current share price of €39 – based on the break-up value of holdings in subsidiaries and other companies. He suggested that a European alliance could reduce this discrepancy. Kohlhaussen considered these statements dangerous, since they increased fears about a break-up of Commerzbank:

> I agree that our share price could be higher but I cannot understand how you can come up with a share price of €50. In my opinion it is irresponsible to talk about this figure. Moreover, you've declared today you won't exercise a direct influence on the bank's strategy. But from your speech I assume that you want to urge the bank into an alliance with a strong partner. You are contradicting yourself!

Kohlhaussen denied that Commerzbank needed to rethink its strategy along Cobra's lines. He planned to continue and expand opportunities for cooperation with other banks in areas such as investment banking, production, or settlement.

Talks between No. 3 and No. 4

In June 2000, Commerzbank started merger talks with Dresdner, the third largest bank in Germany – only weeks after the latter's merger talks with Deutsche Bank had ended.

The two banks planned to establish a holding company and five daughter companies. Insurance company Allianz, Dresdner's main shareholder, aimed to take responsibility for the asset management. The market value of the merged bank would put it at No. 21 worldwide. Insiders believed a full merger would bring substantial cost savings and create a bank with critical mass in Germany.

However, after the merger plans became public, Commerzbank's share price fell and Dresdner's moved up. At the same time rumors were heard that Cobra was willing to sell 8% of its share. Cobra denied this, and it was believed that the two banks were in fact behind the rumors to weaken the investor.

Hofmann viewed the merger talks with Dresdner Bank with skepticism and threatened to block the merger. In his eyes a merger with a German bank would result only in cost reductions. He favored a merger with an international institute to increase shareholder value.

However, Cobra was effectively left powerless when the German banking regulator, Bundesaufsichtsamt fuer Kreditwesen (BAKred), withdrew Cobra's voting rights on July 14. This was the first time that the regulator had ever made such a decision. The press reported Hofmann's tax fraud history as a reason, but the BAKred never officially confirmed this.

It seemed as if the BAKred's decision removed the pressure to close a deal for the moment. However, the share price fell 4.3% to €36.96. Analysts were convinced that the takeover premium on the bank's share had evaporated and that the share price would continue to be weaker and the merger ratio for Commerzbank lower. The two dozen private investors behind Cobra threatened to vote individually if Cobra was not allowed to vote for all of them together.

On July 26 the talks between Dresdner and Commerzbank collapsed over, among other reasons, valuation differences. Commerzbank was pushing for a 45:55 merger ratio, whereas Dresdner was aiming for more like 60:40. For the media, the withdrawal of Cobra's voting rights had failed to provide enough momentum for the merger. Cobra and Hofmann welcomed the development and emphasized the unique opportunity for a cross-border move for Commerzbank. However, one analyst reasoned:

> I'm skeptical whether Commerzbank will be a takeover target. Why should Commerzbank be interesting for a buyer? It has the same problems as all the other German banks in the area of retail banking and its investment banking isn't great either. Commerzbank's return on equity is too small for it to be interesting for a foreign buyer.[4]

Shortly afterwards, the media reported that Cobra had tried to sell its stake in Commerzbank. Apparently some of the investors behind the group were disappointed about the low share price while they still had to pay interest on the money they had borrowed to invest in the bank. Rumors spread that Dresdner CEO Bernd Fahrholz was interested in buying these shares, since this would have enabled Dresdner to accomplish a hostile takeover of Commerzbank. However, Dresdner's main shareholder – Allianz – voted against Fahrholz's plan, and Cobra kept its stake.

---

[4] Dahinten, J. (2001). Update 2: Cobra sells Commerzbank stake to mystery buyers. *Reuters News*, 8 January.

Help from friends?

It was not long before Commerzbank was back in the news. Kohlhaussen had invited the Italian insurance company Assicurazioni Generali and the Spanish bank Banco Santander Central (BSCH) to take part in a capital increase ex rights. Together both partners would then hold about 20% of Commerzbank. The media interpreted this strategic move as a way to further weaken Cobra's influence. Commerzbank emphasized the need for a capital increase and the opportunity to offer universal banking and strengthen the relationship with Generali.

Analysts lowered price expectations for Commerzbank shares to around €30. Merger talks no longer had a positive influence on the share price. Kohlhaussen replied to comments that the only thing that increased the share price was merger or takeover speculation:

> I wonder why serious analysts lamented that the takeover fantasies for Commerzbank no longer exist. The management is not responsible for nurturing such fantasies. Our duty is to improve the share price by showing we are a successful bank.

Analysts also feared that instead of having one big shareholder, Commerzbank would now be faced with three, with different interests. They saw a danger of getting caught in a web of cross-holdings.

In the end only Generali increased its stake in Commerzbank to 10%, but talks with BSCH bore no fruit. Instead, Italian Mediobanca SpA nearly doubled its stake from 1.2% to 2%.

Shareholders were concerned about the dilution of ownership. Generali had subscribed for the shares at market price without any discount. Commerzbank argued that a general capital increase was not to be achieved under these favorable conditions. Furthermore, the capital increase did not prejudice shareholders who were opposed to the dilution of ownership. In the end, the validity of the capital increase was confirmed in four court cases. The bank dismissed calls for an extraordinary shareholders meeting at the end of December and proceeded with preparations for the 2001 AGM.

Getting ready for Kohlhaussen's last AGM

In January 2001, Cobra reduced its stake to 9.98%, split in two 4.9% packages, which were controlled by two unnamed investors. The BAKred no longer considered Cobra a significant shareholder and reinstated its voting rights.

The 40 private investors involved with Cobra and additional supporters had requested a number of counter-motions at Kohlhaussen's last AGM in May, including a vote of no confidence in management and a call for a special audit of the capital increase. Hofmann accused Kohlhaussen of acting against shareholders' interests with the capital increase. Kohlhaussen, by contrast, accused Cobra of never openly discussing its intentions and agenda. This behavior had discouraged potential investors from buying a stake in Commerzbank. Hence, Cobra was to blame for the bank's declining share price (refer to Figure 4.3 for share price development).

The public awaited an even bigger clash than the year before. If necessary, the AGM would be held over two days in order to deal with all the items on the agenda. However, Kohlhaussen was convinced that he had acted in the best interests of the bank and was confident that he would be able to stand up to Cobra.

******

Kohlhaussen was elected to the supervisory board with a vote of 99.9%. Cobra withdrew all its extra items from the agenda. The AGM came to a peaceful conclusion after approximately five hours.

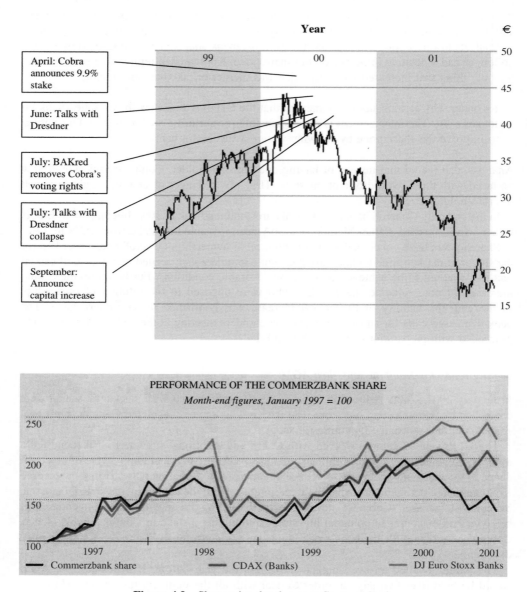

Figure 4.3   Share price development Commerzbank
Source chart: www.handelsblatt.com.; Company information.

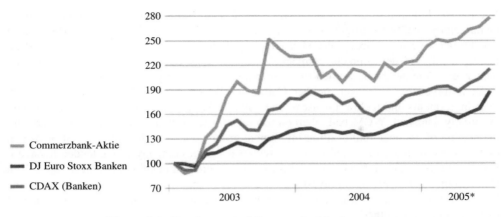

Figure 4.4 Development of Commerzbank's share prices
Source: Commerzbank.

PART B

In August 2005, Martin Kohlhaussen was still head of Commerzbank's supervisory board and the bank continued to generate speculation over a possible takeover. As a result of this, Commerzbank's shares had increased 60% in the preceding 12 months.[5] Three factors had caught the attention of investors. First, restructuring efforts had considerably improved the return on equity ratio of 8% (selected top performers in Europe topped 20%). Second, there were few options for foreign banks interested in expanding in Europe's largest economy through acquisitions – Deutsche Bank, Germany's largest bank, was too big and expensive; the Postbank and Sparkassen were not for sale; and Italian Unicredit had already snapped up Bavarian HypoVereinsbank. Third, Commerzbank itself was on an acquisition spree, now offering more attractive assets and potential for success.

Commerzbank's CEO Klaus-Peter Mueller was struggling with a threat similar to the one his predecessor had faced. London-based hedge fund groups Toscafund and Lansdowne acquired 2% stake each. Former members of the investment group Cobra still either owned, or were said to have access to, roughly 10% of Commerzbank's shares and signaled readiness to join any opposition to management.[6] Would history repeat itself? Would investors try to raid their own company – again?

For the time being, the high share price seemed to discourage foreign investors (refer to Figure 4.4 for an overview of the share price development until August 2005). A Toscafund spokesman confirmed that no influence on the operative management was planned and that the investment was indeed long-term. Cobra managers, for their part, were likely to remember the first attempt to raid Commerzbank, which had failed horribly.

History repeating itself?

In 2002, following in Cobra's footsteps, German investment group WCM AG increased its stake in Commerzbank to 9.9%, making it the fourth largest shareholder after re-insurer

---

[5] Hedgefonds nehmen Commerzbank ins Visier, Spiegel online, 24 August 2005.
[6] Commerzbank: Heuschrecken statt Cobra? Boerse. ARD.de, 13 September 2005.

Munich Re, Italian insurer Assicurazioni Generali, and Cobra. Founded in 1766 as a textile manufacturer, WCM Beteiligungs- und Grundbesitz-Aktiengesellschaft subsequently became a real estate investment group. WCM also had equity interests in other real estate investment, management, and development companies, as well as in nursing homes and a packaging maker, but Commerzbank seemed to be interesting as its next prey.

As it turned out, however, neither Cobra nor WCM reached their original goal with their investments and had to downscale their stakes. Support of the investors behind Cobra eventually vanished. WCM had taken on too much when buying a stake in Commerzbank; the decline of the once multi-billion investment group continued. It sold off most of its real estate assets to Blackstone, and a merger with a daughter company was intended to save it from bankruptcy. Several law suits and tax burdens were still pending in August 2005. With Commerzbank reappearing on investors' radar screens and history likely to repeat itself, the basic question remained: what are the responsibilities of owners on the one hand, and of management on the other?

5

Codes of Conduct – The Value-Added beyond Compliance

5.1 CODES OF CONDUCT AS A PANACEA?

Codes of conduct are sets of principles to which a company agrees to adhere within the context of its activities. They are voluntary, but as there are strong stakeholder expectations and competitors too would have adopted such codes, they may eventually not be that voluntary after all. In terms of contents, their aspects may cover a broad range of principles – ranging from, for instance, trade practices such as non-bribery rules, other corporate conduct and ethics guidelines, to environmental standards, working conditions, or human rights. They can aim to cover a variety of principles, thus preventing crises and misconduct to fostering peak performance. They need not only apply to employees of the issuing company, but also to suppliers and other partner companies.

There is a core dilemma with codes that is generally called the 'transnationality trap'. Transnational companies try to achieve two aims simultaneously, namely to adapt locally while integrating internally for reasons of efficiency and cost. One element of integrating the entire organization is found in the use of codes for the entire organization to streamline a range of behaviors. Simultaneously, one needs to bear in mind the saying, 'when in Rome, do as the Romans'. It becomes a dilemma when a global company is not only active in 'Rome'. What should the response be when it is unclear what the 'Romans' really did? Is such behavior acceptable 'outside Rome'? Trying to integrate and control the behaviors of employees with codes while trying to conduct business in a diverse, local setting may well overwhelm local managers and the company headquarters. On the one hand, local managers may have imposed growth goals and on the other, they nonetheless have to comply with local 'Roman' business practices. Codes of conduct may provide a means to try to give an answer as to which principles and values apply in a specific company, but which may also be 'myopic' towards local idiosyncrasies. Issues relating to codes of conduct or corporate ethics are often diffuse, ambiguous, uncertain, and shaped by culturally different 'moral' or personal ethics, interests (e.g., headquarters vs. subsidiary), and may reflect conflicting goals. If this is not the case, it may well be a case for criminal prosecution... Bad habits often evolve over time and those involved do not necessarily perceive their crossing of the line consciously, especially if they operate in a local environment. Issues regarding codes of conduct could be quite uncertain, but they may concomitantly have far-reaching consequences. It also may only become apparent at a later stage that something was really wrong in the bigger scheme of things. But by then such errors may have had a damaging impact on careers: supervisors of wrongdoers are normally good scapegoats, in that senior managers can demonstrate that they took action 'to clean up' and to prevent the case from exposing matters that may be uncomfortably close to top management.

Codes may thus create managerial dilemmas, which we understand as a situation where two or more (legitimate) goals are in conflict with each other. It is accordingly impossible to achieve both at the same time with the given resources. A priority decision then needs to be taken, which, however, could leave an ongoing tension in its wake. One should remember Murphy's Law: 'if things can go wrong, they will go wrong'. The key question then arises: can the relevant individual(s) and the company draw on a buffer of goodwill that has been accumulated through previous positive actions?

The situation is worsened in today's global fishbowl situation, where the interconnectedness and alert media reveal any corporate misbehavior and thus place this under the spotlight. The media, but also corporate pressure groups, today follow global companies' every step across the world and report every 'mishap', whether they are merely perceived, actually real, or just material which could serve as the basis for a great headline. Every action is immediately made public and is often depicted visually. There is no place to hide and one could maintain that there should not be any such place either. There is an ever-increasing risk of exposure and discovery through stepped-up enforcement of anti-money-laundering, anti-bribery, anti-trust, and tax evasion laws (often related to the 'war against terror'). In this connection, 'whistle-blowers' – in other words, those who report wrongdoings – are increasingly better protected. Tough reactions by clients ('black listing') and the stock markets may well follow. The potential damage to companies' and individuals' image may be considerable, and internally such damage could often be more lasting and may affect employees' motivation.

Owing to peer and stakeholder pressure, there may be no choice other than to act. Therefore, companies nowadays need to have codes of conduct in place. They should, however, be advised to be alert to additional repercussions. Codes may indeed increase bureaucracy. They could also impede risk-taking behavior. They may, in addition, spoil and poison organizational cultures with suspicion and intrusive controls. They may negatively affect the image of companies and top managers if there are contradictions between nice-sounding declarations by top management, whereas they also need to deal with the daily pressure to make the numbers at all cost. In our field research we obtained the impression that companies are far from mastering this skill. The overall process of professionalization regarding how to really benefit from all the potential of codes has not made substantial progress. Our empirical study on hundreds of international companies also revealed the main motivations behind using codes, as portrayed in Figure 5.1. Our research shows that the main focus of codes remains compliance and safety. They are considered as a 'must-do' means to an end. The focus is not necessarily on both compliance and the peak performance of employees.

In analyzing the actual success of the use of codes, we find the situation portrayed in Figure 5.2. Companies only realize initially what real business value they could create. The real 'litmus test' will be, however, when companies are confronted by the question: 'Can one sacrifice business to comply with the code of conduct?'

Learning nuggets from the cases

The first of the two case studies deals with a series of ethical lapses in the US aviation and defense systems giant Boeing in the time period from 2002 until 2005. As early as December 2003, the series of misconducts around Boeing seemed to culminate when CEO Phil Condit stepped down after a series of high-profile ethical scandals. Within only 12 months, Boeing was in the spotlight of public and media attention due to several serious incidents relating to Boeing's business conduct.

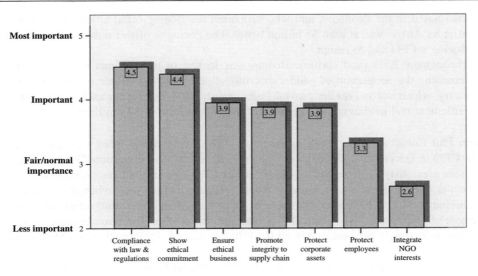

Figure 5.1   The motives for codes of conduct

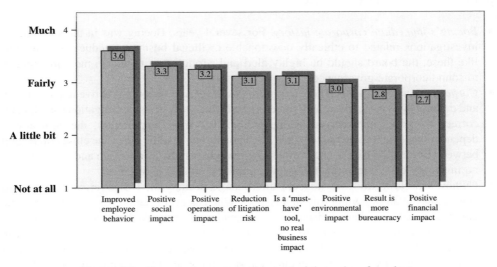

Figure 5.2   The actual success and impact of the codes of conduct

- July 2003: Boeing was convicted of industrial espionage in a public bidding process against competitor Lockheed Martin, which resulted in the Pentagon withdrawing contracts worth $1 billion and imposing a ban against awarding new contracts, which was lifted two years later.
- November 2003: In another public bid for a $23 billion contract, Boeing was convicted firstly for funding the campaign of Senator Ted Stevens who helped the deal to pass through the US Congress; and secondly for hiring a former Air Force executive who was

then based in the Pentagon, and who supported the Boeing offer, although he knew the offer by Airbus was at least $5 billion better. The Pentagon officer was imprisoned, while Boeing's CFO had to resign.

- Throughout 2003 (and earlier): Boeing was locked in negotiations with trade unions regarding the accusation of gender discrimination by paying female employees a lower salary, which internal studies proved. Later, in July 2004, Boeing agreed to an extrajudicial settlement and paid aggrieved employees a compensation of $73 million.

With Phil Condit stepping down as Boeing's CEO, Harry Stonecipher was appointed the new CEO in December 2003 and was charged with the 'ethical turnaround' of the company. He was previously chief operating officer under CEO Condit until his retirement in 2002. However, the ethical scandal relating to Boeing reached its final peak when Stonecipher was dismissed in March 2005 after admitting to an extramarital, consensual affair with another (female) Boeing executive – only 15 months into his tenure. The issue became especially delicate as Boeing's performance in all fields had increased significantly since Stonecipher's return to office.

This case study has several objectives. It deals with an issue from the field of corporate governance and thus firstly aims at raising awareness of the sensitivity and importance of this field for modern companies, especially the members of supervisory and management boards. The key learning points are:

- *Boeing's immediate corporate history.* For several years, Boeing was in the spotlight of investigations related to ethically questionable or illegal business conduct. In situations like these, the board should be highly alert and strongly committed to measures related to sound corporate governance.
- *Corporate governance particularities of Boeing's industry.* Boeing is active in the aviation and defense systems industry and, therefore, subjected to a stronger obligation for ethically correct business, as perceived by the public. And more importantly, the company is dependent on contracts awarded by the Pentagon through public bids. The close connection between Boeing's business and politics ensures constant media attention and consequently no misbehavior by the company or its employees remains unobserved.
- *Culture and corporate governance.* Culture and especially the US governance and board culture played an important role in this case. Whereas every region has its own corporate governance culture characteristics, US companies in particular are known for promoting a very puritanical and politically correct business conduct, which does not mean they actually follow this. Additionally, a generally stronger intrusion in the privacy of employees (e.g., by asking for personal information or forbidding same-sex or workplace relationships – for example, Wal-Mart) is perceived as justified – contrary to many other countries.
- *The effect of the composition of the Boeing board.* The Boeing board was composed of members representing the 'classic' US board and corporate governance culture described above. Of 11 board members in total, only two were female, with the average age being 59 years. In previous discussions of the case, female executives articulated far less concern about the underlying affair than males did. Accordingly, a more diverse board including more non-US members and females could well have been more alert in their decisions.
- *The 'tone at the top'.* The ethical tone set for the company by its top managers is also the benchmark for right and wrong regarding their personal behavior. This tone represents

the (high) ethical standards with which the CEO's private life is measured and evaluated. In Boeing's case, after Stonecipher's return to office, the company began to strongly promote its ethical standards and way of doing business (e.g., by introducing a code of conduct). Furthermore, the ethical standards of a CEO's individual leadership style are also reflected in such a code. So even though Stonecipher's amorous affair did not represent an explicit violation of the code of conduct, the CEO's behavior was judged against this background.

The second case presents another dilemma when trying to introduce codes of conduct into practice. Connect-U2 has a clear code of conduct in place, which clearly prohibits bribery. But Connect-U2 faces several dilemmas. The first is that even if such codes have to be signed by all employees or posted regularly, they may not really be generally known. They may also be a summary of neat and politically correct phrases. The question arises as to whether it is really a tool to steer employees so they can steer the company out of trouble and enable it to reach peak performance? The main dilemma Connect-U2 faces is that it is caught in the aforementioned transnationality trap. One element of integrating the entire organization is found in the use of codes for the entire organization. This has legal reasons, but trying to impose one set of rules on the entire organization poses problems mostly in its peripheral areas. Doing business locally requires companies to make a decision whether to really adapt to those local conditions or not. In the presented case, local adaptation equals bribery. The latter, however, is not perceived as negative in the target country. The less efficient economies could succeed in their own way, since those 'other means of succeeding' (i.e., bribery) actually allow companies to operate efficiently. And as in real life, one deals with additional factors, such as delayed information and a great deal of ambiguity about what is supposed to have really happened. When a company is faced with strong competition, there may well be no choice whether to bribe or not, since a company is simply not short-listed in the case of non-compliance with local standards. This clash of cultures obviously causes tremendous tensions between the headquarters and the subsidiary. This case teaches course participants that it will only be possible to avoid such dilemmas by taking a priori decisions.

5.2   CASE STUDY: BOEING HITS TURBULENCE – IS IT WORTH LOSING A SUCCESSFUL CEO FOR A CODE OF CONDUCT?

[By Ulrich Steger, Wolfgang Amann, and Jochen Brellochs]

I am proud of the strategies that have transformed Boeing into the world's largest aerospace company. I will watch the progress of Boeing with great pride.

These were the words of Phil Condit, chairman and CEO of Boeing, shortly before leaving the company in December 2003.[1] For years, he had vied with his president and chief operating officer Harry C. Stonecipher for control of Chicago-based Boeing. Eventually, Stonecipher retired as an executive in 2002. But ongoing scandals reached a point where the

---

[1] www.boeing.com.

board had to release Condit from his duties and brought back 67-year-old Stonecipher out of retirement in sunny Florida to clean up Boeing's tarnished image and restore credibility.

In February 2005, 15 months into Stonecipher's tenure, Lewis Platt, Boeing's chairman, confronted him about the risk of a further scandal. After a short investigation period of just 10 days, Stonecipher was ousted for having an extramarital affair. The knight in shining *armor* turned out to be the 'knight in shining *amour*'.[2] 'The board concluded that the facts reflected poorly on his judgment and would impair his ability to lead the company.'[3]

But what had really happened? Stonecipher had not stolen documents from competitors in order to gain a competitive advantage, as had happened in his predecessor's era. He had not offered jobs to Pentagon staff to earn contracts worth billions. In fact, Boeing shares gained 52% during his 15-month tenure! It was after all just an affair, to which he openly admitted. The female executive involved did not report to him directly. She did not receive any financial or career advantages, nor was she under any pressure from Stonecipher, who could have taken advantage of his powerful position in the company. So, were the board members being overly sensitive and overreacting? Was their attitude unnecessarily puritanical? Could they even be doing more harm than good?

Company background

Boeing was founded during World War I and benefited substantially from military contracts from the very beginning.[4] In addition to its core business of manufacturing airplanes, Boeing also provided training courses for pilots, setting up airfields and maintenance. In the aftermath of World War II, Boeing increasingly shifted its focus from the defense industry to commercial jets, first marketing short-range jets and subsequently, in 1960, the first jumbo jet. Boeing firmly established itself as a key player by manufacturing Air Force One for the US President in 1962, and in 1969, by joining the Apollo program, after entering the spacecraft industry. The company grew both organically and through mergers and acquisitions with companies such as McDonnell Douglas, the space and defense business of Rockwell International, and Hughes Space & Communications.

Since the 1970s, Airbus, the emerging European competitor worldwide, had been increasing its product range, starting to offer an aircraft in every class that Boeing did. The industry felt the price pressures. In order to ensure fair competition, Boeing filed a complaint at the World Trade Organization in October 2004, claiming that Airbus had violated a 1992 bilateral accord based on unfair subsidies from the European Union. After a round of counter-complaints over Boeing's tax breaks and investment subsidies from Japan, Boeing and Airbus settled outside the WTO courtrooms.

At the end of the 2004 business year, Boeing generated revenues of $52.5 billion, net earnings of $1.9 billion, and $2.24 earnings per share with its two major divisions: Boeing Commercial Airplanes (40% of the revenues) and Integrated Defense Systems (60% of the revenues). While this was not a significant improvement on the previous five years' figures,[5] the company was determined to remain among the industry's market leaders. Its 'Vision 2016' foresaw Boeing as a firm with 'people working together as a global enterprise for

[2] Richman, D. (2005). Knight's shining armour turns out to be shining amour. *The Age*, 9 March.
[3] Wayne, L. (2005). Boeing chief is ousted after admitting affair. *New York Times*, 8 March.
[4] For a full review of the history, refer to en.wikipedia.org/wiki/Boeing.
[5] www.boeing.com.

aerospace leadership'.[6] Future challenges would include not only coping with competition from Airbus, but also with the expected entry of China, which together with Brazil looked likely to create a third new player of global scale.

The beginning of the turbulence: Phil Condit's era

Condit, a trained pilot and aeronautical engineer, joined Boeing in his mid-twenties as an engineer. Ten years later he honed his management skills at MIT, before rejoining the company, this time at management level. After working his way up and gathering experience in a variety of divisions, Condit was appointed president of Boeing at the age of 51, and chairman a year later. Following a manufacturing crisis and the depression across Asian markets, Condit decided to spread risk, decreasing the company's dependence on commercial aircraft and ultimately turning Boeing into a diversified aerospace company with 150,000 employees across the globe and customers in nearly 150 countries.

However, the business environment soon turned unpleasant for Condit: SARS, September 11, and the Iraq war negatively impacted markets and in 2003, for the first time ever, European archrival Airbus sold more planes than Boeing. Several acquisitions did not pay off as planned, but even more worrying was the number of scandals that seemed to have reached new scopes. In addition to allegations of accounting lapses throughout the 1990s, a number of other issues came to light in just a few months during 2003:

- In July, Boeing was suspended from receiving new rocket-launch contracts. The Air Force accused the company of improperly obtaining over 25,000 proprietary and confidential documents from Lockheed Martin Corporation, enabling it to win a 1998 contract for a booster-rocket program.[7] Hiring away an engineer from Lockheed Martin, who brought along these documents as well as crucial insights on cost and pricing information, was very damaging to Boeing's hitherto positive image. To make matters worse, the government transferred business worth $1 billion from Boeing to Lockheed Martin. The suspension was only lifted two years later.
- In November, CFO Mike Sears resigned amid allegations that he sought to hire former Air Force weapons chief Darleen Druyun while they negotiated a $23 billion contract for as many as 100 refueling aircraft tankers.[8] Investigations revealed that leasing the planes actually cost $5 billion more than purchasing them would have done. Druyun, working on the bid at the Pentagon, knew that the Airbus proposal was anywhere between $5 and $17 million cheaper than the final offer from Boeing. Subsequent investigations revealed that Boeing executives personally contributed to the campaign funds of Senator Ted Stevens, who helped the deal through congress. Other congressmen were promised profitable contracts in their constituencies in return for their support of Boeing. Some Boeing executives, along with Druyun, were imprisoned.

Another lingering, but highly explosive, issue was whether female employees were paid less than men. Internal studies, which had been conducted for more than a decade, confirmed the discrimination, which not only comprised pay differentials – women earned on average

---

[6] www.boeing.com.
[7] Richman, D. (2005). Analysis: Boeing conduct code worked properly, expert says. *Seattle Post*, 8 March.
[8] Ibid.

$3741 less for entry-level managerial positions – but also advancement opportunities. $100 million would have been a conservative estimate regarding the potential cost to Boeing of court settlements.[9] (Later, in July 2004, Boeing agreed to pay $72.5 million to resolve these allegations.[10])

A week after these revelations were made, Condit, under pressure from the board, resigned in December 2003. He was seen more as a brilliant engineer than a leader, which had caused him to rely on his president, Stonecipher, for tough calls. Condit was also often criticized for his lavish lifestyle as an executive. For example, he introduced an entire fleet of business jets for Boeing executives, including one with a personalized interior for himself. He also remodeled the Boeing suite at the Four Seasons luxury hotel in Seattle according to his own liking – at Boeing's expense. However, he was never directly accused of any involvement in the scandals with the Pentagon. Stepping down, he nevertheless admitted:

Accountability starts at the top.[11]

The knight in shining armor

Stonecipher had considerable experience with the company and with the industry. He not only served as president, COO, and member of the board after the merger with McDonnell Douglas in 1997, but also as vice chairman from May 2001 until his retirement in June 2002. He did keep his board assignment, which would eventually expire in 2006 when he was 70. Starting as the new CEO in late 2003, Stonecipher's mission was clear: remedying the poor business prospects, cleaning up the company's tarnished image, and restoring credibility, especially with Boeing's most important client, the US government. Stonecipher had been steering Boeing's ethical recovery with great care. Among other initiatives, he introduced a code of conduct that all staff members had to sign every year. Henceforth, no employee should 'engage in conduct or activity that may raise questions as to the company's honesty, impartiality, reputation, or otherwise cause embarrassment to the company' (refer to Figure 5.3 for the full document).

It wasn't just an 'ethical turnaround' that was needed; Boeing's stock had fallen 6.5% under Condit, while Standard & Poor's 500 stock index climbed 61.8% during that time.[12] Stonecipher's leadership style was well known – he was so decisive that he had earned the nickname 'Hatchet Harry'.[13] He had proven many times in the past that he could rise to the occasion. For example, during his time as CEO of McDonnell Douglas before the merger with Boeing, its financial performance had soared, with stock increasing from $18.48 – prior to his arrival – to more than $70 just before the company merged with Boeing in August 1997.[14]

In addition to building great relations with internal and external stakeholders, Stonecipher was also widely respected in American society and the respective industry associations. Several awards underpinned his achievements: Wings Club Distinguished Achievement Award for 2001; US Army Association's John W. Dixon Award for more than 40 years

[9] Holmes, S. and France, M. (2004). Coverup at Boeing? *Business Week*, 28 June.
[10] Richman, D. (2005). Analysis: Boeing conduct code worked properly, expert says. *Seattle Post*, 8 March.
[11] Boeing, Boeing, gone. *The Economist*, 3 December 2003.
[12] Phil Condit – Boeing. *Business Week*, 14 January 2004.
[13] Wayne, L. (2005). Boeing chief is ousted after admitting affair. *New York Times*, 8 March.
[14] www.boeing.com.

Boeing
Code of Conduct

The Boeing Code of Conduct outlines expected behaviors for all Boeing employees. Boeing will conduct its business fairly, impartially, in an ethical and proper manner, and in full compliance with all applicable laws and regulations. In conducting its business, integrity must underlie all company relationships, including those with customers, suppliers, communities and among employees. The highest standards of ethical business conduct are required of Boeing employees in the performance of their company responsibilities. Employees will not engage in conduct or activity that may raise questions as to the company's honesty, impartiality, reputation or otherwise cause embarrassment to the company.

Employees will ensure that:

- They do not engage in any activity that might create a conflict of interest for the company or for themselves individually.

- They do not take advantage of their Boeing position to seek personal gain through the inappropriate use of Boeing or non-public information or abuse of their position. This includes not engaging in insider trading.

- They will follow all restrictions on use and disclosure of information. This includes following all requirements for protecting Boeing information and ensuring that non-Boeing proprietary information is used and disclosed only as authorized by the owner of the information or as otherwise permitted by law.

- They observe that fair dealing is the foundation for all of our transactions and interactions.

- They will protect all company, customer and supplier assets and use them only for appropriate company approved activities.

- Without exception, they will comply with all applicable laws, rules and regulations.

- They will promptly report any illegal or unethical conduct to management or other appropriate authorities (i.e., Ethics, Law, Security, EEO).

Every employee has the responsibility to ask questions, seek guidance and report suspected violations of this Code of Conduct. Retaliation against employees who come forward to raise genuine concerns will not be tolerated.

Figure 5.3   Boeing's code of conduct
Source: www.**boeing**.com/companyoffices/ aboutus/ethics/**code**_of_**conduct**.pdf.

of defense and aeronautical industry leadership; Rear Admiral John J. Bergen Leadership Medal for Industry from the Navy League; the Air Force Association's John R. Allison Award for outstanding contributions to national defense by an industrial leader; and the Air Force Association's General Ira C. Eaker Historical Fellow Award. He was also named a Fellow in The Royal Aeronautical Society.[15]

---

[15] www.boeing.com.

Under Stonecipher's leadership, Boeing rebuilt bridges with Washington and tackled the slide in commercial jet market share. It took Airbus on in a more serious way again (e.g., with the new 7e7 jetliner green lighted by Stonecipher). Shares rose by more than 50%, while Stonecipher's actual pay as an executive remained noticeably low – $1.5 million base pay and incentives of $1.8 million (Stonecipher still owned substantial shares in Boeing). For the outside world, he was undoubtedly the CEO Boeing needed after Condit stepped down.

So when the 68-year-old father and grandfather resigned in March 2005, both Wall Street investors and officials in Washington were shocked. Nobody saw this coming, not even within the company. But the board decided that an extramarital affair with a long-term employee, a female executive, could not be tolerated, especially since they were afraid that details could leak through to the public. Substantial evidence from e-mails with 'very graphic'[16] content sent to the company's ethics officer was screened by the nine male and two female board members. It all began when an anonymous employee used internal communication channels put in place for cases where codes were violated (whistleblower hotline). The identity of the female executive was not revealed and she remained with the company. If she had been the victim of sexual harassment, it would have created a hostile or offensive workplace situation and thus been illegal, but that was not the case. Passion and performance reviews were clearly separate matters. So why then did Stonecipher have to leave Boeing?

'Boeing CEO out in sex scandal'[17]– but who was really the culprit?

An office romance can mean many things: sizzling passion, a date for Saturday night, a lifetime commitment, but for Stonecipher, it meant his ouster.[18] He left the company and Boeing immediately appointed chief financial officer James Bell, 56, as interim president and CEO, and later Jim McNerney as chairman, president, and CEO. Commenting on the second CEO that had to leave Boeing under a cloud in less than two years, Platt explained:

> The investigation determined that the relationship was consensual and had no effect on the conduct of the company's business. It's not the fact he was having an affair – that is not a violation of our code of conduct . . . In my first conversation with him he stepped up and said he was having a relationship. You could not have expected someone to be any more open or honest.[19]

Boeing's share price appeared not to be too troubled by the shake-up after the announcement, but the incident triggered wide public response, partly understanding, partly disapproving. Two journalists commented on the irony of the story:

> Stonecipher's case is unusual for many reasons, not least of which is how career-suicidal his actions were:

> - He had established an ethics office at Boeing.
> - He had established a code of ethics that all employees were required to sign each year.

---

[16] Thomas, L. and Boselovic, L. (2005). Boeing exit shows appearances still count. *Pittsburgh Post-Gazette*, 9 March.
[17] Isidore, C. (2005). Boeing CEO out in sex scandal. *CNN/Money*, 7 March.
[18] Hymowitz, C. and Lublin, L. (2005). Many companies look the other way at employee affairs. *Wall Street Journal*.
[19] Teather, D. (2005). Boeing chief fired for office affair. *Guardian*, 8 March.

- He had established a mechanism for reporting violations that included a toll-free 'ethics hot line'.
- He had said that the code applied to all employees and promised to punish infractions even at the highest levels of management.

And working at a company that had been damaged by revelations that came from email correspondence between Boeing and Air Force officials in 2002, he sent emails to the woman with whom he was having an affair on the company system.[20]

But for Freada Klein, a sexual harassment researcher and consultant in San Francisco, things were crystal clear:

When it's extramarital, it raises the character question . . . Boards are profoundly and legitimately confused about the line between personal and business and whether anything the CEO does, especially with anyone else at the company, is private or not.[21]

Brad Agle, director at the Berg Center for Ethics and Leadership at the University of Pittsburgh's Katz Graduate School of Business, commented:

Whatever happened is happening in a much more sensitized environment than a few years ago . . . there is no question management and boards are much more sensitive to this than they were a few years ago.[22]

Others, in support of true emancipation of women and no discrimination of any type, criticized the fact that different standards were applied for both parties:

Why did Boeing force Stonecipher to resign but not the woman with whom he was having an affair? If his act was enough to lose him his job, shouldn't she have paid the same penalty? Does this give the message that the 'crime' is worse for a man than it is for a woman?[23]

More criticism of the dismissal was raised by pointing to a different, but no less important question:

So what is right for the shareholders? . . . From the time Stonecipher took over, they have been rewarded with a 50% return. Is the board really doing the shareholder right by getting rid of Stonecipher? Warren Buffett and his wife separated way back in 1977, and rumors of an affair were rampant back then. Would Berkshire Hathaway shareholders have been better off if the board had run off Warren back then? Berkshire stock was a few hundred dollars a share. Now it's about $90,000 a share. What is good and right is

---

[20] Thomas, L. and Boselovic, L. (2005). Boeing exit shows appearances still count. *Pittsburgh Post-Gazette*, 9 March.
[21] Hymowitz, C. and Lublin, J.S. (2005). Many companies look the other way at employee affairs. *Wall Street Journal*.
[22] Thomas, L. and Boselovic, L. (2005). Boeing exit shows appearances still count. *Pittsburgh Post-Gazette*, 9 March.
[23] Gaudette, P. The Stonecipher/Boeing affair. http://divorcesupport.about.com/od/cheatings pouse/a/stonecipher.htm.

one thing. I still lose a lot of respect for a guy who is disloyal to his wife, but it's not the same thing as what is right for shareholders.[24]

Cai von Rumohr, an analyst with investment bank SG Cowen, argued in the same direction, pointing to the negative impact on the positive dynamics at Boeing:

> I think under other circumstances it's possible this is something the board might have overlooked. They're gonna get good points for that. But I think the issue is that Harry had done enough good things in terms of commercial (aircraft) marketing and cash redeployment that it will be difficult to maintain that momentum in this transitional period.[25]

Platt tried to justify his decisiveness:

> We felt that if details were disclosed it would cause embarrassment to the company ... This was a very difficult decision for the board given Harry's strong performance ... The board felt this was a right and necessary decision, given the circumstances ... We have fought hard to restore our reputation.[26]

And so, as well as losing a high-performing CEO who had led Boeing out of difficult times, the company continued to generate negative headlines on 'sex scandals', 'code violations', and 'leadership crisis'. Ironically, critics claimed, Stonecipher had achieved Boeing's 'ethical turnaround' and his success as CEO of the company was apparent. But code of conduct norms apply to top management as well, as Stonecipher himself pointed out. So, wasn't it the board itself that was responsible for these headlines by being hypersensitive and overreacting? Or are such strong puritanical morals necessary to steer Boeing – and for that matter any other company – clear of turbulence?

5.3   CASE STUDY: CODES OF CONDUCT AT CONNECTU2 – ADDING VALUE, COST, OR NOTHING AT ALL?

[By Ulrich Steger, Wolfgang Amann, and Jochen Brellochs]

VIENNA, 15 AUGUST 2005, 14:00. Dr Ansgar Kuhn, the 37-year-old corporate secretary and general counsel of Connect-U2, a mid-sized Austrian telecom company, sat in his office flipping through the pages of the corporate code of conduct (refer to Figure 5.4). He sighed – loud enough for his secretary in the adjacent room to hear him through the open door. She immediately got up and went to see whether she could help with the problem he seemed to be struggling with. 'Tough day?' Frowning, Ansgar looked at her.

> Do you know what our code of conduct really says? I mean, have you actually taken the time to reflect on the content, as opposed to just reading and taking note of it?

---

[24] Cf. http://www.beggingtodiffer.com/mt/mt-comments.cgi?entry_id=2455.
[25] Isidore, C. (2005). Boeing CEO out in sex scandal. *CNN/Money*, 7 March.
[26] Ibid.

Code of Conduct
for
Connect-U2 Aktiengesellschaft
and its Subsidiaries
Adopted January, 2004

1. Introduction

Our code of conduct ensures that we continue to be a good corporate citizen in all the environments we are active. The supervisory boards of Connect-U2 passed this Code of Conduct (the 'code'), which summarizes the standards that must guide the actions of all our employees. While covering a wide range of business practices and procedures, these standards cannot and do not cover every issue that may arise in the headquarters or subsidiaries, or every situation where ethical decisions must be made, but rather set forth key guiding principles that represent our policies and establish conditions for employment at our Connect-U2.

We must strive to foster a culture of honesty, accountability and transparency. Our commitment to the highest level of ethical conduct should be reflected in all of the Company's business activities including, but not limited to, relationships with employees, customers, suppliers, partner companies, competitors, the government and the public, including our shareholders in all countries. All our employees must conduct themselves according to the language and spirit of this code and seek to avoid even the appearance of improper behavior. Even well intentioned actions that violate the law or this code may result in negative consequences for the company and for the individuals involved.

One of our most valuable assets at Connect-U2 is our reputation for integrity, professionalism and fairness. We should all recognize that our actions are the foundation of our reputation and adhering to this code and applicable law is imperative.

2. Conflicts of Interest

All our employees have an obligation to conduct themselves in an honest and ethical manner and act in the best interest of Connect-U2. All our employees should endeavor to avoid situations that present a potential or actual conflict between their interest and the interest of the Connect-U2.

A 'conflict of interest' occurs when a person's private interest interferes in any way, or even appears to interfere, with the interest of Connect-U2, including its subsidiaries and affiliates. A conflict of interest can arise when a colleague takes an action or has an interest that may make it difficult for him or her to perform his or her work objectively and effectively. Conflicts of interest may also arise when a colleague (or his or her family members) receives improper personal benefits as a result of the covered Officer's position in the Company.

Although it would not be possible to describe every situation in which a conflict of interest may arise, the following are examples of situations, which may constitute a conflict of interest:

- Working, in any capacity, for a competitor, customer or supplier while employed by Connect-U2.
- Accepting gifts of more than modest value or receiving personal discounts (if such discounts are not generally offered to the public) or other benefits as a result of your position in Connect-U2 from a competitor, partner company, customer or supplier.
- Competing with Connect-U2 for the purchase or sale of property, products, services or other interests.
- Having an interest in a transaction involving Connect-U2, a competitor, customer or supplier (other than as an employee, officer or director of Connect-U2 and not including routine investments in publicly traded companies).
- Receiving an unusual loan or guarantee of an obligation as a result of the position with Connect-U2.

Figure 5.4   Connect-U2's code of conduct

Source: Connect-U2.

- Directing business to a supplier owned or managed by, or which employs, a relative or friend, leading to disadvantages for Connect-U2. Situations involving a conflict of interest may not always be obvious or easy to resolve. Any employee should report actions that may involve a conflict of interest to their superior or the Corporate Secretary/General Counsel of Connect-U2.

In the event that an actual or apparent conflict of interest arises between the personal and professional relationship or activities of a colleague, the colleague involved is required to handle such conflict of interest in an ethical manner in accordance with the provisions of this code.

3. Quality of Public Disclosures

Connect-U2 has a responsibility to communicate effectively with shareholders so that they are provided with full and accurate information, in all material respects, about the Company's financial condition and results of operations. Our reports and documents filed with or submitted to any stock exchange commission and our other public communications shall include full, fair, accurate, timely and understandable disclosure.

4. Compliance with Laws, Rules and Regulations

We are strongly committed to conducting our business affairs with honesty and integrity and in full compliance with all applicable laws, rules and regulations. No employee of Connect-U2 shall commit an illegal or unethical act, or instruct others to do so, for any reason. In case an employee believes that any practice raises questions as to compliance with any applicable law, rule or regulation or otherwise has questions regarding any law, rule or regulation, he or she shall contact his or her superior or the Corporate Secretary/General Counsel.

5. Compliance with this Code and Reporting of Any Illegal or Unethical Behavior

All employees are expected to comply with all of the provisions of this code. The code will be strictly enforced and violations will be dealt with immediately. Violations of the code that involve illegal behavior will be reported to the appropriate authorities and may lead to an immediate dismissal. Situations which may involve a violation of ethics, laws, rules, regulations or this code may not always be clear and may require difficult judgment. All colleagues should promptly report any concerns about violations of ethics, laws, rules, regulations or this Code to their superiors or to the Corporate Secretary/General Counsel or, in the case of accounting, internal accounting controls or auditing matters, to the Audit Committee of the Supervisory Board after its establishment.

Any concerns about violations of ethics, laws, rules, regulations or this Code by a Member of the Management Board should be reported promptly to the Corporate Secretary/General Counsel who shall notify the Chairman of the Supervisory Board. Any such concerns involving the Corporate Secretary/General Counsel and a Member of the Management Board should be directly reported to the Chairman of the Supervisory Board. Connect-U2 encourages all employees to report any suspected violations promptly and intends to thoroughly investigate any good faith reports of violations. All employees are required to co-operate in internal investigations of misconduct and unethical behavior.

Connect-U2 recognizes the need for this code to be applied equally to everyone it covers. The Corporate Secretary/General Counsel with the assistance of the Internal Auditing Department (Revision) will have primary authority and responsibility for the enforcement of this code, subject to the supervision of the Audit Committee of the Supervisory Board after its establishment in the case of accounting, internal accounting controls or internal auditing matters. The Company will devote the necessary resources to enable the Corporate Secretary/General Counsel and the Internal Auditing Department to establish such procedures as

Figure 5.4   (Continued)

may be reasonably necessary to create a culture of accountability and facilitate compliance with this code. Questions concerning this code should be directed to the Corporate Secretary/General Counsel.

6. Whistleblower Protection

On the basis of our values and the Code of Conduct of Connect-U2, all employees may turn to their supervisor or the Corporate Secretary/General Counsel confidentially for advice and help, in the event that legally dubious incidents occur in their field of work. In all questionable affairs that concern the integrity of our financial reporting, direct contact with the Audit Committee of the Supervisory Board may also be taken. Due to legal regulations (Para 806, Sarbanes Oxley Act) as well as to internal guidelines (Para 4 Sec 4 GO for the Audit Committee) all parties providing confidential information have special personal protection with regard to the use of their information and their person.

7. Waivers and Amendments

Any waivers (including any implicit waivers) of the provisions in this code may only be granted by the Supervisory Board. Any waivers (including any implicit waivers) of the provisions in this code will be immediately disclosed as required by applicable law or applicable stock exchange regulations.

Contact:
Dr Ansgar Kuhn
Corporate Secretary/General Counsel
Connect-U2 AG

Figure 5.4   (Continued)

She smiled wryly:

> Do you want the politically correct answer or the truth? In the course of my duties I've certainly seen the document many times; it has passed through my hands like all other company documents. I even remember signing that I had taken note of its content when I started here more than a year ago. It's all about acceptable behavior to avoid embarrassment and trouble for the company and us, isn't it? I suppose that legally we are required to have one. But you are the expert, why don't you tell me? And why on earth are you worrying about this now?

But Ansgar's mind was already on something else. He was thinking about the auditing committee's upcoming meeting that he had to prepare. He was still feeling extremely uneasy about the 'Bucharest' incident – a feeling he just didn't seem able to shake off. Was it truly a case of bribery? Wasn't the code of conduct clear enough? If the rules and codes had indeed been clearly laid out, how come Connect-U2 was facing the risk of a scandal, a damaged reputation, and severe consequences for certain key people?

Company background

Connect-U2 was the rapidly expanding and internationalizing number two company in the Austrian telecommunications market, which had benefited substantially from Austria's general upward economic slope of recent years. Primarily a mobile phone network provider with 3816 employees and a turnover of roughly €380 million, Connect-U2 was still only a mid-sized company in Austria, even though its growth rates had been quite positive and steady ever since its inception in 1993.

Realizing that the competitive pressures and commoditization of simple voice-based phone services would eventually mean the complete erosion of its margins, Connect-U2 aggressively pursued a variety of ways of cooperating with upstream and downstream partners. Securing a successful distribution system, and engaging content providers for value-added content solutions, became Connect-U2's strategy for its sustained future success. Connect-U2 relied heavily on outsourcing for its future value creation, believing that emerging specialists would create innovative services that could then be offered in highly modern value webs. Upcoming hardware devices' technical progress, functionality, and information-processing capability would serve as another magnet to motivate Connect-U2's customers to continuously allocate energy, attention, and funds for future purchases. Soon mobile phones would integrate even more functions, even though 99% of mobile phone owners use less than 1% of the available gimmicks.

As with most telecommunication industry players, growth was the name of the game for Connect-U2. Given Austria's attractive location for – and experience with – Eastern European markets, Connect-U2 decided to avoid the direct competition in the developed Western European markets and worked with a variety of collaborators in Eastern Europe. However, Connect-U2 chose not to buy major stakes immediately, nor to take over Eastern European players in the privatization phase, but favored alliances by means of minor cross-shareholding instead. This market entry strategy was better suited to Connect-U2's limited cash resources. Connect-U2 also believed in keeping local management and in fostering emerging entrepreneurial spirit and organizational culture in alliance partner companies, instead of turning a foreign subsidiary into a bureaucracy solely responsible for implementation. As Markus Mittermaier, head of corporate development, had stated during the previous month's executive committee meeting:

> Our industry is moving too fast. We need to tap any innovation potential and speed up all the advantages that we can exploit. Our expansion strategy is therefore absolutely right and is the only way to bypass direct competition with the main players that are only interested in dominating the acquired targets instead of thinking in terms of win-win. To date we have had good experience in attracting local talent as well, especially those who are interested in creating something themselves, not just in a large company's perks.

The corporate secretary/general counsel's role at Connect-U2

Over time, Ansgar's role at Connect-U2 had expanded to the point where it barely resembled the original job description, which mostly encompassed administrative functions. Up to now, Ansgar thought of himself as a high performer, creating a very positive image throughout the entire organization, and especially to the supervisory board members, who relied on him heavily for his crucial input on a considerable variety of topics. Ansgar's opinion was highly valued when key decisions were to be made. His law studies had given him a very sober, crisp way of thinking. He also became the troubleshooter for the CEO. In recent weeks, though, he had begun to wonder if he had too much on his plate and whether it was time to change his role. Ansgar felt quite comfortable with all governance-related issues. However, he couldn't help feeling that the decision of whether or not Connect-U2 should do business in those few markets where it had any chance to grow – as a consequence of the 'Bucharest' incident – should be a corporate development issue, not a corporate secretary/general council matter. Such interference would surely mean trespassing on someone else's terrain, wouldn't it?

The 'Bucharest' incident

Two weeks previously, Ansgar had received a phone call from Petre Ruxandra, the senior project manager in Romania. Petre was second in command of the negotiations that would lead to the crystallization of Connect-U2's alliances in the fast-growing Romanian cities, especially Bucharest. Petre had become what Ansgar had feared in a large organization such as Connect-U2: the first whistleblower with a serious case, and not just an attention seeker.

   Before saying anything, Petre strongly insisted on being protected from dismissal. What he had to say was definitely bad news for Ansgar, and most likely for Connect-U2 as well. Apparently, Nico Panzaru – Connect-U2's country manager in Romania and Petre's superior and the first in command of the Romania negotiations – had unofficially used substantial bribery to accelerate the alliance negotiations. Ansgar's initial reply was:

> Petre, you know that bribery is always illegal. We don't want to be involved in scandals of any type. While we do know that some of our international competitors use certain financial and non-financial means to speed up negotiations, we agreed to keep our hands clean. This is how we developed our good reputation for probity that in itself has lowered barriers for further expansion for us. But I guess you are the wrong one to talk to about this.

Ansgar decided against acting too impulsively, wanting to gather more information before informing the executive committee or even the board. The following day, Ansgar called Nico to inquire about input for the next board meeting. At the end of the conversation, Ansgar casually commented:

> Nico, I am very happy to hear that in Romania we are moving ahead in record time. The board will be very happy, but let's make very sure that nothing spoils our success story. I've heard that in many other industries they make use of special treats, or plain financial promises to get things going. I trust that we are smarter than that.

Ansgar paused, hoping to find out from Nico's answer whether there were any skeletons in his closet. Personally, Ansgar differentiated between 'grease' payments to ensure that operations run smoothly, and real 'greedy' bribery in the form of payments to influence decisions or gain advantages over rivals. In his job in the corporate world, however, his personal distinction did not really matter; both options were to be avoided. Zero defection was his goal.

   Nico had a strong Romanian accent and spoke in an ebullient, extrovert way as if the two of them had been buddies since childhood, although they had only met on professional occasions. He immediately replied:

> Ansgar, my friend, don't you worry. I will be bringing in good money soon. Relationships with our partners are better than ever. We are already like a big family, very very friendly with one another. We even help our partner to negotiate access to loans, so that the

modernization can proceed faster. I know the market, just let me do my job and don't you worry.

For Ansgar, that was one 'don't you worry' too much. Something definitely felt not quite right. He looked at his watch: it was already late afternoon and it would be wonderful to leave the office on time for once, but he simply had to lay the matter on the table again.

Listen, Nico, the grapevine says that Connect-U2 may be involved with . . . Well, let's call a spade a spade: we may be involved in bribery in Romania. Do you know anything about this?

Angrily Nico answered:

Are you questioning my leadership skills, Ansgar? I'm shocked and very offended. There's nothing untoward to report about events in Romania. We do, of course, have certain local practices, but when in Rome, we do as the Romans do, right? I was sent here to get the job done. Who cares about anything else? Who told you about these rumors? I hope it wasn't that lazy underperformer Petre Ruxandra. I've wanted to fire him for a long time already, but he knows the project and I won't be able to find a substitute in the short term. And he can at least do his job after I've explained it three times. Let me take care of him and his stories this week – I should have done so much sooner!

Nico hung up before Ansgar could reply. He had an unpleasant feeling in the pit of his stomach.

There goes the quiet, romantic dinner with my wife tonight! How can I distance myself mentally from this if I don't know what is really going on?

The dinner turned out to be less of a fiasco than he anticipated, but the next morning Ansgar decided to ring someone on the project management team in Romania whom he knew well personally.

Irina Gheorghe, a former trainee at the Vienna Headquarters and now an up-and-coming fast track manager, was easy to reach. She immediately recognized Ansgar's number on her phone's display and greeted him warmly. Ansgar learned that, in spite of the government's official policy to eradicate bribery, it was indeed still widespread, especially where bigger deals were involved. Irina explained:

Only bribe money talks in these cases – I'm referring to business in general, of course, and not to a specific case. Without it, you simply don't get any business done. There's no point in trying to fool us. It happened before privatization, and it's happening now. This is known in the headquarters as far as I know. I can also understand why headquarters draws up its nice code of behaviour in order to prevent bribery, but out here we're dealing with reality, not theory. If we don't adapt to the local way of doing business to some extent, we won't ever be shortlisted for key projects. Therefore, no sales, no business! We've even encountered our first Chinese competitors here. They build their guanxis no matter what. They simply don't shy away from business opportunities, but grab them. Most Western companies don't realize that Chinese companies simply fly in below their competitors' radar screen to win deals. One fine morning, when it is too late, people will understand the webs of investment companies that have been spun to disguise the Chinese players' massive and aggressive mercantilism.

Overall Irina remained vague, since she did not want to appear to be taking either Nico or Petre's side. She just admitted that there was tension between the two, even once a major fight. She concluded:

> Dr Kuhn, it was great to hear from you. Let's meet for lunch next time I am at headquarters. I am really sorry that I can't be of more help in helping you to find out what is really going on here.

Ansgar decided to issue a warning to the head of corporate development and the members of the audit committee. After a rather brief coordination with the CEO, he also e-mailed Nico asking him to refrain from taking action on this matter until further notice. He then invited the HR director, the head of legal affairs, the head of internal auditing, and two outside consultants – one on corporate governance and one on HR – to a two-hour workshop on the codes of conduct the following week. He wanted to obtain comprehensive feedback on their use of these codes before the next meeting of the audit committee, which would take place two days after the workshop.

The day Ansgar sent out the invitations for this workshop, he received an e-mail from Nico, cc-ing several top managers, with a press clipping attached reporting that the alliance with a Romanian second-tier telecommunication service provider had been concluded at amazingly favorable conditions for Connect-U2.

The code of conduct workshop

The two external consultants were asked for their feedback first and did not hold back. Henri Badescu, the corporate governance expert, commented:

> In its current form, your code of conduct is nothing but a collection of nice-sounding phrases colourfully expressing nothing more than hot air. And, as I deduced from our phone conversation, you never measure its success either. By this time you should know my motto: what you can't measure, you can't improve.

Andreas Baumueller, the gray-haired, extremely tall partner of a renowned Austrian HR consulting company, added:

> Bear in mind that codes are much more than just a means through which to ensure compliance. They should be a great tool with which to program employees' minds and – if I may say so – a unique tool with which to enhance organizational culture. They must, of course, be embedded in a variety of other initiatives, but that is obvious. In its current version, Connect-U2's code of conduct fails in all these respects. It is very general indeed, and even if the staff were to know about it, how could it enable them to do the right thing when they're in doubt? Compliance is a must, codes are a must, but if you've already spent time and money on developing one, please consider a holistic solution that will tap all the potentials available. By the way, my company has had good experiences in

assisting with the successful revision of a number of codes in other industries. We would be more than happy to help.

Breathing laboriously, Connect-U2's HR director, the heavily overweight Cuno Michelis, nodded continuously while Andreas was talking. Too often, projects were thrown over the divisional or functional walls and then he and his team had to do the best implementation possible. He was responsible for, among others, incorporating any code-related aspects into HR selection and development programs. His impression that Connect-U2's codes were merely legal 'must-haves' had been confirmed far too often. Cuno clarified:

Codes are now getting the attention that Mission and Values received a few years ago. But just because we have a code doesn't guarantee or assure the right outcomes. It's all about leadership at the top. This is what ultimately determines ethical behavior.

Andreas mentioned another aspect of codes:

By the same token, let me also point out that many codes are poorly implemented. How rigorously do you monitor the impact of our code? Have you ever followed up on what was going on whenever you planned to or had successfully entered new markets? Ansgar, you mentioned that no one ever used the installed helpline for whistleblowers or the website on the intranet before. Is there really the organizational culture in place for reporting?

59-year-old Thomas Egi, head of internal auditing, interrupted in a slightly stressed voice:

You can be sure that we do follow up and monitor, of course. We are very tough on our actions and there have never been and there will never be any holy cows in this company.

Ansgar sighed softly, knowing that it was high time for Connect-U2 to embark on substantial reforms of its code. But in what direction? To his mind, matters got more complex when companies operated in a plethora of cultures. What was accepted as legal and ethical in one country might not necessarily be regarded as either legal or ethical in other countries. He realized that his thoughts were wandering and once again focused on what the others were contributing.

At that point, Henri, the only top management consultant Ansgar knew that had an earring, which he kept from his student days back in the late seventies, commented:

You know, Ansgar, after all the corporate scandals in the US and the rest of the world, corporate governance needs to be professionalized and to evolve. The must-do changes and those transformations that could be done quite painlessly were handled first. The art is now to also master the greater challenges. In order to ensure ongoing compliance throughout the organization and to enable true value added, I suggest that you reform your codes as well. TINA – there is no alternative. Especially given the, how should I put it, the temptations of the Eastern European markets where the pressure to give way to 'local customs' may be too strong. But don't get me wrong: practices are gradually improving in most East-European markets. Traditionally, bribery was simply a means to make progress. We could regard it as part of inefficient markets' and control systems' dark side. What's more, Eastern Europe isn't alone in facing this problem because even Switzerland, which has one of the lowest street-crime rates in the world, is placed high on several corruption rankings – right next to the usual suspects. And don't forget Germany with Volkswagen's bribery scandal in India, or the scandals around Infineon, Commerzbank, Mercedes and even BMW, all of which led to arrests and criminal prosecutions.

Guenter Amrhein, head of legal affairs, finally joined the discussion:

I am a lawyer by training and by choice. I'm therefore not as familiar with cultural programming, training etc. as you are. My first and foremost interest is in ensuring compliance with the codes so that Connect-U2 keeps its nose clean. This may sound like a modest goal, but I think it is actually of the utmost importance.

Ansgar nodded.

A truly tough call

Since the workshop had turned into a first discussion and feedback session, Ansgar was now back at his desk. He was deep in thought again. How badly did Connect-U2 need to reform its codes? Wasn't it perhaps more a question of implementing the current ones more strictly? In which direction should he steer the audit committee's upcoming meeting, given the ambiguity on the one hand and the lack of readily available solutions on the other?

More important was, what should he recommend to the audit committee regarding Petre and the 'Bucharest' incident, which must certainly have entailed very creative accounting practices to hide the bribes? What should he say to Nico during their next phone call, which would inevitably take place soon? And while whistleblowers should enjoy protection, how could one prevent red herrings from distracting the company's attention, while at the same time ensuring that clear examples would in future leave no uncertainty as to the right approach to take?

Next to potentially tarnishing his image if he made the wrong decisions, the 'Bucharest' incident could have greater repercussions. Two more deals in Bulgaria and Moldowa were in the process of being finalized. And Connect-U2 hoped to be considered in the next phase of privatization in Latvia's telecom industry in 2006. Being involved in scandals would throw back Connect-U2 substantially in this cutthroat competition. On more practical terms, how to substitute the head negotiator in the Bucharest deal if the rumors really turned out to be true? Alternatively, dismissing the number two would spread like wildfire in the industry, as would the reason for the dismissal. More importantly, how soon can one fire someone under whistleblower protection? Ansgar heaved a sigh:

This would be a feast for the competitors, either way.

That evening, Ansgar felt that it would in no way be possible to have the weekly romantic dinner that he had promised his wife before their wedding. He would be too preoccupied with thoughts of his company, and in particular with the question: what should Connect-U2 do now?

6
Board Evaluation

To monitor and even explicitly evaluate the CEO's and the board's performance are increasingly crucial tasks. We decided to apply a more integrative discussion of Farni plc in the following, explaining the patterns as we present the case step by step.

Imagine a 'mid-cap' Northern European company with approximately €8 billion in sales and 21,000 employees. It is strongly rooted in the technological tradition of its industry and its segment – regarded as a 'national' champion. However, in the last 15 years, it has become increasingly global, and now has operations in 40 countries and nearly half of the employees are non-nationals. Contrary to many peers in the industry, its top management team reflects that international diversity. In business terms, the main concern is growth as internal growth has been sluggish over the last decade. Most of the company's growth emanates from acquisitions of national operations in the technology industry. Its global integration, however, is still low. The business is reasonably profitable and cash generating, which also provided the economic base for the acquisition. Although there is no deep crisis in sight, some board members feel uneasy about the company's slow growth.

Accordingly, one early spring day, the board convenes (see Figure 6.1 for the composition of the board). Professor Dirks, a non-national and non-executive director, chairman of a prominent science foundation, and a highly respected economist, proposes at the end of a pretty dull meeting:

Why don't we evaluate our board's effectiveness?

citing recent trends in corporate governance as a need to embark on such an endeavor to improve the effectiveness of the board's work. The chairman, Jan Glistrup, is absolutely enthusiastic, whereas other board members only mildly support this. In raising questions, these indicate some concerns or lack of knowledge. The CEO, Peter Wulf, remains silent maintaining his usual, somewhat frozen, smile. But in the end, the board agrees and requests Professor Dirks to lay a proposal on the table.

Two months later, the board's minutes contain a draft of a questionnaire survey focusing on the board's effectiveness as a group. Based on a concept of an international business school, it focuses on the board's effectiveness factors in three areas:

- Degrees of fulfillment of the board's responsibility.
- Board vs. management relationship.
- The effectiveness of the board processes and meetings, broken down into individual indicators.

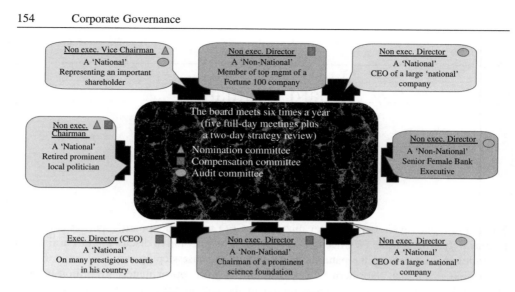

Figure 6.1   Composition of the board

Apart from the effectiveness rating, an 'importance of factor' score is also attached (see Appendix I at the end of this chapter for the full survey for the group level). The first reaction of most board members is:

Too long and too complicated.

But when asked by Professor Dirks:

Which question is less relevant and should be eliminated?

no one makes a specific suggestion deleting one. A rather abstract debate evolves on the importance of various factors. As a result of the survey, a debate on the priority of the board's work erupts for the first time. The chairman summarizes:

Obviously all questions are regarded as important, although some more than others. But let's try to work with this. We see from the results – most of the performance metrics and the importance of topics metrics – where we stand and what is regarded as important. Obviously we have different views here.

This is unanimously agreed.

Lesson 1: Obtain buy-in for the methodology. Otherwise the results will be criticized, not necessarily in content, but in informal terms.

The survey was administered by the company secretary under the guidance of Professor Dirks, since the board did not wish to have an external person or body involved, at least not in the first round. When the results were collated and aggregated by the company secretary, the message was clear: opinions differed widely among board members, revealing different mental models of what board work involves and what the benchmarks and reference models for a high-performance board are. Figure 6.2 shows tables from the company secretary's presentation.

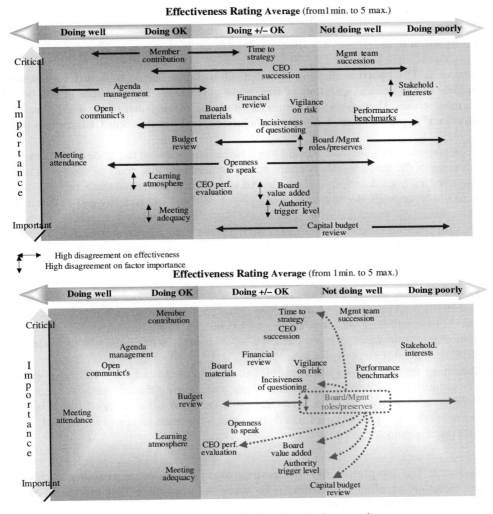

Figure 6.2   Results of the board evaluation exercise

Overall, the board was judged – at best – 'moderately' effective on critical factors. In the following debate on the board's results, it became clear that differences in opinion and evaluation centered around two issues:

- The role of the board vs. management, which includes the division of labor, CEO performance evaluation, value-added by the board, and the authority allocation clarifying what needs to be approved by the board.
- And the expected behavior of directors in a board.

Now that we all know where we stand,

commented Professor Dirks,

the need for action is clear,

to the chairman in the debate. Jan Glistrup couldn't agree more.

Lesson 2: The board evaluation revealed – but did not generate – different mental models of the central question of corporate governance and the role of the board in most cases. They typically center around the management/board relation and directors' expected contributions and behavior (e.g., scrutinizing CEO proposals).

The company secretary alerted the board that it had a charter, called the 'code of governance', which some of the board members remembered vaguely, and that many of the issues under debate were not even described in the code. An agreement was reached that a revision of the code would be urgently needed, loops had to be closed, and more clarity had to be created for the roles of the board and management.

The chairman volunteered, with support from the company secretary, to draft the changes and to circulate them amongst all directors. The following chapters were changed significantly:

- Responsibilities, management tasks and the board were described in much more detail (e.g., written preparation of board meeting points, at least one week before the meeting), and decision authority was clarified (e.g., what was meant by 'investments').
- Committees' role was specified. Each was given a subcharter of tasks in the code with schedules and sufficient explanation.
- Regarding the meeting agenda, the roles of the chairman and the CEO in proposing and setting agenda items were defined. Recurring meeting themes, such as succession planning and strategic reviews, were identified and time slots allocated over the year. Furthermore, the rights of board members to propose agenda topics were codified, along with process guidelines.

Lesson 3: The temptation to refer to structural features or organizational rules as the 'solution' is often irresistible, even when it is plausible that the cause of the problem might lie elsewhere.

However, despite greater clarity on paper, only minor changes were observed in practice. The strong CEO resented even the soft questioning or challenges by board members on every important issue – from succession planning to performance targets and strategic thrusts. It was clear that he regarded the board as 'too intrusive'. Not all board members participated in the attempt to better hold the CEO to account. For instance, the bank executive was especially reluctant, as her bank was the main source of M&A advice to the CEO. The chairman too often protected the CEO, as he was concerned that he might quit his job. Being a prominent national figure due to his previous sports career, well connected and on four other boards of prestigious companies, the probability that he might 'jump ship' was always latent in the mind of Jan Glistrup. In a psychological interpretation one could argue that as an ex-politician the chairman felt a bit inferior to the business tycoons.

> **Lesson 4: Long-held beliefs, mental models, and interpersonal relationships are not changed by one board evaluation. Ingrained attitudes and behaviors do not change quickly. Interpersonal relationships may impede the independence of the board. The actual state of mind and consequent action are more important than a legal description of 'independence'.**

In the following year's evaluation process it was stated that not much had changed in practice. It was, therefore, suggested that every board member should meet one-to-one with the chairman:

- To discuss perceived roadblocks towards a high-performance board.
- To give direct feedback to the chairman on his handling of the board.
- And to direct personal feedback on each other's contribution via the chairman.

Jan Glistrup agreed and carried out this work-intensive task. The collected results in the three areas could be summarized as follows:

- The majority of board members demanded more openness about problems, more discussion, and fewer management presentations, as well as more tolerance from the CEO when professionally challenged by the board.
- The chairman was regarded as too diplomatic and too protective of the CEO. He had to support the board members more in challenging the ideas of management and monitor the progress with commitments more closely.
- Surprisingly, no precise feedback was given by any board member on each other's contribution. As it is implausible that all board members were so satisfied with their peers, this could only be interpreted as a culture issue, which could not be overcome as yet.

The chairman presented the results to the full board – without consulting with the CEO beforehand. Some practical improvements were agreed on. One of them comprised fewer and shorter presentations. But it was obvious that most of the issues could not be collectively decided on through rules and regulations, as they represented deeply rooted individual behavior which proved to be a roadblock to a high-performance board. Could a supportive chairman be turned into a challenger? Would a strong CEO accept challenges without causing a crisis? This all proved that when it comes to human behavior, the road to progress is slow and painful.

Summary of the learning nuggets

Board evaluations normally do not lead to drastic changes in behavior, but they do make matters clear. They create transparency and openly acknowledge what everybody thought. They create some pressure to act, which, in the first round, is often directed towards organizational or internal regulatory issues. Evaluations need to be a continuous process, and only then can ingrained mental models and individual attitudes – which are the most important roadblocks to high-performing boards – be tackled.

APPENDIX I: QUESTIONNAIRE FOR BOARD EVALUATIONS AT THE GROUP LEVEL

Importance of factor (from 1, lowest to 3, highest)	Board Effectiveness Factors	Effectiveness rating (from 1, lowest to 5, highest)

PART I DEGREE OF FULFILLMENT OF THE BOARD'S RESPONSIBILITIES

1. The board devotes a high enough percentage of its time to in-depth discussions of issues related to the company's strategy and its long-term competitiveness.
Comments:

2. The board reflects its understanding of the company's vision, strategies, and plans in its discussions and actions on key issues throughout the year.
Comments:

3. The board reviews and adopts an annual operating budget. It effectively monitors performance against budget throughout the year and ensures corrective action is taken if deviations occur.
Comments:

4. The board regularly monitors the company's income statement, balance sheet, and cash flow, and effectively reviews business and financial risk factors.
Comments:

5. The board reviews and adopts an annual capital budget and receives regular written or oral reports of performance against it throughout the year.
Comments:

6. The board and/or the audit committee is vigilant regarding the management of risk, and ensures that the company's control systems and procedures are regularly updated.
Comments:

7. The board regularly considers the performance of 'best-in-class' peer companies in tracking the company's performance, and uses them as benchmarks for management.
Comments:

8. The board and/or the compensation committee regularly consider the correlation between executive pay and company performance.
Comments:

9. The board discharges its responsibilities in relation to the succession of the CEO and maintains a contingency succession plan up to date.
Comments:

10. The board reviews succession plans for the members of the senior management team on a regular basis.
Comments:

PART II QUALITY OF THE BOARD/MANAGEMENT RELATIONSHIP

11. The board has discussed and clarified its role vis-à-vis management (i.e., it has defined the respective boundaries of board and management powers and preserves).
Comments:

12. In its relationship with management, the board is vigilant to take into account and defend the interests of a broad range of constituencies and stakeholders.
Comments:

13. The board has established appropriate and clear trigger levels for board or committee involvement in major business policies and decisions.
Comments:

14. The board knows and understands management's vision, strategies, operational priorities, and key performance issues.
Comments:

15. The board ensures that it has multiple opportunities to be exposed to the company's management, staff, products, and operations.
Comments:

16. The board tries to maintain an appropriate balance in the time horizon of its efforts, between reviewing the past, addressing current issues, planning for tomorrow, and anticipating the future.
Comments:

17. The board is eager to seize all the opportunities it has to add value to management through its experience, expertise, or contacts, and management fully uses that opportunity.
Comments:

18. The board discusses and approves the CEO's personal objectives, and regularly reviews the performance of the CEO against his stated objectives.
Comments:

19. The board and the compensation/organization committee regularly review the capabilities, performance, and ethics of the senior officers.
Comments:

20. The process in place for setting up the board agenda is a transparent one that represents equally the interests and issues of the board and of management.
Comments:

PART III EFFECTIVENESS OF BOARD PROCESSES AND MEETINGS

21. The frequency, duration, and scheduling of board meetings are adequate to ensure a proper coverage of all the board's responsibilities.
Comments:

22. Board members receive adequate advance board meeting materials, in terms of relevance, content coverage, information detail, and 'reader-friendliness', and receive them sufficiently in advance.
Comments:

Importance of factor (from 1, lowest to 3, highest)	Board Effectiveness Factors	Effectiveness rating (from 1, lowest to 5, highest)
	23. Board members make a point to attend all board meetings, and they generally come well informed of the agenda and well prepared on the issues to be discussed. **Comments:**	
	24. Board agendas are realistic in terms of the topics to be discussed given the time available and are managed effectively given the relative importance of the topics under discussion. **Comments:**	
	25. Board meetings are conducted in a manner that ensures open communication, meaningful participation, and timely resolution of issues. **Comments:**	
	26. Board members are not subject to 'group-think'; board meetings leave room for critical thinking and incisive questioning. **Comments:**	
	27. The board is a genuine working group or team; it is neither fragmented nor split among different interest groups or constituencies. **Comments:**	
	28. All board members feel free to speak their mind without having to suppress their true feelings, and the CEO feels comfortable discussing bad news, anticipated bad news, and risks with the board. **Comments:**	

Part III
Corporate Governance in Specific Contexts

Corporate Governance Dynamics in M&A

7.1 WHY GOVERNANCE AS USUAL IS NOT AN OPTION IN M&A

Major M&A activities are the 'litmus test' of corporate governance. The high-stake and stressful situation during M&A activities can lead to dramatic circumstances, stretching decision-making processes to – and often beyond – their limits. The need for corporate governance is therefore nowhere more dire than in M&As. Study after study confirms that the majority of M&A deals – between 60% and 80%, depending on the study – did not create value for the acquiring company. In many cases, all the value went to the owners of the target company. Although not all failed M&As were necessarily ill-intentioned, their implementation usually left much to be desired. The guiding questions include: can good corporate governance lead to better decisions? If so, how? What is the role of the board before as well as after the M&A deal?

Pre-deal situation

M&A deals are often either triggered by pitches from investment bankers, or a company planning a deal contracts an investment bank's services. As with any other advisor, there is a principal–agent situation here: the advisors know more about the topic (that's why they're hired), but they also have their own interests at heart – to earn the deal fee as quickly as possible. Consequently, if pressure is applied skillfully and dramatically – 'this is the chance of your lifetime' – this often leads to a persuasive situation with management ready to take decisions that it may later regret. Other situations in which this could occur are during frenzied bidding wars or high-profile hostile takeovers. Game theory has coined the expression 'the winner's curse', which applies to such situations. The winner can never financially recoup the price paid during such dramatic escalations. Although in commercial terms it would often be far preferable not to go through with a deal, psychologically, this is not an option that the combatants and their advisors will ever consider.

When can the board's supervisory or non-executive majority step in? If management has already committed itself to a deal, there are only two clear-cut options: either agree to the deal even though there are strong reservations regarding the wisdom of the deal, or let the deal fall through at the very end – accepting the massive collateral damage that will be done. Clearly, the CEO, among others, will have to go. To avoid the latter, decidedly unpleasant alternative, the board should beforehand define the 'scope' an M&A will be given. Certain types of strategy are built on the assumption that organic growth will not be adequate for the company's survival in a consolidating industry. This is a questionable assumption, because many successful companies only grow organically.

Company strategy should clearly spell out what types of acquisition are required under which conditions in order for the strategy to be successfully implemented. The board must also be clear that this strategy is the benchmark according to which management will be assessed. Without such a predetermined benchmark, management too is likely to fall victim to an onerous M&A process, and it would be hard for the board to evaluate any deal's price tag. Management and the board need a concrete benchmark before they are carried away by the dime-a-dozen advisors who are able to identify sufficient potential synergies to justify almost any premium paid for the target company.

In setting such a predetermined, pre-emptive benchmark, the board needs to be involved in the strategy formation process. Management tends to keep its options open and tends to not agree voluntarily to benchmarks, as it may later have difficulties in explaining its deviations.

The second option is for the board to get timely and honest information about the M&A negotiations. This will enable the board to provide feedback from a sufficiently early stage. It would also require frequent meetings – even international ones – and absolute confidentiality. Nevertheless, few successful CEOs would agree to such a process subsequent to their appointment.

The board involvement in the DaimlerChrysler 'merger of equals' is worth serious consideration, as it deviated from what was regarded as 'normal'. Once again, the legal specifics were not really decisive for corporate governance in this large merger, but they needed to be reported as part of the contingency analysis.

Chrysler's CEO, Bob Eaton, informed his board – which was much smaller than that of Daimler-Benz – early on, and his board kept him informed throughout. He could bank on confidentiality, given the heavy personal penalties that any breach in confidentiality faces in the USA. In addition, he had important shareholders' representatives on the board, having previously fought off a bloody takeover attempt by these shareholders. In the process, Eaton made Chrysler a decidedly shareholder-friendly company, and he did not want to risk any further adversity.

Jürgen Schrempp, Daimler-Benz's CEO, was in a different position. He was credited with a rapid turnaround, shedding most of the unprofitable parts of the former technology conglomerate, and forming a successful automotive and transportation company. His position was therefore stronger, and his main concerns were momentum and confidentiality. This was therefore less a matter of co-determination than that of Chrysler (there is no empirical evidence that Daimler-Benz's labor representatives leaked more information than the owner representatives did), but the sheer number of staff involved in the preparation of board meetings (both at the supervisory and management levels) and in disseminating the results made the operation more a grand opera than anything else. This is probably the reason why Schrempp informed his management board and supervisory boards of the M&A so late. There are indications, however, that he informed the chairman of the supervisory board (at that time the largest shareholder with some veto rights) and the deputy chairman (also the head of the Works Council) at an earlier stage.

The post-merger phase

Once the deal has been done, implementation and integration are crucial. The dynamics of this process often limits even an involved board to a bystander role. Swift decisions that often have a high degree of uncertainty have to be taken. If there had been no time for planning and deliberations before this stage, or if the planning and deliberation were inadequate, by this stage it is too late to rectify the situation.

The board should, however, ensure that it is kept sufficiently informed during this stage, so that it exactly understands what is occurring and will know if or when to step in. During the

DaimlerChrysler merger, the management's compensation was addressed during this stage. The upper management compensation was much higher at Chrysler than at Daimler-Benz (partly due to differences in fringe benefits). The potential increase in the German salaries to equal that of the USA led to a public outcry and threatened to dominate the general assembly. This led to the chairman of the supervisory board intervening. He proposed a staggered compensation scheme with a strongly variable, performance-related payment. Both the supervisory board and the general assembly accepted this alternative (although it is an open question whether the general assembly has voting rights on such issues).

Although any major M&A deal contains rich learning opportunities, surprisingly little post-deal reviewing is done. Mistakes are often made during the high-speed, high-uncertainty M&A context. If management is in a 'combatant' mode and therefore biased in its observation, the board can initiate a post-deal review once the integration nears completion. This can only be done if such a review is regarded as a learning opportunity, rather than a 'naming and blaming' exercise. However, as the board has to monitor and evaluate management's performance, this may be easier said than done. Nevertheless, a confident management may prefer a systematic, comprehensive evaluation rather than one driven by gut feel.

Learning nuggets from the cases

Corporate governance considerations are rarely observed or analyzed in detail during M&A. The 'drama' is much 'juicier' than determining the rules of decision and the establishment of accountability and transparency. High-stake, nerve-wracking situations test any corporate governance system's resilience. Do checks and balances still work in dynamic situations in which high risk and ambiguity are prevalent? The characteristics of the DaimlerChrysler M&A are those of a cross-cultural merger. The case is thus not a decision-making case, but one that simply describes corporate governance's main characteristics.

Corporate governance is contingent by nature and the board can do very little after the deal has been made if it did not determine economically viable benchmarks beforehand. It is obvious that very few boards are truly in control; how else can one explain why so many M&A deals destroy more shareholder value than they create?

In the post-merger integration, there is equally little that the board can do if it had neglected this beforehand. After the integration has been achieved, the board should conduct a post-action review to ensure that the learning from the M&A deal is covered.

The situation at DaimlerChrysler, now again Daimler and Chrysler as separate entities, clearly showed what happens if such a post-merger evaluation and constant reality check are ignored. If synergies are planned, they need to be tracked. Synergies in one part of a system usually come with negative synergies in other parts of the system if not managed well. At that time ongoing tension, unexpected negative synergies, too many taboos, and a lack of reality check led to a loss of trust among investors. The actual merger represented substantial additional work, but it did not end there. In today's impatient investment community, there was simply no time for a decade-long integration to really create tremendous synergies. A new CEO, Dieter Zetsche, cleaned up and simplified not only the organizational complexity, but also the governance.

Suggested further reading

Morosini, P. and Steger, U. (eds) (2004). *Managing Complex Mergers*. FT/Prentice Hall, London, chapters 1, 2, 7.

7.2   CASE STUDY: THE DAIMLERCHRYSLER MERGER – THE INVOLVEMENT OF THE BOARDS

[By Fred Neubauer, Ulrich Steger, and George Raedler]

> In the final stage of the merger negotiations [with Chrysler Corporation], a maximum of 20 to 30 employees were involved.
>
> (Jürgen E. Schrempp, former CEO of Daimler-Benz AG, now co-chairman of DaimlerChrysler AG[1] after completing the $40 billion merger with Chrysler in only four months.)

On 7 May 1998, at a press conference in London that had been called on very short notice, the CEOs of Daimler-Benz AG and Chrysler Corporation, Jürgen Schrempp and Robert Eaton, announced that their two companies had decided 'to get together in a merger of equals'.

The combined company would have $132 billion in annual revenues; it would be the fifth largest auto-maker in the world, employing 428,000 people – about one-half in Germany, one-third in North America, and the rest spread across 200 countries around the world. Although it was the largest industrial merger the world had seen to that date, the announcement took most observers by surprise. Negotiations had been conducted under strict secrecy, with only a very limited number of persons from each company involved.

At the London press conference, both CEOs explained the rationale for the merger. In their opinion, both companies were too small on a global scale to prosper in the long term. This handicap, they felt, could be overcome by joining forces; their product ranges and geographical reach made the two enterprises near-perfect partners (refer to Figures 7.1 and 7.2). At the press conference, the CEOs also publicly announced as one of their guiding principles that this move would be 'a merger of growth; there will be no layoffs'. They also stressed their determination to increase shareholder value, to obtain $1.4 billion in savings during the first year of the merger, and to complete the integration process within three years.

After the dust of this 'big bang' had settled, some of the details of the merger's secretive preparation became known. The marriage had indeed had a most interesting courtship.

Mercedes-Benz AG: too small?

After taking over as CEO of Daimler-Benz AG in 1995, Schrempp implemented a number of far-reaching changes. Severe operational inefficiencies, caused by loss-making units acquired since the mid-1980s, had led to the largest corporate financial loss in German history. The company sold or liquidated 12 of its either unprofitable or non-core subsidiaries. Schrempp saw himself as a protagonist for shareholder value, and in response to the loss, he initiated a cultural change program in order to make the employees in Daimler-Benz pay more attention to profitability. One of the arguments for stressing shareholder value was the fact that the shares of Daimler-Benz had been introduced on the New York Stock Exchange in 1993, a first for German industry. To take advantage of this move, the company not only had to publish its results according to US-GAAP, it also had to live up to the expectations of the international investor community with respect to the return on the Daimler-Benz

---

[1] Glöckner, T. (1998). Quartett der Macher. *Focus*, **34**: 210.

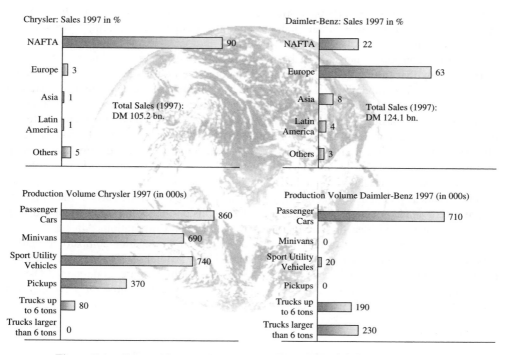

Figure 7.1   Geographic spread of Chrysler Corporation and Daimler-Benz AG
Source: DaimlerChrysler AG.

Market Segment							
	Compact	Medium	Upper Level	Luxury	Pickup	Minivan	Sport/ Utility
High	A-Class ⬤	C-Class ⬤	E-Class ⬤	S-Class ⬤		Town & Country ⬤	M-Class / Grand Cherokee ⬤
Medium	Neon ⬤	Cirrus/ Stratus ⬤	Intrepid/ Concorde ⬤	LHS/ 300 M ⬤	Ram ⬤	Caravan ⬤	Durango/ Cherokee ⬤
Low	Neon ⬤	Breeze ⬤			Dakota ⬤	Voyager ⬤	Cherokee/ Wrangler ⬤

⬤ Mercedes-Benz models   ⬤ Chrysler models

Figure 7.2   The combined product portfolio of DaimlerChrysler AG
Source: DaimlerChrysler AG.

shares. The restructuring efforts paid off, and Daimler-Benz was finally out of the negative news. The rather spectacular turnaround substantially strengthened Schrempp's position in the company and vis-à-vis the board.

Putting the company's house in order was necessary, but it was by no means sufficient. Schrempp saw that further consolidation in the automotive industry was inevitable, in spite of the fact that his company was the most profitable company in the entire industry. He and his colleagues were concerned about the growth limitations of Daimler-Benz's passenger car division with basically one brand, 'Mercedes-Benz', in the premium sector (refer to Figure 7.3). The car-making division of Daimler-Benz AG manufactured Mercedes-Benz. The Mercedes-Benz brand was also used for commercial vehicles. In 1997, Schrempp commissioned, in addition to internal strategic studies, a study by an investment bank of ways this weakness might be remedied. The investment bankers suggested Chrysler and Honda Motors as potential complementary partners, particularly on the basis of their product mix and geographic coverage. Since Honda was not considering giving up its independence, Schrempp pushed the idea of joining forces with Chrysler Corporation. Already back in 1995, both firms had evaluated the possibility of establishing a separate company to market cars outside their home markets in Europe and the USA. A total of 30-plus taskforces had been evaluating ways to achieve that goal. The proposed joint venture, code-named Q-Star, had stopped before it got off the ground. Neither company could agree on personnel and financial issues. Instead, they had agreed, as Schrempp put it, to 'be friends'.

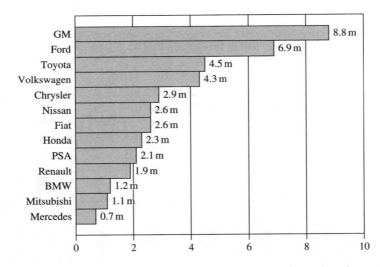

Figure 7.3 The global players in the automotive industry; 1997 annual sales of passenger cars (in million units)
Source: Deutsche Bank AG.

Same procedure as every year: contacts at the Detroit Auto Show

When Schrempp went to the North American International Auto Show in Detroit in January 1998, his official reason was to make a speech on the future challenges of the automotive industry.

Besides delivering his speech, Schrempp contacted Robert Eaton, the chairman of Chrysler Corporation. Chrysler was not a stranger to Schrempp. From the previous abortive round of discussions, Schrempp had gotten the clear impression that Chrysler, as the smallest of the 'Big 3' auto-makers, also had concerns about its size relative to General Motors and Ford. Schrempp decided he would suggest an outright merger with Chrysler.

The initial meeting between Schrempp and Eaton in January 1998 lasted 17 minutes, and Eaton promised to let Schrempp know within a few weeks his reaction to the idea of a full-fledged merger. Adds a source close to Schrempp:

> Eaton was obviously well-prepared. He had done similar studies as Schrempp, and he knew that although Chrysler was highly profitable, it was still too small and too domestic compared to its competitors. They did not have to convince each other anymore – the writing was on the wall.

'The deal these guys pulled off was on nobody's radar screen before the news broke'

Only a few days after their initial meeting, Eaton called Schrempp and expressed his interest in further talks about the possible merger. As he was afraid of leaks – 'we were worried that if word leaked before most of the details were worked out, it might have fallen apart'[2] – Schrempp initially informed only two executives about the talks: Dr Eckhard Cordes, the member of the management board who was responsible for corporate development and directly managed businesses and Dr Rüdiger Grube, senior vice president of corporate strategy and planning (a close associate of Cordes). At that point, Schrempp, Cordes, and Grube were the only three who knew about the intended deal at Daimler-Benz. As the talks continued, secrecy became an obsession. Soon afterwards, Cordes became the key dealmaker behind the merger.

On 12 February 1998, the first meeting between Schrempp, Cordes, Eaton, and Gary C. Valade, CFO of Chrysler, took place. The discussion focused on the state of the industry as well as possible synergies that might result from combining the companies. Potential economies of scale were discovered in R&D, purchasing, and manufacturing.

At the same time, Ford also approached the Stuttgart-based company regarding a closer cooperation. On 13 and 14 February 1998, Cordes, Jürgen Hubbert (management board member and head of Mercedes-Benz passenger cars) and Dr Dieter Zetsche (management board member for sales and distribution) flew to London where they were confronted with the idea of a possible merger. Ford was actively trying to expand its share of the premium market, and Alex Trotman, Ford's CEO, later visited Schrempp in Stuttgart to disclose that the proposed merger could no longer be pursued due to the veto of the Ford family. At this point, the merger talks with Chrysler were quite far along.

External advisors enter early

On February 17 and 18, the representatives of Daimler-Benz and Chrysler met again. This time, Daimler-Benz was represented by Cordes and Grube and representatives of Goldman Sachs, the investment bank. Chrysler was represented by Valade, Thomas P. Capo

---

[2] Ingrassia, L. (1998). How executives at Daimler, Chrysler hammered out deal. *Wall Street Journal Europe*, May 8.

(vice president and treasurer), and William J. O'Brian (general counsel of Chrysler). Credit Suisse First Boston (CSFB) acted as financial advisor to Chrysler. In addition, corporate lawyers were involved.

In these discussions, the representatives of Daimler-Benz stated that:

> . . . it was important to Daimler-Benz that any potential transaction maximize value for its stockholders, that it be tax-free to Daimler-Benz's German stockholders and tax efficient for DaimlerChrysler AG and that the surviving entity of any combination be a German stock corporation. (DaimlerChrysler AG prospectus, p. 47)

Chrysler stated its strategy in a similar fashion:

> . . . it was important to Chrysler that any potential transaction maximize value for its stockholders, that it be tax-free to Chrysler's US stockholders and tax efficient to DaimlerChrysler AG, that it have the post-merger governance structure of a 'merger-of-equals' [this was essential for saving tax on goodwill]. (DaimlerChrysler AG prospectus, p. 47)

During these meetings, various tax, corporate, and management issues were discussed.

The Geneva Auto Show in early March 1998 was a good opportunity for the chief executives of both companies to meet again. During the meeting at a restaurant in neighboring Lausanne (secrecy was still a major issue), Schrempp and Eaton, accompanied once again by Cordes and Valade, looked at corporate governance and organizational structures. In order to avoid massive tax bills, it soon became very clear that locating the merged company in Germany was the only option for Chrysler's American stockholders and Daimler-Benz's German stockholders.

At this point a limited number of small working teams were established. They worked intensively on the key issues during March 1998. These teams were supervised by Cordes and Valade.

Involvement of the boards

According to the classical corporate governance doctrine, the board has the ultimate responsibility for the company. The approval of the boards of both companies to a step as massive as the merger was therefore eventually necessary.

The way both CEOs managed the timetable of the approval process and the degree of involvement of their respective boards shed an interesting light on the corporate governance practices in the USA and in Germany. (Refer to Figure 7.4 for the different timelines according to which both companies proceeded in getting the approval of the merger plans from the appropriate bodies. *Note*: Please keep using Figure 7.4 as a reference while reading the following paragraphs.)

The involvement of the Chrysler board

Before looking into the details of the involvement of the Chrysler board in the merger decision, a few general remarks on US corporate governance practices are appropriate.

As a typical US corporation, Chrysler had been run by a so-called 'unitary board'. This meant that the Chrysler board was composed of executive and non-executive board members.

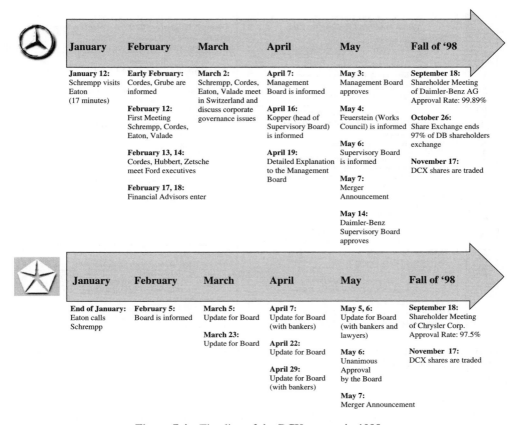

	January	February	March	April	May	Fall of '98
	January 12: Schrempp visits Eaton (17 minutes)	**Early February:** Cordes, Grube are informed	**March 2:** Schrempp, Cordes, Eaton, Valade meet in Switzerland and discuss corporate governance issues	**April 7:** Management Board is informed	**May 3:** Management Board approves	**September 18:** Shareholder Meeting of Daimler-Benz AG Approval Rate: 99.89%
		February 12: First Meeting Schrempp, Cordes, Eaton, Valade		**April 16:** Kopper (head of Supervisory Board) is informed	**May 4:** Feuerstein (Works Council) is informed	**October 26:** Share Exchange ends 97% of DB shareholders exchange
		February 13, 14: Cordes, Hubbert, Zetsche meet Ford executives		**April 19:** Detailed Explanation to the Management Board	**May 6:** Supervisory Board is informed	**November 17:** DCX shares are traded
		February 17, 18: Financial Advisors enter			**May 7:** Merger Announcement	
					May 14: Daimler-Benz Supervisory Board approves	

	January	February	March	April	May	Fall of '98
	End of January: Eaton calls Schrempp	**February 5:** Board is informed	**March 5:** Update for Board	**April 7:** Update for Board (with bankers)	**May 5, 6:** Update for Board (with bankers and lawyers)	**September 18:** Shareholder Meeting of Chrysler Corp. Approval Rate: 97.5%
			March 23: Update for Board	**April 22:** Update for Board	**May 6:** Unanimous Approval by the Board	**November 17:** DCX shares are traded
				April 29: Update for Board (with bankers)	**May 7:** Merger Announcement	

Figure 7.4   Timeline of the DCX merger in 1998
Source: DaimlerChrysler AG Prospectus, company sources.

In the case of Chrysler, Robert Eaton and Robert A. Lutz were the executive directors; in addition, there were ten non-executive directors on the board. Members came from industry and finance, and many of the companies they came from represented 'household names' in US business (refer to Figure 7.5 for a list of board members). As is typical for many US companies, the position of the chairman of the board and the chief executive was held by the same person: Robert Eaton.

US board members are elected by the shareholders annually; they can be re-elected until they reach the age of 70, typically the retirement age for board members.

In a litigious society like America, it should come as no surprise that US board members are under substantial threat of law suits by shareholders for any wrong-doings on a board. As a result, they are usually particularly careful in handling the business of the board they are on and maintain strict confidentiality. A breach of confidentiality or a leak of business information will trigger much more severe sanctions on the American board member than in any other country.

Boards in the United States meet rather frequently. In 1997, the Chrysler board held 15 meetings (down from 18 in 1996); this indicates that the board was rather close to what was going on in the company. This closeness is not unusual for US companies. One of the

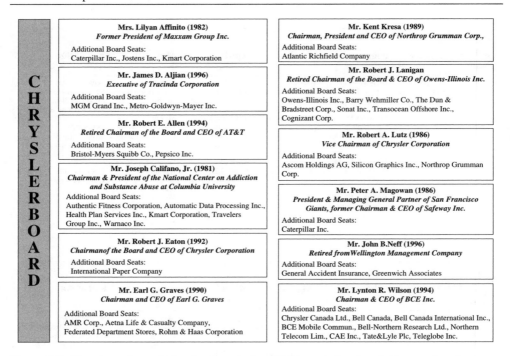

Figure 7.5   Board members of Chrysler Corporation 1998 (year in brackets indicates when the person joined the Chrysler board)
Source: Chrysler Corporation, Annual Letter to Shareholders 1998.

reasons for this closeness is that for the last decade or two, many US corporations have been under great performance pressure from their shareholders, whether institutional investors or individual shareholders. Both categories of investors play a role in Chrysler's case.

For quite some time, a 'thorn in the thigh' of Chrysler has been Kirk Kerkorian, a self-made American billionaire. Kerkorian regularly puts the company under tremendous financial pressure, and at one point, he even embarked on a bitter takeover battle. In April of 1995, with the help of Lee Iacocca, the former Chrysler chairman, Kerkorian attempted to take over Chrysler in a $23 billion bid. He later withdrew his bid, but increased his stake to 13.6% of equity. Moreover, Kerkorian has constantly fought to increase the maximum limit of equity a Chrysler shareholder can hold – first to 15% and later to 20%. Eaton was strongly opposed to this and publicly accused Tracinda, Kerkorian's investment company, of trying to obtain 'creeping control'.[3] James D. Alijian, an executive of Tracinda Corporation, represented the views of Kerkorian on the Chrysler board.

The Chrysler Corporation not only experienced the increasing influence of Kerkorian, but also that of other financial intermediaries. Mutual funds have become very popular in the USA, and with them, the power of fund managers has grown substantially. The influence of the financial side has led to changes in the dividend policy in a number of companies,

---

[3] Simonian, H. and Waters, R. (1996). Chrysler's backseat driver: the battle between Kirk Kerkorian and the car maker over the company's cash is coming to a head. *Financial Times*, January 16.

also in Chrysler. In order to raise the earnings per share, Chrysler started a share buyback program. Between 1995 and 1997, Chrysler spent $5.2 billion on repurchasing roughly 22% of outstanding stock. As a result, the shareholders had higher quarterly earnings per share. In 1997, the dividend yield on common stock reached 4.5%, equivalent to three times the average for Standard & Poor's (S&P) stocks. The top management continued to stress the importance of the interest of shareholders more heavily, and information dissemination to shareholders was considered one of the best in America. As Eaton stated, 'Chrysler is one of the most shareholder-friendly companies in America'.[4]

Eaton contacted his board of directors about the merger talks with Daimler-Benz roughly a week after confirming his interest to Schrempp.

Thereafter, the Chrysler board was regularly updated on the progress of the merger talks on March 5 and 23, and on April 7, 22, and 29 (refer to the timeline in Figure 7.4). The April 7 meeting was of particular relevance: at this meeting, it was decided that DaimlerChrysler would be incorporated in Germany.

After another update on May 5 and 6 – the investment bankers and the lawyers attended this meeting as well – the Chrysler board unanimously approved the merger plans. This meant the green light for the merger from the US side – provided the Chrysler shareholders would also agree.

The involvement of the Daimler-Benz boards

Exactly as in Anglo-Saxon corporations, in German stock companies the ultimate fountain of power is the shareholders meeting. Major differences in the governance systems of both countries occur at the board level. German corporations are governed by a two-tier board system, consisting of the board of management ('Vorstand') and the supervisory board ('Aufsichtsrat'). No overlapping board membership is allowed.

The management board is responsible for running day-to-day operations of the company. Corporations with a paid-in capital of more than $3 million require at least two members on the board of management. The contracts for members of the management board usually run up to five years.

The supervisory board was originally conceived as an institution that was essentially supposed to appoint and control management. As a consequence, members of the supervisory board are not allowed to take part in the actual running of the business. This rule, however, is not without exceptions. The company may, for instance, stipulate in its bylaws that the supervisory board has the right and duty to approve certain categories of management decisions with far-reaching consequences. Typically they are – among others – major acquisitions (of subsidiaries, for instance). In this context, a particular legal 'wrinkle' is of importance: if the board of management decides on a matter that would require the approval of the supervisory board, but fails to secure that approval, then the decision is, in principle, legally binding. The board of management has, however, violated its duty vis-à-vis the supervisory board (and has to bear the responsibility for this step). Obviously, a board of management will not behave in this way as such a violation would ruin the relationship with the supervisory board and jeopardize any reappointment of the management board members. Nevertheless, the possibility exists.

---

[4] Simonian, H. and Waters, R. (1998). Unlikely fellow travellers. *Financial Times*, May 9/10.

In line with this somewhat laid-back, control-oriented view of the role of the traditional German supervisory board, this group normally meets only four times a year. Daimler-Benz normally met five times per year, though in 1998 it held 11 meetings.

One additional important feature of the German board system has to be mentioned here: according to the German Co-Determination Act/Law of 1976, half of the members of the supervisory board are elected by the shareholders and half of them represent the employees. Members of the supervisory board for the capital side are elected for five years by the shareholders at their annual meeting. All employee representatives are voted in by employees. The law stipulates a carefully balanced split among the representatives for blue and white collar employees of the firm, and it also requires one representative of senior management who is not a board member. As a special twist, the Co-Determination Act also requires that in corporations above a certain size, at least three employee representatives be delegated to the supervisory board by the union. (In the case of Daimler-Benz, there were actually three union representatives on the board.)

The possible danger of a paralyzing situation on a German board due to the 50:50 parity between the representatives of the employees and of the capital side is overcome with the help of the 'casting vote' (double vote) of the chairman (who, by the way, always comes from the capital side). It can be used to break a stalemate, should it occur.

Besides the workers' representation on the supervisory board, a second channel of co-determination exists in Germany at the management level, namely the system of works councils. Some observers feel that for practical matters the influence of the employees through the works council is much more effective than through supervisory board representation. The chairmen of works councils typically wield great influence and are accordingly courted by management; they are also frequently elected to the supervisory board as employee representatives. This is also true in the case of Daimler-Benz, where the chairman of the works council, Karl Feuerstein, is not only a member of the Daimler-Benz supervisory board, but in accordance with German law, also its vice chairman.

In order to make the works council system effective, large companies have to provide fully paid absences for some of the council members. This gives the council the ability to play its role vis-à-vis management effectively and to discuss human resources issues. Moreover, some management measures have to be approved by the works councils, such as output-related pay rates, pay structures, hiring, and change of pay. If management and works councils disagree, management can either change its proposal or take it first to an arbitration court and then to the labor court. Although all of this may sound rather stringent to an outsider, 76% of German managers believe that works councils are more flexible than unions.[5]

(The two 'benches' on the Daimler-Benz supervisory board – the representatives of capital on the one side and employee representatives on the other – are shown in Figure 7.6.)

Back to the DaimlerChrysler merger

On the Daimler-Benz side, the merger talks were also thought to be progressing well. The sequence of steps to get other key parts of the corporation involved in the decision-making process differed, however, markedly from Chrysler's approach (refer to the timeline in Figure 7.4).

---

[5] Weidenfeld, U. (1997). Zum letzten Gefecht. *Wirtschaftswoche*, **19**(1.5): 52.

(A)

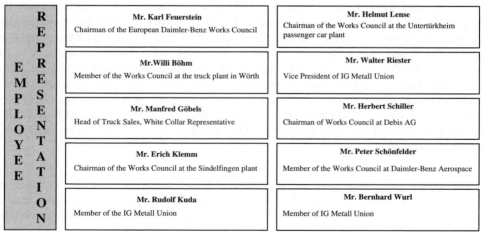

Mr. Hilmar Kopper *Chairman of the Supervisory Board of Daimler-Benz AG* Additional Board Seats: Deutsche Bank AG (Chairman), Mannesmann AG (Chairman), Bayer AG, Akzo Nobel NV, Solvay SA, Unilever, Xerox USA	**Dr. h.c. Martin Kohlhaussen** *Chairman of the Management Board of Commerzbank AG* Additional Board Seats: GKN Automotive International GmbH (Chairman), Bayer AG, Bertelsmann AG, Hochtief AG, Karstadt AG, Schering AG, Winterthur Swiss Insurance
Mrs. Dr. h.c. Birgit Breuel *Commissioner of the World Exhibition EXPO 2000* Additional Board Seats: Gruner+Jahr AG, Novartis AG, J.P. Morgan GmbH	**Mr. Jean-Marie Messier** *Director of Compagnie Generale des Eaux* Additional Board Seats: Compagnie de Saint-Gobain, LVMH, Strafor Facom, Havas, Canal+, UGC
Mr. E. John P. Browne *Group CEO of British Petroleum Company plc. (BP)* Additional Board Seats: SmithKline Beecham, Intel Corporation (both non-executive)	**Dr. Manfred Schneider** *Chairman of the Management Board of Bayer AG* Additional Board Seats: Metro AG, RWE AG
Dr. Michael Endres *Member of the Management Board of Deutsche Bank AG* Additional Board Seats: Deutz AG (Chairman), Heidelberger Printing, Mannesmann Arcor	**Mr. Bernhard Walter** *Chairman of the Management Board of Dresdner Bank AG* Additional Board Seats: Degussa AG, Fresenius Medical Care AG, Metallgesellschaft AG, Rheinmetall AG, Rütgers AG, Thyssen AG
Mr. Ulrich Hartmann *Chairman of the Management Board of VEBA AG* Additional Board Seats: Degussa AG (Chairman), Munich RE Insurance (Chairman), RAG AG (Chairman), Hochtief AG, IKB Deutsche Industriebank AG, Henkel KgaA	**Dr. Mark Wössner** *Chairman of the Management Board of Bertelsmann AG* Additional Board Seats: Gruner+Jahr AG

Left margin label: **C A P I T A L   S I D E**

(B)

Mr. Karl Feuerstein Chairman of the European Daimler-Benz Works Council	**Mr. Helmut Lense** Chairman of the Works Council at the Untertürkheim passenger car plant
Mr.Willi Böhm Member of the Works Council at the truck plant in Wörth	**Mr. Walter Riester** Vice President of IG Metall Union
Mr. Manfred Göbels Head of Truck Sales, White Collar Representative	**Mr. Herbert Schiller** Chairman of Works Council at Debis AG
Mr. Erich Klemm Chairman of the Works Council at the Sindelfingen plant	**Mr. Peter Schönfelder** Member of the Works Council at Daimler-Benz Aerospace
Mr. Rudolf Kuda Member of the IG Metall Union	**Mr. Bernhard Wurl** Member of IG Metall Union

Left margin labels: **E M P L O Y E E** **R E P R E S E N T A T I O N**

Figure 7.6   Board members of Daimler-Benz AG: (A) capital side; (B) employee representation (1998)
Source: Daimler-Benz Annual Report 1997.

Key dates in the decision-making process of Daimler-Benz follow.

On Tuesday, April 7, the management board of Daimler-Benz held its regular weekly meeting. At this gathering, Schrempp, as the head of this board, together with Cordes, informed their colleagues of what had happened during the past few months. No formal decision on the merger was, however, made by the board of management at that point. Moreover, Schrempp explained that he had seen a study evaluating the success of attempted mergers. This study revealed that total secrecy was necessary for ensuring successful mergers.

On April 16, Hilmar Kopper, the chairman of the supervisory board of Deutsche Bank AG (the largest equity holder of Daimler-Benz, with a stake of 22%), in his role as chairman of the Daimler-Benz supervisory board, was officially informed by Schrempp about the possible merger.

Although no details are known to the public, it can be safely assumed that Schrempp had revealed general considerations of such a merger much earlier to Kopper. As one aid to Schrempp put it:

> Schrempp and Kopper have a special relationship. Kopper's role as head of the supervisory board is very different from that of the other members. Kopper and Schrempp meet about twice a month in Frankfurt, and Schrempp has open discussions with Kopper.

On May 4, Schrempp met with Feuerstein to inform him about the merger. Since Daimler-Benz and Chrysler promised that the merger would not lead to any job losses (and since the logic of the merger made sense to him), Feuerstein agreed to the plans. With the leading figures of both benches on the Daimler-Benz supervisory board 'in the boat', Schrempp did not have to expect much opposition from the rank and file board members.

After Kopper was informed, Schrempp and Cordes set up a second meeting about the merger for the management board on April 19. After this extensive second round of discussions, the board of management met again and unanimously approved the merger – on May 3. The merger was announced on May 7, with the proviso that the supervisory board and the shareholders of Daimler-Benz must agree. On May 6, the same day the *Wall Street Journal* reported on a potential merger between Daimler and Chrysler, the supervisory board met in Stuttgart and was informed of the deal. This meeting did not include a vote, but rather a discussion of the reasons behind the move. The actual vote took place on 14 May 1998 – a week after the deal had been announced. One member of the Daimler-Benz supervisory board remembered:

> You cannot tell a story like this to 20 people. This is different from the US situation. A typical US board consists of 7–8 members and their liability is by far higher than in Germany. If you only whisper something about a deal of this magnitude, you are dead!

DCX: role model for convergence

The extraordinary shareholder meetings of Daimler-Benz AG and Chrysler Corporation on the merger decision took place on the same date: 18 September 1998. Both shareholder groups agreed to the merger in an overwhelming fashion: 99.89% of the Daimler-Benz stock owners, and 97.5% of the Chrysler share holders approved of it. This gave the deal the official imprimatur.

The modalities of the deal

Here are some of the key modalities of the deal:

- DaimlerChrysler AG is incorporated in Germany. Tax reasons (mainly the loss-carry forward of Daimler-Benz AG) spoke compellingly for this solution.
- In a complex, multi-step deal, each share of Daimler-Benz AG was de facto exchanged for one share of DaimlerChrysler AG.
- In a similar procedure, each share of Chrysler Corporation was exchanged at a rate of 1 to 0.62 for each new share of DaimlerChrysler AG. This exchange ratio was equivalent to a premium of 28% over Chrysler's share price on the day the exchange ratio was fixed (April 16).
- The composition of the shareholder body of DaimlerChrysler at 'Day One – November 18' was split equally between American and European shareholders. Both groups held 44% each of the outstanding shares. Chrysler only had 6% foreign shareholders, while the former Daimler-Benz AG had 25% of its shares in non-European hands (the State of Kuwait was the biggest shareholder, with a total of 13%).
- The supervisory board of DaimlerChrysler is composed as shown in Figure 7.7). A particularly sensitive point in this context was the representation of the US employees on the

Supervisory Board:

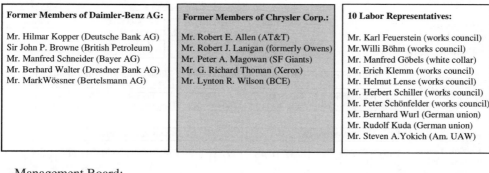

Former Members of Daimler-Benz AG:	Former Members of Chrysler Corp.:	10 Labor Representatives:
Mr. Hilmar Kopper (Deutsche Bank AG)	Mr. Robert E. Allen (AT&T)	Mr. Karl Feuerstein (works council)
Sir John P. Browne (British Petroleum)	Mr. Robert J. Lanigan (formerly Owens)	Mr. Willi Böhm (works council)
Mr. Manfred Schneider (Bayer AG)	Mr. Peter A. Magowan (SF Giants)	Mr. Manfred Göbels (white collar)
Mr. Berhard Walter (Dresdner Bank AG)	Mr. G. Richard Thoman (Xerox)	Mr. Erich Klemm (works council)
Mr. Mark Wössner (Bertelsmann AG)	Mr. Lynton R. Wilson (BCE)	Mr. Helmut Lense (works council)
		Mr. Herbert Schiller (works council)
		Mr. Peter Schönfelder (works council)
		Mr. Bernhard Wurl (German union)
		Mr. Rudolf Kuda (German union)
		Mr. Steven A. Yokich (Am. UAW)

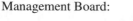

Management Board:

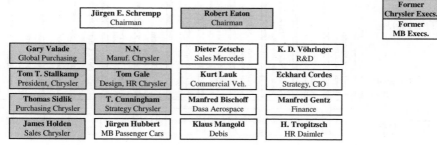

Figure 7.7   Management board and supervisory board of DaimlerChrysler AG
Sources: DaimlerChrysler AG, various newspaper articles.

DaimlerChrysler board. Stephen R. Yokich, president of the American United Auto Workers Union (UAW), initially demanded four seats for representatives from the American and Canadian factories of Chrysler. According to German law, the union can only claim 3 out of the 10 seats for the employees. As the supervisory board could not be enlarged, Yokich realized that his demand for four seats was unrealistic. To solve the problem at least partially, the German metal workers union, IG Metall, gave up one of its seats to allow Yokich to move in. He now represents Chrysler's 74,000 members of the UAW. Yokich stated in public his desire to bring some of the German co-determination practices to America. In addition, his announced goals included unionizing DaimlerChrysler's plant in Tuscaloosa (production site for the Mercedes M-Class) and improving the contracts at Freightliner Trucks, a subsidiary of DaimlerChrysler.

- The board of management of Daimler-Benz AG and the top management of Chrysler have been combined to form the management board of DaimlerChrysler (18 members, although one seat was vacant).
- Schrempp and Eaton serve as co-chairmen of the management board; it was also agreed that Eaton would stay up to three years. At the latest by 2001, Schrempp would be the only chairman.
- The post-merger integration will be handled by an organization shown in Figure 7.8. The structure consists of the chairmen's integration council (CIC), with a total of 8 members and the board of management (10 members). The integration council oversees the post-merger integration phase. It has been left small in order to keep track of progress.

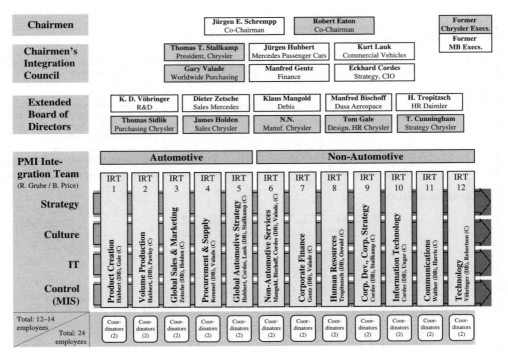

Figure 7.8   Post-merger integration structure of DaimlerChrysler AG
Source: DaimlerChrysler AG.

However, all 17 management board members are involved in the integration. Each member of the management board (except for the chairmen) is responsible for at least one issue resolution team (IRT). These teams are used to identify and realize the synergies between both companies. Each team is jointly run by a management board member from Chrysler and one from Daimler, and they report directly to the CIC. Due to the heavy workload of the board members, each team also has two coordinators who are in close contact with their counterparts from other issue resolution teams. The coordinators form the so-called 'post-merger integration team' and exchange their experiences in the integration process.

Payment of dividends: the parent companies had different approaches to paying out their dividends. In accordance with their national habits, Chrysler paid a quarterly dividend, while Daimler-Benz paid out their dividend only once a year. After the appropriate decision was made at the annual shareholders' meeting, DaimlerChrysler will pay an annual dividend.

Compensation: the differences in absolute amounts and in the structure of the compensation at different levels of the two firms varied markedly. There is a major integration task awaiting DaimlerChrysler in this area. This vast problem can be exemplified with the situation at the top management level. In 1997, Robert Eaton as chairman of Chrysler, earned more than the whole management board of Daimler-Benz combined. Eaton's salary reached almost DM 20 million (DM $1 = \$0.55$), while Schrempp earned only DM 3.5 million (including DM 1 million from stock options). The business combination agreement states that employees would not be worse off, in financial terms, during a transition period of two years. How this aim and the goal to reward equal work with equal pay will be achieved simultaneously is not yet very transparent from the outside. The company has been rather reluctant to divulge many details (refer to Figure 7.9).

Closeness to shareholders: in order to signal to the former shareholders of Chrysler (94% of whom were American before the merger) that the newly formed company would be as close to them as Chrysler had been, a shareholder committee was set up. Both chairmen are members of this committee, in addition to the 10 shareholder representatives from the supervisory board. This composition was chosen to give this new circle some weight in the eyes of the shareholders. The committee will meet every two months. One of its tasks will be to discuss the business strategy directly with the shareholders. (Access to this committee is, of course, open to all shareholders, not only the former Chrysler owners.) Overall, the company wanted to transfer some financial reporting tools from Chrysler. Kopper stated:

> The American reporting system is very concise. The management regularly updates the board on sales, profit levels, extraordinary items, tax, and net income. Moreover, the audit committees in American companies are much more involved in internal audits than their German counterparts.

Condemned to succeed?

The key question at the point of this writing is, of course, what the chances are that the merger will succeed. Nobody will be able to answer this for some time to come. Most observers feel, however, that combining these two companies is a matter of such significance that a failure would have extremely far-reaching consequences.

(Presented by Mr Hilmar Kopper, chairman of the Supervisory Board, Shareholders Meeting 1999)

The new method of remuneration is identical for all members of the Board of Management – irrespective of nationality and location. (...) Total remuneration for the Board of Management is made up of four different components. These are: a basic salary, an annual bonus, the three-year performance plan as a medium-term incentive and stock options or stock appreciation rights as a long-term incentive. The latter three components are the variable elements.

The fundamental component of total remuneration is the basic salary, as all the other elements are related to it. Basic salary was arrived at by comparing with the relevant data of around 15 selected international corporations and also by means of a process of analytical job evaluation. This resulted in differing basic salaries for the individual Board of Management members. In this way the system reflects the differing levels of strategic and operative responsibility of the individual members. In order to ensure that these basic salaries remain competitive, they will be examined every year in the context of the relevant figures for the group of international companies.

The second element of remuneration is the annual bonus. This is a variable cash payment, related to the basic salary and determined by the operating profit achieved by DaimlerChrysler AG. Depending on the particular situation of the company, additional possible goals can be shareholder return and growth in revenues. Furthermore, the Supervisory Board is free to consider other specific performance factors when determining the level of the annual bonus, factors which are not necessarily reflected in the performance of the Group as a whole. In general it is true that the target values for operating profit are determined annually in advance, based on the approved planning.

An element of remuneration that is new for our company is the so-called three-year performance plan or mid-term incentive. The main idea behind this component is that medium-term corporate developments should also be reflected in the level of remuneration. Consequently, the mid-term incentive is linked to the performance goals set by the operative planning for return on capital, return on sales and growth in revenues. Furthermore, the quality of our vehicles and customer satisfaction will also be considered.

The fourth element of remuneration is the stock option as a long-term incentive. Nowadays this is an essential element of any system of remuneration that is to be internationally competitive. We are compelled to design stock option plans according to our national legal system. The current legal situation in Germany since the share law amendment was passed has not quite put an end to the previous uncertainty. For this reason, we have decided at first to award stock appreciation rights for 1999, the design of which is independent of the new share laws. We will have to tackle the new legal situation during the course of this year so that we can present a stock option plan at the Annual General Meeting in the year 2000, a plan which on the one hand can be regarded as internationally competitive and practical, and which on the other hand also fulfills the requirements of German law.

Figure 7.9   Statement on the subject of remuneration for members of the board of management
Source: DaimlerChrysler AG.

7.3   CASE STUDY: DAIMLERCHRYSLER BOARD – AFTER THE DEAL IS DONE

[By Ulrich Steger, Fred Neubauer, and George Raedler]

At the annual shareholder meeting on 19 April 2000, the CEO of DaimlerChrysler AG (DC), Mr Jürgen Schrempp, proudly reported DC's financial results for its first year:

- Revenues up 14% to €150 billion.
- Operating profit up 20% to €10.4 billion.
- Net income up 16% to €6.2 billion.
- Earnings per share up 11% to €6.21.

At the meeting, Schrempp proposed a shareholder dividend of €2.35 per share (refer to Table 7.1 and Figure 7.10 for the financial results). This was among the highest dividend paid by any German company listed on the DAX (the German share price index representing the 50 largest public companies according to market capitalization). Besides the financial success, DC seemed to be on track. The integration had been completed in one year instead of two, and DC had achieved synergies valued at €1.4 billion. Schrempp commented:

Working together has been more demanding than we anticipated. Integration projects made heavy calls on our time and energies. But we got on with our day-to-day business, kept our eye on the ball, and simultaneously set in motion a process of profound change.

Table 7.1 DaimlerChrysler key financial data as of 31 December 1997–1999 (in € million)

	1997	1998	1999	Percentage change (1998/1999)
Revenue	**117,572**	**131,782**	**149,985**	**+14**
European Union	38,449	44,990	49,960	+11
Of which Germany	21,317	24,918	28,393	+14
NAFTA	63,877	72,681	87,083	+20
Of which USA	56,615	65,300	78,104	+20
Other markets	15,246	14,111	12,942	−8
Employees (at year end)	425,649	441,502	466,938	+6
R&D costs	6,501	6,693	7,575	+13
Investments in property, plant, and equipment	8,051	8,155	9,470	+16
Cash provided by operating activities	12,337	16,681	18,023	+8
Operating profit	**6,230**	**8,593**	**11,012**	**+28**
Operating profit (after one-time adjustment)	–	8,583	10,316	+20
Net operating income	4,946	6,359	7,032	+11
Net income	**4,057**	**4,820**	**5,746**	**+19**
Net income per share	4.28	5.03	5.73	+14
Dividend per share	–	2.35	2.35	+/−0

Note: Exchange rate 1€ = US$1.0070 (31 December 1999).
Source: DaimlerChrysler.

Although the Chrysler integration was officially complete and Chrysler was now operating as the 'Chrysler Group' within DC, Schrempp still had to deal with the ever-changing nature of the industry (e-commerce, brand separation, etc.). Further occupying his attention was a letter of intent he had just signed to acquire a 34% stake in Mitsubishi Motors. According to Schrempp, DC was well positioned, but above all, he wondered how to turn around the 40% decline of the stock over the past 12 months.

The auto industry – 'eat lunch or be lunch'

Industry observers commented that the global auto industry had entered the last stage of an endgame situation. Overcapacity, hyper-competition, and value-hungry customers had put incredible pressure on car companies. Some car companies had started to sell out altogether

Mercedes-Benz Passenger Cars & smart mini-car

	1998	1999	Change in %
Operating Profit	1,993	2,703	+36
Revenues	32,587	38,100	+17
Investments in Property, Plant and Equipment	1,995	2,228	+12
R&D	1,930	2,043	+6
Unit Sales	922,795	1,080,267	+17
Employees	95,158	99,459	+5

Chrysler Group (Chrysler, Jeep, Dodge, Plymouth)

	1998	1999	Change in %
Operating Profit (adjusted)	4,255	5,190	+22
Revenues	56,412	64,085	+14
Investments in Property, Plant and Equipment	3,920	5,224	+33
R&D	1,695	2,000	+18
Unit Sales	3,093,716	3,229,270	+4
Employees	126,816	129,395	+2

Commercial Vehicles (MB, Freightliner, Sterling, Setra, Thomas Built Buses)

	1998	1999	Change in %
Operating Profit	946	1,067	+13
Revenues	23,162	26,695	+15
Investments in Property, Plant and Equipment	832	770	−7
R&D	714	827	+16
Unit Sales	489,680	554,929	+13
Employees	89,711	90,082	0

Services (Financial Services, IT Services)

	1998	1999	Change in %
Operating Profit (adjusted)	949	1,026	+8
Revenues	9,987	12,932	+29
Investments in Property, Plant and Equipment	285	324	+14
Employees	21,272	26,240	+23

Aerospace (Commercial, Military, Space, Satellites, Defense and Civil Systems, Aeroengines)

	1998	1999	Change in %
Operating Profit	623	730	+17
Revenues	8,770	9,191	+5
Investments in Property, Plant and Equipment	326	336	+3
R&D	2,047	2,005	−2
Employees	45,858	46,107	1

Others

	1998	1999	Change in %
Operating Profit (adjusted)	(224)	(221)	+1
Revenues	3,526	5,852	+66
Investments in Property, Plant and Equipment	797	588	−26
R&D	307	700	+128
Employees	28,945	41,522	+43

Figure 7.10   Detailed performance overview according to divisions
Source: DaimlerChrysler.

(Volvo), while others moved up-market and full-range (Volkswagen), or formed strategic alliances with bigger manufacturers in order to reap economies of scale (Fiat). After a year of rapid mergers and acquisitions, only six key players had survived (refer to Table 7.2 for an overview of the Big Six).

The survivors in this endgame had announced plans to move increasingly into higher-margin businesses, such as car financing, insurance, and after-sales services, but their individual strategies varied vastly.

Table 7.2 The Big Six

	GM Group	Ford Group	Toyota	Volkswagen Group	DaimlerChrysler	Renault/Nissan
Global market share	24.7% (incl. Fiat)	13.2%	9.8% (incl. Daihatsu)	9.1%	10.5%	8.4%
Production	13.95 million vehicles GM (8.5 million) Fiat (2.7 million) Suzuki (1.65 million) *10% owned by GM* Fuji Heavy (0.6 million) *20% owned by GM* Isuzu (0.5 million) *49% owned by GM*	Ford 7.4 million (including Volvo, Jaguar, Aston Martin) Mazda (0.8 million) *33.4% owned by Ford* Land Rover (0.2 million)	5.5 million vehicles Toyota (4.7 million) Daihatsu (0.7 million)	4.7 million vehicles VW (3.15 million) Audi (0.6 million) Seat (0.5 million) Skoda (0.4 million)	5.8 million vehicles Mercedes (1.1 million) Chrysler (3.2 million) Mitsubishi (1.5 million)	4.7 million vehicles Renault (2.3 million) Nissan (2.45 million) 36.8% *owned by Renault*
Strengths	Massive scale, global reach	Robust profits in North America	Dominant position in Japan, strong in North America	Dominant player in Europe, hot products turning heads in the USA, solid foothold in China	Premier luxury unit in Mercedes-Benz; healthy profits in North America with Chrysler; technical leadership; flair for design	Hot products in Europe
Challenges	Delivering on the potential to boost profitability. Problems at its European subsidiary Opel AG	Weak European and Latin American operations. Needs another Asian Partner	Weak in Europe	Still a bit player in North American market. European profitability undermined by price competition	Making their own merger work; developing a volume presence in Europe; turning around Mitsubishi	Stopping the slide at Nissan

Source: Simison, R.L., White, G.L., and Ball, D. (2000). GM–Fiat deal leaves auto world dominated by six super-groups. *Wall Street Journal Europe*, March 14.

The big American car manufacturers (GM and Ford) were both successful financially in 1999, but had lost market share in Europe. In a move to streamline operations, both companies spun off their component units. Although GM had reported impressive profits of around $5 billion, it had recorded a market share of less than 30% in the USA for two years in a row. The company hoped to overcome its problems in Europe by taking a 20% stake in Fiat, led by the new CEO Richard Wagoner.

Ford had acquired Aston Martin, Jaguar, Volvo, and recently Land Rover, and its strategy for the acquired companies was simple: Ford believed in significantly stretching the brand by moving into lower segments. For example, sales of Jaguar had increased from 23,000 units in 1992 (the first year of Ford's involvement) to 80,000 units in 1999. Jaguar's brand potential was estimated at 200,000 units. In the case of Volvo, sales were expected to increase from 400,000 units in 1999 to around 750,000 units in 2004. In addition, Ford had also acquired Kwik-Fit, a large UK-based car repair chain. However, between 1995 and 1999, the market share of Ford in Western Europe had fallen from 11.6% in 1995 to 9.5%.

Toyota, Japan's premier auto-maker, had been hit hard by the ongoing recession in Japan and had hence focused its resources on international markets. In 1999 the company had record sales both in Europe and North America. Nevertheless, auto analysts had been stunned by the company's announcement, in early 2000, that it planned to start a finance division (offering loans and mortgages to Japanese consumers) and buy a 13% stake in a mobile phone company.

DaimlerChrysler in the endgame

DC reacted to the competitive pressures by streamlining its portfolio.

Non-automotive activities

- The aerospace division (DASA) had been brought into the newly formed European Aeronautic Defence and Space Company (EADS). This company also included the activities of Aerospatiale Matra (France) and CASA (Spain). EADS was going to become the third largest air and space company in the world. DC owned 30% of the total company and had become its largest shareholder. Airbus was the biggest part of EADS, so DC now had to decide whether to approve a decision of the EADS board to invest €12–€14 billion in the new Airbus A3XX plane.
- Debitel (a mobile phone operator) was sold to Swisscom.
- The IT services of debis (DaimlerChrysler Services) entered a joint venture with the IT business of Deutsche Telekom. DC kept the financing division of debis.
- ADTRANZ, the railroad business unit of DC, underwent a massive 'global restructuring program' for its future profitability.

Automotive activities

DC had signed a letter of intent to acquire 34% of Mitsubishi Motors' equity. Due to the minority stake, DC was not required to consolidate any of Mitsubishi Motors' massive debt of €16.75 billion. The acquisition of a stake in Mitsubishi had raised the question of how to 'reap economies of scale'. Newspapers reported that DC did not want to integrate Mitsubishi, rather, it wanted to cooperate with the Japanese company. DC called the cooperation with Mitsubishi Motors an alliance.

Mitsubishi held a 5% stake in Hyundai Motors. Due to the restructuring of the South Korean automotive industry, some executives saw a strategic fit to increase this shareholding. Ford and GM were both very interested in expanding their position in Korea, and declared an interest in the bidding process for Daewoo. Meanwhile, DC announced their acquisition of a 10% stake in Hyundai Motors with an option to increase their stake to 15% after three years.

Mitsubishi was strong in the small car segment. Some shareholders thought that the competence of Mitsubishi Motors in small cars would enable DC to reap economies of scale in the small car segment. This was one of the few growth segments in the auto industry. However, other shareholders worried about diluting profits in this low-cost segment. In 1999, losses at 'smart mini-cars' had been estimated anywhere between €200 and €400 million. DC executives were fast to point out that mini-cars would help DC achieve the Europe-wide self-regulation standard of reducing carbon dioxide emission by 25% between 1995 and 2008. Mr Hilmar Kopper, chairman of the supervisory board, cautioned: 'You have to have a viable strategy, or you are out of business in 2007.'

- Together with Ford and GM, DC had announced plans to start an Internet platform for purchasing parts. The annual purchasing volume of the three companies was estimated at around $246 billion. Shortly after the announcement, the Federal Trade Commission (FTC) raised concerns about price fixing in this 'virtual' purchasing platform. In the meantime, Renault/Nissan and Delphi announced plans to join this platform, called Covisint.
- The arrival of the Internet and the high distribution cost of cars (around 30% of total cost) made manufacturers and dealers very vulnerable. New competitors such as CarsDirect bypassed traditional dealers. Although the share prices of these 'new entrants' had declined significantly, they still posed a threat to the manufacturers. In response, DC appointed e-commerce/e-business managers for both MB and the Chrysler Group as well as on a corporate level.
- Top executives at DC were increasingly concerned about the North American market. In the first quarter of 2000, revenues of the Chrysler Group had risen by 24%, but operating profit had gone down by 7%.
- In the market, there were mixed opinions about the financial aspects of the small car strategy. Moreover, financial analysts were concerned whether MB was able to protect its premium brand and pricing.
- So far, establishing Chrysler in Europe had failed as the existing contracts allowed Chrysler dealers to veto any company-owned dealerships. DC had to initially withdraw from its plan to build 12 Chrysler company-owned dealerships in Germany. Later on, the company reached agreement with its dealers and was able to proceed with establishing company-owned dealers.
- DC remained the world's leading producer of commercial vehicles with 1999 sales of 555,000 units, but the recent merger of Volvo and Renault's truck divisions was likely to increase competitive pressures. For trucks, Asia was still a weak spot and Mitsubishi's truck operations were not included in the deal. Should DC bid for another Asian truck manufacturer?
- For the three years up to 2003, DC planned to invest €50 billion in new products. The company was rumored to have 60 new models in the pipeline within the next five years.

Schrempp explained:

> We achieved a lot over the past five years. What was a 'technology conglomerate' with 35 subsidiaries is now a strategically well-positioned company. The former holding structure is now a 'World AG' and sets the benchmark in many industries. Our vision of becoming a global player is turning into reality with our planned strategic alliance with Mitsubishi.

Due to the strategic moves towards the core product 'automobiles', analysts tended to value DC like a typical North American car company.

Corporate governance

Because DaimlerChrysler was incorporated in Germany, it had to maintain the management and supervisory boards while satisfying shareholder pressure on both sides of the Atlantic. Corporate governance was organized as follows.

- *Board of management.* In a September 1999 restructuring, this board had been reduced from 17 to 14 members and the responsibilities had been shuffled. Mr Robert Eaton, the co-chairman, left DC on 31 March 2000 and hence 13 board members remained (refer to Figure 7.11 for the new management board). The management board met either in New York or Stuttgart.
- *Supervisory board.* Besides adding one ordinary meeting (so there were now five instead of four), the supervisory board dealt more with strategic issues. The supervisory board discussed and defined action categories (a catalogue thereof), which were subject to approval by the supervisory board in addition to the legal requirements (refer to Figure 7.12 for the members of the supervisory board).

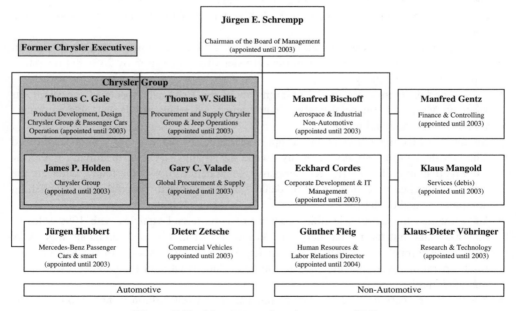

Figure 7.11   Management board structure of DC
Source: DaimlerChrysler (as of 1 April 2000).

Capital Side	Employee Representation
Hilmar Kopper (Chairman) Chairman of the Supervisory Board of Deutsche Bank AG	**Erich Klemm (Deputy Chairman)** Chairman of the Corporate Works Council, DC AG and Group
Robert E. Allen Retired Chairman of the Board and CEO of AT&T Corp.	**Willi Böhm** Member of the Works Council; Wörth Truck Plant
Sir John P. Browne CEO of British Petroleum (BP) Amoco plc.	**Manfred Göbels** Chairman of the Management Representative Committee, DC Group
Robert J. Lanigan Chairman Emeritus of Owens-Illinois, Inc.	**Rudolf Kuda** Retired Head of Department, Executive Council, German Metalworkers' Union
Peter A. Magowan Retired Chairman of the Board of Safeway, Inc. President and Managing Partner of SF Giants	**Helmut Lense** Chairman of the Works Council, Untertürkheim Passenger Car Plant
Dr. Manfred Schneider Chairman of the Management Board of Bayer AG	**Gerd Rheude** Chairman of the Works Council, Wörth Truck Plant
G. Richard Thoman President and CEO of Xerox Corporation	**Herbert Schiller** Chairman of the Corporate Works Council, debis AG
Bernhard Walter Chairman of the Management Board of Dresdner Bank AG	**Peter Schönfelder** Chairman of the Works Council, DC Aerospace
Lynton R. Wilson Chairman of the Board of BCE Inc.	**Bernhard Wurl** IG Metall, Head of Department, Exec. Council German Metalworkers' Union
Dr. Mark Wössner Chairman of the Supervisory Board of Bertelsmann AG	**Stephen P. Yokich** President of United Auto Workers (UAW)

Figure 7.12 Members of the supervisory board of DaimlerChrysler
Source: DaimlerChrysler (as of 1 January 2000).

- *Shareholder committee.* This committee, a first in Germany, consisted of the 10 members from the capital side of the current DC supervisory board plus 4 former members of the previous boards (Daimler-Benz AG/Chrysler Corp.). The shareholder committee met on the day before each supervisory board meeting plus another twice. This committee discussed aspects of the financial markets, and paid particular attention to the stock price development (refer to Figure 7.13 for trends in the stock price) and recommendations from analysts. Moreover, some of Chrysler's traditional board issues (product quality) were also discussed.

From its peak of €102 on the day of the merger announcement (7 May 1998), the share had fallen to as low as €57.90 in early June 2000

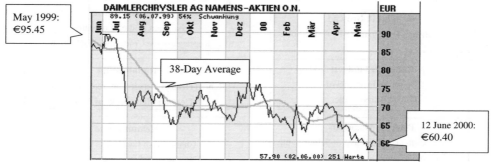

Relative performance of General Motors, Ford Motor, and DaimlerChrysler, indexed, at 26 October 1998

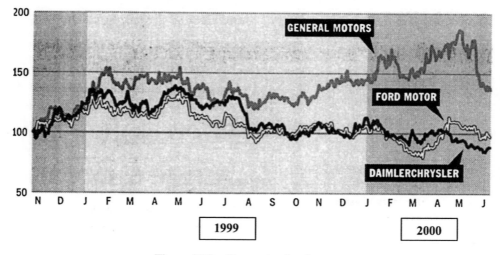

Figure 7.13   Share price development
Source: Comdirect/Teledata; Datastream.

- *Other committees*. DC also maintained a financial audit committee and presidential committee. Both committees were headed by Mr Hilmar Kopper and Mr Erich Klemm (of the works council). The presidential committee was responsible for compensation issues in relation to the board of management and discussed various questions of corporate governance.
- At the annual meeting, several shareholders complained about the new stock option plan valued at €6 billion. The plan entitled the 6500 top managers to exercise their options after the share increased by 20%. Shareholders wanted the plan to be benchmarked against industry indices.

As the supervisory board prepared to discuss the allocation of the investment budgets, they knew that their shareholders also expected record profits in the future. Schrempp's plan for the future was simple: 'We want to become the Number One car company in the world.' In the process, DC combined corporate governance practices from the USA and Germany. The model became a benchmark for other European companies, but was there any chance for DC to obtain higher valuations than traditional car companies?

Corporate Governance in and with Subsidiaries

[By Ulrich Steger, Jochen Brellochs, and Wolfgang Amann]

8.1 TENSION FIELDS AND CENTRAL ISSUES

The wave of corporate governance scandals – and the regulations that have resulted from them – have brought about many changes that have fundamentally improved listed multinationals' governance systems. But what about multinationals' numerous subsidiaries? How good is their governance? Must they change too? Subsidiary governance, which is a more recent challenge on company agendas, encompasses everything not covered by traditional corporate governance, as the latter only addresses the boards of group headquarters and their connections to the outside world.

Multinational groups operate through networks of globally dispersed subsidiaries. In large multinationals, the total number of subsidiaries can be very high indeed: groups like Siemens or DaimlerChrysler in Germany, Total in France, or ABB in Switzerland easily have approximately 1000 legally independent entities. This leads to several key subsidiary governance issues.

Firstly, while subsidiaries are run by their own management teams, corporate governance problems always first impact the group headquarters negatively. In a best-case scenario, this 'only' involves reputational damage. The worst case is far more frightening, as exemplified by Dutch Royal Ahold whose overseas subsidiaries falsely declared profits to the tune of US$500 million. This led to the insolvency of the group as a whole. Clearly, subsidiary governance issues can substantially threaten an entire group's success and financial health.

Secondly, subsidiaries often comprise the lion's share of a group's assets, turnover, and financial success. When problems emerge at subsidiary level, headquarters cannot just divest and acquire a new investment. We examined a Scandinavian pharmaceutical multinational that had a strategically important product trapped in an early development phase in an overseas R&D joint venture. The local board could not handle the dilemma, but the project was too important and the capital invested too substantial to disregard.

Finally, there is also the issue of ethical obligation: subsidiaries are group headquarters' investments on behalf of their shareholders. It is therefore part of the group management's responsibility to ensure good subsidiary corporate governance with its associated costs and benefits. Local environmental issues are a case in point.

The core of the dilemma is clear: the headquarters must achieve subsidiary compliance (i.e., the subsidiary management's compliance with the headquarters' interest). It is, however, surprising that neither group headquarters nor outside investors have as yet addressed subsidiary governance. At the headquarter level, the scandals and new regulations of the past few years have led to a shift towards the checks-and-balances governance model – which has not happened at the subsidiary level.

The reasons for this include:

- Subsidiary shares are normally not publicly traded and their share price cannot fall due to bad governance. Institutional investors and shareholder activists are moreover not yet demanding improvements in subsidiary governance.
- Subsidiaries are subject to far fewer governance regulations: they are mostly not stock corporations but 'limited' in their form; they are also not subject to public listing regulations. Consequently, most subsidiaries are not subject to the majority of present-day corporate governance regulations. Furthermore, in times when compliance with regulations often requires entire teams of experts, there is little time for additional efforts.
- Finally, group headquarters as well as group shareholders (largely erroneously) believe that subsidiary governance is addressed by subsidiaries' management.

Ultimately, subsidiary corporate governance simply emerged and grew over time, although it has not necessarily improved over the past few years. Three basic subsidiary governance models are found in practice, each of which is differentiated by differences in ownership and the nature of the local boards:

1. There is a supervisory board that controls and supervises subsidiary management. This model is mostly found in joint ventures and subsidiaries with multiple owners (e.g., investments in China and India).
2. There is a subsidiary board but its role is purely formal – a 'rubber-stamp board'. Such boards, often required by law, only deal with official issues such as the legally required reporting.
3. In the third model – the one most frequently found in practice – there is no board. A board is not required by law, the headquarters prefers a 'no frills' approach, and direct interaction with the subsidiary's management.

Overall, subsidiary corporate governance differs greatly from efficient, 'classic' headquarters corporate governance. Figure 8.1 summarizes the subsidiary governance systems found in multinationals.

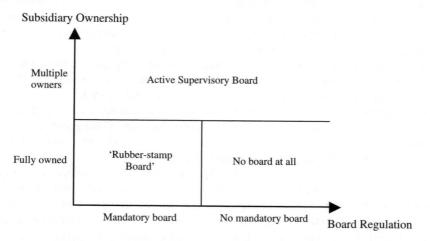

Figure 8.1   Subsidiary governance systems in multinationals

It would appear that the most common subsidiary model is also the most problematic: the subsidiary is fully owned and there is no active supervisory board. The task at hand for multinationals is to solve this subsidiary governance dilemma and improve the quality of subsidiary governance. We next outline ways to achieve this, as well as providing concrete examples.

Recommendations for subsidiary governance

The key question in subsidiary governance is the nature of the relationship between group headquarters and subsidiary management. It is important to bear in mind that there can be no 'one-size-fits-all' approach. Since the characteristics and needs of subsidiaries differ, so too do their governance systems. Key questions that could highlight contingency factors within subsidiary characteristics include: How big is the company? How important is corporate governance to its inner life? Decisions also become more complex when there are numerous stakeholders.

Clear competences and responsibilities must therefore be in place. In respect of the subsidiary environment, aspects like shareholder rights and managerial liability are crucial from the legal side. From the business side, the governance atmosphere and the host country's culture must be taken into account.

In principle, group organizational capacity should offer subsidiaries the benefit of possibilities and options, including subsidiary governance mechanisms. Headquarters can, for example, employ expatriates as subsidiary managers at any point in time, or it can implement a subsidiary compliance bonus system for subsidiary management, which should help create subsidiary management adherence. Overall, group corporate culture is without a doubt the most important subsidiary governance mechanism, and the goals of corporate governance must be integrated and professionalized throughout the group. Every employee must know which goals, ethics, and managerial behavior are desirable and which are not. Specific measures to achieve this could include inviting subsidiary managers to attend governance workshops at the headquarters, or introducing specific subsidiary manager meetings. Private equity funds also implement subsidiary governance manuals (i.e., written standards to help ensure that the local management meets their expectations).

There is therefore no point in expecting general solutions to specific problems. The best governance approach on paper cannot provide good results if it does not match the subsidiary's attributes and that of its local environment. If, for example, the subsidiary environment is complex and challenging, the local management needs more independence. If the subsidiary also faces serious legal challenges in that environment, however, business principles and codes of governance are required. The subsidiary environment includes factors like group organization, positioning, and timeous reporting. One underestimates these factors at one's peril. The group headquarters must shape this subsidiary environment to achieve the best results.

Ultimately, the big picture indicates a strategy: only an overarching, strategic approach that frames the subsidiary governance concept within a larger context makes sense. Punctiform, or 'spots-in-the-dark' approaches are risky, and the next step must be to provide the missing link between corporate governance and corporate strategy.

This means that larger multinationals have to search more intensively for all-encompassing solutions (e.g., group-wide expert teams), while smaller groups can achieve much by simply re-engineering their group organization. The golden rule is: individual adaptations where necessary, and group-wide standardization where possible. The particularities of individual subsidiaries are therefore not necessarily weaknesses. If, for example, a local subsidiary board has been mandated, why not use it for governance purposes? The boards of joint ventures demonstrate just how significant supervisory board contributions can be. The best solution, rather than tight control and supervision, could well be local independence and responsibility.

Subsidiary governance's final imperative is to manage expectations. In theory, headquarters should know exactly what is going on in all its subsidiaries, but this is not necessarily the case in practice. Complete information and complete control are worth striving for but are hardly realistic; if, for whatever reason, they are unachievable, alternative solutions are required. Where, for example, a local CEO dominates the board and makes information inaccessible to the group, regaining local control will be very difficult. In this case, governance risks must be transferred to the local level, also legally if necessary. Options include drafting a subsidiary code of governance and conduct as well as expanding local management's responsibility through contract expansion (all key people would be required to sign and commit to it). All relevant group stakeholders would need to be made aware of this, in case problems emerge. If problems do emerge, swift investigation and prosecution – as well as transparent communication with company externals – can prevent the escalation of subsidiary governance issues into the group as a whole.

Learning nuggets from the cases

Subsidiary governance is part and parcel of corporate governance, and the next step in multinationals' governance evolution is to drive value-adding governance throughout all levels. Consequently, subsidiary governance, similar to traditional corporate governance, must protect the subsidiary shareholders as well as the headquarters. Owing to its importance, subsidiary governance requires a group-wide, strategic, and long-term approach with both individual and general solutions. Particularities need to be considered, without forgetting the complexity that the group headquarters faces in managing the entire organization. Finally, expectations and subsidiary stakeholders need to be considered when addressing subsidiary governance.

The following case study, that of a research and development joint venture involving a large multinational, sheds light on a number of subsidiary governance aspects.

Suggested further reading

Gillies, J. and Dickinson, M. (1999). The governance of transnational firms: some preliminary hypotheses. *Corporate Governance – An International Review*, pp. 237–247.

Kim, B., Prescott, J.E., and Kim, S.-M. (2005). Differentiated governance of foreign subsidiaries in transnational corporations: an agency theory perspective. *Journal of International Management* **11**: 43–66.

Steger, U. and Brellochs, J. (2006). Herding your subsidiaries towards good governance. *Financial Times*, Mastering Financial Management Series, Issue 2, pp. 2–3, June 2.

Strikwerda, J. (2003). An entrepreneurial model of corporate governance: devolving power to subsidiary boards. *Corporate Governance – An International Review* **3**(2): 38–57.

8.2   CASE STUDY: PHARMAGROUP INT. AND FLUVERA – WHEN SUBSIDIARY GOVERNANCE MEANS LOSING COMPETITIVE GROUND

[Ulrich Steger, Jochen Brellochs, and Wolfgang Amann]

In July 2006, the management of the German pharmaceutical giant Pharmagroup Int. pre-pared for its last meeting before a short summer break. The meeting, to be held at the company's Stuttgart headquarters, was a crucial one. Despite enormous efforts, the company had failed to gain control over what was considered to be the most important investment in a long time. Pharmagroup had developed the first efficient serum to immunize poultry and other animals against the dangerous influenza virus H5N1. But more than that, Pharmagroup had teamed up with US-based Biovent to develop a revolutionary new system, Fluvera – a hand-held device that farmers could use themselves to quickly vaccinate their threatened livestock and prevent the virus from spreading! For Pharmagroup, Fluvera was the most strategic product in its pipeline. Its presence on the market could put a halt to a poten-tial global pandemic for poultry and, hence, prevent the virus from spreading to humans. Its financial success promised billions. However, the project seemed to have come to a standstill.

Since the beginning of the R&D joint venture with Biovent in 1998, there had been numerous problems: development was troublesome, timelines were postponed, and com-munication between the partners worsened. In 2003 Pharmagroup's only solution turned out to be the full acquisition and integration of the Fluvera operations as a subsidiary. And it was about time: Kaufmann Medical, Pharmagroup's toughest competitor, was expected to launch its comparable 'InfluAid' vaccination system within the next 12 to 18 months.

The Pharmagroup managers worried: governing a subsidiary had never been an issue so far, but this project had been troublesome from the start. The goal was clear: timely and controlled, but also efficient, completion of the Fluvera development and market launch. But how could this be achieved without strict control from Germany that would prob-ably impede the innovative work of the US-based scientists, the key to the product's success?

Pharmagroup Int. – forerunner in influenza treatment

Headquartered in the south of Germany, Pharmagroup was of notable size in the pharmaceu-tical industry with international production facilities and customers in numerous countries. The group looked back on a proud tradition and is one of the forerunners in the study of – and research on – influenza vaccination. The company grew quickly in the 20th century and strengthened its international position by a merger in the 1990s. It achieved a global turnover of around €4 billion in 2005 (net income €200 million), half of which was generated in Europe, another 25% in North America, and the rest in Asia-Pacific. In 2006 Pharmagroup maintained subsidiaries on every continent and employed around 21,000 employees. Growth was stable and by far the most important source of revenue came from influenza treatment, representing more than 50% of the company's global turnover. Pharmagroup was listed on the German stock exchange in Frankfurt.

Influenza products – a 'market of the future'

Influenza, or 'flu', is an infectious disease caused by the influenza virus, which is hosted in birds and poultry. It is spread by droplet infection and attacks the respiratory tract.[1] Symptoms start 24 to 48 hours after the virus enters the body. While common influenza is a fairly mild illness with symptoms such as fever, a sore throat, runny nose, and cough, real influenza can be serious and sometimes fatal among frail and elderly people. The flu vaccine is recommended for those at risk, but its effectiveness is highly variable.

The most important factor is the mutability of the virus, which means that a particular flu vaccine formulation gives protection for no more than a few years. The World Health Organization (WHO) recommends appropriate contents of the vaccine each year regarding the most likely strains of the virus that will probably attack the following year. Still, the greatest threat posed by influenza is that of a human pandemic. In the 20th century alone, three such pandemics have occurred in Europe. The most well known, Spanish Flu (H1N1), occurred in 1918/1919, infecting more than 500 million people and killing more than 40 million. Each time a pandemic has occurred, it has been as a result of a major genetic change in the influenza virus – which is exactly what happened in 2003, when the highly pathogenic H5N1 influenza virus appeared in Southeast Asia.

H5N1 led to the death of countless birds throughout Southeast Asia. It spread through migrating wild birds all over the world and led to the killing of more than 33 million birds and poultry in Europe alone in 2003.[2] It also affected pigs and other mammals, including, to everyone's horror, humans. Once humans are infected, the disease follows an aggressive course with symptoms including high fever, vomiting, abdominal pains, and bleeding from the nose and gums, and ultimately leads to death.[3] Then, H5N1 disappeared but originated again in China in 2005, spreading across the migratory routes of birds worldwide. It arrived in Russia in July 2005, in Turkey in October, and in Germany, Israel, and the UK by April 2006 (refer to Figure 8.2).

H5N1 is highly fatal and led to 148 deaths since its emergence, where the last human death was reported from Indonesia in July 2006.[4] It is not well researched and understood so far, and it represents the major pandemic threat to humans today (refer to Figure 8.3). The WHO, on global pandemic alert, warns:

> The risk of pandemic influenza is serious. With the H5N1 virus now firmly entrenched in large parts of Asia, the risk that more human cases will occur will persist. Each additional human case gives the virus an opportunity to improve its transmissibility in humans, and thus develop into a pandemic strain.[5]

If such a global pandemic should occur, UN and WHO estimate the number of possible human casualties between 5 and 150 million worldwide.[6] But even in a normal year, influenza kills between 250,000 and 500,000 people. And there is only one product against H5N1 on the

[1] World Health Organization, www.who.int/mediacentre/factsheets/avian_influenza/en, 17.7.2006.
[2] Bird Flu Statistics 1959–2003, *Medical News Today*, http://www.medicalnewstoday.com/medicalnews.php?newsid=6306, 3.3.2004.
[3] Avian influenza fact sheet, World Health Organization, 17.07.2006, p. 4.
[4] Avian influenza – situation in Indonesia – update 22, World Health Organization, 14.07.2006.
[5] World Health Organization, Avian influenza frequently asked questions, 17.7.2006, p. 4.
[6] United Nations Press Conference by UN System Coordinator for Avian and Human Influenza, David Nabarro, http://www.un.org/News/briefings/docs/2005/050929_Nabarro.doc.htm, 29.9.2005.

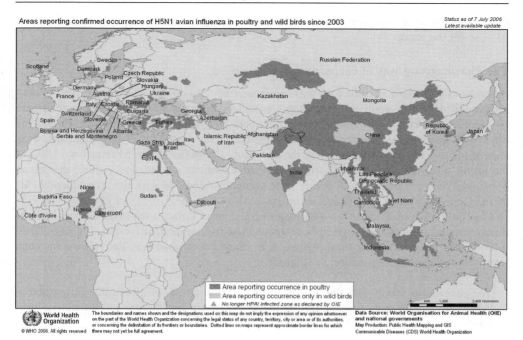

Figure 8.2   World Health Organization global H5N1 spread
Source: World Health Organization, 17.7.2006.

Inter-pandemic phase	Low risk of human cases	1
New virus in animals, no human cases	Higher risk of human cases	2
Pandemic alert	No or very limited human-to-human transmission	3
New virus causes human cases	Evidence of increased human-to-human transmission	4
	Evidence of significant human-to-human transmission	5
Pandemic	Evidence of sustained human-to-human transmission	6

Figure 8.3   World Health Organization influenza pandemic phases
Source: World Health Organization, 17.7.2006.

market, a pill marketed by a Swiss pharmaceutical group. Although it is low-efficiency (i.e., limits symptoms only), the Swiss are unable to meet market demand: pandemic stockpiling by governments led to further sales increases of 37% again in 2005, and Swiss production capacities were increased 10-fold since 2003. Overall, the influenza vaccination market is estimated to grow from $1.6 billion to $3 billion by 2010.[7] Consequently, Pharmagroup's

---

[7] Pandemic threat reignites influenza vaccine market, Pharmaceutical Business Review Online, 20.04.2006.

Fluvera would be a huge step away from a global pandemic and an equally huge financial success for the group.

The Pharmagroup way of corporate governance

Pharmagroup's board of directors was composed of 20 people, who carried the overall responsibility for the group, with Matthias Gering (65, grandson of the founder) as chairman. As per German law, half of these board members were employee representatives and the other half shareholders. The executive management team, made up of five members, took care of the day-to-day management of the company. Dr Stefan Heim (51) had been CEO of the group since October 2001. Pharmagroup had a two-tier governance system, that is, no one could be a member of both bodies. The company complied with the recommendations of the German Code of Corporate Governance.

The company took pride in its 'Pharmagroup Business Values', the codified backbone of the group and symbol of the group's determination for comprehensiveness and excellence in corporate governance. In these values, subsidiary governance was determined for each legally independent group entity, as follows:

> We govern our group with the goal of aligning the interests of all entities (in particular subsidiaries) with those of the group headquarters, while considering and respecting local interests.

And furthermore:

> Each Pharmagroup unit must have a clear definition of purpose, accountabilities and decision powers and constantly work on steps to achieve further performance improvement. (. . .) Each unit manager must establish, maintain and manage procedures in his/her unit in order to live up to respective laws, regulation, and other relevant non-legal commitments.

The business values also aimed at employee representation, strong commitment to social issues, and improving the living conditions of its customers. Since its foundation, the company actively contributed to its local and international environments and donated considerable amounts every year to NGO research on specific global health issues.

Vaccination by self-administration – Biovent's business case

Biovent, a US-based biotech start-up founded in the 1990s, developed drug delivery systems, such as those used by patients for self-administration. Hence, Biovent began the development of the Fluvera system, which consisted of the injector device itself and little flasks containing the vaccination serum. The vaccination was delivered by a subdermal injection and was commonly painless. The device was reusable and could be used for countless applications and drugs and, in particular, was suitable for use by individuals with no medical background, for example, for diabetics injecting insulin. Fluvera, therefore, had the potential to revolutionize the treatment of avian influenza, since farmers could use the device to protect their threatened livestock.

Like many start-ups, Biovent had difficulties in financing the commonly long product-development phase, which for Fluvera was estimated at 10 years before it could be launched onto the market. Biovent realized that completing the development independently would be financially impossible. Pharmagroup, for its part, was determined to invest in new drug delivery technologies and was eager to invest in existing R&D efforts to win time against competitors.

Pharmagroup–Biovent cooperation

In 1998, Biovent entered into a contractual joint venture agreement with Pharmagroup. The aim was to develop Fluvera together until its marketing. The project was managed on Pharmagroup's side from the Stuttgart headquarters and by Biovent on location in the USA. Consequently, the Fluvera operations were run independently by Biovent, but the R&D progress was reviewed periodically by Pharmagroup in Stuttgart. Everything seemed to go well at first.

However, around 2000 the first signs of problems appeared: R&D development deadlines demanded by Pharmagroup were not met by Biovent, and communication was impeded by these and other problems. The management and working style of the young US start-up, which was still run by its founders, now conflicted with Pharmagroup's Germanic leadership approach. The main issue was the step from a functioning Fluvera prototype to a device suitable for mass production. In brief, the complexity and risk involved in the Fluvera project began to worry Pharmagroup and the project's success became increasingly threatened.

The problems culminated in 2003, when the H5N1 virus emerged again, and a mandatory Fluvera test trial had to be ended early. The successful conclusion of this test phase would have meant launching the product about 12 to 18 months later. And competitors had made good progress with comparable devices and announced positive results. The biggest threat came from Kaufmann Medical and its comparable vaccination system called 'InfluAid'. But with the existing arrangement, Pharmagroup felt it could not change anything. So, at a quarterly R&D evaluation at the Stuttgart headquarters, the Pharmagroup management was determined to act.

The acquisition of Biovent's Fluvera operations

There seemed to be only one solution left – full control over all operations. Knowing Biovent's financial needs, Pharmagroup would acquire the whole Fluvera program (manufacturing equipment, buildings, and so on) and establish a new US subsidiary. The agreement was announced in December 2003 and the deal cost Pharmagroup $70 million. Biovent's CEO, Dr Minder, commented:

> Biovent will henceforth no longer be responsible for any costs until commercialization, estimated at around $100 million over several years. We will continue to have a long-term interest in the device with a 5% royalty on all future earnings from Fluvera. It is a very positive step from Pharmagroup to acquire the operations and still allow us that share of future revenues, particularly as no concrete timeline until market launch is foreseeable.

Biovent's financial future was secured, but the return on investment that Pharmagroup's managers had promised their shareholders was not yet in sight. They had to make sure that now, being in full control, they got Fluvera onto the market as soon as possible! In January 2004, Pharmagroup Delivery Technologies (PDT) was established in the USA in the same location as Biovent. Its sole objective was to develop the Fluvera system and it was positioned under Pharmagroup's US sales organization (refer to Figure 8.4). PDT took over

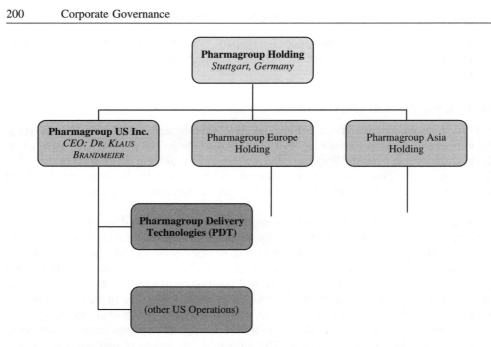

Figure 8.4 The Pharmagroup group organization and US operations

all 200 Biovent employees working on the Fluvera project. A local board was implemented and the CEO of Pharmagroup's US operations, Dr Klaus Brandmeier, became its chairman. The other board members were a controller from Pharmagroup US, PDT's CEO Erwin Fryer, and an employee representative from Biovent. The day-to-day management was taken care of by an executive committee composed of six people (refer to Figure 8.5), headed by its CEO, Erwin Fryer, a former Biovent manager.

This preliminary board's task was to take control over the Fluvera operations, facilitate integration of the entity into the group, and – of capital importance – re-establish confidence in the project's success, both in Stuttgart and with the local scientists in the USA. After all, it was these scientists and their creativity that were the key to Fluvera's development success.

Pharmagroup in control – getting Fluvera to the market

When announcing the Fluvera acquisition, Pharmagroup CEO Dr Heim said:

> We are confident to have made the right move with the acquisition and that the transition will be smooth and both Pharmagroup and Biovent will benefit from the new structure.

But in the course of the next few months, the transition had still not been concluded and a timely completion of the Fluvera development was far from certain. There were successes, for example in July 2005 positive testing results were announced, which suggested that the Fluvera device was found suitable for the quick short-time delivery necessary for H5N1 vaccinations. But to identify a course timeline until market launch was still not possible.

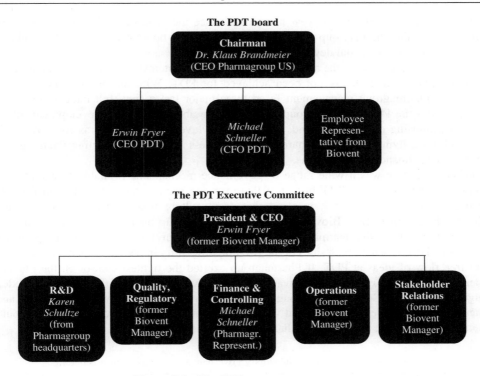

Figure 8.5   The PDT governance structure

Pharmagroup's chief research officer, Dr Ruppen, reported after one of his visits to the US firm:

> When we asked them to streamline the Fluvera prototype to get it ready for mass production, they came back with a completely new system again. And this one was even more complex than the one before!

In the meantime, competitors had been busy: Kaufmann Medical's vaccination system InfluAid was recommended for use by the US health authorities in October 2005 and by the European Medicines Evaluation Agency in November 2005. Experts now expected InfluAid to be on the market in the next 12 to 18 months. Now, in summer 2006, Fluvera was still one important clinical testing phase behind Kaufmann, exactly where it had been in 2003, when Biovent had to stop testing. It seemed at first that technical problems were to blame, but of rather a simple nature and not the sort of mistakes that happened to a quality leader like Pharmagroup. Clearly, Pharmagroup had fallen behind in conquering this lucrative market.

Designing subsidiary governance for PDT

Over the years, Pharmagroup had gradually built up its control over the Fluvera development from a mere contractual joint venture to a fully owned overseas subsidiary. Product development took place in PDT, a subsidiary held by Pharmagroup's US sales organization (refer to Figure 8.4). Over one year had passed since the acquisition, but the issues were still the same: the Pharmagroup representatives on the local board had 'no traction', and had little influence on the actual development of Fluvera.

Subsidiary governance – the alignment of subsidiaries' interests and aims with their head-quarters' goals – had clearly not been achieved for PDT. With the preliminary board in place, the Pharmagroup management faced three major tasks: first, full integration of the business into the Pharmagroup group in order to be able to steer the development into a success-promising direction; second, finishing the Fluvera development as soon as possible; and third, living up to the 'Pharmagroup Business Values' and meeting Pharmagroup shareholders' financial expectations.

Of course, there was a wide range of governance mechanisms available to control and coordinate (refer to Table 8.1); in fact, if Pharmagroup wanted, they could fire all Biovent managers in a second! But it was not that easy: culture was a success factor for the Fluvera development (i.e., Biovent's entrepreneurial start-up methods now conflicted with the working style of the pharmaceutical giant from Germany). Confidence in the project's success had decreased on both sides of the Atlantic; insecurity impeded efficiency, creativity, and free flow of ideas at PDT. If Pharmagroup exerted the tightest control on the Fluvera operations now, the rest of the innovative and creative environment the scientists needed might be destroyed. So could the strong influence from Stuttgart even work? PDT board and management were clearly crucial, but which competencies should they have? What should their composition be, and should it change after a transition phase?

Table 8.1   Selection of subsidiary governance mechanisms in practice

Governance mechanism	Characteristics/operation mode
Subsidiary supervisory board	Influence in strategic planning, performance monitoring, etc.
Personal supervision by HQ management	Visits to the subsidiary, production site inspection
Centralization of competences	Level of local decision-making competences, 'freedom' degree
Planning	E.g. budgeting, target costing, scheduling
Performance reporting to HQ	Analysis and evaluation of subsidiary data or reports
Employment of expatriates in key subsidiary positions	Direct monitoring of actions and behaviors in the subsidiary; also, transfer of values and culture into subsidiary
Incentives for subsidiary management	Rewards directly linked to subsidiary performance aims
Formalization, standardization	Written guidelines, rules, standard processes, etc.
Socialization/corporate culture	Employee transfer, executive training, rewards

On 15 July 2006, the US drug authority surprisingly revoked its approval of InfluAid and announced another six-month reviewing period. It seemed that, by chance, Pharmagroup had been granted some more time. Entering the management board meeting room in Stuttgart, the Pharmagroup managers knew they would need every second of it. . .

Corporate Governance in Developed vs. Emerging Markets

9.1 THE WILD, WILD EAST? THE WILD, WILD SOUTH?

In the previous chapters we have outlined that the main tasks, challenges, and dilemmas of CG lead to patterns that recur rather independently of different countries' specific legal settings. When trying to solve them, one has to bear these differences in mind to better understand where each board comes from. We thus caution that individual country settings should not be evaluated or even discarded due to their particularities or possible and likely differences. The main goal is to create a high-performance upper echelon and governance system. This diversity among systems has often been deemed too complex, which is why the international investment community has been pushing hard for convergence efforts, which would reduce the local diversity and render systems more understandable. There has been progress with this convergence, while substantial differences still remain. In the following, we outline and compare where the main countries or country cluster systems come from and compare them with a typical developing economy situation. We will review these systems based on examples from the USA, UK, Germany, France, the Scandinavian countries, Japan, and a typical emerging country. The dimensions for the comparisons include shareholder influence, the roles and structure of boards in relation to the top management, regulations, and employee influence. Subsequently, two case studies illustrate how these specific CG traits matter in real life.

Basic features of corporate governance systems: USA

Shareholder influence	Little, as institutional investors, who dominate the stock market, mainly stay passive (to avoid becoming an 'insider'), despite some activities by shareholder activists, low importance of general assembly (e.g., new proposal for directors only after a proxy fight), non-binding votes, but legal leverage via liability suits, low barriers for takeover despite many takeover bills
Board	Central organ, represents the company, all major decisions need to pass the board (who can decide to ask the general assembly for approval), recently, a majority of independent, non-executive members in approximately 75% of S&P500: CEO and chairman of the board united
Top management	Strong position of the CEO, leads to very personal accountability, in recent years shrinking tenure, next in line: CFO, dominant background: business/finance, high degree of variable compensation (e.g., in the form of stock options), even though the relation to increased, long-term performance is questionable, often 'golden parachute' as personal protection against job risks

(Continued)	
Regulation	Sweeping changes through Sarbanes–Oxley Act, focused on transparency/reporting and compliance, strengthening of independent auditing (both external and internal). Incorporation laws: state (dominant: Delaware), therefore Federal law tilted towards trading shares (opposite: UK)
Employees	No significant influence of organized labor or institutionalized employee involvement in corporate governance

Basic features of corporate governance systems: UK

Shareholder influence	Similar to USA (both have highly developed capital markets, leading to dispersed ownership, but now dominant role of institutional investors), shareholder rights somewhat stronger than in USA, especially of approval rights in general assembly
Board	Central organ, similar to the USA, but in most cases role of chairman and CEO are separated, majority of independent, non-executive directors, leading to a 'checks and balances' system vs. the CEO-centered US system, extensive description of role of board and directors through the 'Combined Code' (outcome of various Royal Commissions)
Top management	CEO generally not as strong as in the USA, weaker personal accountability, important role of CFO, dominant background: business/finance/liberal arts, high degree of variable compensation, more diversity than in continental Europe
Regulation	'Arms-length', a lot of 'soft regulation' (e.g., 'Combined Code' with principles, deviations should be explained: 'comply or explain'), weak takeover barriers, increasing influence of European regulation
Employees	No significant influence of organized labor or institutionalized employee involvement in corporate governance

Basic features of corporate governance systems: Germany

Shareholder influence	Greater, as many 'block holders' exert considerable influence (but mostly without multiple voting rights), and growing disentanglement of cross-shareholdings and bank holdings, but still little influence of institutional investors due to shortage of stock market tradition and risk-averse retail investors, rights of minority shareholders significantly improved (EU-Standard)
Board	Split into supervisory board and board of management as central organs, supervisory board approves more than initiates items, often regulated in detail in the corporate by-laws, on average larger size (due to co-determination), usually strong position of the chairman, the chairman's committee (which approves top management compensation and contracts), and the audit committee (except in the USA, not a new development), often pre-meeting of shareholder and employee representatives
Top management	Board of management can take binding decisions for corporations (even when supervisory board does not approve), legally a collegial body, but especially in global companies, the CEO is often more than the 'first among equals', dominant technical background of management, but the role of CFO has increased, recently more performance-based payment (but less use of the stock options)

Regulation	As always in Germany, pretty detailed, although often based on EU directives, but not as bureaucratic as Sarbanes–Oxley, recently increasing use of codes, stock market listing requirements, etc., low liability risk
Employees	Unique system of co-determination: 50% of members of the supervisory board are employee representatives including union representatives, the chairman has a casting vote. Problem: representatives are only elected by German employees, no other country has introduced a similar far-reaching system, but no empirical evidence of limited competitiveness of German companies. In addition: Works Council as partner for management of social and HR affairs, but no wage negotiations

Basic features of corporate governance systems: France

Shareholder influence	Considerable, as many big companies have block holders with multiple voting rights, influenced by the government (declining, but still visible especially in pre-election times), increasing minority shareholder and transparency rights through the EU influence; growing foreign shareholding, mainly by institutional investors, leading to conflicts between block holders and minority investors (relatively to, e.g., Benelux and Germany) as general assemblies were previously mere formalities
Board	Option to go for one-tier or two-tier board (60:40, the top tier has mostly opted for two-tier), dominant position of the 'president and director general', who often chairs the board also in the two-tier system, but increasingly boards are becoming more active, but so far few have ousted a president/director general due to the tight network among the French elite
Top management	Dominated by graduates of the 'Grand École', with technical and administrative background, often service in government, more hierarchical organizations, lower degree of viable compensation (also growing)
Regulation	Detailed, based on traditional mistrust of market forces, most driven by EU directives, only slowly emergence of 'soft regulations' (e.g., codes)
Employees	No relevant involvement of organized labor as also the unions want to have clear division of responsibilities

Basic features of corporate governance systems: Scandinavia

Shareholder influence	Greater, as still many block holders with multiple voting rights (except Finland), in Norway: government influence on the dominant oil industry and other very large companies, slow emergence of institutional investors, rights of the general assembly higher than in the Anglo-Saxon system
Board	Dominantly led two-tier system (partly the CEO can also be a member of both boards), works similar to the German supervisory and management board system, however less formal, but also consensus oriented. Chairman normally low profile. In Norway: quota for women on boards
Top management	Strong technical background, due to country size forced to go global early, more decision making in teams by consensus, more diversity (especially women) than in continental Europe
Regulation	Medium, still relies on consensus and agreed social standards, backed by codes; increased influence of EU directive (even Norway although not a member)
Employees	Employee representatives at the supervisory board level but fewer than in Germany (roughly one-third)

Basic features of corporate governance systems: Japan

Shareholder influence	Only beginning of broader shareholder participation and activities of (non-governmental) institutional shareholders. Although eroding, 'keiretsu' still have considerable influence through cross-holding. Expect any change to be slow and gradual
Board	Most still large size, more celebrity members than real decision making, which in Japan is consensus-driven and more emergent than formalized. First pioneers like Sony or Asahi have tried to install a professional board, but Toyota still prefers the traditional way with slow adaptation
Top management	Seniority principles are eroding, but still influential. However, the more companies are forced to act globally (and do not only export), the more pressure is on them to professionalize management along 'western' standards and processes. The (individual) accountability for performance and supervision is key to this
Regulation	Despite capital market reforms and privatization, the government's influence is still stronger than even Latin-European countries (sometimes more informal, but not less effective)
Employees	No formal co-determination process, but still pressure for consensus

Basic features of corporate governance systems: emerging markets

Shareholder influence	Mostly family or government controlled business with stock market listing; control often based on different voting rights. Minority rights a permanent issue, often hampered by lack of legal enforcement. Similar: transparency regulations are not always enforced. Effective capital markets and other 'capitalist' institutions still in early development
Board	Often dominated by insiders, e.g., family members and friends, which makes management control less efficient. Reluctance for transparency, strong relation-based decisions
Top management	Often still part of 'friends and family', interested in risk diversification through conglomerate building to buffer volatile business development, little culture of (personal) accountability in many countries
Regulation	Even if laws are 'perfect', lack of enforcement, e.g., due to corruption and independent judiciary makes any law implementation uncertain and decisions of authorities often arbitrary
Employees	Not at all

As these summaries of the main characteristics evidence, an international investor or board member getting involved in a different country setting has to cope with diversity. Especially in developing countries, many main institutions of checks-and-balances are lacking – for now. There is an increasing understanding in these countries that governance reforms are needed, which will provide them with the stability, transparency, and thus further momentum for progress.

Learning nuggets from the cases

The following case studies describe specific cases where these differences materialize. China Prime presents a typical Chinese company interested in tapping the potential of sound corporate governance for a variety of reasons. At the helm of the company, corporate governance establishes clear structures of accountability, responsibility, transparency, and defines the role of boards as well as management. The case will outline some of the intransparency challenges. The upper echelon can act as a role model in professionalizing itself, a trend which could subsequently cascade down the entire organization. On the cross-company level, such governance reforms make China Prime more transparent and interesting for joint venture partners and M&A efforts. Investors would certainly feel more confident once they can understand much better who really drives and controls the strategizing process, as well as the entire organization. Combined efforts by Chinese companies towards more governance reforms thus also further the transition to a market economy, achieving more economic stability, and ensuring future growth for the sake of all players and stakeholders involved.

The second case study takes the reader to Latin America and presents a concrete challenge often found in developing countries. Power structures in governance settings are established and may not resemble what one may expect in an ideal situation. Any board member new to this situation has to clarify what can be done in a realistic scenario and how this can be achieved, if at all. This case goes far beyond our suggestion for a board member to be a 'party pooper', once a year asking the really fundamental questions. Corporate governance in real life may often deviate from the ideal setting of perfect harmony. Increasingly, being on a board is much more demanding than the retirement activity of a previously established, experienced CEO may appear to be. Failures will happen, even with 'best practices', but good boards limit the negative impact of such failures. There are often no easy answers to the posed dilemmas, but studying such challenges can at least train the current and future board member and leader to be ready for similar occasions.

The third case takes place in Eastern Europe. Privatization is the name of the game for many companies. The unprecedented opportunities due to the European Union expanding eastwards call for rapid professionalization of corporate governance settings, and this often means adaptation, convergence, and homogenization of governance systems. As in any change process, there are people who may feel they are winners or losers as emotions rage. Board members constantly need to reflect on the patterns to be detected in their setting. South East Bank is a case in point, where the decision to professionalize has been taken. Roles are changing and some understand this faster than others. As the old saying goes, some people make things happen, some watch things happen, and some wonder what happened. As outlined in Chapter 3, different agendas can complexify the progress to be made. It takes the reader through a real-life challenge of how to really start this professionalization process. Which questions need to be asked first? Which must-win battles need to be fought and are the right people even on board? South East Bank is also a great example of how legal settings and formal governance structures may change, while the real pattern at work may persist. We therefore encourage the reader to look closely for these patterns, 'to see the forest, not the trees'. There is also an administrative heritage regarding corporate governance, and involved players have to evolve if things are to move on.

9.2   CASE STUDY: CHINA PRIME – CORPORATE GOVERNANCE WITH CHINESE TRAITS

SHANGHAI, 15 AUGUST 2004, 2PM. Lu Wei, chairman of China Prime, looked at his fellow directors gathered in the main meeting room at the company's headquarters and said:

If we agree on this proposal to evolve our corporate governance structure, this will fundamentally change the way we work. It is a huge commitment for all of us. But if we want to play in the world's champions' league, we must do it.

The directors were all nodding in agreement. But the question for Lu and his team was how to actually move forward. They looked at the list of options in front of them:

- Should China Prime create management boards?
- What are the roles and responsibilities of boards of directors in the (partly publicly quoted) subsidiaries?
- What power should they have, and what responsibility should remain at the corporate level? These questions were truly vital as Lu tried to transform the sprawling conglomerate into a single integrated company.
- How to measure and improve the performance of boards and top management?
- What were the roles of boards compared with those of other players, such as management, supervisors, the Agency for State Property, and the Chinese Communist Party (CCP)?
- And, above all, where specifically will corporate governance really add value for China Prime?

Company background

China Prime, with approximately 130,000 employees, was a mid-sized company by Chinese standards. It was still state-owned, but had been pushing for privatization and was trying to attract foreign capital for its ambitious growth plans. Some of its subsidiaries were quoted on the stock market (refer to Figure 9.1), with the Technical Textile and Fiber division and the Textile Machines division being the major growth areas. The Chemicals division was another important part, as it was an internal supplier positioned as a 'cash-cow'. The high growth divisions received substantial R&D investments and would meet the export growth targets. In these areas, China Prime had already made some smaller acquisitions of foreign companies and more were to follow.

Corporate governance systems

Several corporate scandals in the West had led to a proliferation of codes of conduct, which in turn led to the fallacy that mere compliance constituted the entire challenge of corporate governance. Questions of leadership and truly adding value also had their place when talking about corporate governance entities. During the economic crisis in Asia, problems with disclosure, transparency, supervision, and ignoring risks were key governance flaws that contributed to Asia's slide, before its current resurrection. Corporate governance structures differed widely from Western models and were more complex (refer to Figure 9.2). The government, along with its various ministries, state-owned organizations, personal relationships and, most importantly, the respective interests, added an additional layer of considerable complexity. From a Western investor's perspective, the 'rules of the game' were often unclear, the content input and monitoring role of the board rather weak, the efficiency of the board process was limited, and the transparency with regard to foreign investments was almost totally lacking. A comparative survey on global standards confirmed

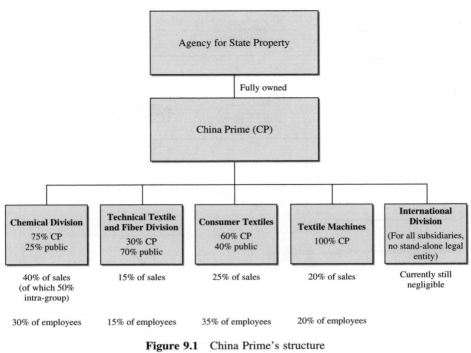

Figure 9.1   China Prime's structure
Source: Company information.

this for China Prime as well. Lu acknowledged this problem and was determined to solve it quickly.

At China Prime, Lu questioned whether the board really worked together as a team. Given the expansion plans, part-time assignments for board members with limited involvement and contribution were not an option. Lu also wondered about the right alignment of behaviors of the board members in subsidiaries. He complained:

> Whenever people serve on a subsidiary board, they forget their 'corporate hat' and act only in the interests of the subsidiary. Also, there is no professional risk management, and things are not transparent for the overall board.

Trying to delve into the details of corporate governance, Lu became increasingly aware that China Prime's practices were not consistent. The question of who appointed top management in subsidiaries and to whom they reported – the president or the board – remained confused, as Lu had to admit. In addition, tension over compensation arose. In order to attract and retain internationally experienced managers, salary differentials widened. Rumors about the sudden wealth of some managers spread too easily among a workforce that had been deprived for so long. Increasingly, China Prime relied on recruiting key managers from joint ventures in China, where they earned much more than the average upper echelons in state-owned enterprises. In one case, China Prime offered US$150,000 to a new hire, while the president earned only $100,000 and peers at board level roughly $75,000.

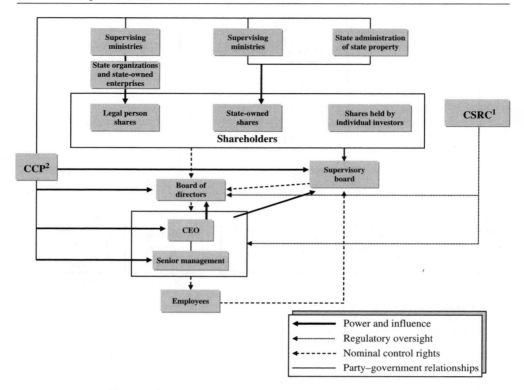

Figure 9.2   Current corporate governance structures in China
[1]Chinese Securities Regulatory Commission. [2]Communist Party.
Source: On Kit Tam. *The Development of Corporate Governance in China*. Edward
Elgat Publishing, 1999, p. 100.

Lu also realized that the board composition of subsidiaries showed inconsistencies. Of the board chairmen of the subsidiaries, three were internal – most of them presidents of other divisions – one was a retired executive, and one was external (ministry official). Most of them spent only five days per year at official board meetings. One-third of board members were internal people, one-third were government and party officials, and one-third were experts; they met no more than three times a year. Supervisors came from within the organizations and only met for a maximum of two days a year.

Lu knew that the business press in China, especially the emerging key publication *Caijin Magazine*, was starting to scrutinize companies and he wanted to avoid any bad press. The fact that China Prime was aiming for internationalization was a challenge for Lu, since he not only intended to 'clean up' the corporate governance systems that were already in place, but also to 'leapfrog' intermediate steps to reach world standards. Lu looked at the directors gathered in front of him and asked them:

Where should we start?

After exploring several options, the group was unanimous that the board must be able to ensure alignment of the emerging organization and therefore needed a framework. The

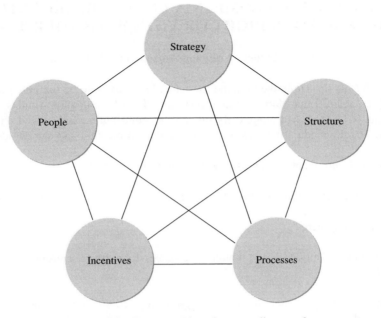

Figure 9.3   How can a board ensure alignment?
Source: Adapted from Galbraith, J. (2001). *Designing Organizations*. Jossey-Bass, San Francisco.

board agreed on the Star Model (refer to Figure 9.3) to create a frame of reference and to keep complexity at a tolerable level. According to this model, different strategies required a different type of organization, which could be seen as more than just structure. To achieve effectiveness, individual but interdependent aspects such as processes, incentives, and people needed to be aligned. Lu was convinced, though, that clear priorities had to be identified for the board. Any duplication of the work of other executive managers had to be avoided. Core processes in governance and management had to be identified, so that a critical degree of standardization could take place.

As China Prime grew its structure over time, Lu had no doubt that, while staying within the legal framework, a one-size-fits-all approach of corporate governance without adaptation to China Prime would not make sense. Also, roles and people might shift over time, so the new corporate governance systems would have to be flexible enough without compromising any monitoring or controlling function.

Lu realized that they had been debating intensively all afternoon and that the traditional and quite lavish banquet would start 30 minutes later. He decided to break up the meeting and to continue the next day. He set the clear goal that by the end of the following day, they would have agreed on the cornerstones of the new corporate governance systems. But what would they be? How should they go about designing a corporate governance system? What would be the value-added? What were the priorities? And which incentive system and performance drivers would ensure its success?

9.3   CASE STUDY: COMPANIA UNIDAS DE ARGENTINA – FIGHT FOR YOUR RIGHT OR VOTE WITH YOUR TEETH?

[By Ulrich Steger, Wolfgang Amann, and Helga Krapf]

Paulo Silva bit his lip. He looked around the table, but seemed to be the only one who had noticed. Once again, Luis Martinez, chairman and CEO of Compañías Unidas de Seguros de Argentina (CUSDA), had completely ignored his contribution and moved on to the last item on the board agenda – the upcoming annual general meeting and shareholders.

Does anybody *not* want to stand for re-election to the board?

Martinez surveyed the assembled board members and his gaze finally came to rest on Silva.

What am I doing here?

Silva asked himself. But on second thought, the successful software entrepreneur felt a sense of obligation:

I have never run away when things got tough. I accepted the mandate, and now I have to stay and fight.

But what were his options for success? What could he as an individual board member do to shake up this change-resistant company? What was his real obligation? How should he involve IFC? Who could be an ally?

Company background: CUSDA

CUSDA emerged as the No. 2 insurer in Argentina after a phase of consolidation in the early 1990s. It had a stronghold in towns with populations less than 100,000 due to the strength of its tight agent network, regarded as one of the most powerful, yet expensive, sales machines. CUSDA had added Property & Casualty insurance to its portfolio several years earlier, and had recently added asset management, but its funds were not top performers.

The company was very stable in every aspect. The agents achieved a high customer retention rate. Products and services changed as slowly as the turnover of the board – the average service was more than 10 years.

The most important asset in insurance is reliability,

was Martinez's deep conviction. CUSDA was not an outperformer in its industry, but it had not experienced any severe troubles either. Ownership was widely fragmented: four institutional investors held 10% together, IFC held 15%, the rest was owned by individuals as a 'widow-and-orphan-paper', a secure stock with a continual stream of dividends.

CUSDA's board had 13 members, most of them in their late fifties/early sixties, apart from the younger powerful sales boss, Juan Ramirez – who clearly had ambitions to succeed Martinez – and former chairman and CEO, Roberto Iglesias – who was in his seventies. One of the reasons IFC nominated Silva to the board was to tip the balance in favor of non-executive members. This was, however, rather euphemistic because three of the eight 'non-execs' were former corporate officers and not inclined to challenge their former colleagues. Only Iglesias still seemed to exert a considerable level of influence behind the scenes. The five corporate executives on the board were under Martinez's tight control – he was the unchallenged boss. CUSDA had no formal evaluation system in place – either for the CEO/chairman or for the directors on the board. Among the reasons that IFC chose to nominate Silva to the board were local knowledge, a solid education, unique IT expertise (felt valuable for someone on the board of a financial service provider), and a modern business approach. In addition, Silva demonstrated a critical degree of integrity in a previous board assignment for IFC.

Silva and one other board member, Carlos Junto, a banker, had to fly in for the meetings; all the others lived within driving distance of the Buenos Aires headquarters. Despite this closeness, the non-executive board members had little contact with each other outside the four to five board meetings per year. It was also not customary to seek direct contact with CUSDA employees, customers, or other outside parties.

Finding a place in an established board

Living further south, near the beautiful city of Bahia Blanca directly on the coast, and married to a famous novelist, 38-year-old Silva was indeed the 'odd-one-out' in this circle of older men. He had his own IT business, which was booming despite the technology bear market. The artificial intelligence on which his special program relied identified patterns of suspicious cases in the millions of transactions on the global financial markets. Because of new security legislation in several Latin American countries, many companies – not just financial service institutions – were eager to install his software.

Silva's first interactions with the board went well – socially. Everybody was interested in his career and his wife, and asked a lot of questions over lunch. In the meetings he asked only one or two, more factual, questions; otherwise, he listened and tried to learn about and understand CUSDA's business model. He felt that there was not much time for discussion anyhow, since more than half of the time was spent on issues for which information and decisions by the board were required for regulatory reasons. Silva never understood the deeper logic of all this – except that one older colleague explained to him:

In Argentina, when something goes wrong, the regulators know whom to sue . . .

The rest of the time was filled with presentations and a couple of questions afterwards. Everybody seemed to be happy with the routine of meeting early in the morning and finishing with a good lunch in the executive dining room.

Silva remembered only two interactions with board members outside the board meetings: Iglesias had invited Silva to dinner the evening before his second meeting. He tried to explain a bit about the history, culture, and business of CUSDA. He added some background information on some of the people on the board. Iglesias was a 'Grand Seigneur' and Silva enjoyed the evening with him. The other occasion was when he and Junto happened to be on the same flight home after the memorable fifth board meeting.

The fifth board meeting: a watershed

At this meeting, a so-called IT strategy was on the agenda. As usual, a board file arrived a couple of days before the meeting. Due to time pressure, Silva read the proposals only on the way to the meeting. They seemed to be merely a costly extension of the existing mainframe, which Silva thought to be slow, expensive, and too centralized to allow quick access to relevant information from every part of the organization. In particular, the proposed system was not capable of serving customers online, neither for information nor anything close to 'e-business'. Because of the legacy systems, Silva assumed that several interfaces still had to be bridged by entering data manually.

Immediately after the presenter – a technical expert in his mid-fifties – had finished his talk, Silva explained that he really didn't understand it. After his passionate five-minute intervention, he suddenly noticed the disbelief in the eyes of his colleagues. Into the silence, Ramirez said coldly:

> Please note that we are not in information services, but in insurance, and I don't let my agents become victims of the latest fleeting fashion. We have seen where this has landed our competitors.

Silva was perplexed, but hit back angrily:

> If you are not able to manage different sales channels, you will be out of business pretty soon.

Martinez stepped in:

> I think our IT people have done a great job in the past and will continue to do so in the future.

Silva was desperate – after all, he had been brought to the board partly because of his IT background. He made it clear:

> On the contrary, from what I can see, CUSDA is an absolute laggard in IT. You will have to go through a massive renewal process, not just some extensions, to stay competitive.

Martinez went red in the face, but kept his cool:

> Thank you for your opinion. I don't see any further intervention, so we'll proceed to the next item.

Silva slumped in his seat. He knew he was right, but he knew also that he had made a mistake. Iglesias's words came to mind:

> Never challenge Martinez in public.

Also:

> Nobody at CUSDA likes surprises.

But it was too late. And from then on, Martinez consistently ignored Silva's input. The lunch was over more quickly than usual, with only minimal small talk. Silva realized,

Now I am an outsider.

On the way back, Junto was not particularly inclined to talk to him. But Junto's parting words as he took his first-class seat on the plane – before Silva made his way to the economy section – were:

Remember, you are on this board as a courtesy to IFC. You should be careful about offending the rest of the board.

Fall from grace

At the next board meeting, Silva did not hesitate to give his opinion on different items on the agenda. However, Martinez ignored him completely. While the meeting continued, Silva continued to ponder his options. Could he have avoided the situation? Was it too late to repair the relationship? Could Iglesias serve as a mediator? Or, failing this, he thought defiantly:

But I can also live happily as a maverick in this circle. Or if I approach IFC and the institutional shareholders, we could probably organize enough pressure to influence or replace all the executives, except Iglesias. Then there would be six non-executives on the board, who should have no reservations in challenging executive management.

What was his real obligation to the company? To IFC? What information should he share with IFC (or other outside investors)? What information *can* he share with them? Would IFC really step in? Or would it all just be a big waste of his time?

9.4   CASE STUDY: STARTING FROM SCRATCH – CORPORATE GOVERNANCE AT SOUTH EAST BANK EUROPE

[By Ulrich Steger and Wolfgang Amann]

16 AUGUST 2005.The newly appointed chairman of the supervisory board of South East Bank Europe (SBE), Laurentio Bunescu, looked rather skeptically at his CEO Dr Cornelius Cojacaru, who was obviously regretting his emotional outbreak. It was late evening and they were in Cornelius's office debating about how the bank's corporate governance should be organized during its privatization phase in what was one of Eastern Europe's fastest growing economies. Cornelius was finding it difficult to control his emotions – in his opinion corporate governance was not only about roles and tasks, but also about power. For more than six years, he had been both the chairman of the board of directors and head of the managing committee. Laurentio understood perfectly how difficult it was for Cornelius to let go of the reins of power, but the majority of shareholders were in tune with the law regarding corporate governance, which was crystal clear. Moreover, the privatization agency, which had pushed vigorously for the sales of shares to both domestic and international investors,

demanded transparency as well as better checks and balances. Cornelius swallowed, shook his head and said:

> I sincerely apologize for suggesting that your proposal will create a communist bureaucracy, but I still think that the supervisory board has too much power. The management's authority is minimal and you can't run a bank successfully with such a division of power and such tremendous reporting requirements.

Laurentio contemplated his options. The first meeting of the supervisory board was to take place the following day. He very much wanted a consensus with the successful CEO, but doubts remained. Was Cornelius really ready to face the new realities and accept the division of responsibilities? Would the supervisory board monitor him and his top team sufficiently? Or too much? Should he go for a detailed internal regulation or rely on general board guidelines? What were his priorities for the next morning? What could be postponed? In cases of real conflicts, should the supervisory board meet alone and just confront management with its decision? Should he avoid such confrontational meetings or did they help establish his authority?

The birth of a privatized, professional bank

In 1993 the monopolistic, state-owned bank system was dissolved, which led to the creation of six smaller banks. SBE started with what many considered a handicap: it inherited most of the rural branches. The farming community had been very reluctant to accept the transformations and reforms, although almost all industries suffered on their way to a market economy. The required reforms had been tough. SBE soon embarked on getting a foothold in towns and cities, mostly with small and midsize businesses in the newly developing service sector and those of the emerging middle class. Car loans and credit cards were amongst the most profitable new fields. Lending mostly to smaller customers, SBE had been able to steer clear of the legacies of non-performing loans. The latter had too often been caused by political intervention aimed at avoiding even higher unemployment figures due to huge state-run companies going bankrupt. Currently, SBE was the second largest bank in the country, but clearly the most profitable one with the highest growth rate (refer to Table 9.1 for some key figures).

Table 9.1   Financial highlights (€ thousand)

Corporate performance	2001	2002	2003	2004
Total number of customers	16,495	21,444	30,021	45,031
Total assets	139,658	210,813	286,019	354,329
Profit	2,019	8,084	9,448	16,764
ROE	13.46%	27.23%	22.99%	24,87%
ROA	1.45%	3.83%	3.30%	4.73%

Source: SBE.

SBE's CEO Cornelius Cojacaru

Much of SBE's success could be attributed to Cornelius's leadership. Coming from a modest rural background, he had chosen the politically rather neutral engineering profession. However, he 'jumped ship' when the market economy was introduced and became a rising star among the brand managers at SBE and a member of the managing committee shortly thereafter. He was the mastermind behind SBE's dual strategy to expand into new market segments, especially in the cities, while preserving the strategic core of being a retail bank. Furthermore, he suggested investing massively in order to increase the efficiency of the back office processes to ensure a state-of-the-art system, which included:

- Risk management, which needed to preserve its independence and integrity while being integrated into the portfolio management and growth processes. Policies and procedures were communicated throughout the organization and integrated into the development programs of SBE's organizational culture. Key control processes, risk measurement criteria, and certain risk mitigation strategies were established and used to monitor performance. The latest techniques in applicant scoring and behavioral monitoring and scoring were implemented at SBE. With the help of a consulting company, intensive benchmarking was done on a global scale. SBE also started to employ experts in market risks, such as equity risks, foreign exchange rate and commodity price risks, interest rate risks, debt-specific risks, credit spread risks, etc. Core processes for liquidity risks, insurance risks, and other operational risk rounded off the highly professional efforts initiated by Cornelius, who had been convinced that these were worthwhile investments. Those that were first to commit would lead the industry within a matter of years.
- The latest record management software to enable SBE to view real-time information on all SBE subsidiaries, to facilitate a decentralized approach to updated information and, eventually, regulatory fillings. Cornelius believed that software was central not only to managing subsidiaries, but also to better, timelier, and more accurate reporting and monitoring. In his opinion, information was essential to provide an outstanding service and to build lasting, profitable client relationships. He felt that this was even more the case in an environment where few of the bank's competitors were able to deliver excellent service due to their lack of experience in the previous, generally low, service environment in which the markets had not been the primary mechanism.

Since becoming CEO and chairman of the board in late 1998, Cornelius had been accelerating the bank's expansion, without losing sight of profitability. He had also developed the bank's asset management and home loan products. He started to set up subsidiaries in neighboring countries, basically to support agricultural exports, and started bond emission and trade, hitherto still limited to government and public bonds. He had so far succeeded in steering clear of overt government intervention and from lending that had been 'directed', thus making SBE one of the few commercially very successful banks in the country.

People that worked for him admired not only his mastery of detail, but also his ability to think strategically. He was a great networker and had charisma. However, he was never afraid to make difficult decisions and see them through.

A member of the executive committee observed:

He is clearly the alpha male at SBE, but recently his patience seems to be running out. He's stopped listening.

The new chairman Laurentio Bunesco

Laurentio went a different route. In 1968, while only in his second semester at university, he had organized a students' protest and walk-out. As a consequence, he was jailed for a short period of time but was allowed to leave the country after six months. He studied in the USA and worked mostly as an economist for international organizations. He returned after the breakdown of communism and – following the election cycles – held senior government positions and worked as a consultant in the EU. He was brought back to government assignments after the previous election to support the rise of the corporate governance legislation and its implementation. He sat on the 'Blue Ribbon Panel', which created the blueprint for the legislation, and advised the privatization agency on these issues, particularly on how to make the country's companies more attractive for foreign investors. His assignment with the SBE gave him the opportunity to prove himself.

The new corporate governance framework

Like other companies, SBE was now confronted with a 'two-tier' corporate governance law. Before this attempt to modernize and professionalize corporate laws, managers basically ran companies while being more or less supervised by government agencies. Personal relationships with key people in politics and society mattered more than corporate governance. These relationships amounted to a non-transparent web of personal relationships spun across all industries, offering advantages to some groups, but not others. However, spurred by the privatization process, the growth of domestic companies required more systematic and transparent governance standards. Contrary to the Anglo-Saxon model with a one-tier board, a clear division between the non-executive supervisory board and the management board was established in all companies and industries. The supervisory board would be elected by the shareholders and owners and basically had three tasks:

- To elect, evaluate, and terminate the management board.
- To monitor performance and ensure compliance.
- To approve major investments, budgets, and strategic plans.

The law was not very prescriptive about the details of the corporate governance system for two main reasons. First, there was a substantive lack of experience and no established practice to build on. Second, the variety of size, ownership, and industry specificities made it difficult to describe details. Following a huge financial scandal a few years earlier, additional laws and regulations had been set down for the financial services industry. Since a substantial number of people had lost their savings during that time, supervisory boards in financial service companies were made responsible for additional aspects:

- The approval of any loan, credit, bond, etc. which exceeded 1% of the nominal capital of their company.
- An obligation to sign off and permanently monitor the risk management system, especially for trading activities.
- Approval of all non-traditional banking activities like hedging or derivatives.

- Scrutinizing and acting upon all reports from external auditors (including the so-called management letters, in which the auditors elaborate on risk, special findings, etc. and make recommendations – e.g., for improving the financial and reporting system) and internal auditors, including the approval of the internal audit plan.

Recognizing the importance of the human factor, Laurentio contemplated this in detail, including the very specific requirements that involved training and developing people as well as testing by means of checks and balances in order to ensure that personnel-building would be complied with. New board members would get a jump-start by means of orientation and education programs.

Nevertheless, he realized that the differences between a one-tier and a two-tier board were not really significant in practice, although they were in theory. Future one-tier boards would be predominantly composed of a majority of independent directors and, to an increasing extent, also headed by a non-executive chairman. Thus, the differences between the two systems would become increasingly irrelevant. Regardless of the organizational structure, the shareholders expected either the independent directors or the supervisory board to control companies' management effectively, as well as to monitor performance and compliance. Simultaneously, there had to be close cooperation between the top management and the non-executives, or supervisory board members, to avoid tension and conflicts that could paralyze the organization. Hence, personalities and actual behaviors maintained their crucial importance in both systems. Laurentio knew that setting up modern structures would be just the beginning.

Setting the right tone from the beginning – but how?

When Laurentio left Cornelius's office, he was still thinking about the supervisory board's constituting meeting the following day. Good relationships were important for Laurentio, but not at any price – certainly not at the cost of his principles nor of ensuring a bright future for SBE. Corporate governance was a critical success factor for such a future. Laurentio felt that he had a tremendous responsibility towards the shareholders, but even more importantly, he wanted to do what was right. If only he knew how to open the supervisory board's meeting, how to manage the flow of the discussion, and what to prioritize when Cornelius became imposing. Arriving back in his office, he sat down, loosened his tie, and started to think about what he was going to do.

Responsibilities in Alternative Forms of Governance

[By Ulrich Steger, Christoph Nedopil, and Wolfgang Amann]

10.1 DIFFERENCES IN NON-PROFIT ORGANIZATIONS

Although this book deals with the governance of profit-based corporations, it should not be forgotten that a significant part of the economy is organized differently. Often called the third sector, non-profit organizations are positioned between the private sector and the core public administration, resulting in a vast diversity of organizations that cover between 15% and 25% of the economy. In many countries the church, for example, is the single largest employer. Organizations such as the Red Cross can match any company regarding revenue and a global presence.

Three groups of non-profit organizations can be distinguished:

- The first group is organizations that have owners, but have a different goal system than companies. The owner can be a local city council that outsources services such as waste management to another company or a church that runs a conglomerate of childcare centers, hospitals, senior citizen homes, etc. Although the goals are different, many corporate governance processes can be applied, as non-profit organizations also need to deploy their resources as efficiently as possible and have accountable management and transparent bookkeeping.
- The second group is membership organizations that do not have property-based owner- ship. Members from the organization are selected on a one-person-one-vote principle. Mutual or cooperative associations are typical examples. Not too long ago, stock market exchanges were member associations (e.g., broker companies). In many countries, hous- ing cooperatives and a large part of the agricultural/handicraft sector are also organized on this basis. Once these organizations become global, however, their management teams have to be professional. Individual members also do not have a greater say than individ- ual shareholders do. Nevertheless, whether non-profit organizations are global or local, their goals and behavior are often still similar (e.g., the Dutch agricultural cooperative Rabo Bank). These organizations' corporate governance processes are again very simi- lar, as they often compete with for-profit cooperations and have to meet similar market standards, as their business scope lies far beyond mere membership.
- The third group refers to instances when organizational design and ownership are 'reversed' and other mechanisms dominate the organization's governance. This happens where the professionalized membership organizations own the top organization, as is the case in the mutual banking system or with various international organizations that are formed by a single national organization. Here the 'subsidiaries' sit on the board, which could lead to a conflict of interest between the local and global organization. Other,

similar organizational forms are based on shared beliefs or goals, but have a looser control mechanism. Greenpeace International's headquarters are in Amsterdam and licenses its logo to national, mostly volunteer-based organizations. Withdrawing the license is therefore the only 'weapon' that the headquarters has. Consequently, if things go wrong, as with Greenpeace in the USA, there is little that the headquarters can legally do. These organizations need governance too – they are after all quite large (it is estimated that Greenpeace has a turnover in excess of $200 million per year worldwide) and donors hold the leadership accountable. However, the mechanism to ensure governance probably differs widely between the various organizations.

In line with most of the relevant literature, this book deals with economic, profit-based organizations in which the fundamental, decision-making rights are vested in the ownership. This is the most dominant pattern in a market-based capitalist society. However, if these organizations embark on certain (service) activities for their members or society at large, they often organize these activities as different types of corporations with different goals. Serving the members may nevertheless dominate the thinking. As resources are not unlimited, the management of such companies needs to ensure that the decision-making criteria and processes meet the organizational goals. The owners have the same basic task to ensure that managers do not fulfill their own goals or serve their own interests rather than the owners' not-for-profit goals. The principal–agent theory is therefore as relevant for not-for-profit organizations as it is for profit-based organizations. Studies of such companies reveal that there are many similarities in the corporate governance's mechanism, processes, and failures. These companies can easily fail, as management can repeat mistakes, miscalculate funds, or abuse their positions.

In the above-mentioned cases, the owners' goals differ from those of capitalists, but ownership is still the defining criterion of the ultimate decision-making power. Another option is not ownership, but membership. This can be found in many countries where cooperatives or associations are still strong in agriculture, some financial areas, or even retail. The organizational principle is one member one vote, regardless of the capital involved. (Many cooperatives require an equal, predetermined capital contribution per member that cannot be exceeded.) The supervision activities of those who operate a cooperative or association's activities are uncomplicated if the operation is small and local. However, cooperatives are often specifically national or even global in size to match their competitors' market power or reap the benefits of economies of scale. Consequently, individual members' alienation from 'their' organization largely equals that of individual shareholders in respect of 'their' company. This is revealed when members of such large organizations have to vote for representatives: the turnout is very low, often below 20%, which is similar to that in many stock companies (if bank representatives are not mistaken for stockholders). The principal–agent issues are also largely similar. The same rule that applies to stock market-listed companies with large numbers of shareholders is therefore applicable: the more members there are, the greater the management's dominance.

An exception to the rule occurs when members themselves form associations, which often happens in international organizations or federations, but also on national levels (e.g., industry-focused associations form the national employer federation). This leads to a tricky constellation: the members are the 'objects' of the federation's management, as well as the 'subjects', as they sit on the board and are on a higher level than management. It is small wonder that these organizations are extremely political, slow in decision-making, and minorities often block change.

In some organizational forms, the owners are also the employers. This is often the result of a crisis during which contributions from employees saved the company from bankruptcy. United Airlines, the second largest airline in the USA, is one example. In some parts of Eastern Europe, especially in the former Yugoslavia with its 'workers' self-government', there are still several examples of worker ownership of major, internationally active companies. As Adria, a successful Slovenic producer of motor homes and caravans, demonstrates, such constellations can work if the employees manage to disguise their role as owners and workers sufficiently to develop a 'normal' organizational culture. The board therefore acts as representatives of the owners in respect of the management and the management acts as leaders in respect of the employees. In this case, many of the corporate governance issues are similar to those in other organizational forms.

Learning nuggets from the WWF case

In the following, we present the case of the World Wide Fund for Nature (WWF) – formerly World Wildlife Fund – from a corporate governance perspective. The rich description of the issues will clarify that building great governance systems is no longer a challenge restricted to managers in for-profit organizations. The case nevertheless illustrates the main idiosyncrasies of NGOs though. The dilemmas emerge from a lack of formal, streamlined authority at the upper echelon. WWF is just one example of a rising number of globally active institutions forced to professionalize every corner of their operations and governance, much like regular companies do. The WWF case exemplifies another must-do aspect of great governance (i.e., the need to adapt and develop governance structures and processes further), if possible as proactively as possible when the entire organization is reshuffled. All pieces of the puzzle must fit together perfectly. Obviously, if one piece of the puzzle changes its shape, others have to be adapted in order to ensure a perfect fit.

10.2   CASE STUDY: WWF INTERNATIONAL – A TRULY WORLDWIDE ORGANIZATION

[By Ulrich Steger and Christoph Nedopil]

I want to thank you all for this great effort over the last years to create the new structure of the network management and the establishment of the Network Executive Team!

Now we have to keep on moving forward and we really need to think about how we can make our organization more accountable, how we have to adjust our corporate governance and how we need to redefine the role and responsibilities of our board!

These were the words that Paul Steele, COO of WWF International, had used half an hour earlier at a meeting with representatives of WWF's National Organizations and Programme Offices. Most participants thought that the meeting would just be a summing-up of the major restructuring of WWF's network decision structure, which had involved all parts of the organization and took place over the last four years. Nobody had expected such a far-reaching proposal.

The reorganization had become necessary because the company with the panda logo had not only built a global reputation since its establishment more than 40 years earlier, but also an expansive organization. With activities in over 100 countries organized through 30 National Organizations and Programme Offices around the globe, decision making had become a lengthy process with competencies spread between the National Organizations, the International Organization's Programme Offices, and WWF's International Secretariat.

Paul and Thomas Schultz-Jagow, Directors of Communication of WWF International, were surprised by the strong reaction of the assembly. They were back in Paul's office when the phone rang. It was the board's vice president, The Hon. Mrs Morrison, on the line. She said in her polite English way:

> Paul, I don't necessarily agree with your idea. I believe the board has – considering its structure – performed well in the past and will perform even better now that the NET will have to report more in detail! But I am interested: what changes were you thinking about exactly?

WWF International: a truly worldwide organization

Birth and growth

The WWF was founded in 1961 after Sir Julian Huxley returned from a trip to East Africa appalled by the destruction of wildlife he had witnessed. With the help of a small group of experts, the charity organization with the panda logo was born soon after to help stop the destruction of the environment. By 2006 this small group of experts had grown to over 4000 people operating in over 100 countries in four associated offices and 30 independent WWF National Organizations.

WWF's agenda was determined by its purpose 'to conserve the natural environment and ecological processes worldwide' and its mission statement was to 'build a future in which humans live in harmony with nature'. WWF focused its activities on three key areas: forest, freshwater ecosystems, oceans and coasts.

Major accomplishments through the work of WWF included the institution of the 'debt-for-nature swap', where governments could 'repay' their debts through investment in conservation projects. Furthermore, the ban of the ivory trade and other trade of endangered species through WWF's partner organization TRAFFIC, as well as the creation of numerous protected parks in Africa, South America, and Asia.

The WWF network

WWF was founded as a fund. The center of WWF International is the Secretariat, which is located in Gland, Switzerland, and the 'subsidiaries' are 30 National Organizations and various Programme Offices located around the world (refer to Figure 10.1).

The 30 National Organizations were established as independent entities with their own management structures and boards, and were responsible for fundraising to sponsor WWF International projects and to run conservation projects. In 2006 around 60% of WWF International's funds came from the National Organizations. In exchange, the National Organizations were allowed to use the panda logo, thereby benefiting from the reputation of WWF and were also allowed to run their own projects. The National Organizations varied

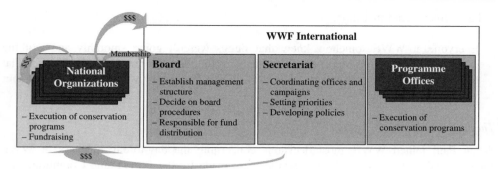

Figure 10.1 WWF organization
Source: WWF.

greatly in size – the smallest, in New Zealand, employing 14 people; the largest, in the USA, employing 300 people. Each had its own group of supporters and donors whose goals and aims for nature conservation did not necessarily conform with WWF's International strategy. The conservation programs of some smaller or poorer National Organizations were supported by WWF International or in a bilateral manner from other, wealthier National Organizations.

In some of the countries where no National Organization was operating, WWF International sponsored and operated Programme Offices, which also executed conservation programs, but were not directly engaged in fundraising.

The Secretariat of WWF International was located in Gland, Switzerland, and in 2006 employed around 140 people, who were responsible for:

- Coordinating various offices and National Organizations.
- Developing program priorities.
- Developing WWF's policies.
- Coordinating international campaigns.

Conserved for too long

In 2001 there were increasing complaints about inefficient structures in the network, time-consuming procedures for making decisions and getting resources, missing standards on program development, execution and reporting as well as a weighty administration. As a result, former WWF Director General Claude Martin initiated a review of WWF's operations – despite some reluctance from the independent National Organizations – in order to analyze the status quo of the decision structure, which had grown organically since WWF's establishment.

This was also the time when Paul came to WWF International to serve as chief operating officer. Before his job at WWF International, he had held senior positions at various industrial companies such as The Virgin Trading Group, the Hilton Hotel Group, and Pepsi Cola International. With his great interest for nature conservation as well as his working experience in various countries, he was just the right person to deal with the structural problems at WWF. It was a difficult task since he had to take into consideration all the various ideas and needs of the different and independent parts of the organization.

Paul remembered that time:

> Everyone at WWF somehow knew that things weren't going smoothly and that the environment for NGOs had changed and become tougher. But nobody really knew at that time what exactly our problems were here at WWF and how we needed to react – but we were to find out.

The old structure

When Paul joined WWF, most decisions concerning the day-to-day business of WWF International and the network as a whole were made by the Programme Committee and its subcommittees. The purpose of the Programme Committee was to align all National Organizations to work according to WWF's principles and conservation goals. However, the decision processes were lengthy and the Programme Committees had no authority to enforce the strategies, rather it was at the discretion of the National Organizations to follow the agenda. That is why some National Organizations preferred to work bilaterally or multilaterally with other National Organizations to get things done, without having to go through WWF International, who was responsible for the Programme Committees. Hence, many National Organizations – especially the bigger ones – had been following their own programs and had their own ideas on how to spend their funds.

Operations review

For four years after Claude had initiated the review process it was the task of the Operations Review Team to uncover the problems and issues of WWF's current structure.

Internal issues

Stagnation in fundraising

Fundraising in the WWF network had not been growing during the past few years and had stagnated at around US$500 million, despite growing efforts by the National Organizations. This meant that for every dollar as a donation, more and more money for fundraising activities was needed. This situation gave both WWF International and the National Organizations less leverage to expand their programs and growth of the network was stalled.

Inefficient resource allocation

It became clear during the operations review process that the procedures of sharing resources between the different independent organizations were lacking efficiency. Similar areas of expertise were being built up in various parts of the organization due to a lack of information and communication about already existing expertise in the network because there was no central human resources department. This also resulted in unsatisfactory career possibilities for WWF's employees.

In addition, communication about the various projects that were run throughout the network was inefficient. When Paul and Robert Napier, CEOs of WWF UK, discussed the issue, Robert clearly stated:

> It often seems to me, that you guys at WWF International have no idea of what we are doing here at the National Organizations. How do you want to make sound decisions and give directions with this structure and information level at WWF International?

Paul replied:

> I understand that: We need to make our processes much more transparent. We need to know what the others are doing and they need to be able to find out what we are working on. It is just a waste of resources if every organization builds up its own expertise just because we don't know what is going on in the network and can't coordinate properly!

The lack of transparency also led to accountability problems, since not only was the information on WWF's engagement not readily available, but also the aggregated numbers of the different National Organizations were not accessible. This created discord in the relations with the various stakeholders, who were interested in what WWF was working on.

External pressures

The market for NGOs
NGOs set up new foundations almost on a daily basis. Despite some trigger events – like the tsunami at the end of 2004, which prompted an unprecedented public generosity – donations for NGOs worldwide did not grow as fast as the number of new NGOs. Paul pointed this out at one of the task force meetings:

> We have to compete with more and more NGOs for the same resources, such as donations and media coverage!

Paul also mentioned – not without envy – that organizations such as Nature Conservancy or Conservation International had been able to expand quickly during recent years and to raise a considerable amount of funds, while WWF's fundraising was stagnating.

Need for transparency
Accountability and transparency were hot topics not only in the shareholder world but also for NGO donors. In the past, donating money had been much more philanthropic, but donors were increasingly demanding precise information about how and where their money was being spent. They wanted to see concrete results and some even tried to exert a direct influence on how their donations were being used. The demand by stakeholders for transparency was given a voice through organizations such as the One World Trust, which evaluated and tracked the transparency of various NGOs.

In fact, from the point of view of the One World Trust, WWF rated poorly against other NGOs in terms of its accountability. This rating sent a clear signal to WWF International that change, in terms of transparency, was urgently needed. In addition, donors approached WWF International to express their concern about the lack of transparency and accountability. Kristian Parker, trustee at the Oak Foundation, a group of charitable and philanthropic organizations, once told Paul:

> We really want to know how you at WWF manage your money, especially how much money is spent on the different programs to be certain about the value and impact of our donations. It is just not enough for us to see your total spending and your project expenditures, much more we want to know your program expenditures, the developments of this spending and we would appreciate getting information on the impact of our donations.

Planning evolution

When the operations review process was finished in 2005, it was more than evident to all members in WWF's International Secretariat that the current structure of WWF was no longer viable in today's environment and that changes in the organization of WWF International and the WWF network were urgently needed to adapt to the size and scope the organization has grown to and to cope with the external pressures.

Since the closure of the operations review process, some urgent changes had already been implemented, like the abolishment of the Programme Committees. But to clearly communicate the changes throughout the network, a meeting of the newly established Assembly was called with representatives from National Organizations and Programme Offices, as well as from WWF International. It was up to Thomas to present the changes the task force had developed for the network.

Structural changes
The structural changes were the most comprehensive to be implemented, and dealt with the decision-making authority in the WWF network as well as the relationship between management and the board of WWF International.

Previously, decisions concerning WWF's 3- to 5-year planning horizon had been made by the Programme Committees. Now, decisions were to be made by a Network Executive Team (NET) with Paul as secretary and up to nine members from the top donor countries as well as other members from National Organizations and Programme Offices.

The functions assigned to NET were:

- Develop the network business plan and conservation strategy.
- Make strategic and tactical decisions for the network, such as fund allocation.
- Facilitate cooperation in the network.
- Monitor WWF's performance.

In order to fulfill these functions, NET was supported by four expert groups as illustrated in Figure 10.2: Programme, Global Partnerships, Marketing, and Operations & Network Development. The members of the expert groups were to come from the National Organizations, the Programme Offices, and WWF International's Secretariat. These members could therefore be classified as 'dual citizens', since through their work in NET they were part of their National Organization as well as of the WWF network as a whole.

The other structural change dealt with the interaction between the management and the board of WWF International. In the old structure, WWF's Director General James Leape, Paul as COO, the Program Director, as well as relevant staff attended board meetings. With the new structure, board meetings were to be attended by the secretaries of the four expert groups, Paul, as the secretary of NET, and WWF's Director General. In this way, the board would be provided more directly with information on all topics relevant to the WWF network.

Role change
The role of WWF's Secretariat (a name that did not reflect its role appropriately) was somewhere between managing, serving, supporting, and coordinating the Programme Offices and the National Organizations. With the new structure, behavioral as well as cultural changes were necessary in the Secretariat itself as well as in different parts of the network as a whole. For example, National Organizations – the main donors to WWF International's project – had to begin to see themselves more as shareholders of WWF's operations and to

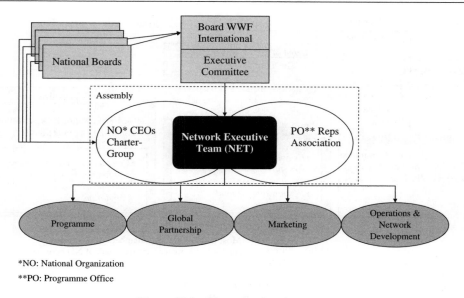

*NO: National Organization
**PO: Programme Office

Figure 10.2   Network executive team
Source: WWF.

stop regarding themselves as managers of the projects. Therefore, they were to give more discretion and control of the projects to other members of the network and were asked to stop following their own individual agendas. The Secretariat, for its part, had to step up and change its role from implementing to more orchestrating the work of the National Organizations and Programme Offices.

Changes in performance management
In order to motivate people working for WWF to better organize and evaluate the contribution of the various parts of the network and to make NET work, a new performance management was developed. This included the introduction of Key Performance Indicators (KPIs), for example for targets on fundraising, brand awareness, and program alignment.

WWF International board organization: an issue just for Paul?

While Thomas was presenting these changes to the assembly, Paul was sitting in the front row. He had been part of the development team for the new structure, and he knew every detail of it. He also knew that one central issue had so far been avoided: the board of WWF International.

The board of WWF International
In 2006 the WWF International board consisted of 25 trustees, of whom 17 were nominated for this post through their National Organizations – of which they were also trustees. The remaining eight trustees were co-opted by the board (refer to Figure 10.3). All members were – by the rule of the statutes – 'of high-standing and special competence in fields useful to the foundation'. The statutes further specified that none of the trustees were to be reimbursed for their acquittals as trustees of WWF International, and neither should they be a member

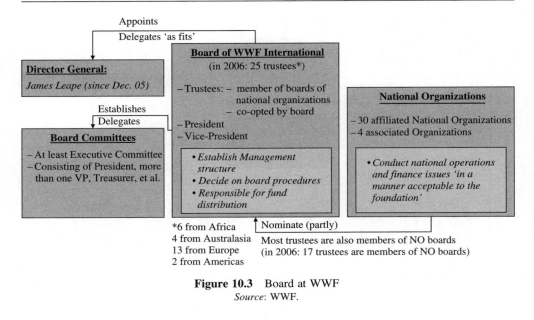

Figure 10.3   Board at WWF
Source: WWF.

of the paid staff at WWF International or – if possible – at their National Organizations. The board members of WWF International indeed worked for philanthropic reasons.

In recent years, the WWF International board had met around twice a year to fulfill its vast duties of being responsible for fund distributions in the network as well as for WWF's overall strategy. More specifically, the board was responsible for the policies, management, and finances of the organization as outlined in Figure 10.4. The board was also responsible for appointing the Director General, a post held by James Leape since December 2005. For better decision making, it was specified in the statutes of WWF that committees had to be established by the board, at least an executive committee.

An invisible board?
Paul was wondering what effects the new decision structure at WWF would and should actually have on the board, when he suddenly remembered what Robert had said during their previous discussion:

> What has the board of WWF International actually decided in the last years? What did the board contribute to stop the stagnation of the network growth? Many of us at the National Organizations have the perception that this board doesn't even really exist!

Paul pondered: what actually *was* the role of WWF International's board? Just nodding or helping to make sound decisions? What would it take to bring more decision power to the board? And how could it help to make the organization more accountable and transparent? What kind of restructuring and changes were necessary to the operation?

Paul kept on thinking, but it now became clear to him that with mounting pressures for more accountability from the outside, it would just be wrong to stop here with the restructuring, something should be done about this ancient board structure.

Taken from the WWF statutes:
8. Management of the Foundation

(a) The Board is responsible for the conduct, administration and representation of the Foundation, and defines its Mission and policies.
(b) The Board is responsible for establishing the management structure of the Foundation, and shall appoint a Director General and approve the appointment of such senior members of the staff as shall be determined by the By-Laws.
(c) The Board may delegate to Committees (see Art. 11), the Director General and to other bodies or individuals such functions and responsibilities as it sees fit.

Adapted from WWF: The Role and Structure of WWF Boards and Committees:
WWF boards should inter alia

– Financial

  o oversee the budget process and approve the final budget
  o monitor financial performance on an ongoing basis through clear, accurate and timely financial statements (quarterly and preferably monthly)
  o establish an accessible reserve fund sufficient to cover at least six months' normal expenditure to reduce problems resulting from a severe downturn in income
  o establish policy on fundraising and investment
  o ensure that an audit of the annual financial statement is undertaken

– Goals and Strategies

  o agree on planning process and provide Board commitment
  o ensure proper action plans are developed to enable implementation of the strategy
  o review progress

– Enhancing WWF's Public Image

  o build and review communication objectives
  o promotion of WWF
  o measure effectiveness of promotion
  o help CEO in promoting and making relevant announcements

– Establishing Policies

  o establish clear process to develop policies to guide the activities of the organization
  o participate in the preparation of such

– Promoting WWF Network Cohesion

Figure 10.4   Responsibilities of the board
Source: WWF.

Living r-evolution

When Thomas's presentation to the Assembly was over, some of the Assembly members took to the podium and were full of praise for the new structure. One of them was Ravi Singh, the CEO of WWF India:

What Thomas has just presented here shows us that NOs and POs will continue to be the backbone of the organization, as will the programme elements of conservation implementation. Through the new structure our global key targets can be streamlined and reached much easier in addition to our national goals. The challenge is on us now to implement this new structure and strategy, the completion of which will take WWF into a new and successful future.

Robert was also very positive about the new decision structure:

This is a brilliant step forward! This leaves the decisions in the network to where the money is made – the National Organizations!

Then, Paul went to the podium, asked for attention, and said what most people in the meeting thought was going to be just the final note:

Five years ago we all knew that things weren't going smoothly, but nobody had a clear understanding of the problems and issues we had to solve. It was only after the operations review that we really recognized the need for change. Now that we have defined our charter and set the goals, we have come a long way.

Paul hesitated, but he knew that he must continue: he must make it clear to the Assembly that this had just been the beginning of the structural changes in the network!

Part IV
Corporate Governance in Special
Ownership Situations

11

Corporate Governance in Family Businesses

11.1 GOOD NEWS FOR FAMILY FIRMS

There is good news for family businesses with regard to corporate governance. For the most part, family businesses can ignore the plethora of new corporate governance regulations such as the Sarbanes–Oxley Act or the Hicks Report, as these mostly do not require private companies to comply. However, this privilege lulls many family firms into becoming complacent about governance. Family firms should use this freedom to regard questions of governance in greater depth, because they encounter many of the same dilemmas as their non-family counterparts do, plus a few others that can be even more complicated and challenging.

Before examining some uncommon views of corporate governance, a little background on Sarbanes–Oxley is necessary. During the 'new economy' stock market bubble, most family businesses were, by definition, old economy. They were condemned to a shadowy existence on the fringes of the new virtual business world. Although many had existed for generations, they were just not 'cool', nor were they attractive enough to investment bankers in terms of fees.

When the bubble eventually burst, the 'day after' revealed the darker side of public market capitalism – greed. Greed had misled and cheated many investors. Furthermore, rogue investment practices had at times even included fraud. None of this was really new. Every market implosion since the Dutch Tulip Bubble during the 17th century (one of the earliest significant commercial disasters) has destroyed value. These catastrophes redistribute wealth to early adopters and wipe out the savings of latecomers. Such high-stakes diversions have always been followed by a 'moral hangover' when the party is over. When the 'new economy' bubble burst, investors likewise lost trust, prosecutors discovered malpractice, and the media made sure that everyone knew.

The recession that mostly follows a bubble reveals what outsiders and auditors often choose to ignore when things are booming. This time, too, the backlash was swift and severe. Regulators and politicians all over the world created new far-reaching rules. American regulators led with the Sarbanes–Oxley Act. The focus was corporate governance, a term barely used in public parlance five years ago. Even notorious laggards in stock market regulation, such as Greece, jumped on the bandwagon. Thereafter the Parmalat case convinced lukewarm continental Europeans that corporate governance was not just an Anglo-Saxon affair.

The results of these efforts are visible. Just about every publicly quoted company now faces a barrage of new and complex regulations, stock market listing requirements, directors' fiduciary liability rules, and voluminous codes of conduct, the latter often with the mandate, 'comply or explain'. No wonder there is a renewed interest in private ownership. The motivation to avoid the high costs of public ownership has never been greater.

Is this good news for privately held family businesses? Yes. Contrary to conventional wisdom, however, we would amend this answer to include '... and no'. The answer is yes because avoiding the new regulations' compliance costs is another source of competitive advantage. Corporate governance reforms routinely cost millions. Moreover, an often-overlooked consequence is the time and energy spent by CEOs and boards to ensure compliance – an expensive distraction.

The answer is also no, however, because it would be naïve to ignore the fact that private family businesses have their own corporate governance problems. In the absence of compliance sanctions, family firms might feel no need to embrace good governance practices. While most questions of corporate governance are universal, the answers are specific. Without legal compliance as a benchmark, many private family companies might also struggle to develop appropriate governance solutions in the present-day environment.

The purpose of this chapter is not to repeat mainstream thinking and research. Our goal, rather, is to provide some views that could be considered contrarian, views based on research done at IMD. We will attempt to challenge some common corporate governance myths.

The fit is everything

The first myth to address is the assumption that corporate governance regulations really drive the way a company behaves. Instead, there are four situational factors that really mold business behavior (which we will examine below). The result is that there is no such thing as a singular generic 'best practice' in corporate governance. What counts is the governance system's fit in respect of the specific company. The fit is what creates value.

For family firms the question of fit is even more complex. Conventional thinking makes the board of directors the locus of governance. There are, however, also other key players such as owners. Furthermore, the market's knee-jerk approach to establish complicated, legalistic, and rigid governance structures could be especially harmful for family businesses. When fit is the key to value, and the business environment is dynamic, rigid rules or protocols designed to restrict flexibility attack the very strength of family-owned enterprises – their ability to adapt and act in their long-term best interests.

Factors shaping corporate governance practice

Regulators, academics and, curiously, the wider public hold a strong belief that corporations require tighter regulation to drive new rules for corporate behavior. One question being considered is whether one-tier or two-tier boards protect shareholders best. The first, typical in the Anglo-Saxon world, unites executive and non-executive members of the board in a single entity that is ultimately responsible for the company. In the two-tier system, predominant in Northern Europe, responsibility is shared by a non-executive supervisory board and an executive management board.

The board of British Petroleum, for example, is legally a one-tier board with an independent chairman and a majority of non-executive directors. In practice, these individuals act as though there is a two-tier structure, determining the 'space' in which the CEO and the top team can work independently, setting targets, evaluating performance, and debating major decisions that affect the company's future.

In Germany, there have been examples of the non-executive chairman of a supervisory board effectively running a company. This may not be in accordance with German law, but strong CEOs with a great track record tend not to let go easily when they retire and become chairmen of supervisory boards.

Another example is the tendency for power to shift to executives in global companies. The more global a company, the more complex the business becomes. According to research done at IMD, maintaining a global enterprise is the leading indicator of organizational complexity, rather than sheer size. In the 1970s, for example, American steel companies were huge, but nevertheless simpler operations than global businesses. This increased complexity makes it very difficult for a non-executive board member to understand all relevant risks, know different markets, and assess investment opportunities. This inevitably shifts the balance of power towards full-time company executives, regardless of regulation and ownership. As information on strategic issues can be imprecise, even diffuse, top management often has abundant opportunities to present its action plan in the best light without legally misleading the board.

What then are the most important factors shaping corporate governance practice, if not regulation? IMD research has identified four primary factors:

- *Personalities matter.* Whether regulators like it or not, effective CEOs inevitably shape the way the corporate governance system works. Through personal initiatives, by leveraging influence, and wielding individual power, the CEO dominates the interpretation of facts and determines the governance process, the dissemination of information, and the timing. This can happen irrespective of whether a two-tier or a one-tier board system prevails. When a strong personality is combined with concentrated ownership – as in a family business – the leader may wield inordinate power.
- *The strategy/business model.* In different stages of the corporate life cycle and in different industries, different corporate governance systems are appropriate. A start-up in a volatile high-tech industry has different requirements (i.e., more coaching and risk management by the board) than a more mature business in which the board needs leverage to fight complacency and bureaucracy. An aggressive growth strategy based on mergers and acquisitions would require different supervision than a more gradual, organic approach.
- *The business environment.* The unwritten dos and don'ts can be as important as the established rules and regulations. They can shape the political environment, social norms, traditions, and/or public expectations. Families with high name recognition may face additional requirements, especially if they are private companies. A lack of legal corporate governance sanctions and financial disclosure is a hurdle for corporate governance that is at least as high as that faced by non-family, publicly listed firms – if the family brand is to be protected.
- *Ownership/capital markets.* Institutional investors, who regard themselves as representatives of a wider shareholder group, have driven many previous and current governance rules. Private owners can shape appropriate governance practices even more fervently than the fragmented owners of public companies.

These brief sketches make it pretty clear that there is no generic, one-size-fits-all corporate governance best practice. This is, however, the implication of many codes of conduct. The needs of family businesses require a specifically tailored approach.

The role of the board in family business

With no best practices to set the standard, the various roles that the board plays and the various roles that outsiders play in the family business governance system need to be examined. There are four different types of governance system:

- The CEO-centered model – often found in the USA. Here the role of the CEO and chairman of the board is combined, and one person dominates the governance system and its decisions. As mentioned earlier, the more global and complex a company, the more the power shifts to the executives and is centralized in the role of the CEO. Even in governance systems in which the management board is legally equal to a CEO and bears a fiduciary responsibility, 'imperial CEOs' have nonetheless developed.
- The checks-and-balances model – the current favorite of regulators and even investment bankers, who had previously favored the CEO-centered model. Most of the recent changes in corporate governance regulations are intended to strengthen the role of the board and independent directors in order to better control and supervise management.
- The consensus model – culturally ingrained in many Asian and northern European systems. This model emphasizes harmony on the board, as well as harmony within the business environment and among stakeholders.
- The owner-centered model – relevant for family businesses and private non-family companies. It is vital to understand the specific role that owners play and the governance implications of this for family business.

IMD Professor John Ward has identified five categories of family firms (operating, governing, active, investing, and passive). The specific implications of this framework for corporate governance are as follows for the respective type of owner:

- *Operating owner.* Management is wholly or partly dominated by the owning family. If there are legal requirements in respect of corporate governance, they are minimal and roles are allocated within the family. The transaction costs are extremely low as trust and informality drive the governance process. The danger lies in the possibility that key decisions might be effected without a thorough examination of their possible consequences.
- *Governing owner.* Often outside managers run the day-to-day operations, but the family dominates the (supervisory) board, directing and controlling the business from there. It is likely that the family will not only select the management team but will also have the final say on important business decisions. Family members' presence has a huge influence on the strategy, portfolio mix, synergies, culture, risk preferences, organization, and performance measurement.
- *Active owner.* More elaborate governance structures are typical in this category, with the family constituting only a part of the (supervisory) board. External trustees play a more important role, especially when there are minority shareholders. However, the owners set the standards and processes for governance, which is often based on a checks-and-balances model and designed to ensure the continuity of the business and leadership.
- *Investing owners or passive owners.* The involvement of the family in the business is often reduced to the collection of dividends. The company is run by the management and the board. However, the stability implied by continued family ownership could have important consequences for the business model and the core strategy.

These governance frameworks have important implications for the board. Figure 11.1 indicates the different options correlating with the owners' level of involvement.

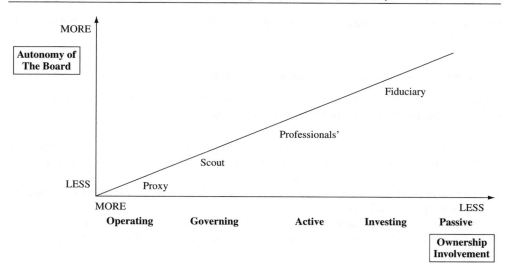

Figure 11.1   Types of owner

- Operating owners often have a 'proxy board' of friends and family. Given the deep involvement of the owners in day-to-day operations, no agency problem exists. If there is any meaningful role for outsiders, it lies in the objective evaluation of the team around the operating owners and the mediation of potential family conflicts. This does not mean that operating owners cannot benefit from outside advisors who really know the company – but few in this position are ready to listen.
- Governing owners depend on a good board, often referred to as a 'scout board'. The role of outsiders is to support owners with advice on industry trends, to challenge management on operational issues, and to help evaluate management performance. External advisors can add valuable insight. Mitigation and reconciliation of conflicts are necessary as their occurrence is likely. Coordination between family governance and business governance becomes more and more crucial.
- Active owners depend even more on formal governance structures, especially as surviving family firms tend to be larger. Often families set the fundamental business values that the external board members must share in order to help operationalize them and support the corporate culture. Boards in this category need to be closely aligned with the owners while maintaining objectivity and independence – a 'professionals' board'. The synchronization of family and business governance at this stage is vital, as the power wielded by an individual family 'tribe' is often sufficiently large to cause trouble. External actors might find themselves in the unpleasant situation of protecting the business from family conflicts.
- Investing or passive owners do not differ much from non-family companies with the exception of strategy. Such uninvolved owners seek and need a 'fiduciary board'. Since a significant portion of individual wealth is tied up in an illiquid asset, risk diversification is a more distinct concern for the family firm.

It should be noted that there is no natural progression to these categories. A family business in the sixth generation may still have operating owners, such as C&A. And, as the Ford Motor Company illustrates, even an investing family might again be called upon to act as operating owners. Therefore, it is important not to look for 'best practices', but rather to seek the best fit.

Additional requirements for governance in the family business

Regardless of the style of the board, the family business has to meet the general imperatives of good, context-sensitive corporate governance rules:

- Clear allocation of duties, responsibilities, power, and accountability – especially the division of labor between board and top management, regardless of whether management ranks are occupied by family or not.
- Transparency in the business model/strategy, the planned and achieved results, and the opportunity/risk preferences.
- Monitoring and compliance, supported by appropriate and rigorous follow-up.
- Professional qualifications and leadership competencies of the directors in line with the industry.

Particularly with regard to performance requirements, there can be no 'discount'. Family businesses must meet the same hurdles for competence and leadership skills as others in the industry. If this standard is not met, declining competitiveness will soon follow.

In a non-family company, every board member has equal rights and standing. Owner members on private family business boards cannot realistically be regarded as equal to non-family board members. This inequality does not mean that arguments from outside board members should be ignored. In every debate, analysis, or evaluation of options, each viewpoint should stand on its own merits, regardless of its advocate. However, it should be clear to everyone that the owners have the final say. In principle, this is the same for a publicly quoted company, but given the fragmented ownership, it is nearly impossible for owners to express a common will. One of the dilemmas in the governance of public companies is that the owners are practically unrepresented. When institutional investors step in, a new agency problem emerges. The managers of these funds have their own interests, which might not be the same as those of the broad class of shareholders. Therefore, responsible ownership should be regarded as good news, even if it leads to some inequality.

All involved in the governance system of a family business have to understand the specific context and what is expected. As described above, depending on the level of ownership involvement, boards play different roles as long as transparency and a mutual understanding of the rules prevail. As no one is obliged to serve on family business boards, such a differentiation should not be an obstacle.

When owner-directors have more power, they also have more responsibility. One of the fundamental obligations of ownership is to set the values and basic rules for the business, as long as they conform with local laws. With values and their impact on norms and cultural attitudes, the board then shapes the life of the company through strategic decision making. An excellent example of strongly held beliefs and philosophy can be found in the abridged version of the values statement of Lehmann & Voss, a fourth-generation Hamburg family business, found in Figure 11.2.

Those who work in the governance system of a family business must share the organization's fundamental values. This does not preclude professional disagreements or differences of opinion. On the contrary, on this foundation of mutual understanding, issues and strategy

---

Lehmann & Voss & Co.

Our Values, Our Guidelines

Our Values
or: what counts for us

As a family business we think and plan long-term. And all of us are responsible for insuring that this finds expression in our daily activities.
That makes us predictable.

The relationship between our managers and our employees is one of trust, as is that between those responsible for the market and our clients and suppliers. We stand by our word.
That makes us reliable.

Our company is happy to incorporate change in order to remain successful. Yet we always hold to our course: our fixed points are mutual respect and a sound, socially-oriented entrepreneurial spirit.
That makes us credible.

Our Guideline
or: who we are and what we want

1. Our Company

As a chemicals company we aim to increase the value of our enterprise without taking dangerous risks or neglecting social and ecological factors.
That makes our activities sustainable.

2. Our Strategy

We pursue three business strands: own production, distribution and trade. Our products and our service are of the highest quality, but there is always room for improvement. We seek the new mainly by developing the tried-and-tested. We are consequently growing our international involvement.
That makes us competitive.

3. Our Clients

We work closely with our clients. Together with them we seek improvements and solutions to problems on a basis of trust and respect.
That makes us successful.

4. Our Employees

Our dedicated employees participate in the company's economic success. The company offers them secure work places and satisfying working conditions and tasks. We prefer direct discussions, as we see problems as opportunities and not a reason for criticism. Our employees work in a responsible and results-oriented way.
That makes us socially responsible and appealing.

5. Our Managers

Our managers have sufficient scope for their own initiatives and decisions, and bear responsibility for the results in their respective sectors. They have a model function, giving encouragement while also making demands. Women and men have the same chances of promotion.
That makes managing in our company an ambitious and varied task.

To achieve the objectives behind our guideline, all of us must make our contribution in our respective fields.
At the end of a working week, we should be able to be proud of what we have achieved.

That makes Lehmann & Voss & Co. a special company.

Figure 11.2   Lehmann & Voss's value statement

can be debated even more rigorously. Principles can be more important than personalities in boardroom discussions. Beware, though. These shared values must not lead to 'group think', which can be a breeding ground for complacency and tolerance of low performance. Family business boards need to guard against such 'group think' by seeking independent and family directors who bring disparate points of view and have the courage to express them.

Learning nuggets from the case

There is one fundamental, but self-inflicted flaw in family business governance, both in the family and business dimension. Dominant, successful personalities in the family constellation can lead to a rigid dynamic that threatens the governance system. In non-family firms, lawmakers and regulators can mandate governance systems that adapt to changing circumstances. In a family business, the way out of ingrained practices can be profoundly difficult.

A typical example can be found in the serious governance challenges faced by the third-generation Bata Shoe Organization of Canada. In the following, we first discuss the case, which is embedded in the key points on corporate governance at which we aim at in this chapter. We subsequently present a more extensive version of the case for the interested reader to delve deeper.

Regarding Bata, the patriarch intended to make the business immortal by setting up a trust and protecting it from the family. The trust did not prevent family conflicts, nor did the trustees prove to be vigilant guardians of the family's heritage. They presided over a declining business for far too long. The law of unintended consequences kicked in.

The happy ending of the Bata drama

Hollywood could not have invented a better story of family and business struggle than that faced by the Bata Shoe Organization following World War II. Uncle and nephew battled for decades to determine who would control the company. The son quit as CEO. But it took hard work, persistence, and dedication to straighten out this corporate governance challenge.

Founded in 1894 in Zlin, Czechoslovakia, the Bata Shoe Organization was set to become the largest global shoe manufacturer despite the turmoil of two world wars. However, the founder, Tomas Bata, left no will when he died in 1932, but instead a 'moral testament'. To make the company immortal and to ensure its future as a source of social benefits, he dedicated its shares to a public trust. But one paragraph could be interpreted as giving ownership control to his half-brother Jan, not to his then 17-year-old son, Thomas J. Bata. The situation did not immediately cause trouble, as Thomas J. was still young and not yet ready to take up the reins of such a vast enterprise. However, after World War II, when Thomas J. was grown up and ready to assume his rightful role in the company, Jan refused to cede control. It took a legal battle that lasted for nearly two decades for Thomas to regain ownership. His persuasion and sheer will led executives in the company's nearly 30 local subsidiaries to embrace him as their leader.

His son, Thomas G. Bata Jr, faced another dilemma in the late 1980s. Well-meaning, but aged trustees watched over a decade of decline in the company which was then structured as self-perpetuating trusts. The trustees supervised the destruction of more than half of the family's wealth – and very nearly the Bata reputation. It took almost another decade of contentious wrangling for Thomas G. Bata Jr, together with his sisters, to develop a corporate governance structure that established clear accountability and responsiveness to the rapidly changing world of a globalizing consumer business.

The dedication of the Bata family to its heritage and the integrity of the family name resulted in a long fight to regain control of the company. The four third-generation siblings developed and staged a turnaround. Things could easily have been worse.

The Bata case is not an atypical example. It is sad that future realities are seldom foreseen in the will or contract. Given the many potential issues, it is not difficult to miss at least one. Nor do provisions always work out as intended. People change over time and what works at one time may not work under different circumstances. Promising young heirs can take unexpected turns, turbulence in the business may require rare turnaround skills, tax rules can change, profitable business models may disappear when knowledge cannot be protected. The list of examples that trigger serious reconsideration of important governance rules is nearly unlimited.

So, what can be done? Three recommendations can help: first, a 'sunset' clause should be the basis of the family and business governance systems; second, focus on a few basic rules to ensure the continuity of core values; finally, include conflict resolution rules.

The first idea is that each responsible generation gives to the next generation a new governance system for the family and the business. It is part of their duty. It should reflect changing circumstances like the growth of the family or the business, foreseeable trends such as industry consolidation and experience gained, including selection criteria for family representatives on boards and managing conflicts of interest.

Secondly, instead of trying to foresee every possible situation, the basic agreement should lay out the core values of the family and the business. Company policies must necessarily follow from these core values. For example, if the goal is to stay independent, then the sales of shares/property rights must be restricted and tightly controlled by the family office.

Thirdly, arbitration rules must be in place in case of conflicts in the family or business and to provide for necessary adaptation of the governance system over time. Historically, the family is the primary source of contentious debate. In the business sphere, the rules for conflict resolution are generally much clearer and often anticipated. Disagreements are not necessarily bad. Innovation cannot be born without conflict. Different perspectives legitimately shape divergent viewpoints. Those who run the family businesses are often more ready to invest in new ventures than those who simply want to enjoy the benefits of a steady, robust cash flow. The issue then is adopting a fair process to resolve these differences. In the past, conflict resolution was frequently the purview of the 'family elder' who considered each argument and then rendered a decision.

The decline of patriarchal structures in families makes conflicts within the family more likely. No one really has the power to discipline dissenters. Therefore, either court cases are pursued (mostly an unpleasant experience, dividing the family further) or neutral parties are selected to mediate and resolve crises. To be effective, trusted outsiders must be appointed *before* any conflict arises. Many families do not like people outside the family deciding their destiny. But this reticence could increase the pressure to find a solution within the family first. The difficulty in finding external people who know the family and the business yet are not tied to any of the 'family tribes', could bring the warring factions together.

Where does the value-added come from?

It is conventional wisdom that dedicated and responsible ownership considerably lowers transaction costs. However, the way ownership rights and responsibility are exercised in varying contexts differs widely. The identification of a value-added governance system has to be more specific and based on the merits of the individual situation and the closeness of fit in serving the family and business most effectively.

There is one case in which the family as owner can always add value – the transparency and continuity of core business values. Formal and informal corporate policies are derived from these values. The litmus test for the effectiveness of family owners is therefore the readiness and the competence with which they provide a clear set of principles that guide the life of the operation. This differs from the 'motherhood and apple pie' vision and mission statements in most non-family companies, which triggers cynicism and the disinclination to espouse stated values.

Selecting independent directors

As discussed earlier, despite the fact that in some instances family members may assume primary managerial and supervisory responsibility, external professionals need to be involved in the family firm. The best way to incorporate fresh, objective viewpoints into this process is to ensure that strong, competent outside professionals hold seats on the company board. The board bears ultimate responsibility for the long-term direction of an enterprise and so is in a position to play a crucial role. In family businesses, board members can contribute in another important realm. They are also custodians of the family's basic values that ultimately shape corporate culture and the way the firm conducts itself. This is not a trivial issue but it is one that has implications for the board recruitment process.

Gone are the days when the typical board was composed of the CEO, hand-picked friends, and two members amenable to the local community. Frantic efforts have begun to beef up boards with truly independent directors. Many companies have employed headhunters for this purpose, with mixed results. The use of headhunters also puts confidentiality at risk. Such high-level and important searches can take an extended period, as management seeks to be sure of its choice. After all, there is no definitive test for potential board members and headhunters often have difficulty fully understanding the values dimension inherent in the family enterprise. In the past, there were often far more suitable candidates available than vacant board seats, which made things somewhat easier. But the situation has now reversed.

There is a more practical way to approach this issue. One has to admit that personal choices are subjective and the higher one moves up in the hierarchy, the more personal it can get. But two things can help – the transparency of the process and the clarity of the selection criteria. The latter includes not only the core values set by the family but also a kind of job description.

In today's complex world, no one person possesses all requisite skills for successful board functioning. Excellent performance by a board requires a group effort and the composition of the team is vital. Who will complement existing competencies best? Are industry experts who are operational, battle-hardened 'old hands' best, or someone who can liaise especially well with the family? It is important that the board and family ownership agree unanimously on what is needed.

The temptation for family firms is to see the criteria for an effective director as common to all businesses. It is not. The family business seeks directors who have two seemingly contradictory qualities: they remain faithful to values and principles and they challenge fundamental strategic assumptions and performance standards. Special instruction or heed is needed if a search firm is used to be sure this dilemma is well understood and addressed.

The board chairman has a pivotal role. Even if there is a nominating committee, the chairman must be involved and, without dominating the process, play two essential roles. First, the chairman must strike the balance between director empathy for the family's values and the directors' capacity to constructively challenge management's *and ownership's* current thinking. And the chairman must ensure that the family owners present clear values and expectations to the board.

It is unconventional to imagine independent directors as resources and critics to owners, in addition to their customary role as resources and critics to management.

Conclusion

Recent corporate scandals have brought increasingly rigid standards for corporate governance. Family-controlled firms have the privilege to examine those standards and to adopt a governance form suitable to their situation. That opportunity is very valuable as governance that fits the circumstances is surely preferable.

For all companies, the proper form of governance varies with the complexity of the company and the personality of the leader. Government and market laws make acknowledging those differences very difficult. Therefore, family companies have a competitive advantage in governance.

But family owners also have a greater responsibility. They must resist the conventional wisdoms of how the board functions and what to look for in independent directors. Instead, they must take the time and care to design their governance system.

Further, the owners have the challenge to clarify and assert their values as the core of how the business is conducted and what the directors oversee. Yet, with the more powerful force of values, encouraging vigorous debate on strategic issues in the boardroom is both more possible and more difficult. It is more difficult to avoid 'group think'. To overcome that risk, the chairman requires special skills, as do the independent board members.

On the other hand, when core values are the foundation of the governance system, the quality of debate and the conviction to achieve is ever greater. Happily, family firms do not have to follow all the new rules in corporate governance. Instead, they can govern in a way most appropriate to the circumstances in their company. This is the counterintuitive truth: the value from governance comes not from the necessary compliance, but from the fit.

11.2   CASE STUDY: BATA SHOE ORGANIZATION

[By Joachim Schwass, Ulrich Steger, John Ward, and Colleen Lief]

PART A

Thomas G. Bata (Bata Jr) cradled the telephone and gazed down again at the figures he had been studying. The story was clear . . . the millennium strategy was not working.

Bata Jr felt compelled to convince the board and his parents to replace the CEO of Bata Shoe Organization (Bata). Though the family and the board knew things were bad, no one wanted to face another change in leadership. It was October 2000 and Bata Jr had just spoken to the CEO, who had confirmed that he would not be changing the strategy that was centralizing many activities and implementing a global way of doing things.

Bata Jr felt frustrated. Although he sat on the board of directors of the company, his options appeared to be limited. There seemed little he could do to dissuade the CEO from his strategy. He felt helpless to do anything more than urge change. Because of the company's ownership structure, Bata Jr and his sisters were powerless to help save the company that bore their name and represented the culmination of their family's legacy of ten generations of shoemaking.

With the current ownership structure, the family had little direct control over the company. The majority of shares were held in a trust administered by trustees who, although well intentioned, were aged and falling short of the challenges posed by rapid and difficult changes in the industry. The absence of leadership at critical junctures had already cost the company more than half its value. Now, misguided strategy was threatening its future viability. Not only was the Bata reputation at stake, but the family's financial heritage also hung precariously in the balance. The time had come for the Bata family to make a decision – walk away or roll up their sleeves and fix what was wrong.

Bata: from founding to the 1950s

The Bata Shoe Organization grew from its beginnings in Zlin, Czechoslovakia, in 1894 to become one of the largest shoe companies in the world. However, the road from this humble start to finding its place among global industry giants was not without obstacles. The company faced considerable external turmoil during its long history – from the disruptive effects of World War II to the rise of Communism in key markets and the nationalization of its assets in several developing countries. Perhaps the most significant event occurred in 1945, when Communist regimes expropriated the family's holdings in Eastern and Central Europe, which had previously served as its nerve center. Having lost its entire headquarters operation, Bata was left with about 30 different operating companies scattered throughout the globe. The organization founded by Tomas Bata (Tomas) and inherited by Thomas J. Bata (Bata Sr), though, would ultimately become a Canada-based global manufacturing and retailing empire operating in 68 countries with over 50,000 employees selling over 250 million pairs of shoes every year – primarily through company branded retail shops.

Tomas had built a paternalistic organization that reflected the 'moral testament' found among his papers at his death in 1932. Tomas believed that the Bata Shoe Organization should not be a source of private wealth for his descendants but should rather be preserved as a public trust, a means of improving living standards within its communities and providing customers with good value for money.[1] Bata was innovative for its times. One of the first companies to have profit sharing for employees, it also provided housing, education, and a short five-day work week. This was the philosophy that guided the creation of the first family trust in the 1950s.

Bata: from the 1950s to 1984

After World War II, a severe shoe shortage resulted in a sellers' market for footwear manufacturers. Said Bata Jr,

---

[1] Bata, T., with Sonja Sinclair. (1990). *Bata: Shoemaker to the World*. Stoddart, Toronto.

If you could supply, you were able to sell.

Bata operated successfully for years as a loose confederation of about 40 independent entrepreneurial operations. But by the 1980s, the market had begun to change – people no longer simply needed to buy shoes. Functionality was balanced with price, style and, now, brands. The emergence of brands resulted from a shift in industry emphasis from manufacturing to marketing and was underscored by the arrival of competitors like Adidas and Nike. Shoe production also shifted, first to cheaper southern European countries, then to low-cost countries like China. These trends led Bata to reduce its European production capacity (the company went from 18 European factories in the 1950s to none by 2002), while it shifted its focus from manufacturing to distribution.

During this period, too, a critical battle for control of the company took place between Bata Sr and his uncle, Jan Bata (Jan). Tomas had died without a will. But a handwritten memorandum made out to his half-brother, which appeared to sell the business to Jan at a fraction of its value, was discovered. Since Bata Sr was 17 years old when his father died, he could not yet operate this large enterprise anyway, so the issue of rightful ownership remained unresolved for many years. The trouble finally started when Jan refused to initiate an orderly transfer of the firm to Bata Sr once his age and skills had become equal to the challenge of his inheritance. The ensuing court battle was not settled until 1966, when Bata Sr finally won title to the company's shares. It had been unclear in the intervening 19 years who actually owned the business. It was only as a result of the odd and sometimes controversial behavior of his uncle, along with sheer force of personality, that Bata Sr persuaded the operating companies to recognize him as the firm's leader. His extraordinary powers of persuasion enabled him to convince many in the organization, even those senior to him in age and experience, that he was the rightful owner even before the court battle was settled. Once ownership ceased to be an issue, Bata Sr established two trusts in Bermuda to hold the 80% of company shares that were not held by the charitable foundation created by Tomas long ago in furtherance of his social agenda. Domicile in Bermuda assured favorable tax treatment of company profits, which enhanced organic growth and expansion potential and drove its organizational structure (refer to Figure 11.3).

Bata Jr leads the family firm

In 1984 the structure of the company changed when Bata Jr became CEO of the company (refer to Figure 11.4) and the first supervisory board was established in response to Bata Sr's retirement at age 70. Bata Jr had been groomed to take the helm at Bata one day. Years of preparation had culminated in his moving from the deputy CEO position to the firm's chief leadership role. Up until that time, the company had had no formal oversight and Bata Sr counted on the counsel of three or four close advisors. When his son took over as CEO in 1984, Bata Sr stayed on as honorary chairman of the newly created board. A non-family, non-executive chairman, two outside business executives, two trustees, and a representative of the company's charitable foundation were appointed to the board in accordance with the ownership structure. The trustees, who also appointed themselves to seats on the board, appointed these directors.

Structured as a self-perpetuating entity, the trust was put in place to ensure the continuity of the business, in fulfillment of the founder's aim. The family, which in addition to Bata Sr

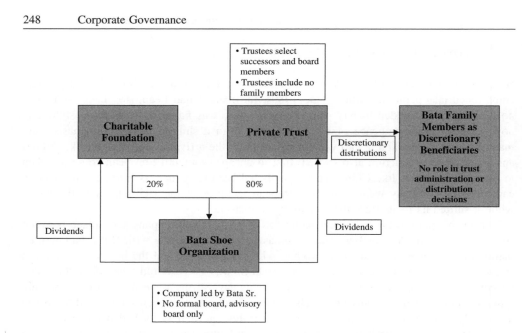

Figure 11.3   Ownership structure from 1950s to 1984
Source: Company information.

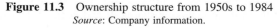

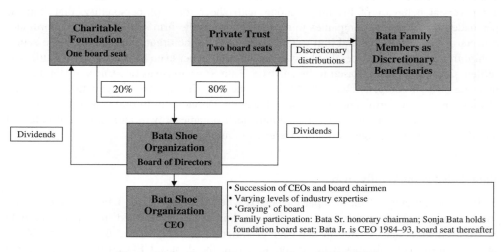

Figure 11.4   Ownership structure from 1984 to 2001
Source: Company information.

and his wife Sonja included their four children (refer to Figure 11.5), did not directly own the firm's shares, but could benefit from its success through dividends paid to the trust. Because of poor company performance and a frugal family tradition, however, dividends were very modest. The senior Batas appointed the first set of trustees; subsequently, the trustees appointed their own successors. The trustees were under no obligation to do what the family wanted. Said Bata Jr:

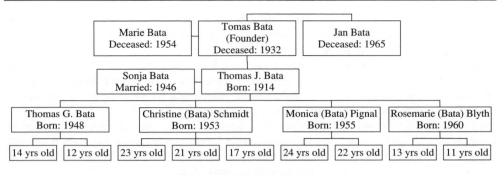

Figure 11.5   Bata family tree
Source: Company information.

The family, like myself, was always kept interested but we never quite understood what our role was because we didn't own any shares. We were consulted from time to time but the trustees had no requirement to do anything we requested or wanted.

However, for many years, Bata Sr exercised some indirect control through his personality and relationships with the trustees, and thereby held informal influence.

As CEO of the company, Bata Jr was accountable to the board. The directors tended to be prestigious individuals, some of whom had been chairmen of large multinational companies, albeit in unrelated industries. The board was procedurally heavy and Bata Jr spent much time preparing for board meetings, where the emphasis was on reporting and process. It was an uneasy relationship – and Bata Jr questioned the wisdom of the existing structure. In an exchange with one of the trustees, Bata Jr said,

The problem between you and me is [that] I can't sleep seeing what's going on.

I can,

responded the trustee, to which Bata Jr replied,

That's why it's wrong, you *acting* as an owner because you *do* sleep at night.

At this time, the Bata Company began to encounter financial difficulties. In September 1990 a new senior vice president of finance and development admitted that the company's return on equity was poor. He said,

My two to three year target is a 16% return.[2]

By then, Bata was a global giant employing 66,000 people and manufacturing and selling more footwear than anyone else in the world. Its dependency on its Canadian domestic market was marginal – 3% to 4% of its revenue – and it was strong overseas. It was then, for example, the largest shoe retailer in Italy, India, and Indonesia. Realizing that manufacturing

---

[2] Collison, R. (1990). How Bata rules its world. *Canadian Business* **63**(9): 28ff.

shoes in the industrialized West was a dying business, Bata Jr systematically transformed the company's operations in Western Europe and North America into 'niche manufacturers' making specialty footwear for various industries.

In earlier decades, national ownership laws forced Bata to list shares of its local subsidiaries on many domestic stock exchanges in the Asia-Pacific region. Bata Jr ultimately saw in this situation an opportunity both to consolidate the company's holdings in the region and to raise much-needed equity for Bata. With a 20% listing on the Singapore Stock Exchange, the firm could have raised $150 million. Bata would have had enough to settle all its bank loans worldwide and to strengthen its balance sheet for the challenges ahead. Bata Jr ardently supported the deal and viewed this potential transaction as key to the firm's future. But his parents opposed the deal on the grounds that selling shares would place the company on a slippery slope, which could ultimately erode the trust's majority stake and the founder's legacy. When the board of directors bowed to their influence and vetoed the deal, Bata Jr resigned as CEO in 1993. This lack of support was the final straw for Bata Jr – the culmination of the frustration of a long series of differences with his parents and the board.

From 1994 to 1999: the revolving door years

Between 1994 and 1999 Bata went through two CEOs and a period with no CEO. First came Stanley Heath,[3] the company's first non-family chief executive, who was previously head of RJR Nabisco's Latin American food operations. Heath, together with several of his senior managers, resigned in 1995 – after only a year – amid growing tension with the senior family members. His efforts to implement a restructuring plan that involved closing large portions of Bata's European operations were not well received. According to the *Financial Times* in June 1996, Bata Sr described Heath as 'a very fine gentleman', but noted that neither he, nor his new management team, were 'shoe people' and that the shoe industry 'is a very, very peculiar business'.

By contrast, one Bata manager, upon resignation in 1995, said:

> . . . You can't appoint a new chief executive and then poke your nose in all over the place.[4]

In 1996 Bata's European operations continued to encounter trouble, as retail stores in Germany, Belgium, and the Netherlands, and one of four subsidiaries in France, were all losing money. Drastic action was required. At the insistence of the younger family members, a new director with retail and merchandising experience, Jack Butler, joined the board in April 1996 and later became executive chairman, working about 40% of the time. He and Bata Jr, who had assumed a board seat upon his resignation as CEO, set up a committee to study the problems in the European operations and recommend corrective action. Although Butler was a valued executive chairman and member of the board, he resigned after only six months. His strong personality led to major disagreements with the family matriarch and trustees. In spite of Butler's early exit, the committee's work was successful. Bata's European operations bounced back in 1997 with a strong balance sheet and the best profit year ever, largely due to the elimination of money-losing operations and the efforts of an excellent regional manager.

---

[3] Simon, B. (1996). Footwear family goes out of fashion. *Financial Times*, June 6, pp. 25ff.
[4] Ibid.

After Butler left Bata, one of the trustees became interim chairman and an internal candidate was chosen to fill the newly created post of president. The company continued without a CEO until March 1999, when Jim Pantelidis assumed the post.[5] Pantelidis's appointment, and the way it was done, proved to be controversial. When the board first formed a CEO selection committee, the four Bata siblings were excluded from the decision-making process, despite the fact that Bata Jr sat on the board. The committee went on to appoint Pantelidis, then in his mid-50s and a 30-year veteran of the oil industry, as CEO. He lacked the support of the Bata siblings and one of the board members, who questioned the relevance of his past experience in tackling the unique but pressing problems before them.

In an interview in January 2000,[6] Pantelidis explained that his strategy aimed 'to position the company in the next millennium – to re-establish it as a major force in the shoe business'. The plan was to streamline operations so that each plant specialized in producing one type of footwear for a global market. At the same time, the company would update and enlarge many of its stores and introduce new styles designed to appeal more to younger and middle-income family shoppers. Pantelidis also aimed to cut 10% of the company's $400 to $600 million costs over five years. Said Pantelidis:

> What needs to happen in this organization . . . is for it to start thinking more globally and start taking advantage of our scale and size.

But there was little momentum behind the strategy, and efforts to explain the new operating model within the company fell short. Senior family members were becoming increasingly nervous about how the business was being run. Even the board, which struggled under the weight of age and inertia, voiced its concern about the strategy to the CEO, who remained intransigent.

Despite a lack of substantive support for the millennium strategy and in direct contra-vention of the company's mandatory retirement age of 70, the CEO and the 73-year-old chairman were both reappointed at the annual meeting in October 2000. Following that meeting, it became clear to Bata Jr that this dire situation required drastic action. The family could agree to the business being sold and not put their own effort into finding a solution. Alternatively, they could take a deep breath and jump into a sea of trouble, and fight to save their birthright. Given the constraints imposed by the current ownership structure, though, Bata Jr wondered what he could, and should, do.

22 NOVEMBER 2001. Thomas G. Bata (Bata Jr), with the support of the new board, fired the Bata Shoe Organization's CEO. But the events leading up to that decision had started in October 2000 and required much effort and dedication on the part of Bata Jr and his three sisters to make it a reality. Changing the ownership structure of the Bata Organization was a revolutionary idea but one that was necessary for its survival.

'Hostile takeover': October 2000

Bata Jr faced a challenging situation. For the last three years an outside CEO had run his family's company with little success or tacit support. Although he was willing to step in and help redirect the company's course, Bata Jr was hampered by an ownership structure that excluded Bata family members from exercising direct control over the organization. To

---

[5] Strauss, M. (2000). Canada: Bata to revamp worldwide operations. *Globe and Mail (Toronto)*, January 17.

[6] Strauss, M. (2000). Canada: Bata to revamp worldwide operations. *Globe and Mail (Toronto)*, January 17.

make matters worse, the incumbent directors and trustees were paralyzed. Although they did not agree with what Jim Pantelidis, the CEO, was doing, they remembered the difficult times earlier without anyone in that role. Who else in their right mind would agree to preside over this colossal challenge?

Since the board members seemed unable to move towards positive change, Bata Jr and his sisters realized the onus was on them to do whatever was necessary to preserve the family's past and their children's future.

The Geneva conspiracy: the creation of a new trust structure

Recognizing the need to reinvent the company's ownership structure, the Bata siblings met in Geneva, Switzerland, in February 2001. In a two-day meeting that came to be known as the 'Geneva conspiracy', the siblings worked with outside advisors to fashion a bold new ownership and governance structure (refer to Figure 11.6). If they had control of the company, they reasoned, they would be free to take decisive action to salvage the Bata name and the company whose value they had watched drop by 50% over the last decade. In their view, the company had lost significant value through a leadership and strategy vacuum at critical points in its development. Bata Jr, who had evaluated many private companies over the years as potential investments, thought the family business still had a good basic platform

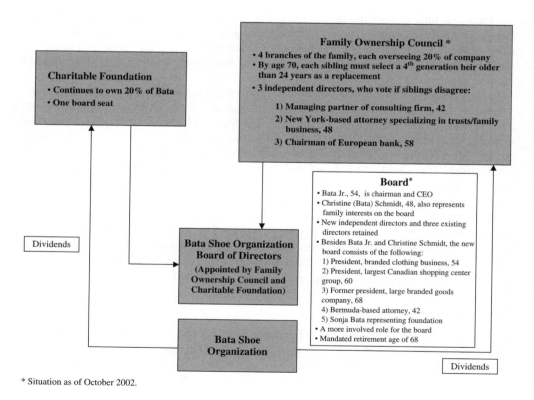

* Situation as of October 2002.

Figure 11.6   Ownership structure: post-2001 (simplified)
Source: Company information.

and business proposition. Major changes were needed to compete effectively in the rapidly changing shoe industry. But the Bata siblings felt that the company, if managed well, could again generate healthy returns, jobs, and products that exceeded customer expectations.

Working together, the siblings convinced their parents and the trustees of the merits of the new structure. The trustees agreed that fundamental change was necessary to keep the company intact. They appeared relieved at the prospect of handing over this grave responsibility – of finding successor trustees, board members, and a capable CEO – to the ultimate beneficiaries. There followed an eight-month legal process that culminated in November 2001. The four Bata siblings would now oversee the shares representing 80% of the Bata Shoe Organization, which were formerly held in the old trust. The charitable foundation maintained its 20% share of Bata and its seat on the board.

On 22 November 2001, Bata Jr, with a new ownership role, fired the CEO with the support of the family and new board and assumed the role of CEO himself. Previously, the trustees had appointed the board members and they often nominated each other. The new seven-member board, which consisted of three Bata family members and four outsiders, was now appointed de facto at the discretion of the Family Ownership Council, with the exception of Sonia Bata, who held the charitable foundation's board seat. The four Bata siblings sat on the new Ownership Council, along with three outside members who could break deadlocks that might occur among the family stakeholders. Not only was the composition of the company's board dramatically different (although three existing board members were retained), but a more informal, participatory spirit had also taken hold. Bata Jr was hopeful that, together, he and the new board could forge a successful path into the future:

> Previously the board, while intelligent, was adding little value because it was orchestrated in a very formalistic manner. It was management but not leadership. Now we have fewer board members and there's a dialogue – an 'us' situation.

> In our business, we have to move fast. So the way the board operates for the time being is more informal. The value we get from our board now is so much greater because members are more knowledgeable and understand the business much better.

So, the company's destiny was once more back in the hands of Batas, fulfilling the family's legacy of ten generations of shoemaking.

12

Corporate Governance Dilemmas in Private Equity Companies

12.1 CORPORATE GOVERNANCE IN PRIVATE EQUITY FIRMS: CAN IT ADD VALUE?

Private equity investment companies are now being confronted with the results of their success: growing to 10%–15% of the total stock market capitalization in recent years, including in Europe, ever more capital is chasing increasingly fewer suitable target companies. This not only requires a change in the way private equity companies (PECs) screen, select, and access potential investments, but also challenges the traditional way in which PECs, in the phase between acquisition and exit, work with their respective partner companies. A new paradigm is emerging: working with partner companies is becoming increasingly important. PECs need to be close to their investments for control reasons, to provide a variety of resources since capital alone is not enough, and, finally, to be a true sparring partner in order to optimize the strategizing process.

One promising area is corporate governance, to which most private equity companies have paid barely any attention so far. Many believe that it is sufficient to meet the legal requirements regarding corporate governance and they do not see the potential value-added that superior corporate governance can offer. Most PECs pursue active ownership, but only few have defined the principles of CG. To detect this value, however, one first has to understand the fundamental differences between the private equity and stock market-quoted companies, which dwarf the legal differences that exist between these entities across Europe. In the second part we specifically look at the role that the board can play in private equity investments.

Understanding the differences

The dominant CG paradigm for stock-quoted companies is the 'principal–agent problem'. The principal (investor) cannot control the agent (management) fully, due to an asymmetry in information. Basically, this means that the management has more comprehensive and up–to-date information about the business than the outside investor and has obtained this information at a lower transaction cost. Whereas management receives information in the course of their daily work, investors have to spend extra time and money. Therefore, all CG aims to align the investors' and management's interests (e.g., via stock options), as well as supervising the management at minimal transaction cost in the shareholders' interest.

There are three basic flaws in this 'principal–agent theory': first, it is pessimistic about human behavior (e.g., money is the dominant motivation, all management will deceive investors if they can). Second, it assumes that currently there is no imbalance of power between investors and management, but equal contractual relations. However, empirical evidence indicates[1] that in complex organizations power shifts to the executive side (which is conveyed by the many flawed stock option plans that favor management despite poor performance). And, third, there is an implicit assumption that investors will not withdraw their investments if transaction costs are low. Although the very notion of the stock market is to make assets liquid by establishing permanent market prices and bringing buyers and sellers together, no individual shareholder is driven to 'voice' his/her concern in companies with 10,000, or even a million, shareholders and become engaged in, for example, improved CG: she/he would have to shoulder the cost, the results are uncertain, and any improvement will benefit everyone else who did not become engaged ('free-rider problem'). Therefore, the incentive is to simply 'exit' the investment in case of dissatisfaction. This loss of 'responsible ownership' is the core of the corporate governance crisis in widely held public companies.

If substitutes (e.g., institutional investors) step in to assume the ownership role in stock market-quoted companies, another set of principal–agent issues arises. As the recent prosecutions and settlements in respect of the (pension) fund industry indicate, fund managers' and individual shareholders' interests are not synchronized. In addition, funds shy away from any involvement that limits their ability to trade stocks; they do not want to be regarded as an 'insider'. This is why they have been pushing for structural CG reforms that would provide features that could be observed from the *outside* (e.g., the number of independent directors, committees, etc.). The bad news is that there is no empirical evidence that such structural features in CG improve company performance at all.

Due to this 'outsider perspective', which is necessary for the permanent liquidity of the asset, the conclusion is drawn that PECs cannot learn much from the current CG debate on stock market-quoted companies, because their CG issues are completely different.

Contrary to 'outside' investors in stock markets, the PECs are 'insiders' in the companies in which they invest. One can argue that this 'insider' position is the compensation for forgoing liquidity and for investments that are 'locked in' the target company for three to seven years. In addition, the companies in which PECs invest are an unfavorable choice: if they were not experiencing problems (poor performance, succession issues, etc.), why would they be sold? And from the PECs' side: if the value-added does not indicate a turnaround, a strategic renewal opportunity, or accelerate new growth opportunities, where is the value-added to be found relative to other financial tools (e.g., a bank loan)? In any case, as a dedicated partner that contributes to a development strategy's implementation and to the enhancement of the competitiveness of the companies in which they invest, PECs have ownership with an insider status. This creates specific corporate governance dilemmas, which differ from those of public companies, but need to be made transparent and managed.

However, the insider status also solves some CG issues. As a more or less majority owner, there is no 'free-rider' problem. Clearly, the information asymmetry is – due to the involvement – lower (simultaneously, making the 'principal–agent problem' less relevant). The transaction costs of the involvement are 'part of the package', and need to be overcompensated by the value-added of their involvement (if not, then the PECs have a different problem).

---

[1] Steger, U. (2004). *Mastering Global Corporate Governance*. John Wiley & Sons, p. 45.

Corporate governance issues in private equity

The list of potential CG issues to be managed in PECs is as follows:

- The PECs represent a strong shareholder and they may undermine the board. The PECs' involvement can blur the clear responsibility and accountability of the owners, boards, and management (especially if the legal requirements of the boards are described in more detail and members are personally liable). Hence, there is need for clarification.
- If there are minority shareholders, the shareholder agreement might not have foreseen all potential sources of conflict. The mechanism for aligning interests might therefore be insufficient.
- Within the specific PEC framework, the 'usual' governance issues need to be solved:
  - Where does a board, besides in PECs, add value? The latter includes strategy development and implementation, recruiting and rewarding the top team, as well as ensuring and monitoring the results and compliance in the relevant industry.
  - Does a board work effectively as a team: interacting with one another, the management, and the individual PEC? What is the role and contribution of the chairman and the individual board members? What impacts do mentality and a relevant (mid-term) timeframe have?
  - Which are appropriate CG processes, besides those of reporting the committees' work (especially the audit committee), etc.? How should board members be recruited, remunerated, and evaluated? What are board members' specific requirements in respect of PECs? How can potential conflicts of interest (e.g., between board responsibility and employment at the PECs) be solved?
  - How should likely, but unpredictable, events (time-wise) – such as, e.g., acquisitions, changes in the top team, exit, etc. – be dealt with?

A board's function in a private equity framework

One thing is clear: there is more complexity in the 'triangle' shown in the relation between the PEC, board, and management than in the 'usual' hierarchical relation between the board (as representatives of shareholders) and management (see Figure 12.1). Simultaneously, reducing this complexity by staffing boards with the PECs' full-time employees leads to other disadvantages:

- If a company were to have a diverse portfolio of investments across industries, which occurs frequently, it would be very expensive to employ widely experienced board members with industry knowledge.
- PEC representatives may quite often only have financial expertise and have no need or opportunity to develop qualifications to serve on boards.
- PECs with a larger number of investments tend to have more opportunities for learning than others.
- PECs' specific role in M&A and exit can lead to conflicts of interest if a partner company's board is dominated by the PECs' employees.

Given this special profile demanded from board members, organizing an appropriate pool of candidates for board assignment remains challenging. At the same time, ensuring the

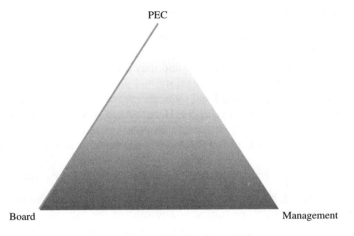

Figure 12.1   CG triangle at PECs

board's performance in the 'triangle' can be a PEC's true value-added service. PECs are always obliged to capture learning, so that their overall investment decision and interaction patterns in the top PECs' four major disciplines improve over time: defining the investment case; measuring the essential – not everything; improving the portfolio company's balance sheet considerably; and making the shareholder the crux of activities – i.e., ensuring value acceleration through joint efforts for the active shareholder.[2]

With the ultimate withdrawal decision in mind, three tasks crystallize for boards:

- Monitor and assess the (financial) performance as well as the business's conduct, based on a business case rather than on very short-term measures.
- Recruit, remunerate, and release the top team.
- Add value to corporate development through input and feedback to the strategy and its implementation, the organizational design to support the strategy, and other key issues (e.g., acquisitions and de-investment) as they emerge.

A well-performing board has to realize these three responsibilities, but there should be no overlap and redundancy between its work and what the PECs are doing in an active ownership role. This is no trivial task, and the details of the circumstances are important to find an optimal division of labor, which should be transparent to all involved.

If one looks at the three tasks in detail:

- The first task is ongoing and probably on every meeting's agenda, but should not consume too much time. The audit committee's preparation is therefore vital (and a lot depends on the PECs' separate scrutiny, especially if they have established a special 'link' to the CFO, often with additional reporting requirements).

---

[2] See Rogers, P., Holland, T. and Haas, D. (2002). Value acceleration: lessons from private-equity masters. *Harvard Business Review* **80**(6): 94–101.

- The second task is usually done through an (annual) appraisal of the top management, which forms the basis for the calculation of the bonuses as well as other decisions (e.g., whether to extend the contract or not). Again, this is an issue of coordination with PECs.
- The third task is often dealt with at an (annual) strategy retreat, a special board strategy committee, and specific tasks. Individual board members could even serve in an expert advisory capacity. The PECs could probably contribute additional input here, too.

It is vital for the PECs to build a network of capable board members from which one could quickly select a new board as an investment opportunity arises. However, as always, when it comes to personal decisions, matters become fuzzy. And the higher up you go in a corporate hierarchy, the fuzzier they become. And a lot depends on intuition, experience, and judgment (including the prejudices which often guide these decisions). There is no 'psychology test' available to indicate suitable board members. But at least two elements can be made transparent: the set of criteria which the (new) board member has to fulfill (and agree to), and the process of selection (and discharging). The potential board members will fulfill the different criteria to different degrees (e.g., a brilliant industry expert might be a very poor communicator), therefore much depends on the ability to create a 'diverse portfolio' of board members so that as a team they can deliver the highest performance. A significant question is, however: are there differences between 'normal' board members and those employed by the PECs?

Boards often charge a specific committee (more specifically, the remuneration or corporate governance committee) with the task of recruiting new board members. This committee then frequently employs a headhunter in the search. The goal is to prevent new members only coming through the chairman, or even worse, the CEO's network. However, the experience with headhunters has not been an unmitigated success – besides having its own share of embarrassment because it normally generates too many suitable candidates, who then have to be rejected. If there are leaks in the process, rejection might specifically cause frustration and resentment on both sides. Once again the question needs to be clarified: what role can the PECs play in this process?

As a matter of good practice, the board has to evaluate its own performance on a regular basis. This can again be done internally by the chairman or the chairman of the committee in charge, or with the help of a neutral outside moderator. The evaluation can be limited to the general board performance on a team level, or can specifically ascertain individual board members' contribution, especially that of the chairman. As the latter plays a pivotal role in the board's effectiveness and performance, an evaluation based on a multidimensional framework is encouraged in almost all cases.

Although there is a growing consensus that there should be an evaluation of board performance, there is still a lot of – often hidden – resistance, especially when it comes to the evaluation of board members' individual performance and contribution. Experience has indicated, however, that inefficiencies in boards' function are revealed by such evaluation, making intervention possible. A two-step approach might be advisable for boards that are not used to evaluation: start with the general board evaluation and when everybody is comfortable and familiar with the process, which mostly only occurs in the second round, move on to the next level. Board evaluation should in any case be part of the shareholder agreement and the letter of engagement.

The crucial board–management relationship

If the 'checks and balances' principle is applied, and the board is separated from the management, the question of the division of labor (and power) arises as one of the key questions in respect of CG. Please note that this question too is not concerned with the board's legal composition: in practice, a one-tier board with an 'independent' chairman and a large majority of outside directors functions exactly the same as the two-tier board with its separation of the supervisory and management boards in relation to the CEO/top management. The sensitivity is obvious: every tremor at the top can trigger an earthquake within the organization.

First, the relationship is often guided by the 'CEO life cycle'. A new top management is intensively scrutinized, but if it has a positive track record, the board often takes a less assertive position, although it should be more assertive before the CEO dominance becomes counterproductive, which normally occurs after 10 years. This pattern might be less relevant for PECs, as they should sell earlier.

Second, the different responsibilities should be clearly defined (e.g., in a 'code of governance' – the content of which would very much depend on the type of board the PECs, as the responsible owner, expect).

Third, the board should clearly define its information needs and the delivery process. Much time is wasted and communication required because management has no idea of what the board really wants and the board does not take the trouble to define what it thinks is needed for its work.

And, fourth, there should be some rules in respect of 'emergency situations' so that, for example, the chairman of the board and the chairman of the responsible committee could make or approve decisions if a dramatically urgent situation were to occur and only inform the full board later.

As difficult as it may seem, our experience has proven that if everyone involved understands the complexity of the 'triangle' and cooperates to find a workable solution to which everyone adds the best value in respect of their specific competencies, it is possible for great corporate governance to work. The benefits of superior CG are clear:

- A sounder and more realizable strategy.
- Better coaching and professional support of management.
- Quicker adjustments to new situations, emerging risks, and opportunity.
- Greater transparency about management performance, which is important not only for replacing non-performers, but also for rewarding high performers adequately.

This is the bottom line that investors expect.

Learning nuggets from the cases

In order to address the highly dynamic development the private equity industry has taken, we outline several tension fields in corporate governance in three cases, which complement each other. The first one, Automotive Machine Tool (AMT), describes the transition from a family business to a private equity investor-owned company. As with many distressed companies or firms that hope to fund expansion by accepting a private equity involvement, perceptions differ drastically when adopting the previous management's point of view on the one hand, and the view of the private equity investor on the other. In order to illustrate these discrepancies, we have written the very same situation from these two perspectives. Where you stand on an issue depends on where you sit. Part A describes the corporate governance dynamics from the established management's view. The subsequent part B provides the insightful view of the private equity investor as the story and real-life dilemma unfolds. The first main insight is that reality is multifaceted. Trying to fully understand the other's point of view is crucial.

The second main case on private equity elaborates on a situation where the investor really aims to add value beyond hidden agendas and returns. The private equity investor really aims to function as a strategy and corporate governance coach. It differs from the first case in the way that the investor is clearly not harsh, deceitful, opportunistic, and egoistic. Quite the opposite. We felt that both segments deserve attention in this book on corporate governance as both entail interesting dynamics until Murphy's law kicks in and the things that can go wrong actually go wrong. This investment body is interested in real growth and local development. The investor was happy with an observer status on the board, believing in management and its capabilities to make it happen – until it dawned that the investor might be the one being played in the truest Machiavellian way. It describes reality as it happened in a real-life event, with only minimum degrees of disguise in order to protect real-life people. What is important though is the pattern at work. Biocast is a high-growth biotech company in Brazil, which faces several corporate governance dilemmas. Established power structures oppose any noteworthy involvement or checks-and-balances influence from the representative of the private equity investor, frequent exchanges of this representative, as well as risky business decisions. The main insight here, beyond rendering the reader sensitive to the dilemma, is that corporate governance problems usually never come alone – and never at a convenient point in time. If the fish starts smelling at the top, the likelihood is that several construction sites need attention and anything you try to fix will take longer and cost more than you thought.

The third case, on Asian Car Part Holding, represents an exercise on what to do if board processes are suboptimal, but the financial side and returns on investments remain positive. Should the 'ideal' investor nonetheless insist on sound governance? Should the investor optimize? How can the investor transfer lessons learned by his or her colleagues in order to prevent poor governance from repeating itself elsewhere? This third case presents a specific challenge based on this dilemma.

12.2   CASE STUDY: AUTOMOTIVE MACHINE TOOL GMBH&COKG – FROM AILING FAMILY BUSINESS TO ACCELERATING PRIVATE EQUITY?

PART A

[By Ulrich Steger and Wolfgang Amann]

SINDELFINGEN, GERMANY, 14 NOVEMBER 2005, 21:46.

On paper everything looked so good when they acquired us,

thought Dr Jürgen Leitl as another of Benjamin White's aggressive e-mails popped up on his laptop. It read:

> I am deeply disappointed. Your HR director didn't get it. He is too slow in reducing headcount. He should be part of the layoffs too – as soon as possible. New horses for new courses.

The e-mail ended with the usual epilogue:

> Our battle cry: 15% EBIT!

Jürgen thought bitterly,

> He ignored my advice completely – again!

Benjamin represented D3 Capital, a British–European private equity company, named after the three Ds in the three founders' first names (David, Dennis, Dustin). On 1 October 2005, D3 Capital had acquired AMT after the Badische Gemeindebank decided to divest due to the upcoming strict Bale II credit regulations. Jürgen had been running AMT as its managing director since the beginning of 1999, and the bank brought him in 'to stop the bleeding' and to turn AMT around.

Why could he not get along with the new owners? Why did they ignore his advice and extensive experience within AMT nearly all the time? Did he still have a chance to influence decisions at AMT, or would he sooner or later have to go? Should he pre-empt this by leaving immediately? Could he have prevented them assuming all the power and turning him into a messenger boy? He closed his laptop to go home. But then he realized: time to answer these questions was rapidly running out . . .

The ups and downs of a family business

AMT was a typical mid-sized Swabian company with a strong record in technological excellence, exactly what you would expect from the 'Land of Tüftler und Bastler'. Founded in 1901 by Dieter Laibinger, it had been producing machine tools ever since. In the late 1960s it bought another machine tool company and focused increasingly on specific machine tools for the automotive industry. As the acquisition relied heavily on bank loans, the profit margin became very small. In the 1980s the third generation of the family – eight cousins – fell out as each had a very different vision of AMT. Decisions were blocked and opportunities missed. Investments slowed down and AMT went through a series of restructurings, cutting the workforce down to 1500 from 2500. Jürgen took over in 1999 after Badische Gemeindebank ousted the owners by buying the company. AMT relied too heavily on loans and eventually became too exposed to the bank. AMT was not the only company in Germany for which the established concept of a Hausbank, one main and supporting bank per company, ended.

Like so many other German managers, Jürgen had a technical background. He had earned a PhD in electrical engineering and subsequently worked his way up from the research laboratory of one of Germany's Blue Chips to head of manufacturing at a large plant. However, tired of bureaucracy, he had been more than happy to jump ship at the age of 42 to become one of the three managing directors of another Mittelstand's company, in charge of manufacturing. Five years later he was hired to turn AMT around.

A successful turnaround – by German standards

After a huge battle with the unions, Jürgen closed one of the acquired company's sites, laying off nearly 300 workers within a year, but he had no other option. He restructured the company into two major business units: one developing and producing the machine tools for the car and related industries, and the other concentrating on developing complex custom-made software for the machines, installing them in older and newer machines, as well as doing the necessary maintenance services.

Using the distribution center near Bratislava in Slovakia as a springboard, he repeatedly shifted low-skilled manufacturing tasks to this Eastern European low-wage country. This relocation cost another 350 jobs in Sindelfingen, but as it was gradual and partly compensated by the build-up of the service units, it went smoothly. AMT's overall 65% vertical integration in manufacturing was still rather high (in comparison with an industry average that was 5% lower), but Jürgen was convinced that the car giants' very specific demands required in-house flexibility and know-how for a wide variety of components too, otherwise quality standards would not be met. And for the company's cutting technological edge, he clearly needed Germany as his home base.

Since 2001, AMT had stopped losing money and had steadily increased its profits (refer to Table 12.1 for key figures). Jürgen was convinced that a continuous improvement process was working well, improving the quality gradually, thus developing a lean manufacturing and a more efficient customer relation management. He was sure that AMT's current profitability – at around 3% of the industry average – would continue to grow, and the EBIT could develop from the nominal 10% (average 7% after extraordinary items) to 12%–13% (10% after extraordinary items – the move to Slovakia and a change in location sites weighed heavily on the results). This would be the upper quartile of the industry and probably top for those mid-sized companies that were continuously being squeezed by their powerful customers.

Table 12.1 Economic development of AMT

	1999	2000	2001	2002	2003	2004	2005[3]
Employees	1500	1400	1100	1050	1000	950	950
Turnover (in € million)	110	112	103[4]	110	118	123	129
Profit as % of turnover	−3	−1	0	0.5	1.4	1.8	2.1
ROCE (before extraordinary items)	−15.6	−5.3	0	3.2	7.1	9.2	10.1
Gearing (relation of debt to equity)	94%	89%	81%	75%	68%	63%	59%

However, there was one big obstacle to these financial goals: the investments needed to go to China – Jürgen's real dream. The automotive industry was not only booming there, but also in other Southeast Asian countries like Thailand. Through a partnership with a Chinese distributor, AMT held the biggest market share of close to 30% for the machine tool investments in Chinese auto-manufacturing plants, roughly also a third of its turnover. AMT's US market activities had conversely contracted considerably in the last few years. Jürgen knew that distribution was not a sustainable solution. He was planning a JV with the current Chinese partner, increasing the manufacturing in China in the same manner as in

---

[3] Budget in October 2005.
[4] Due to plant closure and streamlining of product.

Slovakia, and ensuring that the status of the service (including the intellectual property rights for the software) was legally unambiguous. He knew the local content regulations would also cover such investments, and that the emerging domestic Chinese automotive industry was looking for domestic suppliers.

Up for sale

However, when Jürgen presented the investment of approximately €9 million in his three-year plan, the bank owners stopped him. This was the first time it had happened – he was utterly astonished. He could not and did not want to believe it at first. The corporate governance process had so far been pretty straightforward as the GmbH (the German limited liability company) had a simpler structure than a stock market company (refer to Figure 12.2). The supervisory board, the so-called Aufsichtsrat, was identical to an owners' meeting. The combination with a personal incorporation (&CoKG) was simply for tax reasons and included three bank managers, one of them – a member of the management board of Badische Gemeindebank – as its chairman. Their main concern was obvious: keeping AMT profitable enough to service its debt, therefore guaranteeing that the banks would not have to write off the loans. But the strict Bale II regulations and the loss of more advantageous financing privileges, due to public ownership, shifted the focus of interest towards selling AMT.

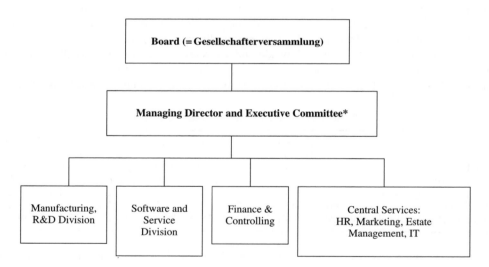

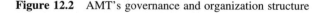

* The head of the four units and the head of the plant in Slovakia formed, together with the Managing Director, the Executive Committee. Purchasing was a task of the divisions as there were no real economies of scale to be made.

Figure 12.2   AMT's governance and organization structure

Jürgen organized an auction with the help of the investment bank arm of the state-owned bank. The exposure to investment bankers was a new experience for him. Surprisingly, eight bidders showed up – including Jürgen's former employer, which he saw as an indication that they wanted him back as CEO for the new entity. This auction was the start of the global engineering company's interesting journey with D3. While the private equity company did not offer the highest price, it won by offering the bank owner other advantages – cash, it required no provisions for liability and would buy the company outright. Jürgen remembered:

> At the end, they were just more alert to the needs of the bank and moved faster.

During the entire well-organized process that was focused on a balanced scorecard, Jürgen felt very committed to serve the bank. His sense of duty was based on a simple recognition:

> Badische Gemeindebank could have easily let AMT go bankrupt and they gave me a chance to show AMT's potential.

He had no real preference for any of the bidders as, on the one hand, he disliked the bureaucracy of the big global company that was bidding, but on the other hand, remained skeptical about the actual industry knowledge that D3's representatives had.

The new owners come in

Jürgen was not involved in the final round of negotiations, although he had guided the process up to that point. While signing the contract on Friday 30 September 2005 he met Dustin Kenburry, an elderly statesman and founder of D3, Ken Livingston, who introduced himself as the CFO of D3 and the new chairman of the board of AMT, and Benjamin White, a partner.

Dustin introduced Benjamin with the words:

> At my age, it is better to stay on the golf course and not to stand in the way of eager young men like Ben. He is a new partner at D3 and will be your main counterpart from the fund.

Jürgen learned that Ben, obviously in his late thirties, had worked in investment banking, mainly structured finance. From the website, Jürgen knew that Ben was not yet on the list of the eight partners who managed D3's diverse equity investments. Ben became one of AMT's board members.

The next Monday morning, October 3, Jürgen was surprised when Ben called him on his mobile, announcing that he would be in Jürgen's office in 30 minutes. Ben usually kept conversations extremely short when he was on his mobile, he hated to accumulate unnecessary expenses and always kept costs down to a minimum. Jürgen was a bit miffed when he saw Ben arrive in a small rented Fiat Punto, and learned that he had spent the night at a rather low-cost hotel. He thought to himself:

> That's definitely not our style. Ben is a real penny pincher, and this could create the wrong impression with customers and suppliers. There must be a minimum level; otherwise he will not represent us well. People will think we are in serious trouble.

There was little time for small talk. Ben came directly to the point:

> We invested our money here in the expectation of earning 15% ROCE – fast. Our normal experience is that you can lay off 20% of the staff without negative impact and reduce

other overhead costs by the same percentage. So, let's go for this first, and then we see how you can streamline the business further. In 2006, however, everything must have achieved 15% ROCE. By the way, we have already hired a new CFO, he will probably be here in a week and he will not only bring the controlling and reporting up to date, but has a direct communication line to D3, too. I am sure you don't mind that. It just makes things easier.

Jürgen had to admit that the current CFO was a bit 'old school', but thought that for a company of AMT's size, this was sufficient. He responded:

You are the owners; you can, of course, appoint new management. Any additional changes?

Jürgen could not prevent a trace of cynicism slipping into his tone. Ben was, after all, 16 years younger. In a firm voice, Ben replied,

Not for the time being – everything depends on performance.

Jürgen then argued about the 20%, explaining the history of the turnaround, the growth plans, and labor laws, and the discussion soon turned acrimonious. In the end, Ben and Jürgen settled for 12.5% in six months instead of three. By then it was 11:45 and Jürgen really wanted to see the IT staff before lunch, which was usually not taken before 12:30. The new ERP system was causing more headaches than expected. But Ben explained:

I'll stay here for the next three days and join all your meetings. I need to get to know the business.

Jürgen was surprised, but again kept it to himself. However, halfway through a meeting something happened that left Jürgen completely perplexed – Ben interrupted the meeting and announced:

Please remember that from now IT is clearly not a core function. It will be outsourced by the end of the year.

All the participants protested and explained that IT was so interwoven with AMT's core processes that it would not make sense at all, especially not in the current critical situation. But Ben was unmoved:

Fix it, but by the end of the year, it is going to be outsourced. My own money has been invested in this company as well, I therefore have to see progress and don't have time to stop and smell the roses.

Jürgen and Ben's lunch started in a frosty atmosphere. No one really focused on the food or noticed what they were eating. Jürgen asked Ben to coordinate with him before meetings to avoid situations in which Ben could undermine his authority.

After all,

Jürgen said,

> you hold me accountable for the results. Right?

Ben agreed and apologized, but repeated that the outsourcing of the IT and other functions was a core D3 strategy – standard procedure so to speak.

> The less unproductive capital you employ, the easier it is to get 15% ROCE,

he explained to Jürgen, as if he were an undergraduate in a business school. He went on:

> I'll return here for two half-days a week. Let's reserve Monday morning as a *jour fix*.

On a personal note he assured Jürgen:

> I really want to achieve a ROCE of 15% with you. But understand: the goal is fixed. We made commitments to the investors who financed this deal. And my own money is at stake as well . . .

On the second item, plans for China, Ben's response was very vague:

> It sounds interesting, but let's ensure a ROCE of 15% first.

Jürgen tried to explain how vital the China plans were and that without this investment, the further growth, if not the company's very survival, were at risk in the cut-throat competitive industry. AMT's window of opportunity would soon close. Ben remained uncommitted.

Jürgen also learned that Ben often talked informally to people throughout the organization, asking them for their opinion on colleague X and Y, and telling them what had to change. Jürgen was sure that this destabilized the organization. People would wonder what would happen next.

One day, he openly confronted Ben:

> Ben, you cannot sit at your desk and design the new organization alone, or decide to fire person A or B without consulting his or her boss. We need to clarify the skill profiles and ensure there is someone who can carry out the tasks afterwards. You are also bypassing the entire formal organization. People are confused about who is really in charge, and there's a risk that they will end up doing nothing at all.

Ben agreed verbally, but his body language told Jürgen that there was in fact disagreement. Nothing really changed afterwards in this regard.

Despite the *jour fix*, there were again situations in which Ben contradicted Jürgen in meetings, or even at one point gave instructions with which Jürgen openly disagreed. The next to go was the complete central marketing function, and the head of the central service unit. Fortunately, Jürgen could prevent HR from being allocated to the CFO. Ben even declined to see customers with Jürgen and the head of marketing, something that made

Jürgen wonder. Except for a short tour of the plant, Ben stayed in the office next door. Jürgen thought to himself:

The best time for me is when Ben is busy with what must be another potential deal.

Unfortunately, D3 was not so successful, and AMT remained Ben's only mandate. Jürgen raised the China issue several times, even trying to put it on the agenda of the next board meeting. Ben declined, 'This is not the right time.'

When do you put your foot down?

In the meantime, the mood at AMT turned more and more sour. The changes and layoffs were heavily resisted by the workers council, which was ready to fight them by all legal means. The swift layoff of 12.5% was not done carefully enough. There was no analysis, no discussion, too little thinking about anticipated capacities. Jürgen thought:

Our competitors would certainly enjoy getting access to some of AMT's talents. The best ones would in fact leave voluntarily before they are let go. They will find jobs the easiest.

Line managers frequently complained to Jürgen about the heavy daily, weekly, and monthly reporting requirement that the new CFO had imposed on them. Jürgen's rough estimate was that reporting requirements had at least doubled for line managers. But what frustrated him even more was the fact that the gearing (the relation between equity and debt) was now back to 85%. It gave him little comfort to learn that quite a few private equity companies' basic business model was to leverage the equity as far as possible. He thought that such a high burden limited AMT's room for maneuver due to the interest rates. And as a Swabian, he just disliked debt. Jürgen did, however, notice good moments with Ben – especially when there was no ambiguity regarding the profit, which was increasing positively.
    And then Ben's next e-mail arrived:

Fire the HR manager! . . .

PART B

HOTEL BRAEUNLINGER HOF, STUTTGART-MOEHRINGEN, GERMANY, 14 NOVEMBER 2005, 21:43. Benjamin White was in the process of writing an e-mail. He thought to himself:

Things have been progressing pretty well and I will in no way allow anyone to lose any momentum. I need to make this crystal clear.

Benjamin's e-mail was to Dr Jürgen Leitl. It read:

I am deeply disappointed. Your HR director didn't get it. He is too slow in reducing headcount. He should be part of the layoff too – as soon as possible. New horses for new courses. Our battle cry: 15% EBIT!

Benjamin represented D3 Capital, a British–European private equity company, named after the three Ds in the three founders' first names (David, Dennis, Dustin). On 1 October 2005, D3 Capital had acquired AMT after the Badische Gemeindebank decided to divest due to the upcoming strict Bale II credit regulations. Jürgen had been running AMT as its managing director since the beginning of 1999, and the bank brought him in 'to stop the bleeding' and to turn AMT around. Ben asked himself:

Why do I have the impression that people at AMT think they can slow down developments that will take place anyway?

Was it now time to replace Jürgen as the managing director, especially since he seemed to think that he could give him a hard time? Would a new person from outside have enough knowledge of the nuts and bolts of AMT? Was it time to communicate the next step? Ben closed his laptop, but AMT continued to occupy his thoughts with imagined scenarios: how he successfully led meetings and discussions during what he called AMT's required fitness program. Each imagined scenario gave him new ideas on how to better phrase things in discussions and lead change. But then he realized: time to answer these questions is rapidly running out . . .

D3

D3 was based in Reading, about 30 minutes from London. It was not at the top in the private equity companies ranking, but actually enjoyed operating without too much public attention. Like many of its competitors, D3 suffered from the common market development that too many potential investors were chasing an ever-decreasing number of really attractive targets. D3 clearly focused on small and mid caps in the European Private Equity universe (refer to Figure 12.3 for an overview). Nonetheless, David, Dennis, and Dustin had a good relationship with their investors and had delivered attractive returns during the last eight years.

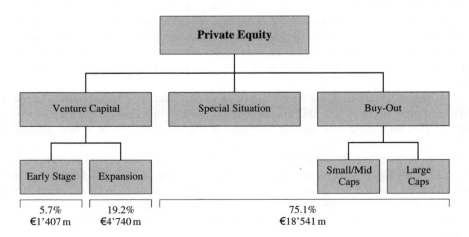

Figure 12.3   The European private equity universe in 2004
Source: Thomson Venture Economics/EVCA; 2004 Survey of Pan-European PE and VC Activity
(Preliminary Data).

Acquiring AMT as a new portfolio company

As Ben learned when preparing D3's bid, AMT was a typical mid-sized Swabian company with a strong record in technological excellence, exactly what you would expect from the 'Land of Tüftler und Bastler'. Founded in 1901 by Dieter Laibinger, it had always produced machine tools. In the late 1960s it bought another machine tool company and was increasingly focusing on specific machine tools for the automotive industry, but since the acquisition relied heavily on bank credit, the profit margin was rather slim. In the 1980s, the third generation of the family – eight cousins – fell out as each had a very different vision of AMT. Decisions were blocked and opportunities missed. Investments slowed down and AMT went through a series of restructurings, cutting the workforce from 2500 to 1500. While studying the company details, Ben also learned that Jürgen had taken over in 1999 after the Badische Gemeindebank had ousted the owners by buying the company even before D3 had been in the picture. AMT relied too heavily on loans and eventually became too exposed to the bank.

Ben studied the managing director carefully. Like so many other German managers, Jürgen had a technical background. He had earned a PhD in electrical engineering and subsequently worked his way up from one of Germany's Blue Chips' research labs to head of manufacturing at a large plant. But tiring of bureaucracy, he had been more than happy to jump ship when he was 42 to become one of the three managing directors of another Mittelstand's company, in charge of manufacturing. Five years later he was hired to turn AMT around. Jürgen was well established and had apparently won the trust of his colleagues throughout the organization quite quickly. People listened to him. Ben thought:

> He has valuable information. I need him on board – at least during the most radical changes at the beginning.

Ben was delighted to learn that Jürgen had closed one of the sites – after a tough and successful battle with the unions – laying off nearly 300 workers in 2000, the first year of his tenure. Jürgen had restructured the company, providing two major business units: one developing and producing machine tools for the car and related industries and another, which concentrated on developing complex custom-made software for the machines, installing and upgrading them in old and new machines as well as providing the necessary maintenance services.

Using the distribution center near Bratislava in Slovakia as a springboard, Jürgen and AMT continued to move low-skill manufacturing tasks to this Eastern European low-wage country. This relocation cost another 350 jobs in Sindelfingen, but as it was gradual and partly compensated by the build-up of the service units, it went smoothly (refer to Table 12.1 for an overview of key figures). AMT's overall 65% vertical integration in manufacturing was still rather high (in comparison with an industry average that was 5% lower), but Jürgen was convinced that the car giants' very specific demands required in-house flexibility and know-how for a wide variety of components too, otherwise quality standards would not be met. And for his company's cutting technological edge, he clearly needed Germany as his home base.

Since 2001, AMT had stopped losing money and had steadily increased its profits. Jürgen was convinced that a continuous improvement process was working well, improving the quality and cutting losses, thus developing a lean manufacturing and a more efficient customer relation management. He was sure that the current profitability – at around 3% of the average in the industry – would continue to grow, and the EBIT could develop from the now nominal 10% (average 7% after extraordinary items) to 12%–13% (10% after extraordinary items – the move to Slovakia and a change in location sites weighed heavily on the results). This would be the upper quartile of the industry and probably top for those mid-sized companies that were continuously being squeezed by their powerful customers. Not enough for Ben though.

Jürgen desperately wanted to invest in China. At first sight, Jürgen's logic made sense. The automotive industry was not only booming there, but also in other Southeast Asian countries like Thailand. Through a partnership with a Chinese distributor, AMT held the biggest market share of close to 30% for the machine tool investments in Chinese auto-manufacturing plants, roughly also a third of its turnover. AMT's US market activities had conversely contracted considerably in the last few years. Jürgen knew that this set-up was not a sustainable solution. He was planning for a JV with the current Chinese partner, increasing the manufacturing in China in the same manner as in Slovakia, and ensuring that the status of the service (including the intellectual property rights for the software) was legally unambiguous. He knew that the local content regulations would also cover investments, and that the emerging domestic Chinese automotive industry was looking for domestic suppliers.

But when Jürgen presented the investment of approximately €9 million in his three-year plan, the bank owners stopped him. This was the first time it had happened – he was utterly astonished. The corporate governance process had so far been pretty straightforward as the GmbH (the German limited liability company) had a simpler structure than a stock market company (refer to Figure 12.2 for an overview). The supervisory board, the so-called Aufsichtsrat, was identical to an owners' meeting. The combination with a personal incorporation (&CoKG) was simply for tax reasons and included three bank managers, one of them – a member of the management board of Badener Gemeindebank – as its chairman. Their main concern was obvious: keep AMT profitable enough to service its debt, therefore avoiding having to write off the loans. But the strict Bale II regulation and the loss of more advantageous financing privileges, due to public ownership, shifted the focus of interest towards selling AMT.

D3 had been one of eight bidders, and although Ben's team had not offered the highest price, it won by offering the bank owner other advantages: cash, it required no provisions for liability and would buy the company outright.

D3 as the new strategy coach

On Friday 30 September 2005, Ben, Dustin Kenburry – an elderly statesman and founder of D3 – and Ken Livingston, D3's CFO showed up to sign the contract for the acquisitions. Dustin introduced Ben with the words:

> At my age, it is better to stay on the golf course and not to stand in the way of eager young men like Ben. He is a new partner at D3 and will be your main counterpart from the fund.

Ben, in his late 30s, had worked in investment banking, mainly structured finance. It was Ben's chance to cement his position as a new partner on probation at D3. Ben remembered an anecdote that Dustin had once told him:

> In my life, I've fired about 15,000 people and earned €100 million. A few years ago, I acquired a Swedish company and immediately fired the CEO. Most of the directors were very unhappy with my decision and unwilling to follow my directives. I fired all of them, and put the second line in command. It was a great success and a large saving in wages.

Ben wanted to deliver results as well! On Monday October 3, the morning after the deal had been signed, Ben decided to act. He called Jürgen on his mobile phone, announcing that he would be in the latter's office within 30 minutes. Despite earning a decent remuneration and having a decent project budget for AMT, Ben preferred to rent a Fiat Punto for the time he would spend with AMT. Once he had pulled into AMT's parking lot, he could see Jürgen standing at the big window of his office on AMT's top floor. Ben thought:

> I have to set the right tone and pace from the very beginning. If we all focus on financial performance, life will be simple for all of us. I therefore also need to bring along the new CFO, as figures never lie. Fortunately, D3 has already picked one.

He decided not to indulge in small talk, and came directly to the point:

> We invested our money here in the expectation of earning 15% ROCE – fast. Our normal experience is that you can lay off 20% of the staff without negative impact and reduce other overhead costs by the same percentage. So, let's go for this first, and then we'll see how you can streamline the business further. In 2006, however, everything must have achieved 15% ROCE. By the way, we have already hired a new CFO, he will probably be here in a week and he will not only bring the controlling and reporting up to date, but has a direct communication line to D3, too.

Ben was glad to hear Jürgen admit that the current CFO was 'old school'. Jürgen's answer confirmed that there was no ambiguity about where the journey was heading:

> You are the owners; you can, of course, appoint new management. Any additional changes?

Shrugging his shoulders, Ben replied, 'Not for the time being – everything depends on performance.'

Ben did not really want to listen to Jürgen's speech about what had been achieved hitherto – the growth plans and labor laws – and the discussion soon turned acrimonious. Even though Ben was an optimist, he did not shy away from trouble. During his studies at Manchester Business School he had learned that 'winners never quit, quitters never win'.

In the end, Ben agreed with Jürgen to settle for 12.5% in six months instead of three. It was now 11:45 and Ben was surprised that Jürgen suddenly had something better to do than continue the meeting with him. Ben asked himself:

Who does he think he is? And what could it possibly be? What is more important than setting goals and talking about how to cascade the goals to other areas? Does Jürgen even get the big picture of what is at stake?

Jürgen explained that he had to see his IT staff before lunch, which was usually enjoyed after 12:30. Ben learned that the new ERP system was causing more headaches than had been expected. He wanted to know more about the problem and told Jürgen:

I'll stay here for the next three days and join all your meetings. I need to get to know the business.

Ben accompanied Jürgen, and what he heard just confirmed what he had feared. He had to step in to clarify his plans:

Please remember that IT is now no longer a core function. It will be outsourced at the end of the year.

As Ben had expected, the first reaction from the staff in this portfolio company was to protest and explain that the IT was so interwoven with AMT's core processes that it would not make sense at all, especially not in the current critical situation. Ben was unmoved and saw no point in having endless discussions:

Fix it, but at the end of the year, it is going to be outsourced.

It was no surprise to him that this negatively impacted his rapport with Jürgen, or that Jürgen asked him to coordinate with him before meetings to avoid situations in which he, Ben, could create the impression that he was undermining Jürgen's authority. Jürgen reasoned:

After all, you hold me accountable for the results. Right?

Ben agreed, acknowledging that Jürgen might need some time to realize that he was no longer first in command, but unequivocally stating that outsourcing of the IT and other functions was a core of D3 strategy. He explained:

The less unproductive capital you employ, the easier it is to get 15% ROCE.

In order to keep the momentum, Ben then suggested:

I'll return here for 2½ days each week and let's reserve Monday morning as a *jour fix*.

On a personal note he assured Jürgen:

I really want to achieve a ROCE of 15% with you. But understand: the goal is fixed. We made commitments to the investors who financed this deal. And my own money is at stake as well . . .

With regards to the second item, the plans for China, Ben decided that Jürgen had heard enough news for that day. He intentionally gave Jürgen a very vague response:

It sounds interesting, but let's ensure a ROCE of 15% first.

What followed was another one of Jürgen's attempts to outline the business case for China: how vital the China plans were, and that without this investment further growth was at risk. AMT's window of opportunity would be closing soon. Ben let him talk, seeing no reason to change his mind. He preferred to remain uncommitted. He, in stark contrast to Jürgen, was not a believer in the China fairy tale and did not want to jump on the bandwagon simply to have to patiently wait for profits in China.

Such investments usually need a lot of crucial capital, returns are uncertain, IP theft is rather likely, and the Chinese player – backed by the government – would sooner or later become more independent, take the lead, and leave AMT out of the picture. He remembered Dustin saying:

Sometimes one has to call a spade a spade, and reality in China has been a sobering lesson for many companies.

Ben clearly wanted to avoid these risks and the slight chances of profits in the long run. His timeframe was much shorter. After all, if his fitness program for AMT really worked out, there would be no shortage of opportunities later on. Even selling AMT to the internationally expanding Chinese players would be an option – why not?

Despite the *jour fix*, there were again situations in which Ben felt the strong need to correct Jürgen in meetings whenever there was a deviation from his strategic path. He was convinced that it was better to put his cards on the table and to continue to correct Jürgen whenever the opportunity presented itself. This would get everybody to concentrate his or her energy on the right strategy. As he had planned, the next to go was the entire central marketing function, and the head of the central service unit. Ben also tried to allocate responsibility for HR to the new CFO, but the opposition he encountered from Jürgen was too strong. He let Jürgen have HR report to him – for the time being. Ben didn't really want to get involved in visiting clients together with the head of marketing and Jürgen. The cost–benefit analysis in respect of the time spent was a knock-out criterion.

Ben needed to take care of D3's internal coordination as well. Several other planned and quite promising deals had slipped through D3's hands at the last minute. Too many investors were now competing for fewer and fewer investments. AMT was his only mandate for the time being. But trying to think positively, he realized that this would allow him to fully focus on AMT, delivering the results that could impress his colleagues, removing the question mark behind his partner position.

As Jürgen did not stop talking about China as AMT's Promised Land, and even attempted to put it on the agenda of the next board meeting, Ben saw no alternative than to clarify,

This is not the right time.

Ben had expected that the AMT staff would not hit new highs in enthusiasm during the restructuring, but this was part of any turnaround and a temporary phenomenon. He was surprised, however, at the resistance the workers council put up against the layoffs that he regarded as crucial. He truly disliked the thought that one's own workforce could dare embark on legal means to block developments that would ultimately take place. He thought:

Why fight? Why even try to resist? It is not their company.

Ben also thought it would be best to accept the situation as normal and downplay the complaints Jürgen forwarded from the line managers about the heavy daily, weekly, and monthly reporting requirements that the new CFO had imposed on them. He felt:

After all, how do you steer a company without the proper information? We need to feel the pulse of the organization pretty much all the time.

Ben needed information and therefore often talked to people throughout the organization before drafting restructuring and staffing ideas.

How else would you learn about what is really going on?

he asked himself, and ignored Jürgen when he confronted him openly:

Ben, you cannot sit at your desk and design the new organization alone, or decide to fire person A or B without consulting his or her boss. We need to clarify the skill profiles and ensure there is someone who can carry out the tasks afterwards. You are also bypassing the entire formal organization. People are confused about who is really in charge, and there's a risk that they will end up doing nothing at all.

Ben agreed to get this distracting 'monkey' off his shoulder. The improving company figures clearly confirmed he was on the right track. Ben dreamed about the future:

One day the employees will be happy to work in a highly competitive company with secure jobs. But they clearly do not yet see it. And D3 will be able to sell a highly lucrative player, which will give a nice exit value.

Quickly moving on to the next step

He also seemed to have disillusioned Jürgen a bit when both of them talked about the gearing (the relation between equity and debt), which was now back at 85%. As he outlined – clearly not to Jürgen's joy – this was not an unusual basic business model. Quite a few private equity companies' basic business model was to leverage equity as far as possible. He didn't care that Jürgen, as a Swabian, might dislike debt as a matter of principle, and he didn't share Jürgen's worries that such a high interest rate burden could limit AMT's room to maneuver – quite the contrary, in fact. He thought:

Room for manoeuvre? What manoeuvre? The strategy is clear and set.

He decided to go ahead with his prepared agenda for the restructuring. The HR manager had resisted change for too long. Ben clicked on the send button to send his e-mail to Jürgen instructing him to fire the HR manager immediately.

He stared out the window of his small hotel room feeling convinced that he was one step closer to the organizational settings that would allow AMT to prosper, to achieve its financial goals, and ensure a reasonable exit value. But would Jürgen be a problem? He needed him. But resistance levels were rising and Jürgen did nothing to appease the staff. What should he do next?

12.3   CASE STUDY: BIOCAST

[By Wolfgang Amann and Ulrich Steger]

PART A: Welcome to the board. I knew your three predecessors well

SÃO PAOLO, 13 AUGUST 2004. Michael Shaw had just left the airport in a limousine on his way to a board meeting at Biocast when, recalling the welcome he had received some months back from a fellow board member, he was filled with great trepidation. At that time, he had taken over as IFC's fourth portfolio manager in just four years. Biocast was one of the hottest biotech companies in Brazil, specializing in biopharmaceuticals, vaccines, and blood tests. Biocast was optimistic about the FDA's forthcoming approval of its newest nucleic acid blood-testing technology, which the Brazilian Red Cross Blood Service would likely use to test the nation's entire blood supply for hepatitis C and HIV. Adelino de Bortoli Neto, Biocast's CEO, repeatedly told its investors:

I'm confident that Biocast's earnings are easily going to exceed expectations.

Michael was more cautious. As an IFC representative, he had observer status at board meetings. IFC was one of the investors that had initially provided Biocast with seed money. Michael's real worries were less about the business potential than the board's ability to act as a counterbalance to the CEO, who seemed to follow a 'take no prisoners' strategy while opportunistically forcing his interests to the fore. Michael said to himself:

One could bluntly call it mucking around with anybody he wants to.

His predecessor had told him what had happened in 2003 when the board decided that the CEO had to be replaced. When the chairman, Rafael de Oliveira, was asked to convey this, Adelino threatened to fire the board and resented Rafael for delivering the message. Matters were complex, since Adelino owned a considerable share of the common stocks and controlled parts of the board. This should have been a warning, but now Michael faced a remarkable new situation: Biocast badly needed to raise money for further expansion or Adelino would literally bankrupt the company. Michael was certain that it was time to clean up the corporate governance at Biocast – but how?

Biocast's heterogeneous investors

Like other start-ups that survive, Biocast went through several rounds of financing. Before August 2004 there had been two major rounds. In the A series, a group of business angels funded Biocast. They were regarded as beholden to the CEO, but not uniformly so. Biocast was an interesting investment target among all the start-ups, since its core competency was highly needed, and jump-starting a biotech industry was expected to have positive spill-over effects for the region in general. One of IFC's goals was to enable companies with great potential, such as Biocast, to have access to capital. IFC itself usually only aimed for a minority stake in such a company, and had a strong non-confrontational culture.

At Biocast only the common shareholders (basically, the founders including the CEO) were entitled to have board members representing their interests, with IFC being the only exception. As a conscious choice, however, IFC chose to take observer status only – even though it had director rights. It was reluctant to exercise director rights as a result of the perceived risk to itself. IFC also used its extensive minority rights to protect its interests, including consent rights regarding all future financing rounds or loans. In addition, IFC strongly believed in job rotation in order to ensure learning and the development of top talent. Crucial insights into emerging markets and industries could therefore be transferred more easily. However, Michael, a 43-year-old Canadian and pharmaceutical expert from Vancouver, was already the fourth outside director in as many years. As an early investor, IFC still enjoyed certain privileges, such as a 2–1 liquidation preference and a right to veto new investors or capital increases. Nonetheless, minority shareholder rights were weak.

The second round of fund raising, the B series, led to a substantially improved capital endowment, enabling Biocast to expand faster. The composition of the board remained unchanged. Besides Michael, the CEO, and the chairman, there were five other board members. Bernardo Waldmann was one of Michael's favorites. He also enjoyed the trust of the other investors of the A and B series, even though he had originally been introduced by Adelino. Francisco Gaudencio was rather neutral, contrasting strongly with Jose Maciel, Rodrigo Preto, and Heitor Megale, who left no doubt about their absolute loyalty towards the CEO, Adelino. This trio usually spoke with one voice. Michael was sure that substantial coordination took place before they arrived at the actual board meetings.

The 'entrepreneurial' CEO

Michael thought that Adelino was up to every trick in the book, and while he had always tried to see the good in him, the signals Adelino sent became increasingly clear. Michael's senior colleagues at IFC also became aware of this. Michael was, however, convinced that start-ups are led to success by an entrepreneurial CEO who sometimes contravenes conventions to innovate and get things done. Adelino, a 51-year-old self-made man, who was usually unshaven, and who had grown up in severe poverty in a small village far from the booming cities, managed his position well – to his own advantage. His stake in Biocast gave him more power than Michael or IFC welcomed. As such, Adelino was one of the permanent people in Biocast's top management team, while the fluctuation among the remaining key positions was unusually high. Michael thought to himself:

Is Adelino a real team player? Is he consensus-oriented? Open to real discussions on what is in the company's best interest? Absolutely not. He clearly thinks in terms of 'me-me-me', he is neither transparent nor honest with the board. There's nothing.

Several incidences supported Michael's skepticism regarding Adelino. At one point during Michael's tenure on the board, Biocast had received a takeover offer. The US$20 million bid could have left IFC with a return of twice its investment. Adelino had, however, insisted on retaining the title of CEO. As this was impossible, the deal eventually failed, postponing the actual payback to IFC to an uncertain time in the future. Adelino also exacerbated matters with his ongoing debates, even wars, with the chairman. He had tried to oust the current chairman Rafael, but Rafael had Michael's trust. Biocast needed new funds to finance R&D and to keep its expansion on a fast track before the competition caught up. Michael knew he had to put his foot down, and made a conscious decision:

No more financing if we cannot find a counterbalance within the board.

But Adelino was more or less bluntly threatening to let the company go bust if he did not get his way, while, of course, making sure that he would receive his paycheck. The current funds would allow the company to die a slow death over an extended period of time, while losing its investments as well as market opportunities. This rendered the next round of financing extremely difficult.

The emergence of a new investor

Michael had just learned about the interest that Diamond Equity, a Palo Alto-based private equity firm, had in providing Biocast's next round of financing. This fresh capital would be highly welcome, as Biocast's current funds were about to dry up and the company's expansion pace could only be maintained through a new capital boost. Michael remembered that IFC had the right to block new investments and saw this as a unique opportunity to trigger corporate governance reforms. He thought to himself:

Perhaps liaising with the new investor to create a strong institutional investor interest representation will finally provide a counterbalance to the overly eager and dominant CEO.

And indeed, initial one-to-one discussions with Diamond Equity's investment directors looked promising. If Diamond Equity insisted on representation on the board of Biocast, Michael felt more confident of having success, perhaps even taking control of the boardroom discussion together with Diamond Equity. After all, Adelino depended on further financing to keep the success story alive. Michael and the other board members realized, however, that the actual progress and business performance did not meet expectations. Diamond Equity was indeed emerging as a value-added investor offering a reasonable valuation. IFC would eventually have to forgo its senior equity position, a 2–1 liquidation preference and significant minority rights to facilitate the deal, but Michael saw the quid pro quo.

Michael wondered if IFC should permit the new investment and forgo its rights. What protection and provisions should he and IFC seek before agreeing to the investment? How could IFC work within the existing policy constraints to facilitate ownership and board structures that promote good governance? Were there ownership structures and board arrangements that IFC had to avoid? What lessons learned could he provide as feedback to IFC regarding the way in which minority rights promote and limit effective governance? Raising more practical questions, Michael wondered what obligations IFC had regarding incoming investors in respect of a fair and full disclosure, even if such a disclosure would not serve IFC's interests? What would be fair, if things were subjective and subject to interpretation, for example, when there was not even full internal agreement on key issues such as CEO effectiveness and integrity? What should IFC do if, in the future, a CEO tried to manipulate the situation and place investors in a very difficult position? More broadly and importantly, how should IFC respond when a more interventionist approach than was typically required of IFC was necessary to protect investor interests? Michael knew there was lots of work to do. He knew that 'pressure creates diamonds – or a lot of dust'.

PART B: All's well that ends well, or losing the entire investment?

SÃO PAOLO, 6 SEPTEMBER 2004. The fine-tuning of the negotiations with Diamond Equity continued. IFC negotiated for a balanced board and effective governance structure within a six-month period in order to forgo its rights. The resulting board would consist of two members from the new C series shareholders, two from the A/B series, three from the common shareholders, including those representing the CEO's interests. Things had proceeded smoothly thus far.

Meanwhile, the more or less latent tensions between Adelino and his chairman Rafael had reached new levels. The chairman, who had verbally arranged with the CEO to step down if necessary, disclosed his willingness to do so to all the investors prior to the new investment. At the next board meeting, however, the board discussed the situation and decided that the chairman would stay on. There was consensus on this matter. In an attempt to make peace, Adelino and Rafael even consulted a psychologist to obtain professional coaching. Promising to improve, Adelino managed to force Rafael to agree to leave the board, even getting a signed and undated resignation from him which he, as CEO, could countersign and enforce as and when he chose. This arrangement was not disclosed to the board. Adelino scheduled a board meeting for 25 September, knowing that the chairman would be on holiday, and presented Rafael's letter of resignation in his absence – to the utter astonishment of the remaining board members. Michael thought that Rafael was one of the very few trustworthy board members and a crucial counterbalance to Adelino.

This is unacceptable!

he protested. There was an awkward silence while Adelino just smiled...

After extensive discussions, Michael realized that his plan for Rafael to maintain his position had failed horribly. Michael pointed out that Adelino's maneuver to oust the chairman was certainly immoral, if not illegal. Michael understood that Adelino had tricked Rafael into signing this letter without the board's consent, or even knowledge of it, and, of course, without keeping to his part of the deal. Acting in good faith, Rafael wanted to fulfill his part of the agreement and stepped down. Michael threatened to make the matter public if Adelino did not retract, but the latter took no notice. As bad news seems to attract more bad news, Michael also learned that Diamond Equity had suddenly lost interest in the deal. They doubted whether they could succeed in:

- Getting sufficient influence on the board after they had been made aware of the governance difficulties.
- Replacing the CEO with someone who would act more in the company's interest, someone who could actually scale the business better.
- Managing to persuade Rafael to return as chairman on an interim basis to facilitate future expansion. Rafael clearly enjoyed Diamond Equity's trust.
- Fostering a culture of learning and honesty, as well as continuous improvement, and assessing risks more accurately at the board level, with the CEO setting the right tone at the top.

Diamond Equity's interest in acquiring a critical part of the common shares decreased, and concerns about a satisfying ROI spread. Relationships at the board level worsened throughout September. Adelino even demanded that IFC and Michael immediately stop their unofficial talks with Diamond Equity behind his and the board's back.

It thus no longer made a difference to Diamond Equity that Michael and the board were initiating a committee to search for a new chairman, but this committee consisted only of three members, one of whom was clearly controlled by Adelino.

> Adelino has certainly managed to gain time . . . once again,

Michael remarked cynically to Bernado, a fellow board member. Distracted by internal governance issues and the unnecessarily prolonged negotiations with Diamond Equity, Biocast missed an opportunity to acquire an attractive takeover target that would have added state-of-the-art manufacturing competencies. But even without this missed deal, business prospects started to look dull. Equity reserves were low and IFC had no interest in investing more funds. The percentage of common stocks now amounted to 60%, B investors and IFC held a 12.5% stake each, and other A series investors 25%.

As Michael left the board meeting and got back into the limousine to return to the airport for his flight back to IFC's headquarters in Washington, he felt very uneasy. He had just one urgent goal: ensuring that IFC recovered its money. But what were his options? What had really gone wrong? What could the IFC and the investors have done differently to prevent this disastrous situation?

12.4   CASE STUDY: ASIAN CAR PART HOLDING – SOLD WITHOUT THE KNOWLEDGE OF THE BOARD?

[By Ulrich Steger and Wolfgang Amann]

Hendrik van Geusen slammed the receiver on the phone. The IFC investment officer had just received a call from Hung Tschin, his regional counterpart in the Southeast Asian office, who was upset that Hendrik had not informed him in advance about the breaking news in Bangkok: Asian Car Part Holding (ACH), one of IFC's biggest investments in the region, had been sold to the Chinese Kanton Car & Parts Group (KCPG). He was stunned to hear that Hendrik had not been consulted prior to information of the sale leaking to the market – after all, Hendrik was sitting on the board of directors of ACH as IFC's nominee director.

> Adith Cheosakul cannot sell ACH without the consent of the board,

Hendrik thought. Or could he? An hour later Hendrik found an e-mail with his invitation to the next board meeting, as usual one week in advance: the sale was listed under the heading: 'Information for the Board', promising more details at the meeting. However, the price tag was already being reported in the press: 15× average operating profit for the last three years with adjustments dependent on the finalization of the due diligence. For IFC this would mean a decent profit, but was this the real issue here?

He called one of the other members of the ACH board, Emmanuel Florido, who represented the Philippine investors. The two directors were on especially good terms, in part because they were the only members of the ACH board who challenged Adith Cheosakul, the chairman and CEO, from time to time. Emmanuel had not yet read his e-mail and was completely at a loss.

But the Singaporean shareholders would be even more shocked, as they have sold out their shares three weeks ago, and for considerably less than the price we are discussing,

he told Hendrik. After the call Hendrik ran down the hallway to the office of his colleague Kazmiro Isheida. He needed a sounding board. What should he do now? And what position should he take on the transaction at the next board meeting? Should IFC just 'take the money and run', or should he represent some broader principles and responsibilities?

Asian Car Part Holding

Asian Car Part Holding (ACH) was the result of a series of acquisitions by Thai Electric, a sprawling conglomerate focused on household consumer products, to harness the market growth in the car industry in Southeast Asia. The strategy of the holding was to become a 'first-tier supplier' for global car companies as they expanded in Asia, with a core competence in all cooling and heat exchange systems. The acquisitions in Malaysia, Singapore, Indonesia, Philippines, and Vietnam were paid mostly in (newly issued) shares, but also cash infusions on the part of Thai Electric, allowing the controlling shareholder to retain a majority stake in ACH. In the process, the percentage of the company's shares that were traded on the stock market shrank from 35% to 12% of the capital (see Figure 12.4 for the ownership structure and company activities). IFC became a shareholder in ACH through its investments in the acquired companies in both the Philippines and Indonesia. As economies of scale are very important in car part manufacturing, IFC agreed to both acquisitions in 2001 and agreed to hold equity in the holding company ACH, which was created at that time. As a condition of its approval of the acquisitions, IFC demanded tag-along rights should Thai Electric ever

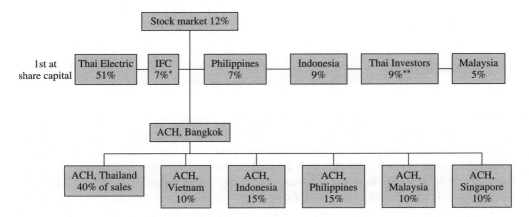

* Plus convertible debt of approx. 4% of capital.
** Thai investors was a group of private individuals, among them the chairman and CEO, Adith, with close ties to Thai Electric. No detailed information about individual shareowners.

Figure 12.4   Ownership and regional structure of activities

decide to sell its stake, and this was formalized in the form of a shareholders' agreement which also included requiring strict observance of IFC's environmental and social policies. In commercial terms, the company was sufficiently successful when juxtaposed with the dominant position of the global car manufacturers. The latter showed a clear propensity to 'squeeze' their suppliers due to the cut-throat competition, even in a growing car market.

Adith Cheosakul – the soft-spoken autocrat

The obvious center of power in ACH was the CEO and chairman of the board, Mr Adith Cheosakul, who served at the pleasure of the family running Thai Electric (he held board seats on some of their other investments) and through the power of his own – undisclosed – shareholdings. Hendrik just assumed that he was the head of the Thai investors.

The board meetings usually ran smoothly. Presentations by the executive committee to the board took the majority of the time, and there was usually very little debate in the boardroom. Executives pretty much stuck to their presentations and provided little additional commentary. The person who was closest to Adith was clearly the CFO, who was always in attendance. The board members (see Figure 12.5) seemed to treat the meetings as mostly a Q&A session or a mere opportunity to provide feedback on financial details. Adith was always polite and soft-spoken – but there could be no doubt as to who was in charge.

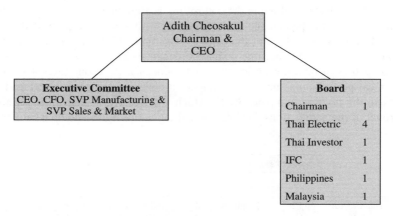

Figure 12.5   Board composition and executive committee

Hendrik remembered only one instance when he – in addition to his usual professional input – really challenged Adith. Roughly a year ago there was an e-mail sent to all board members seeking feedback on the suggestion that stakes in a few private companies which were held by the ACH-Thailand branch be sold to the Thai investors. Although the stakes were not in ACH's core business – hence, the selling could make sense – the prices were suspiciously low. Hendrik's back-of-the-envelope calculations estimated approximately a 40% 'discount'. At the board meeting where the sale was discussed, only Hendrik and Emmanuel Florido, his Philippine colleague, voiced any concern about the price. A week later, the board was informed that the proposal was withdrawn.

Hendrik expected some discussion at the following meeting, and perhaps an icy atmosphere, but nothing of the sort happened; Adith was as polite and soft-spoken as ever. To his surprise, Hendrik learned during the dinner that the directors from Thai Electric had agreed to approve the sale in advance of the previous meeting.

As the deal was also clearly to the disadvantage of Thai Electric, he asked his table neighbor over dessert why he would not confront Adith. His neighbor was astonished and said:

> Have you not realized how carefully Adith is planning every move? He has certainly already talked to the family.

And after a pause, he continued:

> Maybe you folks from IFC see his velvet gloves, but do not notice the iron fist inside...

Thus, the planned sale of the company surprised Hendrik as he had expected that Thai Electric wanted to further increase its holdings, not sell. Three weeks ago, the Thai investors had bought a 3% share from a Singaporean businessman (rumors said with the help of Thai Electric).

Checkmate? Or had the game only just begun?

Coming back from this discussion with Kazmiro – basically a 30-minute lecture in Asian relationship building – he found an e-mail from Adith, asking for a convenient time when they could speak. When they got together on the phone, Adith presented the agreement and sought IFC's approval of the sale as a significant investor. When asked about the opinion of the other shareholders, Adith confirmed that he had spoken only to the owners of Thai Electric and the other Thai investors and was only now contacting representatives of other larger shareholders to individually seek their approval. Assuring Hendrik that all of IFC's legal rights, including the tag-along rights, were to be respected in the transaction, Adith presented the offer and made his case.

Part V
Conclusion

In this book, we have presented what we understand to be the value school of corporate governance. We are currently moving beyond the period of a heavy focus on scandals and crises that characterized not exclusively, but especially, the period between 2001 and 2007. We outlined a multitude of areas where and how corporate governance could add real value. We paid particular attention to the necessity of a contingency approach when presenting our model of board types and roles. No 'one-size-fits-all' model – such as, for example, suggesting a participatory approach for all settings or countries – emerged as a solution. The presented insights took idiosyncrasies and dynamics over time into consideration. They included the main issues and their real causes, ownership settings, country settings, and new developments in corporate governance research and practice, such as optimizing corporate governance in and with subsidiaries, since the upper echelon hitherto received considerable attention and subsequently saw major improvements in their conduct. Instead of national laws, we rather emphasized typical patterns and solutions. We illustrated our points with in-depth case studies and highlighted learning nuggets. This is where our responsibilities end and yours begin. We alerted you to be sensitive to typical dilemmas, traps, and promising avenues forward when value creation is the goal. The adaptations of these insights to your current and future corporate governance settings and challenges will determine your success. As you know, it is reflection on experience that builds competence. Experience alone often only builds (unfounded) confidence – at the price of unhappy stakeholders. Reflection on experience comes in two forms – after the main event or beforehand. If we have been helpful in stimulating new thoughts, we have achieved our goal. Reality, however, is more influenced by your decisions and actions based on the stimuli provided to you.

Index

Note: Page references in *italics* refer to Figures; those in **bold** refer to Tables

ABB   29, 30, 31, 191
ABB case study   49–62
   leadership in decentralized governance
       structure   60–2
   strategy committee   53–9
accountability   4, 27, 31
ADTRANZ   186
Aer Lingus   39, 45
Aerospatiale Matra   184
Air France–Sky Team   45
Air Liberté   47, 48
Air Littoral   47
Airbus   136, 137
airline alliances   *38*
Allianz   126
AMEX   10
Anglo-Saxon model   11, 14
annual meeting   15
AOM   47
ASEA   50
Asian Car Part Holding case study   261, 280–3
Assicurazioni Generali   130
Aston Martin   184
Austrian Airlines (AUA)   37, 39
Automotive Machine tool (AMT) case study
   260–1, 261–76
   governance and organization structure   *264*
   as new portfolio company   270–1
Aventis   60
Axa Australia   114

Badische Gemeindebank   262, 265, 269
Balair   37
Balair/CTA Leisure   39
Balanced Scorecard approach   21
Banco Santander Central (BSCH)   121, 127

Bata Shoe Organization case study   242–3,
   245–53
Berlin Initiative Group   10
best practice   24
Biocast case study   276–9
Biovent   195, 198–201
Blackstone   130
'Blue Ribbon Committee'   9
board   16, 64
   composition   *154*
   contingent role   28–32, *29*
   dilemmas for   23–4
   evaluation   153–60
   information   91–7
   monitoring and supervising   21
   questionnaire   158–60
   selecting, evaluating and coaching top
       management   21
   substantive input in the corporate evolution
       21–2
   types of   20–2, *22*
Boeing code of conduct case study   132–5,
   135–42
   board composition   135
   Code of Conduct   *139*
   corporate governance of industry   134
   corporate history   134, 136–7
   culture   135
   ethical tone   135–6
   Harry Stonecipher as President   138–42
   Phil Conduit as chairman   137–8
Boesky, Ivan   8
British Petroleum (BP)   16, 64, 236
British Steel   114
   merger with Hoogovens   113
Brown Boveri   50

Bullock report   7
Bundesaufsichtsamt fuer Kreditwesen
    (BAKred)   126
business model   17

C&A   238
Cadbury Report   8
Cargolifter   10
CarsDirect   185
CASA   184
CEMEX   64
CEO life cycle   260
'challenger' board   22
checks-and-balances model   30
China
    current corporate governance structures
        in   210
    Prime case study   206–7, 207–11
        company background   208
        corporate governance systems   208–11
        structure   209
Chrysler   63, 64, 65, 68–9, 71, 72–3, 75–6, 87
Citigroup   121
Cobra vs. Commerzbank case study   120–30
code of conduct   16, 27
    Boeing code of conduct case study   132–5,
        135–42
    ConnectU2 case study   135, 142–51
    motives for   133
    as panacea   131–5
    success and impact of   133
Commerzbank
    vs Cobra case study   120–30
    share price development   128–9
    structure   123
Compania Unidas de Argentina (CUSDA) case
    study   212–15
'comply-or-explain' regulation   8, 10
conflict
    between owners   114
    board vs. management   111–13
    board/management vs. owners   113–14
    Cobra vs. Commerzbank case study
        114–15, 120–30
    Elicore case study   115–20
    Germany vs US   78
    'toxic' CEOs   112–13, 114
    within board   113
conflicts of interest,
    Khan AG case study   97–103

ConnectU2 code of conduct case study
    142–51
    Bucharest' incident   147–9
    code of conduct   143–5
    code of conduct workshop   149–51
    company background   145–6
    corporate secretary/general counsel's role
        146–7
continental-European model   11
contingency role of boards   28–32, 29
contingency theory   15, 30
core processes   27
corporate evolution   26
Credit Lyonnais   121
Credit Suisse   48
Credit Suisse First Boston (CSFB)   170
Crossair   37, 39, 48

D3 Capital   262, 269, 271–5
Daewoo   185
Daimler-Benz   7, 9, 63, 68, 164, 169–70
DaimlerChrysler (DC)   63, 64, 164, 191
    alliance committee   66, 81, 82
    audit committee   65
    case study   66–7, 68–87
    chairman's council   84
    chairman's integration council   64–5, 81
    corporate governance at   78–9
    executive automotive committee   65–6
    international advisory board   84
    Issue Resolution Teams (IRTs)   71, 71
    labor committee   83
    management board   79–82
    merger   68–76
    shareholder committee   83
    supervisory board   65, 82, 82
    understanding risks   86–7
    view of financial markets   84–6
    see also Daimler–Chrysler merger case study;
        Daimler–Chrysler post-merger case
        study
Daimler–Chrysler merger case study   164, 165,
    166–80
    after the deal is done   180–9
    board remuneration   179, 180
    external advisors   169–70
    involvement of boards   166–80
    involvement of Chrysler board   170–3, 172
    involvement of Daimler-Benz boards
        173–4, 174

management board and supervisory board
    177
modalities of deal   177–9
post-merger integration structure   *178*
product portfolio   *167*
Daimler–Chrysler post-merger case study
    180–9
    board of management   186
    management board structure   186, *186*
    share price development   *188*
    shareholder committee   188
    supervisory board   186, *187*
Debitel   184
definition of corporate governance   4
Delphi   185
Delta   39, 46
Deutsche Bank   67, 86, 121, 125, 129, 176
Deutsche Telekom   184
Diamond Equity   278–80
diffusion of corporate governance issues
    11–14, **12**
    barriers to   13–14
Disney   20
dot.com bubble   5, 20
Dresdner Bank   121, 122, 125–6
drivers of corporate regulation   13
Dutch Royal Ahold   191
Dutch Tulip Bubble   235

Economic Regulation Act (France)   10
Elicore case study   115–20
emerging markets   **206**
Enron   6, 11, 17
European Aeronautic Defence and Space
    Company (EADS)   184
European Codex for Corporate Governance   11
European Economic Commissions
    Fifth Draft Directive   7
European Union   11
externalities   3

family businesses   235–45
    active owner   237, 238
    Bata Shoes Organization case study   242–3,
        245–53
    board in   236–40
    business environment   237
    CEO-centered model   237
    checks-and-balances model   237
    consensus model   237
    corporate governance rules   240–2

factors shaping corporate governance   236–7
    governing owner   237, 238
    investing owner   237, 238
    operating owner   237
    owner-centered model   237
    ownership/capital markets   237
    passive owner   237, 238
    personalities   237
    role of board chairman   245
    selecting independent directors   244–5
    strategy/business model   237
    value-added   244
Farni plc   153
financial performance   24–6
Finnair   39, 45
Flowtex AG   10
Ford   169, 184, 185, 238
France, corporate governance systems in   205
Frankfurt Commission for Principles on
    Corporate Governance   10
fraud   24

game theory   163
general assembly   15
General Motors (GM)   25, 169, 184, 185
Germany
    Bundesaufsichtsamt fuer Kreditwesen
        (BAKred)   126
    Code of Corporate Governance (Cromme
        Code)   10, 14, 77
    Co-Determination Act/Law 1976   174
    corporate governance systems   204–5
    regulations   9
Goldman Sachs   121, 169
Gramm–Leach–Bliley Act   9
Greenbury Report   8
Greenpeace International   222
groupthink   17
Guinness share-trading fraud   8
Güldner AG   97

Hampel Report   8–9
Hicks Report   235
Highfly Logistics Software case study
    30, 32–6
history of corporate governance   5–14
Hoeschst   60
Hollinger International   22
Honda Motors   168
Hoogovens–British Steel merger   113
HSBC Group   121

Hughes Space & Communications   136
Hungarian Malev   39
Hunter   46
HypoVereinsbank   129
Hyundai Motors   68, 72, 74, 76, 185

ICM case study   104–8, 108–9
ICM Semiconduct   107, 108
IKWGmbH   103
incentives   27–8
information for boards   91–7
   board positions and   93
   influences on   93–5
   quality of   93, *94*
   satisfaction of members with   92, *92, 94*
   sources and potential implications   95–6, *95*
   understanding of board roles and tasks   95
initial public offerings (IPOs)   8
insider trading   8
Integrated Circuit Manufacturing (ICM) case
      study   104–8, 108–9
Internet   10
Intesa   121

Jaguar   184
Japan, corporate governance systems in   206

Kanton Car & Parts Group (KCPG)   280
KapAEG   9
Kaufmann Medical   195, 201
Kerkorian, Kirk   66
Key Performance Indicators (KPIs)   21
Khan AG conflicts of interest case study
      97–103
Kissinger, Henry   22
KLM Royal Dutch Airlines   37
KonTraG   9
KPMG   48
Kwik-Fit   184

Land Rover   184
Lansdowne   129
legal environment   18
Lehmann & Voss   240, *241*
Leuenberger   49
Levine, Michael   8
license-to-operate   3
Lockheed Martin   133, 137
LTU   47
Lufthansa Airlines   78

management   16
   top   27–8
Mannesmann–Vodafone trial   114
McDonnell Douglas   136
McKinsey Switzerland   39
Means–Berle dilemma   5
Mediobanca SpA   127
Mercede-Benz AG   166–8
Mercedes   65
Mercedes-Benz   69
'Merger of Equals' notion   66
mergers & acquisitions
   Daimler–Chrysler merger case study   164,
         165, 166–80
   Daimler–Chrysler post-merger case study
         180–9
   governance in   163–4
   post-merger phase   164–5
   pred-deal situation   163–4
Milken, Michael   8
Mitsubishi Motors   63, 65, 66, 68, 72, 74–6,
         181, 182, 184, 185, 186
Morgan Stanley   121
Munich Re   130

NASDAQ   10
Nestlé   78
Nissan Motors   72, 185
non-profit organizations, differences in   221–3
NYSE   10

OECD CG Guidelines   4
One World Trust   227
one-tier board systems   16
OneWorld   39
organizational risks   66
ownership   18

Parmalat   91, 235
personalities   17
Pharmacia–Upjohan merger   113
Pharmagroup Delivery Technologies (PDT)
         199–202, *200*
Pharmagroup Int. subsidiaries case study
         195–202
   Biovent   195, 198–201
   corporate governance   198
   influenza products   186–8
   Pharmagroup Delivery technologies (PDT)
         199–202, *200*
Philipp Holzmann AG   10

political environment   18
Porsche AG   13, 25
Portuguese TAP   39
Postbank   129
PricewaterhouseCoopers   48
principal–agent theory   5, 14–15, 18, 28, 31,
    114–15, 163, 222, 255
principles of corporate governance   3–4
private equity firms   255–83
    Asian Car Part Holding case study   261,
        280–3
    Automotive Machine tool (AMT) case study
        260–1, 261–76
    Biocast case study   276–9
    board–management relationship   360
    board's function   257–9
    CEO life cycle   260
    corporate governance issues   257
privatization   8
profit   3
property rights   3

Rabo Bank   221
Raffles Hotels   48
Rebon N.V.   124
Red Cross   221
regulation   6–7
    in the 1970s   7
    in the 1980s   8
    in the 1990s   8–10
    since 2000   10–11
remuneration policies   13
Renault   185
responsibility   31
Rhys-Williams, Sir Brandon   7
Rockwell International   136
Roosevelt, Franklin   10

Sabena   39, 46, 47, 48
Sarbanes–Oxley Act (SOX)   7, 10–11, 14, 21,
    22, 28, 63, 76, 79, 83, 235
scandals   6–7, 6, 96
Scandinavia, corporate governance
    systems in   205
Scandinavian Airlines (SAS)   37
Schering Pharmaceuticals   78
'scout' board   22
Securities and Exchange Commission (SEC)
    77
Securities and Exchange Control (SEC)   6, 7
September 11th, 2001   48

Siemens   191
South East Bank Europe case study   207,
    215–19
Sparkassen   129
stakeholders
    benefit of good corporate governance   28
    outside   16
Standard & Poor   51
StarAlliance   39
Stevens, Ted   133
stock market   5
stock market crash
    (1873)   5
    (1929)   5
subsidiaries   191–202
    governance systems in multinationsals
        192
    Pharmagroup Int. case study   195–202
    recommendations for governance   193–4
    supervisory board   192
surprise risks   66
Swissair   17, 24, 30
    acquired holdings   46
    board   40–3, 41
    case study   36–49, 38
    committees   42–3
    consolidated financial results   44
    Hunter strategy   46–8
Swissair Group (SAirGroup)   37–48
Swisscom   184
Swissotel Hotel & Resorts   48

Thai Electric   281–3
Toscafund   129
Total   191
Toyota   25, 184
TRAFFIC   224
transnationality trap   131
transparency   27
Treitschke, Heinrich von   5
two-tier board systems   16
Tyco International   11
types
    of board   20–2
    of corporate governance system   18–20, 19,
        19–20

UK, corporate governance systems in   204
Unicredit   129
Unilever   67
USA, corporate governance systems in   203–4

value, added   26–8
Viénot Report   8, 9
'VIP' board   22
Vivendi   6
Volkswagen   13, 182
Volvo   182, 184, 185

Wal-Mart   134
'watchdog' board   22
WCM AG   129–30
whistle-blowers   132
white space risks   66
winner's curse   163
Winter report   11

WorldCom   11, 17, 91
WWF International case study   223–32
  birth and growth   224
  board   229–30, *231*
  external pressures   227
  fundraising   226
  internal issues   226–7
  network   224–5, *229*
  old structure   226
  operations review   226
  organization   *225*
  planning evolution   228–31
  resource allocation   226–7

Index compiled by Annette Musker